D0229593

Complete Devon

© 1972 Ward Lock Limited

Published in Great Britain by
Ward Lock Limited, 116 Baker Street,
London W1M 2BB, a member of the Pentos Group.

ISBN 0 7063 1378 X

Revised and Reprinted 1978

All rights reserved. No part of this publication may be
reproduced, stored in a retrieval system, or transmitted,
in any form or by any means, electronic, mechanical,
photocopying, recording, or otherwise, without the prior
permission of the Copyright owners.

Drawings by Cetra Hearne and Colin Gibson.
Photographs by Peter Baker, Roy Westlake and British Tourist Authority.
Text filmset in Times Roman.

Plans based upon the Ordnance Survey map with the sanction
of the Controller of Her Majesty's Stationery Office.

Printed and bound by Editorial Fher S.A., Bilbao, Spain.

RED GUIDE

Complete Devon

Describing the main resorts and places of interest

Edited by Reginald J. W. Hammond F.R.G.S.

WARD LOCK LIMITED . LONDON

Maps and Plans

	Page
Devon	8–9
Exeter Cathedral	16
Exeter	24–25
Exmouth	34
Budleigh Salterton	42
Sidmouth	48
Dawlish	72
Teignmouth	78
Central Torquay	104–105
Paignton	122
Dartmouth	136
The River Dart	144
Kingsbridge	154
Salcombe	162
Bideford	182
Barnstaple	196
Ilfracombe	216–217
Lundy	228
Lynton and Lynmouth	232

Contents

	Page
Introduction	11
Exeter	15
Exmouth	35
Excursions round Exmouth	39
Budleigh Salterton	43
Walks and Drives from Budleigh	45
Sidmouth	49
Branscombe and Beer	52
Seaton	57
Walk round Seaton, Sidmouth and Beer	59
Exeter to Tiverton and Bampton	65
The Exeter–Barnstaple Road	69
Exeter to Dawlish	70
Dawlish	73
Walks and Drives round Dawlish	76
Teignmouth	79
Excursions from Teignmouth	84
Newton Abbot	87
Excursions round Newton Abbot	90
Newton Abbot to Chagford	93
Exeter to Plymouth via Princetown	96
Torquay	99
In and About Torquay	101
Excursions from Torquay	110
Paignton	123
Excursions from Paignton	127

CONTENTS

	Page
Brixham	131
Brixham to Kingswear by the Coast	135
Dartmouth	137
A Trip up the Dart	145
Totnes	147
Excursions from Totnes	151
In the South Hams	155
Kingsbridge	156
Excursions from Kingsbridge	158
Kingsbridge to Salcombe	161
Salcombe	163
Excursions from Salcombe	165
Plymouth	168
Plymouth to Tavistock and the North Coast	171
Clovelly	173
Hartland	178
Hartland to Bude by the cliffs	181
Bideford	183
The Bideford District	187
Barnstaple	197
Walks and Excursions from Barnstaple	203
Ilfracombe	209
Excursions from Ilfracombe	214
Combe Martin	221
Walks from Combe Martin	224
Lundy	229
Lynton and Lynmouth	233
Excursions from Lynton and Lynmouth	238
Index	251

Illustrations

	Page
Bishop's Palace and Cathedral, Exeter	14
West Front, Exeter Cathedral	19
Cathedral Close, Exeter	22
St. Mary Steps	23
From the Close, Exeter	26
At Topsham	33
The Sands, Exmouth	36
Sandy Bay, Exmouth	38
The Front, Budleigh Salterton	41
East Budleigh	44
Hayes Barton	45
Jacob's Ladder Beach, Sidmouth	50
Branscombe Church	53
The Beach and Cliffs, Beer	54
Fore Street, Beer	55
Seaton	56
Ladram Bay	58
Old Stocks, Ottery St. Mary	60
Colyton Church	62
Axminster	63
Bickleigh	65
By the Exe at Bickleigh	67
Powderham Castle	71
The Sands, Dawlish	75
Shaldon, Teignmouth	82
Stoke-in-Teignhead	83
Forde House	89
Bradley Manor	92
Typical Dartmoor	94
Postbridge	98
Harbour and Vane Hill, Torquay	102
Torquay Harbour	107
Anstey's Cove, Torquay	111
Cockington	112
Thatcher Rock	114
Oddicombe Beach, Babbacombe	116
Compton Castle	119
The Harbour, Paignton	125
Berry Pomeroy Castle	128
Brixham and the Harbour	130
At Brixham	134
The Lower Dart Ferry	139
Dartmouth Castle	142
The Dart at Dittisham	146
Buckfast Abbey	152
Slapton Sands	155
Kingsbridge	157
Bantham on the Avon	160
At Salcombe	164
Burgh Island	167
Royal Parade, Plymouth	169
Clovelly	172
Clovelly Cove	175
Clovelly main Street	176
Hartland	178
Hartland Quay	180
The Quay, Bideford	181
The Torridge and Bridge, Bideford	185
Appledore	188
The Sands, Instow	191
The Taw, Barnstaple	199
St. Peter's, Barnstaple	200
Pilton Church	202
Chittlehampton	204
Arlington Court	208
The Harbour, Ilfracombe	211
Old Cottage, Lee	215
Combe Martin	221
Great and Little Hangman	223
Heddon's Mouth	226
On Lundy	230
Lynton	234
Lynmouth	237
Watersmeet	243
Countisbury Hill	245

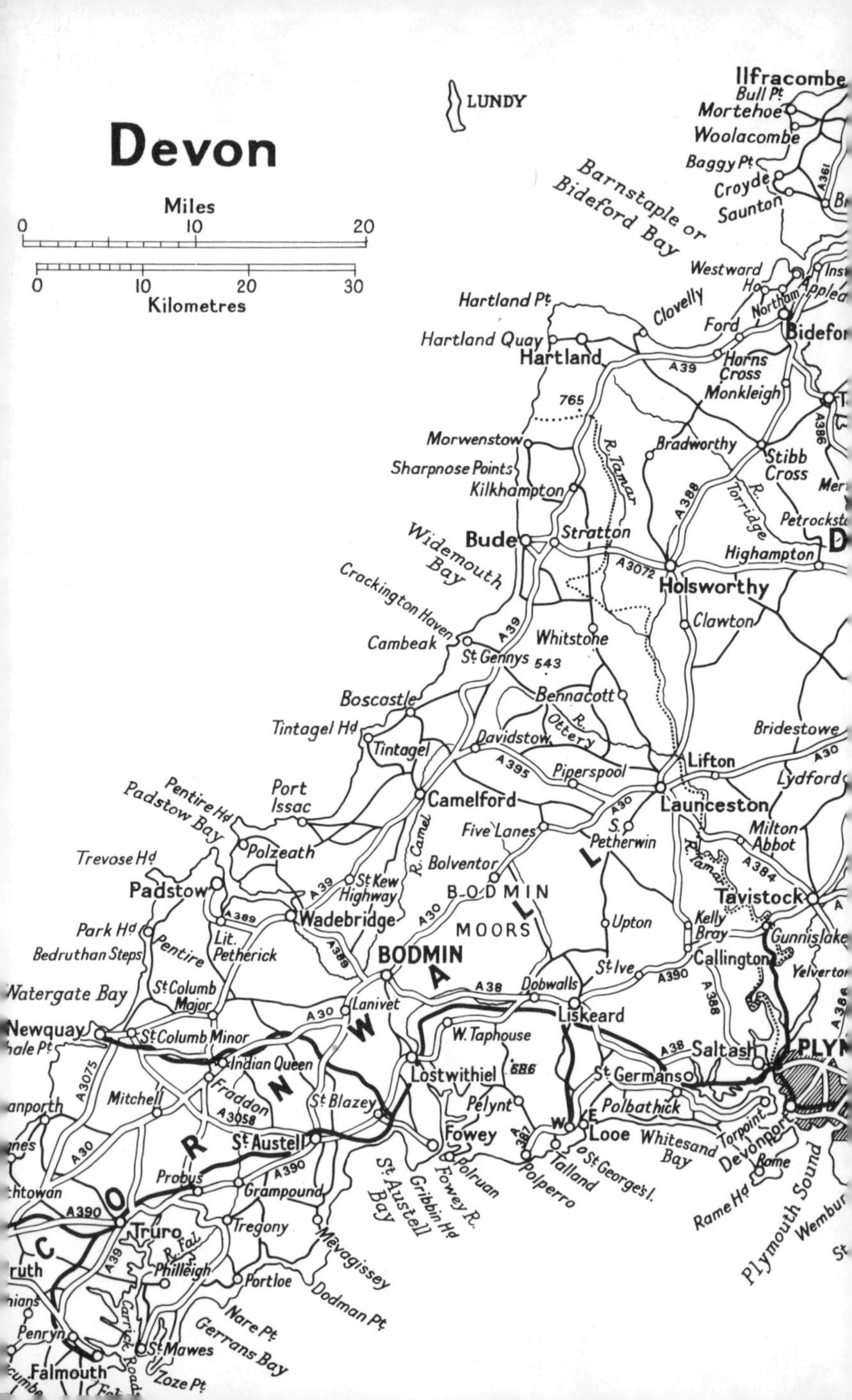
Devon
Miles
0
10
20
0
10
20
30
Kilometres
LUNDY
Ilfracombe
Bull Pt
Mortehoe
Woolacombe
Baggy Pt
Croyde
Saunton
Barnstaple or Bideford Bay
Westward Ho
Northam
Bideford
Clovelly
Ford
Hartland Pt
Hartland Quay
Hartland
Horns Cross
Monkleigh
765
Morwenstow
Bradworthy
Stibb Cross
Sharpnose Points
Kilkhampton
R. Tamar
R. Torridge
Petrockstow
Bude
Stratton
Highampton
Widemouth Bay
Holsworthy
Crackington Haven
Clawton
Cambeak
St Gennys
543
Whitstone
Boscastle
Bennacott
R. Ottery
Tintagel Hd
Tintagel
Davidstow
Bridestowe
Lifton
Lydford
Piperspool
Pentire Hd
Padstow Bay
Port Issac
Camelford
Launceston
Polzeath
Five Lanes
S. Petherwin
Milton Abbot
Trevose Hd
R. Camel
Bolventor
Padstow
St Kew Highway
BODMIN MOORS
Tavistock
Wadebridge
Park Hd
Lit. Petherick
Upton
Kelly Bray
Gunnislake
Bedruthan Steps
Pentire
BODMIN
Callington
Watergate Bay
St Columb Major
St Ive
Yelverton
Dobwalls
Lanivet
Liskeard
Newquay
St Columb Minor
W. Taphouse
Saltash
PLYM
Indian Queen
Lostwithiel
686
St Germans
Fraddon
Mitchell
St Blazey
Pelynt
Polbathick
Torpoint
Devonport
Looe
Whitesand Bay
Fowey
St Austell
Polruan
Talland
St George's I.
Rame
Rame Hd
Plymouth Sound
Polperro
Fowey R.
Gribbin Hd
St Austell Bay
Probus
Grampound
Truro
Tregony
Mevagissey
R. Fal
Philleigh
Portloe
Dodman Pt
Nare Pt
Penryn
Carrick Roads
St Mawes
Gerrans Bay
Falmouth
Zoze Pt
CORNWALL
A39
A361
A386
A388
A3072
A30
A395
A389
A384
A390
A38
A3075
A3058
A387

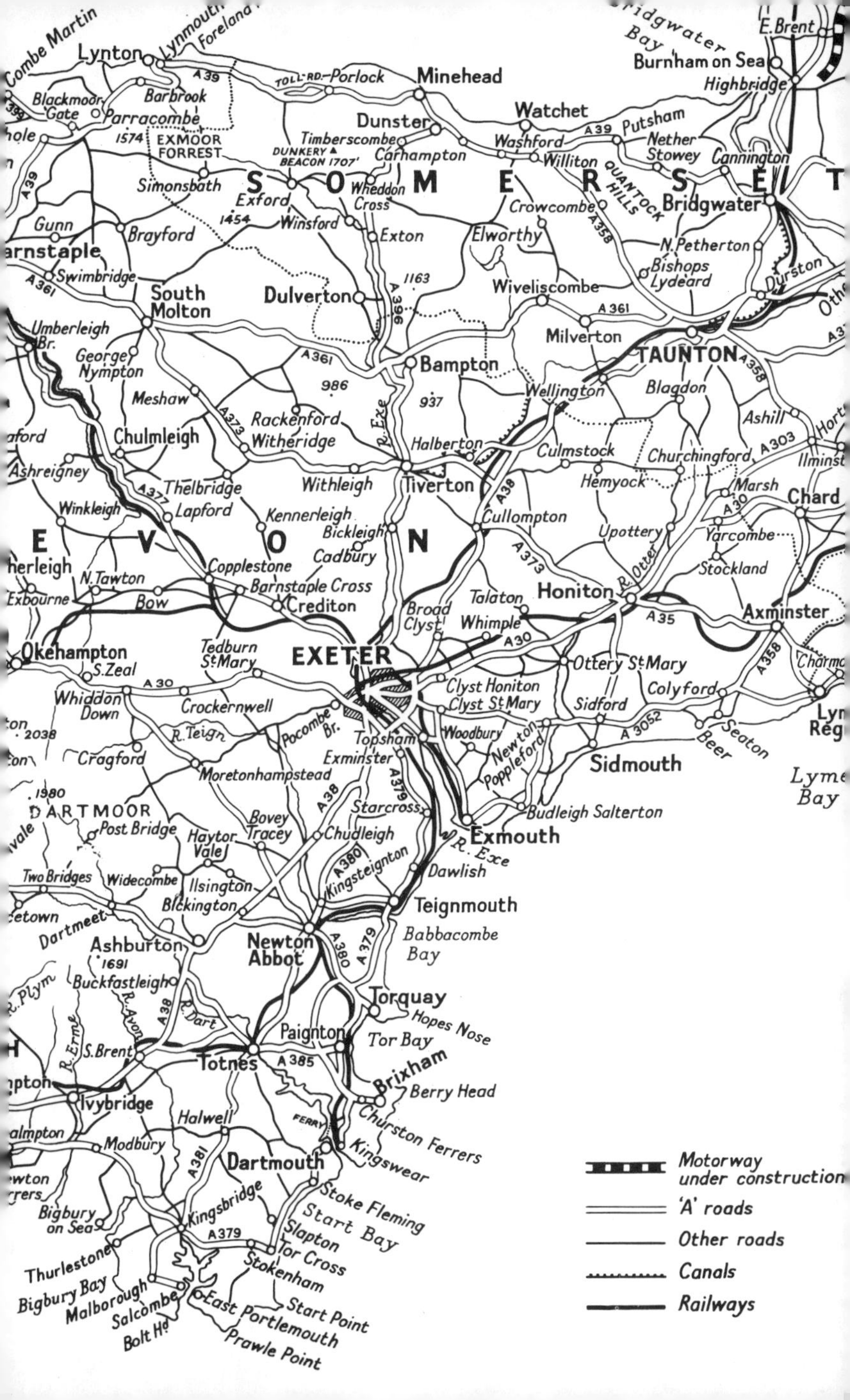
Combe Martin
Lynton
Lynmouth
Foreland
Bridgwater Bay
E. Brent
Burnham on Sea
Highbridge
A 39
Toll Rd.
Porlock
Minehead
Blackmoor Gate
Barbrook
Parracombe
Watchet
Dunster
Putsham
Timberscombe
Washford
Nether Stowey
1574
Exmoor Forrest
Dunkery Beacon 1707'
Carhampton
Williton
Cannington
Quantock Hills
Simonsbath
S O M E R S E T
Wheddon Cross
Crowcombe
Bridgwater
Exford
1454
Winsford
A 358
Gunn
Brayford
Exton
Elworthy
N. Petherton
Barnstaple
Bishops Lydeard
A 361
Swimbridge
1163
Durston
South Molton
Dulverton
A 396
Wiveliscombe
Umberleigh Br.
Milverton
A 361
Taunton
A 358
George Nympton
Bampton
986
937
Wellington
Blagdon
Meshaw
R. Exe
Ashill
A 373
Rackenford
Chulmleigh
Witheridge
Halberton
Culmstock
Churchingford
A 303
Ilminster
Ashreigney
Thelbridge
Withleigh
Tiverton
Hemyock
Marsh
A 377
A 38
Chard
Winkleigh
Lapford
Kennerleigh
Cullompton
A 30
Bickleigh
Upottery
Yarcombe
D E V O N
Cadbury
A 373
Stockland
Copplestone
R. Otter
N. Tawton
Barnstaple Cross
Talaton
Honiton
Exbourne
Bow
Crediton
Broad Clyst
Whimple
A 35
Axminster
Okehampton
Tedburn St. Mary
Exeter
A 30
S. Zeal
Ottery St. Mary
A 358
A 30
Clyst Honiton
Colyford
Whiddon Down
Crockernwell
Clyst St. Mary
Sidford
2038
R. Teign
Pocombe Br.
Topsham
Woodbury
Newton Poppleford
A 3052
Seaton
Beer
Cragford
Exminster
Sidmouth
Moretonhampstead
A 379
1980
A 38
Lyme Bay
Dartmoor
Starcross
Budleigh Salterton
Post Bridge
Bovey Tracey
Haytor Vale
Chudleigh
Exmouth
R. Exe
A 380
Kingsteignton
Dawlish
Two Bridges
Widecombe
Ilsington
Bickington
Teignmouth
Dartmeet
Ashburton
Newton Abbot
Babbacombe Bay
1691
A 379
A 380
R. Plym
Buckfastleigh
R. Avon
Torquay
A 38
R. Dart
Hopes Nose
R. Erme
S. Brent
Paignton
Tor Bay
Totnes
A 385
Brixham
Ivybridge
Berry Head
Halwell
Ferry
Churston Ferrers
Modbury
A 381
Kingswear
Dartmouth
Stoke Fleming
Kingsbridge
Start Bay
Bigbury on Sea
A 379
Slapton
Thurlestone
Tor Cross
Stokenham
Bigbury Bay
Malborough
Start Point
Salcombe
East Portlemouth
Bolt Hd.
Prawle Point
Motorway under construction
'A' roads
Other roads
Canals
Railways

THE RED GUIDES

Edited by Reginald J. W. Hammond

Bournemouth, New Forest
Channel Islands
Cornwall: North
Cornwall: South
Cornwall: West
Cotswolds
Devon, South
Dorset Coast
Isle of Wight
Lake District
London
Norfolk and the Broads
Peak District
Wales N. (Northn. Section)
Wales N. (Southn. Section)
Wales, South
Northern Ireland

SCOTLAND

Highlands of Scotland
Northern Scotland
Western Scotland

RED TOURIST GUIDES

Complete England
Complete Scotland
Complete Ireland
Complete Wales
Lake District (Baddeley)
Complete Devon
Complete South-East Coast
Complete Yorkshire
Complete Cornwall
Complete Scottish Lowlands
Complete Cotswolds and Shakespeare Country
Complete Wye Valley, Hereford and Worcester
Complete Dorset and Wiltshire
Complete Thames and Chilterns

WARD LOCK LIMITED

Introduction

The word "Devon" comes from the name of a Celtic tribe which occupied this south-west corner of England in Romano-British times. The first references to "Defenascir" (Devonshire) are recorded in the Anglo-Saxon chronicles of the ninth century.

Devon in size is the third largest county in England. The Devon coast is broken up in the most unexpected and delightful manner by creeks, estuaries and bays; and in this irregularity and in the variety of the scenery lies its charm. It is a lush landscape of rich pasturage, luxuriant foliage, sheltered combes, extensive moors, and high hedged lanes. Many sparkling streams and rivers intersect the county which is fringed with golden sands, rocky coves, and enchanting bays.

The softness of the air, the glorious rich redness of the sandstone cliffs and soil particularly in the south, the vivid green hinterland and the deep blue sea, combine to make every prospect glow with colour during the long summer days, and there is an all-pervading sense of restfulness and beauty.

The climate is equable and, since much of the area is sheltered by hills and headlands, the winters are mild. Years ago when the rivers were the chief means of communication, Seaton, Sidmouth, Exmouth and Teignmouth were ports of importance. Now, across the mouths of the Axe, the Sid and the Otter, and in lesser degree, the Exe and the Teign, the sea has washed ridges of sand and pebbles, and where commerce once thrived are crowds of holiday-makers boating, bathing or lazing on the sunny beaches.

Exeter, the capital, is a fine city with a magnificent cathedral and many historic buildings of absorbing interest. It is too an excellent centre, for roads lead in all directions and distances are not too great for excursions to be made to any part of the county within the compass of a day's daylight hours.

Torquay has been named "Queen of the English Riviera". Its beautiful setting, sophisticated pleasures, and mild climate make it an all-the-year resort. Paignton with its sands and zoo is frequented by family parties. Slapton, a far-less populated area, also has wonderful sands. Dartmouth combines the delights of a sea, river and market town. Unspoiled Brixham is loved for its picturesque harbour, narrow streets and quaint houses. Salcombe, the most southerly town of the county, provides fine sea fishing and sailing.

Inland, the thriving town of Newton Abbot is another excellent centre for tours. The medieval town of Totnes, with its old walls and gates, its Norman castle, and its Tudor Guildhall, attracts the historian and lover of antiquity. Tucked away in secluded combes, there are many delightful villages.

Plymouth, with a population of a quarter of a million, is the largest city, and in its rebuilt form is a splendid centre for the coast and nearby moors. Its Hoe must surely be one of the finest seaside promenades in the world.

Dartmoor quite apart from its high moorland character embraces lovely gorges, beautiful ravines and deep river valleys. The Moor occupies an area of more than 200 square miles, much of it of a wonderful, subdued colour, a paradise for painter and sportsman, for photographer or just plain idler.

Over the north coast Ilfracombe is the only town of any size. It is well placed among hills and combes. The Torrs to the west, and Hillsborough, nearly 450 feet high, to the east, are connected by a lofty ridge of downs in the south, the whole forming a natural screen which protects and encloses the town, giving it a slightly Continental air.

Barnstaple, the chief business centre of the northern part of the county, presents a pleasing combination of ancient interest and modern industry. All visitors to North Devon go to Barnstaple at some time on their holiday and many stay, for there is good accommodation, and all other places are conveniently reached from it.

Bideford will undoubtedly appeal to Americans. Besides a sentimental interest experienced when walking through the old streets with visions of Salvation Yeo, Amyas Leigh, Sir Richard Grenville, and courtier Raleigh, Bideford is a pleasant, busy little place and its surroundings are extremely beautiful.

There are many smaller coastal places nearby all with their own special appeal. Combe Martin, Lee, Woolacombe, Instow, Appledore, Westward Ho! and Clovelly, whilst inland again are still more attractive villages with fine churches, manor houses and neat farms.

At the north-eastern corner on the edges of Exmoor are delightful Lynton and Lynmouth, the one on its lofty hill, the other nestling attractively in the valley and woods beneath.

Motoring

It is hardly necessary to remark that Devon is one of the most popular motor touring-grounds in the British Isles. The main roads are excellent, but many of the unclassified roads are high-banked, narrow and winding. Modern cars make light work of hills these days but even so there are some gradients that will command respect and care.

As for motor-coaching, it is a case of from everywhere to anywhere. All the resorts, big and little, have their fleets of coaches making day, half-day and shorter trips.

Walking and Cycling

The whole county is admirably suited to walking, since so much of it is open moor and cliff, and so many of the woods have public paths running through them. In fact, with the aid now and then of the coach and bus services, the whole country can be thoroughly explored and enjoyed on foot. Sign-posts are adequate, and hills and cliffs stand out as landmarks. In following the cliff walks, or the many pleasant paths and roads overlooking the sea, care should be taken as the cliffs are crumbling in many places and the incautious may encounter a serious fall or find themselves involved in a small landslide.

The country is good for cycling also, as far as road surface and accommodation are concerned, and many cyclists are to be seen on the roads. They must be prepared, however, to walk up many hills, and even, for the sake of safety, down a few of them.

Camping and Caravanning

Throughout the county there are many places where the caravan can draw up for a day or two or a tent be pitched for even longer periods. The Caravan Club and the Camping Club issue lists of suitable sites and where reservations can be made. There are also many camps where static caravans may be hired for periods. Those towing caravans are warned that some of the hilly by-roads can be quite difficult to negotiate and "Caution" signs should be heeded to the full. For those with tents there are many suitable sites. Permission to camp is usually readily given by landowners or tenants.

Accommodation

Devon has a great many hotels and all resorts have a great range of establishments from luxury to modest boarding house. Even so, as with all popular areas, the demand is tremendous and, where at all possible, advance reservations should be made. Certainly, in the season, it is well-nigh impossible to find chance vacancies in any of the popular resorts. Away from the centres, where hotels cater for the touring motorist, the possibilities are easier, but the accommodation question should always be settled by afternoon. It is frustrating and irksome to search for chance vacancies as darkness descends.

Bishop's Palace and Cathedral, Exeter

Exeter

Angling. – Good fishing in Exeter and Tiverton canals, and in the rivers Exe, Creedy, Culm, and Clyst – for bream, carp, dace, gudgeon, perch, pike, rudd, roach and tench. Pike fishing is not allowed before October 1; for other fish the season is from mid-June to mid-March. Exeter District Angling Association.

Banks. – Branches of all banks throughout the city.

Bowls. – Greens at Belmont pleasure ground. Heavitree pleasure ground, Pinces Gardens and Cowick playing fields.

Cinemas. – *Odeon*, Sidwell Street; *A.B.C.*, London Inn Square.

Cricket. – At ground of *Devon County and Exeter Cricket Club*, West Avenue.

Dancing. – As advertised locally, in hotels and public halls.

Early Closing Day. – Wednesday.

Golf. – *Exeter Golf and Country Club*, Countess Weir.

Greyhound Racing. – County Ground.

Horse Racing. – Haldon Race Club; meetings held at excellent course with 2 mile circuit, just outside city, during August and September.

Hotels. – *Rougemont*, Queen Street; *Great Western*, St. David's; *Royal Clarence*, Cathedral Close; *Queen's*, Queen Street; *Imperial*, St. David's Hill; *Bystock*, Queen Street; *White Hart*, South Street; *Beech Hill*, St. David's Hill; *Devon Motel*, Exeter By-Pass; *Exeter Motel*, Exeter By-Pass, and many others of all grades.

Information Bureau. – 18, Queen Street.

Libraries. – City Library in Castle Street. Cathedral Library, Bishop's Palace. Devon County Library, Isleworth Road, near the Okehampton Road.

Markets. – Cattle market, Marsh Burton Road. General market at Fore Street. Market Day, Friday.

Population. – 93,900.

Post Office. – Bedford Street.

Hunting. – East Devon, Mid Devon, Silverton and Tiverton hunt in the area.

Swimming. – Public covered swimming bath with filtered and heated water, Heavitree Road.

Tennis. – Public courts at Heavitree pleasure ground (8 hard); Pinces Gardens (2 hard); Cowick Barton (3 grass).

Various Sports Clubs. – Archery, badminton, bowls, canoeing, fencing, rowing, swimming, tennis, table-tennis, etc. Apply Information Bureau for particulars of the various clubs.

Exeter is an ancient and fascinating city. In the days of the Romans, and later under the Saxons, it was a frontier outpost whose position – shelving steeply to the river Exe – gave a natural defence against the western Celts.

Later came the Norman Castle, the Cathedral, the Guildhall and other medieval buildings, and the steady growth of the city up to our own times.

In 1942 air-raids inflicted widespread destruction. Much of great beauty and interest was lost, while the main shopping centre was almost wiped out. Much has been rebuilt in a style which is spacious and modern. An inner by-pass and the recently opened M5 have relieved traffic congestion.

The city is not only ancient, but it is charmingly situated in countryside of great beauty, and within a few miles of the sea. From it excellent roads run to all parts of the county.

Those spending only a short time in Exeter should make a point of visiting the Cathedral, St. Nicholas Priory, the Guildhall, the Castle, Northernhay, and walk down the principal streets, with a glance at the old walls and some of the medieval parish churches.

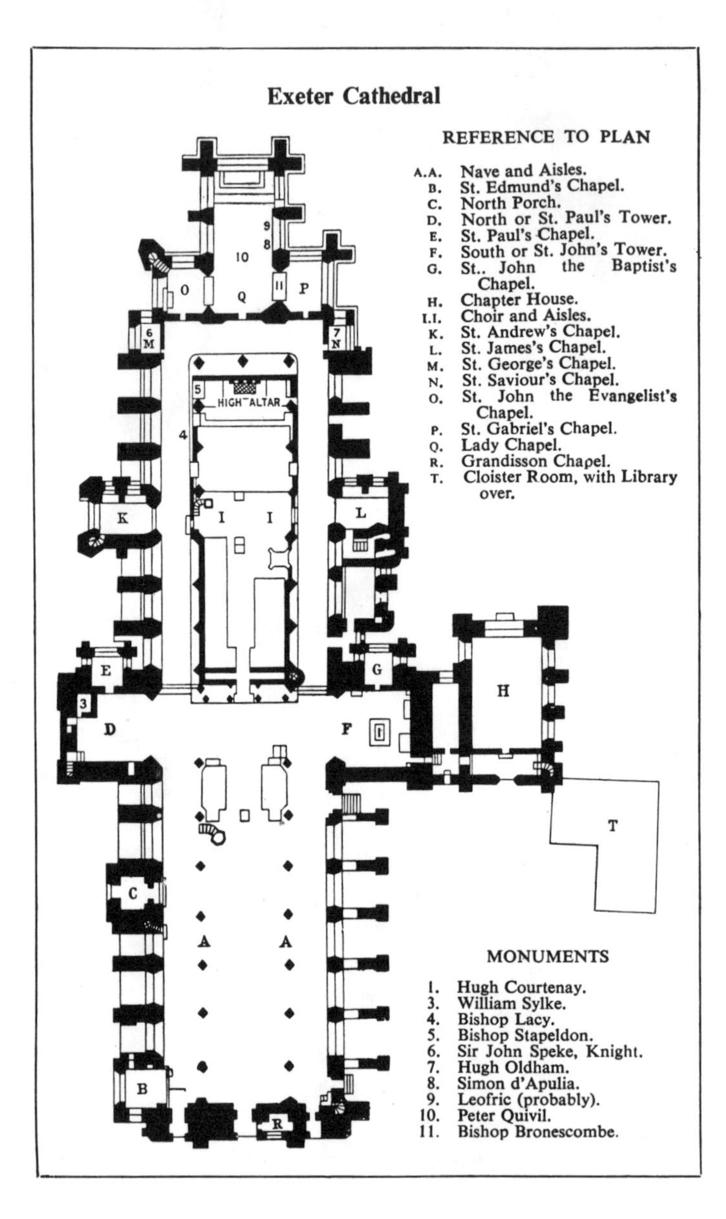
Exeter Cathedral
REFERENCE TO PLAN
A.A. Nave and Aisles.
B. St. Edmund's Chapel.
C. North Porch.
D. North or St. Paul's Tower.
E. St. Paul's Chapel.
F. South or St. John's Tower.
G. St.. John the Baptist's Chapel.
H. Chapter House.
I.I. Choir and Aisles.
K. St. Andrew's Chapel.
L. St. James's Chapel.
M. St. George's Chapel.
N. St. Saviour's Chapel.
O. St. John the Evangelist's Chapel.
P. St. Gabriel's Chapel.
Q. Lady Chapel.
R. Grandisson Chapel.
T. Cloister Room, with Library over.
MONUMENTS
1. Hugh Courtenay.
3. William Sylke.
4. Bishop Lacy.
5. Bishop Stapeldon.
6. Sir John Speke, Knight.
7. Hugh Oldham.
8. Simon d'Apulia.
9. Leofric (probably).
10. Peter Quivil.
11. Bishop Bronescombe.
HIGH ALTAR

Exeter Cathedral

Admission. – The Cathedral is freely open to visitors throughout the day from 7.30 a.m. until 5.30 p.m. or 7, according to the season.
Services on Sundays, 8, 10, 11.15, 3 and 6.30. On week-days, 7.45, 9.30 and 5.30 (Saturdays 3), or as notified.

Dimensions. – The main dimensions are as follows, Total length, 408 ft.; breadth of nave choir, 40 ft.; of the aisles, 20 ft.; of the Lady Chapel, 35 ft. The transept is 140 feet long; the roof of the Cathedral is 68 feet high to the interior vaulting, and the towers, 145 ft.

The Cathedral stands clear of all buildings, in a charming close, so that the grandeur of the architecture and the stone upon stone, blotched black and white by wind and rain and smoke, can be seen without obstruction. The structure is the city's most eloquent memorial of the past, beyond question one of the finest ecclesiastical piles in the country, and one of the most interesting historically. It has been appropriately termed "the pride and glory of the western counties . . . for chaste, correct, and uniform adherence to the best style of English Pointed architecture competing with any cathedral in the kingdom". This is no mere phrase. Every West-Country man is proud of his heritage.

The Saxon monastic church adopted by Leofric as his Cathedral is said traditionally to have stood on the site of the present Lady Chapel.

Westward of this minster, William Warelwast, third Bishop of Exeter and a nephew of the Conqueror, began a newer, larger one, so that by the middle of the twelfth century a Norman Cathedral extended the whole length and width of the present nave – flanked by the great transeptal towers that have ever since been such a unique feature of Exeter – and terminated in an apse at a point where the fourth bay of the choir now ends.

The transformation of this Norman building to its present form was conceived by Bishop Bronescombe about the middle of the thirteenth century. His plan began with the erection of the Lady Chapel clear away to the eastward of the Norman apse, and on the ground where it seems likely Leofric's minster had stood; it proceeded to link this, by the present 100-feet length of Presbytery, to the Norman Choir and Nave, the whole of which was gradually rebuilt in its present lofty Gothic design.

This masterly scheme was carried on by a succession of great "Building Bishops" – Quivil, Bitton, Stapeldon, Grandisson – whose adherence to the original plan, joining up Saxon site and Norman fabric, has given Exeter that consistently harmonious Decorated interior which is so singularly satisfying. The unusual feature of a continuous 300 ft. of graceful roof-vaulting, unbroken from west to east, is due of course to the absence of a central tower; the pair of massive flanking towers, forming transepts in their lower stages, were also fittingly altered, with higher openings and roof-arches corresponding with the rest of the building.

John de Grandisson, who ruled the diocese for over forty years and consecrated the altar in December, 1328, almost finished the edifice as it now appears, except the west front, the east window and the cloisters, which works Thomas Brantyngham (1370–94) completed. Edmund Lacy, who was translated from Hereford in 1420, and died in 1455, built the upper part of the Chapter House. The throne in the choir, the most remarkable thing of its kind in England, and the organ screen, were erected by Bishop Stapeldon (1308–26).

EXETER CATHEDRAL

The Exterior

The best exterior view of the Cathedral is perhaps that which is obtained from the Cathedral yard, or **Close**. The general view of the building does not compare architecturally with that of Salisbury and some other cathedrals, but only the hypercritical will deny that the pile in its old age is imposing.

The Towers. From the exterior the Norman Towers are the most noticeable features. The walls of the north tower are plain to a considerable height; it is then divided into four stages by horizontal bands, and surmounted with an embattled parapet. Each stage is adorned with arcades of round-headed arches, most of which have the zigzag moulding. Some of the arches are pierced with windows, and on the north face of this tower – and the south face of its brother – Bishop Quivil inserted a large Pointed window of six lights, with beautiful and elaborate Decorated tracery, giving light to the transepts, which the towers form in their lower stages.

The towers are almost similar in general form. The south tower is the older and has more Norman arcading than the north tower: each is turned to account in quite a different way.

The North Tower contains an ancient astronomical **Clock**, traditionally supposed to have been presented by Bishop Courtenay (1478).

That there was a timepiece of some sort in the Cathedral as early as Bishop Quivil's time is shown by the Patent Rolls, and by his appointing Roger of Ropeford to repair the organs and "horologe". This is the earliest record of a clock in England, but no part of it survives. In 1376–7 a new chamber was constructed in the North Transept for the "horologe called clokke". The works of an ancient instrument are in the North Transept, the "horologe" being now actuated by a modern movement (1885); the going and quarters portion, combined, are in the chamber behind (mentioned above), and the quarters strike on a small basin bell (1760) just over the dial. The disposal of parts is very much as before, the going and quarters movements being saddled one above the other. The hours are struck – as for centuries past – on the "Peter" bell in the tower above.

There are three other very early clocks in England – at Wimborne Minster; Wells Cathedral; and at Salisbury.

The South Tower contains thirteen of the **Cathedral Bells**. They are the second heaviest peal in England, and very rich in tone. In the North Tower hangs **Peter**, which was given to the city by Bishop Courtenay. It was recast in 1676. The Peter bell weighs 125 cwt. is 76 inches in diameter at the mouth, and 56 inches high, so that it ranks among the largest bells in the kingdom.

The North Porch. Close to the North Tower is the North Porch, which projects a considerable distance beyond the line of the aisles – in fact, as far out as the buttresses of the Cathedral – and is surmounted by a heavy embattled parapet. The portal has a lofty, straight, acute-angled canopy, richly crocketed. Each side is also adorned with arches and niches in which are statues presented in thank-offering for the preservation of the donor's three sons in the 1914–18 war. The largest represents St. George of England, and others St. Denis of France, St. Joseph of Belgium, St. Ambrose of Italy, St. Vladimir of Russia, St. Cyril of Serbia and St. Methodius of Roumania, the patron saints of the allied nations of the First World War. The face of the North Porch in which these figures have been placed was probably added in the fifteenth century to the main portion of it.

The West Front of the Cathedral consists of three storeys. The basement, or screen, containing the three portals, is entirely covered with niches, which are all filled with statues; above this, and receding a little, is the west wall of the nave, in

West Front, Exeter Cathedral

which is a magnificent window, with most beautiful Decorated tracery; and above this, and receding a little in like manner behind the parapet, is the gable of the nave, containing a window of the same style, but of much smaller dimensions. The lower and greater part of the buttresses at this end of the building are hidden behind the projecting storey. The portions seen above are adorned with niches, canopies, and statues. The wall of the nave above the great west window is embattled and surmounted by hexagonal turrets, each with a canopied and crocketed pinnacle. The gable point is ornamented with a canopied niche containing a statue and terminating in a crocketed pinnacle. The screen contains three tiers (except where broken by the windows of the Grandisson Chapel) of figures of saints, kings, and other distinguished persons, somewhat damaged by the soldiers of the Parliamentarian army, and also by the superstition, which lingered long in Devon, that powdered stone purloined from sacred statues possessed medicinal virtues; but much careful restoration has been carried out. On the buttresses above are two other statues – possibly King Athelstan on the north, King Edward the Confessor on the south. On the right of the centre entrance, in the space between the image-screen and the main west wall, is the tiny chapel built by Bishop Grandisson as his mortuary chapel. There are mutilated remains of a reredos on the south wall, and a figure of our Saviour sculptured on the roof. The glass (modern) of the small west window in the south aisle commemorates the Bishop; one attendant holds a model of the Cathedral, and the other that of the Church of Ottery St. Mary, which he converted into a collegiate foundation.

The Interior

The Cathedral consists of a long nave, with two aisles of the same length; north and south transepts under towers dedicated to St. Paul and St. John Baptist; and, at its eastern end, the noble Choir and aisles. The Lady Chapel, and ten other Chapels, connect with the interior at various points (*see* plan).

The Nave. The beauty of the Nave strikes one immediately on entering. The great breadth and length, the rich windows, the uniformity of architecture, the beauty, excellence, and variety of every detail, and, above all, the form and plan of the vaulting, uninterrupted throughout the whole length of the Cathedral, are unrivalled in England. The roof is supported on each side upon an arcade of seven pillars and arches, the former beautifully clustered, the latter wide, but of graceful form, and wrought with mouldings and surfaces. The capitals are exquisitely moulded and of simple design; the bases, consisting of three courses of mouldings, are equally good. Between every two arches is a rich corbel, composed of figures and foliage, of which no two are alike. They support slender reeded columns of stone, with highly decorated and studiously diversified capitals, from which spring the ribs of the vaulting, which are adorned at their intersections with bosses of sculpture of various devices and exquisite finish. This roof, there being no intervening central tower or lantern, is continued across the transept to the eastern extremity of the Choir in one unbroken line, and is the longest known stone vaulting in the Pointed style of architecture.

Projecting from the north wall of the nave is the **Minstrels' Gallery**. The front is adorned with twelve niches, each containing the statue of an angel playing on a musical instrument.

A feature of the nave is the **Martyrs' Pulpit**, erected in 1877 in memory of Bishop Patteson, who suffered martyrdom in the Pacific. It is of Mansfield stone, and is a fine specimen of modern sculpture.

From about here or perhaps a little higher up is the best view of the great **West Window**, with its magnificent fourteenth-century tracery, which formerly was filled with coloured glass in memory of Archbishop Temple (1821–1902), who was Bishop of Exeter from 1869 to 1885. The glass was all destroyed in the raid of 1942 but the new window follows the same lines.

Below to the right is a memorial tablet, in memory of Richard Doddridge Blackmore, the author of that West Country classic, *Lorna Doone*.

At the north-west angle of the nave, immediately to the left of the entrance door, is the **Chapel of St. Edmund the Martyr**, used as the chapel of the Devonshire Regiment. Divided from the nave by a beautiful parclose oak screen dating from the fourteenth century, it has been described as "nearly all window".

In the south aisle is the **Font** of Sicilian marble. It was first used in 1687.

On the south wall, a little to the west of this, hangs the Sledge Flag carried by Captain Scott on his first expedition to the Antarctic, and a little farther east a five-light window commemorates men of Devon who died in South Africa, 1899 to 1902; 467 in all. Below the window are tablets to commanders who earned fame in the same campaign – General Buller, Major-General Kekewich, defender of Kimberley.

The **Transepts** form the lowest stages of the old Norman towers, a feature shared by no other cathedral in England. **St. Paul's Chapel** (the *Children's Chapel*) – to the east of the north transept – and **St. John the Baptist's** – to the east of the south – are fitted up for private prayer and meditation. Beneath the clock in the north transept is the **Chantry Chapel of William Sylke**, a precentor of the Cathedral, his effigy, an emaciated figure in a shroud, being badly mutilated. Nearby are the old works of the clock.

The **Choir Screen** was the work of Bishop Stapeldon, who died in 1326. It is a magnificent example of the style which then prevailed, and is, as a screen, almost unrivalled in England. It is composed of three Pointed arches, richly feathered and supporting an arcade of thirteen compartments. These originally were filled with sculptured panels; they now contain paintings depicting events in Biblical history from the creation onwards; the paintings date from the seventeenth century and are more interesting than artistic. The case of the seventeenth-century organ, built by John Loosemore in 1665, remains, and contains a few of the old pipes. The present organ was erected in 1891. It is a fine sonorous instrument, recently renovated.

The Choir. In the centre of the screen is the door to the Choir. From it the very fine **East Window** may be seen to advantage. It is a nine-light Perpendicular replacement (1391) of the original window, all the other windows being Decorated, of the purest character. Nineteen whole-length figures of saints, patriarchs, and others are portrayed, six of them (three on either side in the lowest row) being survivors from the original window of *c.* 1300.

To the south of the altar are the elaborately and delicately carved sedilia of the fourteenth century, which have been admirably restored. The canopy of the seat nearest the altar, with its wreath of vine leaves, is especially beautiful. The seats themselves are possibly of an earlier date than the canopies; notice the lions which form the elbows.

Probably the most imposing feature of the Choir is the **Bishop's Throne**, of carved oak and with a pyramidal canopy of open carving rising nearly to the height of the vaulting, 52 ft. Round the base are modern paintings of Warelwast, Quivil, Stapeldon, and Grandisson – the four Bishops who did most to make the Cathedral what it is.

The **Stalls** are modern, and elaborately carved with Decorated work. They, too, are of oak, the seats being formed of the old misericords, which, dating from the early part of the thirteenth century, are among the earliest existing in England. Some of them bear very curious carvings.

The **Pulpit** is modern, of oak, replacing a marble one destroyed in the air-raid of 1942.

On the north of the High Altar – the place of honour, as is his due who did so much to beautify the Choir – is the tomb of *Bishop Stapeldon* (d. 1326). The Bishop was Lord High Treasurer to King Edward II and the founder of Exeter College; the effigy of a knight in armour (in the north Choir Aisle opposite) with two squires and a horse is that of his brother, Sir Richard Stapeldon: the bishop was murdered in Cheapside on account of his partisanship of Edward II.

The table tomb nearby, with the indent of a lost brass on it, commemorates Bishop Lacy (d. 1455).

Beyond the Choir and Reredos is –

The Lady Chapel entered from the ambulatory aisle, or Retro-choir, at the back of the High Altar. Thought to cover the site of Leofric's Saxon monastic church, it affords a burial place for several of the Bishops of Exeter. Bishop Bronescombe began the present building, and it was finished by Bishop Peter Quivil, whose

Cathedral Close, Exeter

monument, a slab 9½ feet long with foliated cross and Latin inscription, is in the centre of the pavement. The Lady Chapel has a gem-like appearance, having been carefully restored and enriched with costly gifts as a memorial to the late Dean Gamble. It is 60 feet long, 35 feet wide, and 40 feet high. On the south side of the chapel are the tombs of an early Norman bishop, possibly Leofric himself, and Simon d'Apulia (1223); and on the north monuments of Sir John Doddridge, a judge of the reign of James I, and his wife, Lady Dorothy, the latter famous for the carving of the lace. On the same side the canopied tomb of Bishop Stafford (1419) separates the Lady Chapel from that of **St. John the Evangelist**, and opposite that of **St. Gabriel** is separated in like manner by the tomb and carved effigy of Bishop Bronescombe. The recumbent figure of the bishop, delicately sculptured and coloured, is considered one of the finest in existence.

At the east end of the north aisle of the Choir is **St. George's Chapel**, called also the **Chantry Chapel of Sir John Speke**, who was buried in it (1517); and in a similar position in the south aisle is **St. Saviour's Chapel**, known as **Bishop Oldham's Chantry**, that prelate having built and been interred in it (1519).

The Chapel of St. Andrew – built in the time of Bishop Bronescombe – has windows and vaulting of the same style as the north aisle of the Choir, from which it is entered. Over the chapel is the exchequer room.

St. James's Chapel, originally built at the same time as that of St. Andrew, and following the style of the south aisle, together with its ancient crypt below and the muniment room above, was destroyed during the raids of 1942 but has been rebuilt.

The Cloisters were originally built in a quadrangle south of the Cathedral, in front of the Chapter House, the north walk being designed in Bishop Grandisson's time actually under the nave buttresses. They were destroyed during the Commonwealth, and only a portion, at the south-east angle, was rebuilt in 1887. This has been glazed with stained glass preserved from the great West window when this was replaced by the Archbishop Temple memorial in 1904. The **Cloister Room** gives access to the old library above, which houses the Capitular Archives and Precentor Cook's Collection (admission on application to new Cathedral Library).

The Chapter House, (*shown only on application to the Vergers*), was built by Bishop Bruere (1224–44) in the Early English style of architecture, but the walls were heightened and the present Perpendicular windows and roof placed there nearly two centuries later.

The Bishop's Palace

Stands to the south-east in beautiful grounds which command the best view of the south side of the Cathedral. Here is the new **Cathedral Library**, now administered on behalf of the Dean and Chapter by the University of Exeter. The Library is open to students Monday–Friday, 2–5 p.m. It includes 20,000 books and manuscripts, among which are the "Exeter Book"; a collection of poems in Old English dating from the tenth century; the MS of "Exon. Domesday", the draft of the Domesday text for the south-western counties of England; and the original Foundation Charter of the Cathedral.

St. Mary Steps

Taddiforde Brook
A.3052
NEW NORTH ROAD
VELWELL RD.
VELWELL RD.
Fire Sta.
Reservoirs
St. David's Sta.
HOWELL RD.
HOWELL ROAD
TELFORD RD
CLAYTON RD.
BONHAY ROAD
Technical Coll.
Bury Meadow
ELMGROVE RD.
HELE ROAD
NEW
Clock Tr.
QUEEN'S TER.
Ch.
A377
LOOE ROAD
HAY ROAD
RICHMOND ROAD
QUEEN ST.
Central Sta.
PEEP LANE
ST. DAVID'S HILL
RIVER EXE
HALDON ROAD
LOWER NORTH ST.
IRON BRIDGE
NORTHERNHAY ST.
Ch.
Bus Sta.
PAUL ST.
Sch.
DINHAM RD
Sch.
Ch.
Ch.
NORTH ST.
Weir
Playing Fields
Mount Dinham
NAPIER TER.
EXE STREET
Weir
Cemetery
City Wall
BARTHOLOMEW ST. E.
WATERBEER ST.
Cin.
MARY ARCHES ST.
Ch.
Sch.
Cem.
BARBICAN STEPS
A.377
St. Nicholas Priory
Ch.
Ch.
MARKET ST.
A377
BONHAY ROAD
Sch.
BARTHOLOMEW ST. W.
Tuckers Hall
FORE ST.
KING ST.
SMYTHEN ST.
LYNWOOD AV.
WESTERN ROAD
TUDOR ST.
STEPCOTE HILL
PRESTON ST.
RACK ST.
Sch
Ch.
OKEHAMPTON RD.
Ch.
A3085
MANOR RD.
CAMBRIDGE ST.
BULLER ROAD
OKEHAMPTON STREET
Sch.
NEW BRIDGE ST.
FROG ST.
Ch.
EDMUND
City Wall
ALBION ST.
Sch.
BRUNSWICK ST.
OAKFIELD RD.
COMMERCIAL ROAD
BULLER RD.
CLEVELAND ST.
EXE BR.
CLARENCE RD.
NELSON RD.
CLINTON ST.
MAPLE RD.
A.3084
GERVASE AV.
A.3085
Great Shilhay

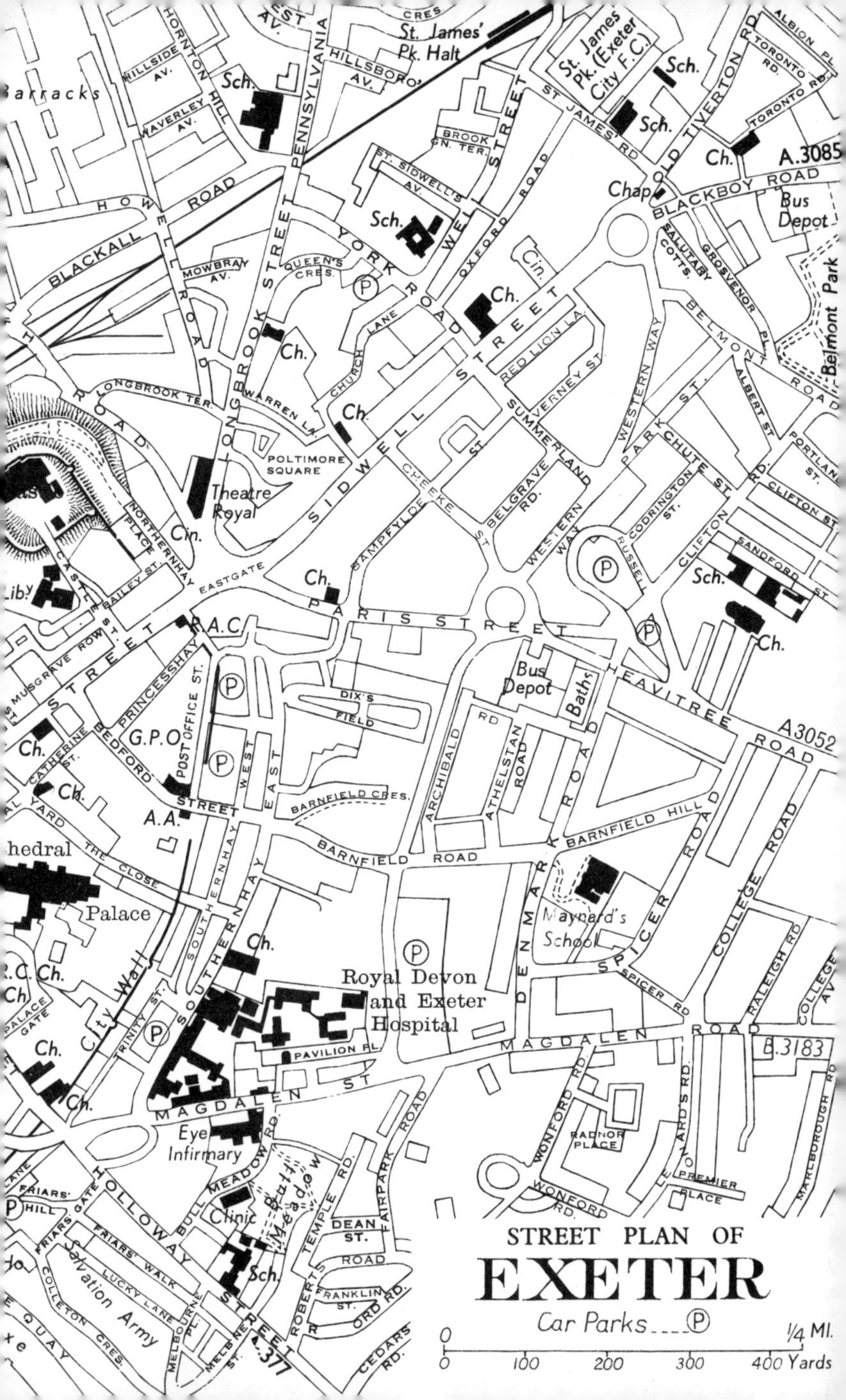
STREET PLAN OF
EXETER
Car Parks ---- P
0
1/4 MI.
0 100 200 300 400 Yards
St. James' Pk. Halt
St. James Pk. (Exeter City F.C.)
Barracks
HILLSIDE AV.
WAVERLEY AV.
HORNTON HILL
HILLSBORO' AV.
PENNSYLVANIA
ST. JAMES' RD
OLD TIVERTON RD
ALBION PL
TORONTO RD.
TORONTO RD.
A.3085
BLACKBOY ROAD
Bus Depot
Chap.
SALUTARY COTTS.
GROSVENOR PL.
BELMONT ROAD
Belmont Park
BROOK GN. TER.
ST. SIDWELL'S AV.
HOWELL ROAD
BLACKALL ROAD
MOWBRAY AV.
QUEEN'S CRES.
YORK ROAD
WELL STREET
OXFORD ROAD
Cin.
RED LION LA.
SUMMERLAND ST
VERNEY ST
WESTERN WAY
ALBERT ST
PORTLAND ST
CLIFTON RD.
CLIFTON ST
CHUTE ST.
PARK ST.
CODRINGTON ST.
RUSSELL ST
SANDFORD ST
CHURCH LANE
LONGBROOK STREET
LONGBROOK TER.
WARREN LA.
POLTIMORE SQUARE
Theatre Royal
SIDWELL STREET
CHEEKE ST
BELGRAVE RD.
SAMPFYLDE ST
Cin.
NORTHERNHAY PLACE
CASTLE ST.
BAILEY ST.
EASTGATE
PARIS STREET
R.A.C.
MUSGRAVE ROW
PRINCESSHAY
POST OFFICE ST.
G.P.O.
BEDFORD STREET
CATHERINE ST.
A.A.
DIX'S FIELD
WEST
EAST
BARNFIELD CRES.
ARCHIBALD RD
ATHELSTAN ROAD
Bus Depot
Baths
HEAVITREE ROAD
A3052
DENMARK ROAD
BARNFIELD HILL
BARNFIELD ROAD
SPICER ROAD
COLLEGE ROAD
Maynard's School
SPICER RD
RALEIGH RD
COLLEGE AV
Cathedral
THE CLOSE
Palace
R.C. Ch.
PALACE GATE
City Wall
SOUTHERNHAY
TRINITY ST.
Royal Devon and Exeter Hospital
PAVILION PL.
MAGDALEN ROAD
B.3183
MAGDALEN ST
WONFORD RD.
RADNOR PLACE
LEONARD'S RD.
PREMIER PLACE
MARLBOROUGH RD
WONFORD RD.
Eye Infirmary
BULL MEADOW RD.
Bull Meadow
FAIRPARK ROAD
TEMPLE RD.
DEAN ST.
ROAD
FRANKLIN ST.
ROBERTS
CEDARS RD.
Clinic
HOLLOWAY STREET
A.377
FRIARS' HILL
FRIARS' GATE
FRIARS' WALK
LUCKY LANE
Salvation Army
COLLETON CRES.
MELBOURNE PL.
MELBOURNE ST.
QUAY
Ch.
Sch.

From the Close, Exeter

The Close

In the Close is a white marble statue by Alfred Drury of **Richard Hooker**, the celebrated divine. He was born at Heavitree in 1553.

Almost opposite the West Front of the Cathedral, on St. Mary Major's Green, is the **Devon County War Memorial**, unveiled by the Prince of Wales in May, 1921. Designed by Sir Edwin Lutyens, a cross of Devon granite, 30 feet high, it bears the inscription: "The County of Devon. To her glorious dead, 1914–1919. Te Deum Laudamus".

In the Cathedral Yard stands the *Royal Clarence Hotel*, built about 1770, and often said to have been the first establishment in England to assume the French title of "Hotel".

When in the Close, time should certainly be spared to visit the beautiful Elizabethan building known as **Mol's Coffee House**, which is believed to have been built in 1596. The "Dutch" gable is comparatively modern. The handsome oak panelling and carving in the room on the first floor are late Elizabethan and among the forty-six coats of arms painted on the frieze are those of Drake, Raleigh, and Gilbert. The building is now used for the display of pictures, china, etc. Admission to view by courtesy. The **Annivellars' Refectory** is a few yards from Mol's Coffee House and is now part of an antique shop. It was built at the beginning of the fifteenth century, the front being added in 1618. These chantry priests were called *Annivellarii* or *Annuellarii* because they celebrated the anniversaries of the deaths of their benefactors with masses. They were suppressed by Edward VI and the chantries abolished in 1549. The hall was then used for various lay purposes. The beamed roof, stone fireplace and original carved screen still remain.

Nearby is the quaint little **St. Martin's Church**, consecrated in 1065, but almost completely rebuilt in the fifteenth century of local Heavitree stone. The fine arch dividing the nave and chancel may be earlier than fifteenth century. The oak barrel-vaulted roof, the west window, font, Jacobean altar rails and west gallery are all of note. In the basement of the bookshop near the Royal Clarence Hotel may be seen, by permission, **St. Martin's Well** 32 feet deep and connecting with underground springs.

In Catherine Street near-by was the small chapel of St. Catherine founded about 1450. This was badly damaged in 1942, and only the walls remain. When the site was cleared, a Roman tessellated pavement was discovered.

Also in the Cathedral Close is the former town house of the Courtenays, now the home of the **Devon and Exeter Instution** for promoting Science, Literature, and the Arts. The hall of the adjacent building has a fine timbered Perpendicular roof with carved corbels, and a minstrels' gallery. The Jacobean oak door beyond, with its wicket gate and the arms of Bishop Cotton above, opens into a picturesque quadrangle, the residence of the Bishop of Crediton; the mullioned windows of the hall and porch, and the tracery of the windows in the chapel, together with the other details, make a charming picture. The **Deanery** is the large house to the south-west of the Cathedral surrounded by a high wall and bearing the official arms of the Dean of Exeter over the entrance door. The building has a medieval hall with a fourteenth-century roof, minstrels' gallery and lancet window. It is not open to visitors. The House of the Archdeacon of Totnes is in the eastern part of the Close, the front being of Georgian design. Of the three houses which once faced this house only one survived the raids of 1942. This was formerly the residence of the Archdeacon of Barnstaple. Below the Deanery stands the **Chantry**, which is a modern replacement and now houses the Cathedral School. The Hall of the Vicars Choral in South Street was almost completely destroyed in 1942.

Old Parish Churches

The medieval Parish Churches of Exeter, with their red sandstone towers, have sadly decreased in numbers. They were restricted to nineteen after the Norman Conquest, and have since been reduced further by disuse, amalgamation, and man's destruction.

Though small, they are of considerable interest. Most still show signs of Norman and pre-Norman work, and are rich in mural monuments that epitomize the history of the city.

The most interesting of the churches that remain are:

St. Petrock, at the centre of the parish of old Exeter, where the four main roads of the city meet. A church has existed here since the days of Athelstan.

St. Martin *(see above)* in Cathedral Yard.

St. Stephen (High Street) which was founded before the Conquest, later fell into disuse, and was rebuilt about 1664 after destruction by fire. It is now united with St. Martin.

St. Pancras (behind Guildhall), a pre-Saxon foundation on the site of the Roman Praetorium. The present church is twelfth century and possesses a fine Norman font.

St. Mary Arches (Mary Arches Street, off Fore Street) is also largely twelfth century, with Saxon work in the east wall, and a double Norman arcade. It has undergone reconstruction after severe bomb damage; the timber to restore the roof came from an American landing barge used on D-day.

St. Mary Steps (p. 30) in West Street.

St. Thomas (p. 30) is a larger church, outside the city walls and across the Exe.

St. Nicholas Priory

Another ancient ecclesiastical building that should not be missed is the Priory of St. Nicholas, in The Mint, turning out of Fore Street. Possibly the last surviving English example of a monastic guest house, the Priory has a fine eleventh-century crypt, an exceptional fifteenth-century guest hall and some sixteenth-century plasterwork. It contains some good English sixteenth-century and seventeenth-century furniture. *April–September inclusive. Weekdays and alternate Saturday mornings.* This building, the entire western range of the original priory, is the only complete "guest house" of an ancient monastery that has survived in the whole country.

The Guildhall

Next to its Cathedral, Exeter glories in the ancient Guildhall. Rebuilt in 1330 and restored about a century later, it is probably the oldest municipal building in England.

Formerly, it is believed, there was a Saxon building on this site. The particularly fine oak roof was erected in 1468. The beautiful Elizabethan portico which projects across the footway was added in 1593. The **Guildhall** is a handsome room with old panelling which has a frieze emblazoned with the armorial shields of ancient incorporated trades of the city and its most famous citizens. On the walls hang several portraits, not the least interesting being that by *Lely* of the Princess Henrietta Anne, daughter of King Charles I, who was born June 16, 1644, at Bedford House, which once stood on what later became Bedford Circus.

Another interesting portrait, also by Lely, is that of General Monk, afterwards Duke of Albermarle. The flags of Canada, Australia, New Zealand, and South Africa were presented to the City by the Dominions. More recent additions are the Polish and American flags – the latter presented in 1943, whilst in the gallery is the white ensign of H.M.S. *Exeter*. This was flown during the battle of the River Plate. Other portraits are hung in the **Mayor's Parlour**, above the porch, where is a mantelpiece made of lava brought from Poltimore, 3½ miles north-east of Exeter. This room, originally a chapel, was used in the Stuart period as a prison. Later it was an assembly room for the merchant adventurers, and after that a council chamber. It contains interesting portraits, furniture and china. On the landing outside may be seen the City regalia, which includes many beautiful specimens of the goldsmith's art, ancient and modern.

Behind the Guildhall, in Waterbeer Street, a Roman pavement was discovered in 1888 during building work, but it has now been covered. Visitors should look for **Parliament Street**, surely the narrowest street in the country; it runs from Waterbeer Street to High Street.

Far older than the Guildhall is –

Rougemont Castle

adjoining Northernhay, close to the Central Station, and approached from High Street by way of Castle Street. Shakespeare tells us that the name raised the fears of Richard III when he first heard it. The Castle – or rather the small piece that remains – was built by the Conqueror, and probably received its name from the red sandstone of which it was composed. A writer of the days of Charles I called it "an old ruyning castle, whose gaping chinks and aged countenance presageth a downfall ere longe"; and the "downfall" then "presaged" was soon afterwards expediated by the unkind treatment the building received at the hands of the Roundheads under Fairfax. The ancient gateway has been restored, and beyond it is the old castle yard, in which stands a full-length *Statue of Hugh, Earl Fortescue.* Behind this statue is the **Devon Assize Hall and Sessions House**, in which is a large picture of "The Judgment of Daniel", painted by Brockedon, and presented by him to his native county. Round the castle yard run the ramparts, on the two outer sides forming part of the old **City Wall**, from which glimpses of the city and surrounding country can be obtained.

Close to the gateway of the castle yard is the entrance gate to Rougemont House and Gardens. The former houses the **Rougemont House Museum** (*weekdays*) devoted to the history of Exeter and Devon. The Rougemont Gardens (*open daily to dusk*) were purchased by the council in 1913, and with their shady paths and terraced slopes make a delightful retreat. Here, too, is part of the castle fosse.

From the Rougemont Gardens an archway in the wall, on the level, or through **Athelstan's Tower**, if the ascending path on the right is taken, gives access to **Northernhay Gardens**, Exeter's famous promenade and open-air resort claimed to be the first public park in England.

The City Walls. Rougemont Castle was the main defence of ancient Exeter, and perhaps the best idea of the old wall may be obtained in its vicinity, but the interested visitor may desire to see more. The original walls were probably built about A.D. 930, and are best seen in Southernhay where the surrounding buildings have been destroyed in the raids. It is possible to make almost a circuit of the walls although the only part of the wall that can be actually promenaded is between New Bridge Street and Bartholomew Street East. Leaving Northernhay by the Queen Street entrance, the road is crossed to Northernhay Street opposite, and a little way down on the left is an arch in the wall itself, which formerly led into Maddock's Row. Close at hand is the legendary site of Athelstan's Palace. On the Iron Bridge, just above where Northernhay Street joins North Street, is a short stone pillar, with a flag-staff, erected to commemorate the Diamond Jubilee and the site of the **North Gate**, pulled down in 1769; a facsimile of the gate is shown with the original weather vane. It is unfortunate that none of the medieval gates remain, but plaques mark their sites. Beyond Iron Bridge, on the city side, is Bartholomew Street, and here one follows the wall itself, the typical rampart of a walled city, with widespreading views across the river to the hills beyond. The **East Gate** stood at the end of High Street, near the modern cinema. Near St. Mary Steps Church in West Street is the space where the **West Gate** stood, as recorded on a tablet. Crossing the inner by-pass and continuing along Lower Coombe Street, one is almost on the wall again, and keeping down Quay Hill and turning sharp to the right under it, what remains of the Water Gate may be seen. By taking

Quay Lane on the left South Street is reached, but there is nothing but a bronze tablet to show where the **South Gate** stood close to Trinity Church. Two sections of the old wall in Quay Lane collapsed in 1927; the remaining parts, cemented and made secure, show a difference in level of some 20 feet between the city wall within the wall and the outside.

Principal Streets

High Street is the chief street of the city, and, under the names of New Bridge Street, Fore Street, High Street, East Gate, Sidwell Street, and Tiverton Road, it extends from the Exe Bridge to the north-eastern suburbs of Exeter. Old Leland declared that "there be diverse fair Streates in Excester, but the High Streate, that goith from the West to the Est Gate, is the fairest". It may have been the main Roman road, and is certainly the most important and probably the oldest street in Exeter. The air-raids of 1942 destroyed many of its ancient buildings and modern shops. Numbers 41 (1564), 46 and 47 remain though much restored and plans to rebuild are in hand. The Red Brick House opposite Queen Street is of seventeenth-century Dutch architecture, of bricks brought from Holland. Other old houses, apart from those in the Cathedral Close and High Street, can be seen at Stepcote Hill; and the Tudor House stands in West Street.

The old waterfront is worth a visit, with its *Custom House* dated 1681, and containing fine ceilings and a Charles II coat of arms. Opposite the Quay is the **Exeter Maritime Museum** (*daily, fee*) with a collection of craft collected by the International Sailing Craft Association.

The centre of Roman Exeter, where North Street and South Street join High Street, was formerly known as the **Carfax** (Lat. *quadrifurcus*) or cross-roads. The western extension of High Street originally bore left at the Guildhall and ran down Stepcote Hill to the river Exe.

A short distance down Fore Street on the right is the **Tucker's Hall,** or the Hall of "The Worshipful Company of Weavers, Fullers and Shearmen", to give it its full title (shown Tuesdays, Thursdays and Fridays 10.30 to 12.30 in summer; Fridays 10.30 to 12.30 in winter). Built in 1471–2 as the "Lady Chapel of the Tuckers and Weavers", it was divided by a substantial floor into lower and upper halls about 1634; the fine roof and panelled walls are still displayed upstairs.

Fore Street and New Bridge Street continue downhill to **Exe Bridge**, across which is the **Church of St. Thomas**, whose vicar in 1549 was hanged on the tower as a rebel.

In the neighbourhood of the bridges, on the east side of the river, there is much that is noteworthy for those interested in church and domestic architecture. In Tudor Street, behind the new block of office buildings stands an Elizabethan merchant's house, fronted with hanging slates.

In West Street is the parish church of **St. Mary Steps**, founded in the twelfth century. The richly ornamented tub font is of this period. The present fabric dates largely from the fifteenth century, when the church was enlarged. Of the screen only three bays, enclosing the south aisle chapel, belong to that century, and even these were not original to the church, but were taken from the medieval church of St. Mary Major when it was demolished in the middle of the last century; the other five bays across the chancel were constructed at that time by Harry Hems. The fine east window of Christ in majesty, by John Hayward, was introduced in 1697. Over the high altar is a tester bearing the Tetragrammaton – the Hebrew letters of the name Jehovah or YHWH. Outside the south face of the tower are clock jacks which strike the hour and quarters. The clock and the central figure date from the early seventeenth century; the other figures are considerably later.

Close by the church some fifteenth-century merchants' houses have been preserved and restored. Two stand at the foot of **Stepcote Hill**, which in medieval times was the main street into the city from the west. The third, thought to be one of the oldest timber-framed houses in Europe, was removed bodily in 1961 from its site in Edmund Street three hundred feet up the slope to its present position on the corner of West Street. Adjacent to this house are the remains of the **West Gate**, and part of the west wall of the city. Further parts of the wall may be seen on the river side of the inner by-pass. Between the West Gate and the river is Edmund Street, built on the arches of the earliest stone bridge over the Exe. **St. Edmund-on-the-Bridge**, rebuilt in the nineteenth century on the site of the bridge chapel, but now in decay, flanks this road.

Turning up Coombe Street into South Street, and continuing into Magdalen Street, we reach the Eye Infirmary. Opposite are the picturesque red stone buildings known as **Wynard's Hospital**, or Almshouses. An archway leads into the cobble-stoned courtyard, round three sides of which the dormer-windowed houses of the twelve pensioners are built, the chapel and the widows' quarters occupying the fourth side. These were built in 1430 by William Wynard, a Recorder of the City of Exeter. Exeter is rich in almshouses; a little nearer Southernhay a stone in the wall on the same side marks the former site of Palmer's Almshouses for four poor women, endowed in 1487, and some distance beyond Wynard's are the rebuilt **Magdalen Almshouses**, the old Leper hospital; still farther, at the junction with Heavitree Road, is **Livery Dole**, with its ancient chapel and newer dwellings, begun by Sir Robert Dennis in 1591. If this does not satisfy interest in such foundations, a bus may be taken to the top of Sidwell Street, in which, at the beginning of Old Tiverton Road, are **St. Anne's Almshouses**. St. Anne's Day, July 26, has been observed here for centuries.

At the junction of Denmark and Barnfield roads is the **Martyrs' Memorial**, commemorating the Martyrdom of Thomas Benet, M.A., burnt at Livery Dole in 1531, and Agnes Prest, who suffered the same fate on Southernhay in August, 1557, the then mayor refusing to allow the sentence to be carried out within the city wall.

By keeping to the left, High Street can be regained *via* Barnfield Road. Bedford Circus, containing the earliest houses of Georgian Exeter, was entirely destroyed by bombing. Much attractive Georgian architecture can, however, still be seen in Barnfield Crescent, in Southernhay West, and in other parts of the City outside the walls. Retracing one's steps down High Street into **Queen Street**, passing the **Civic Hall** on the left, a visit can be paid to the –

EXETER

Royal Albert Memorial Museum and Art Gallery

A Gothic building, erected in 1865–9 as a memorial to the Prince Consort. It houses one of the largest collections in the region with fine paintings and watercolours, collections of costumes, silver and glass, and sections on ethnography, foreign archaeology and natural history. *Open weekdays.*

The Underground Passages

A unique feature in Exeter is the complex of medieval underground water courses from which the growing population of the Cathedral complex and the City were supplied with wholesome water from the Well of St. Sidwella outside the City Walls between Longbrook Street and Sidwell Street. *Weekday afternoons or by arrangement with the Director of Museums and Art Gallery.*

The City Library is in Castle Street. Burnt out in the war a new building was opened in 1965. The search rooms of the City Record Office adjoin.

The University

Developing from the University College of the South West and obtaining full University status in 1955, the University now caters for some 3,300 students taking courses in Arts, Law, Social Studies, Science, Applied Science and Education. Although the original College Building, in Gandy Street in the city centre, still houses the departments of Law, Psychology and Extra-Mural Studies and the Institute of Education, the rest of the University has moved to the 270 acre Streatham Estate, a wooded site, about 1 mile to the north of the city centre.

Exeter School – originally on the site of St. John's Hospital in High Street, was removed to its present site in Victoria Park Road in 1877. Other Grammar Schools are **Hele's School** (boys) **Maynard's School** (girls) and **Bishop Blackall School** (girls). **Exeter Technical College** is in Hele Road and the **College of Art** in Queen Street. **St. Luke's College** is a residential training college for schoolmasters.

The Cathedral Choir School in the Close is a preparatory school. **The West of England School for the Partially Sighted** and the **Royal School for the Deaf** are in Topsham Road.

Another institution of which Exeter is proud is the **Royal Devon and Exeter Hospital** in Southernhay. The **Princess Elizabeth Orthopaedic Hospital**, on the Topsham side of the city, was opened in 1927.

Countess Weir

Three miles down river from Exeter is Countess Weir, set amid delightful surroundings which, time and again, have inspired the painter's brush. The old bridge has yielded to the demands of modern traffic and now forms an important road link although the bridge has been scheduled as an ancient monument. A good way to the Weir is to take the ferry at Topsham and walk up the Canal towpath (west bank).

It is stated that the river Exe once flowed deep with the tide as high as Exeter, but in 1282 it was closed to salt water and sea-going vessels by the erection of a weir, the work of the then Countess of Devon, who thus

Exmouth

Banks. – *Barclays, Devon and Exeter, Midland, National Westminster*, all in Rolle Street. *Lloyds*, Strand.
Bathing. – Safe bathing from Maer Bay and in numerous sandy coves. Large open-air swimming-pool on sea front.
Bowls. – Two public greens at Phear Park. *Madeira Bowling Club* (adjoining Esplanade).
Car Parks. – Along sea front where indicated, and near the Bus and Rail Station.
Cinemas. – *Royal*, off Exeter Road; *Savoy*, Rolle Street.
Clubs. – *Manor*, St. Andrew's Road; *Rotary*, weekly lunch on Mondays 1 p.m. at Clapp's Café, Rolle Street; *Conservative*, Parade; Y.M.C.A., Victoria Road; Y.W.C.A., Imperial Road; also Sports Clubs of all kinds.
Early Closing. – Wednesday.
Ferry. – Motor ferry across the Exe to Starcross.
Fishing. – Excellent facilities from shore or boats. Freshwater fishing in canal at Countess Weir and for trout in River Otter. Apply to Rolle Estate Office, East Budleigh, for trout fishing licences.
Hotels. – *Imperial*, Esplanade; *Devoncourt*, Douglas Avenue; *Grand*, Esplanade; *Cavendish*, Esplanade; *Pencarwick, Bow House, Highcliffe*, Louisa Terrace; *Royal Beacon*, The Beacon; *Manor*, The Beacon; *Moriglen*, Salterton Road, and many others.
Information Bureau. – Manor Grounds, Alexandra Terrace.
Library and Reading-Room. – Exeter Road.
Population. – 26,840.
Post Office. – Rolle Street. Sub-offices – Exeter Road, Littleham Cross, St. Andrew's Road and Withycombe.
Sailing. – *Exe Sailing Club* at Dock entrance. Good mooring facilities and professional service available. Races held regularly.
Tennis, etc. – Public courts (hard and grass) at Phear Park. Grass courts at Undercliff, sea front, *Exmouth Croquet and Lawn Tennis Club* at Cranford has 11 grass and 3 hard tennis courts, 4 croquet and 2 squash courts. Temporary membership arranged. Annual open tournament.

Exmouth is the largest coastal resort between the Axe and the Teign. It stands at the mouth of the river *Exe*, where the sea sweeps in round Straight Point, strewing the shore with yellowish sand that threatens at times to block the estuary. Half-submerged sands stretch from the Warren at the river mouth along the front of Exmouth, leaving a channel for sailing craft of all descriptions.

The present town has developed from the two parishes of Littleham and Withycombe Raleigh, and is now popular as a "family holiday" resort, well liked for its pleasant equable climate, its clean, extensive sands, fine sea front and the magnificent coastal views extending from Dawlish to Brixham and Berry Head. The broad, well-kept **Esplanade** is well equipped with cafés, kiosks and shelters. There is a large Concert Pavilion and opposite, overlooking the sands, are the Beach Gardens.

On the landward side of the Esplanade are the **Madeira and Plantation Walks** forming part of an almost continuous background of green slopes, wooded cliffs, gardens and sports fields.

The Marine Drive, bounded by the Maer on one side and the beach on the other, sweeps on another mile under the cliffs to the red rocks of Orcombe. Practically all along this extensive shore are facilities for bathing. At low tide it is possible to walk round the headland, and a path leads down

The Sands, Exmouth

to this side from the cliffs, a path thronged when the incoming tide drives holiday-makers before it.

The cliffs may be gained from the Drive by paths and steps cut in the sandstone or with less exertion by turning off close to Maer Road.

The Maer, a sandy, tussocky stretch with a path sloping up towards Orcombe is one of Exmouth's greatest attractions. This path gives glorious views. It can be followed over fields close to the cliff and across the peninsula of **Straight Point**, where it is possible to descend to the beach, and by a steep climb up Westdown Beacon to Budleigh Salterton.

In addition to its scenic attractions Exmouth offers a wide variety of amusements and sports. At the Pavilion in the centre of the sea front, dances, concerts and other entertainments are held. For children, there is a large enclosed playground near the lifeboat station where they may safely play in the care of attendants. Near by is the Zoo with a Pets' Corner. Along the sea front, Approach Golf, Putting, Bowls and Tennis are available. Those who prefer to watch the experts can attend the minor county matches at the Cricket Club (near Madeira Walk) or visit the Exmouth Lawn Tennis Club, where international players compete in the annual open tournaments.

Near the Pavilion is the fine open-air swimming-pool. Sea-bathing is good; what is called the "bay" is the recognized bathing-place at high water. Beyond Orcombe Point there is a popular bathing beach at Sandy

Bay Holiday Camp and there are numerous small sandy coves ideal for bathing. Exmouth's shore is safe and pleasant for bathers, but a little to the east of the old coastguard station the current is swift, and caution is necessary.

The boating facilities are excellent. The Exe Sailing Club has headquarters near the Jetty. The harbour provides safe anchorage for yachts. Motor-launches make cruises to adjoining resorts and up the Exe to Turf, and steam-launches make trips to sea or up the estuary.

Excellent sea-fishing can be had at Exmouth, bass, pollack, etc., being plentiful in season. There is a Sea Angling Association. Boats go over the bar every day at the mackerel season, and visitors can usually, for a small gratuity, accompany the fishermen or engage the boat. The docks can also be fished, tickets having first been obtained at the Pier.

The **Docks** – for Exmouth is a commercial port as well as a health resort – lie hidden away behind the western end of the Esplanade. Here Customs officials and steamship agents congregate; the jetty for the Starcross ferry is close by, and the **Pier** stands out into the river channel.

The **Town** is pleasantly laid out with open spaces and well provided with good shops. Near the rail and bus station is the town centre, **The Strand**, where there are attractive gardens surrounding the War Memorial. In the **Manor Grounds**, just beyond, is the Information Bureau. From here, the road uphill leads to the **Beacon** a high open terrace dominated by the fine tower of **Holy Trinity Church**. This is a comparatively modern building, erected on the present site in 1823–5, then restored and enlarged in 1905. On Beacon Hill are the most attractive houses of Exmouth. These were built at the end of the eighteenth century. Lady Nelson lived for a time in No. 6 and Lady Byron in No. 19. Many are now hotels and have fine views out to sea and across to the Haldon Hills. More hotels line the Esplanade and principal thoroughfares.

To the north of the town, at Withycombe, is **Phear Park**, with tennis courts and bowling and putting greens.

Sandy Bay, Exmouth

Excursions round Exmouth

This corner of Devon is rich in historical associations, and no one familiar with the country bounded on three sides by the Otter, the Exe, and the sea, and by the cathedral city on the north-west, will deny its natural beauties. The Otter is not imposing, but it is a pleasant Devon stream. Near its mouth the Exe is broad, if shallow, with many nooks and corners on its tree-clad banks that give delight.

1. Withycombe and St. John-in-the-Wilderness

A favourite walk is from Exmouth to St. John-in-the-Wilderness, a distance of rather less than three miles by way of **Withycombe Raleigh**, now joined to the main town by extensive housing development. The **Church** in this village, in the Early Decorated style, was erected in 1864. At Bystock, a mile and a half to the north-east, is the **Church of St. John-in-the-Wilderness**, first built with a dedication to St. John the Baptist. In 1778 this was pulled down with the exception of the battlemented tower and north aisle, which has windows of beautiful designs and a fine specimen of the old Devonshire wagon-roof. The whole nave has been carefully rebuilt of the old stone with a similar roof. Buses run conveniently to the Church entrance for the Sunday service.

2. To Littleham

At one time Exmouth was part of Littleham; buildings, however, have so extended the town that now Littleham, like Withycombe Raleigh, must be regarded as part of Exmouth. The most pleasant ways of reaching Littleham, which is some two miles east of Exmouth, are by the cliff-path or by way of Douglas Avenue.

Littleham Church (SS. Margaret and Andrew) is interesting; it is the ancient parish Church of Exmouth. It is mainly of fifteenth- and early sixteenth-century date, but the chancel dates from the thirteenth century. The much restored screen is worth notice, and near the organ is a memorial (1746) to Henry Stafford on which is a carving of a three-masted ship. Among the memorial tablets is one in the chantry chapel to the memory of Lady Nelson, wife of the hero of Trafalgar. She lived for many years at the Beacon, Exmouth, dying in London in 1831, and was buried in the churchyard. The same tablet is also a memorial of Captain Nisbet and his wife. (He was her son by her first husband.) Another memorial is to Robert Drake who lived near by at Spratshayes (now a farm).

The return to Exmouth can be made by the high road, by the lane direct to the Maer, or by the much longer route by the cliff; or the walk may be lengthened by steering a course to the cliffs, and thus dropping down into Budleigh Salterton from **Westdown Beacon**, the hill which overlooks that town, and from which magnificent views of land and sea are obtained.

3. To Lympstone

The route is by the Exeter road. In 1½ miles is Courtlands toll house (*bus stop*), where Summer Lane on the right leads past **A-la-Ronde**.

This is a circular house built in 1798 by a Miss Jane Parminter and her cousin Mary Parminter after seeing San Vitale, Ravenna. The rooms range round a central octagonal hall. On the upper floor is the Shell Gallery, decorated with fanciful designs in shells and feathers. There are interesting prints, engravings, silhouettes and samplers. *The house is open on Wednesdays in May and additionally Tuesdays and Thursdays, June to September, fee.*

A little higher up the lane a path on the right leads across an adjoining field to the almshouses and chapel of **Point-in-View** commanding views of great beauty. Over the entrance to the chapel is the inscription "The Point in View". The almshouses were founded in 1813 by two maiden ladies named Parminter, mentioned above. In addition to the four neat little "cottages", a room was provided to serve as a schoolroom for six female children: "the children of Jewish parents shall in all cases be preferred". The "point in view" of the Misses Parminter was the conversion of the Jews to Christianity prior to their promised return to Palestine. A little chapel with a residence and a stipend for a United Reformed minister, is attached to the almshouse. Divine service takes place every Sunday, and as it is a pleasant walk from Exmouth many visitors attend the services. The two Misses Parminter are buried below the organ. The four residents of the cottages maintain their little gardens and are always pleased to welcome visitors and show them over the chapel and almshouses.

The walk may be pleasantly extended to Lympstone by going down the lane again, and continuing across the main road and later turning right, and then left down to the shore and rightwards, alongside the river.

Lympstone is a picturesque riverside village about two miles north of Exmouth, just off the main road to Exeter. One long, straggling street leads down to the waterside. The **Parish Church** was rebuilt in 1864, and of the early fifteenth-century edifice only the tower remains. Fine views are obtained from the top of the clock tower. Lympstone's recreation ground, the **Cliff Field,** now belonging to the National Trust, commands a beautiful prospect to the west over the river, of the distant Haldon hills, and of Powderham Castle.

The pleasant early nineteenth-century house a little to the north and overlooking the Exe, is **Nutwell Court** which until recently was occupied by the descendants of Sir Francis Drake.

Near Nutwell Court, the road to the right leads to the village of **Woodbury**, or this can be reached by the footpaths over the fields and commons. This picturesque village of cob-walled and thatched cottages was probably founded in the seventh century by the Saxons. The **Church of St. Swithin** dates back to the thirteenth century. The fine tower was added in 1409 and the large north aisle in the early sixteenth century. Some of the woodwork is notable.

About a mile east of the village is **Woodbury Castle**, the name given to a series of earthworks of British origin, called by the Romans *Alauna Sylvia*. The camp covers about five acres, is oval in shape, and commands a view of the country from the Blackdown range to Portland on the east, and to Berry Head on the west. It has been the scene of many encounters, and here, in 1549, the first Lord Russell encamped when he came to the relief of Exeter, then besieged by the Cornish rebels, with whom a battle took place in the vicinity. Woodbury Castle is on the spur of high ground running north-east from **Black Hill** – a splendid place for picnics.

4. To Budleigh Salterton

The coast between Exmouth and Budleigh (5 miles) is worth exploring. The rocks about **Straight Point** – half-way – afford good scrambling and a fine view up and down the coast.

An alternative route is to follow the high road for about one and a half miles, and then to branch off to the right along the road to **Littleham** (*see* p. 39), whence a path leads to Westdown Beacon, overlooking Budleigh. The view from the Beacon comprises all that is specially interesting between Exmouth and Budleigh Salterton.

The high road ascends steadily out of Exmouth and presents, looking back, fine views over the Exe estuary to the Haldon range and along the red coast, in the midst of which Dawlish lies in its little combe.

The Front, Budleigh Salterton

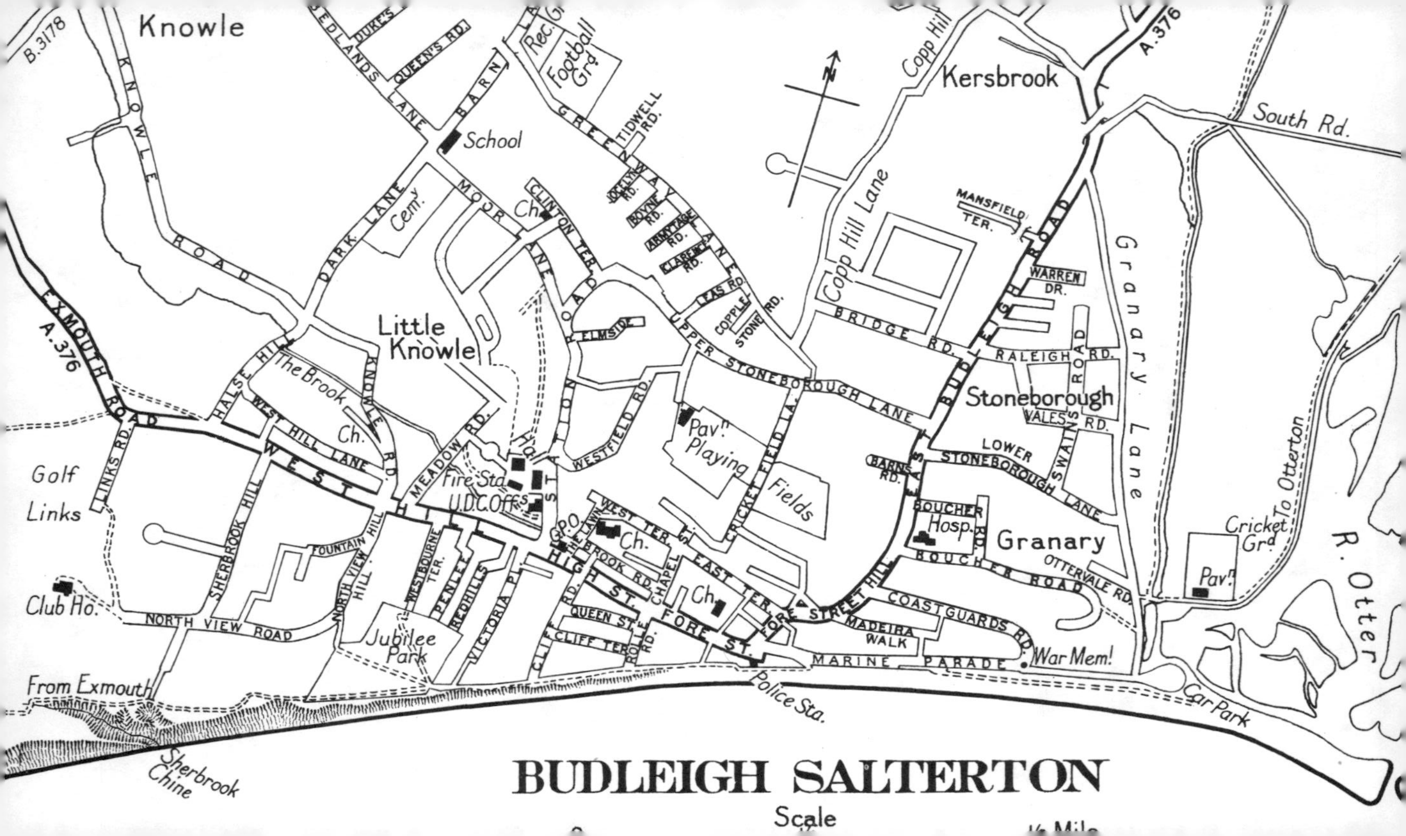
BUDLEIGH SALTERTON
Scale
Knowle
Knowle Road
B.3178
Sedlands Lane
Duke's
Queen's Rd.
Barn Lane
Rec. Gd.
Football Grd.
School
Greenway Lane
Tidwell Rd.
Joslyn Rd.
Boyne Rd.
Armytage Rd.
Clarence Rd.
Leas Rd.
Copple Stone Rd.
Dark Lane
Cem.y
Moor Lane
Ch.
Clinton Ter.
Station Road
Elmside
Little Knowle
The Brook
Halse Hill
West Hill Lane
Knowle Rd.
Ch.
Meadow Rd.
Fire Sta.
U.D.C. Offs.
Westfield Rd.
Upper Stoneborough Lane
Pav.n
Playing Fields
Cricket Field La.
Kersbrook
Copp Hill
Copp Hill Lane
Mansfield Ter.
Bridge Rd.
Budleigh Road
Warren Dr.
Raleigh Rd.
Raleigh Road
Stoneborough
Vales Rd.
Swains Rd.
Lower Stoneborough Lane
Granary Lane
A.376
South Rd.
To Otterton
Cricket Grd.
Pav.n
R. Otter
Barns Rd.
East St.
Boucher Rd.
Hosp.
Granary
Boucher Road
Ottervale Rd.
Coastguards Rd.
War Mem.l
Marine Parade
Madeira Walk
Fore Street Hill
Fore St.
East Ter.
Chapel St.
Ch.
West Ter.
The Lawn
G.P.O.
Brook Rd.
High St.
Queen St.
Cliff Ter.
Cliff Rd.
Rolle Rd.
Victoria P.
Redhills
Penlee
Westbourne Ter.
North View Hill
Fountain Hill
West Hill
Sherbrook Hill
North View Road
Jubilee Park
Police Sta.
Car Park
Exmouth Road
A.376
Links Rd.
Golf Links
Club Ho.
From Exmouth
Sherbrook Chine

Budleigh Salterton

Angling. – Good sea fishing. Angling in river Otter (tickets from Rolle Estate Office, Exmouth).
Bathing. – Pebble beach. Beach huts available.
Banks. – *Barclays, Lloyds, Midland and National Westminster; Devon and Exeter Savings Bank.*
Bowls. – At Games Club and at Lawn Tennis Club in Cricket Field Road.
Buses. – Services to Exeter, Exmouth, Lympstone and Woodbury; to East Budleigh, Otterton and Ladrum Bay; and to Sidmouth.
Car Parks. – Station Road, Fore Street, Brook Road and Beach (east end).
Concerts and Dances. – In Public Hall.
Early Closing Day. – Thursday.
Golf. – *East Devon Club* (18 holes), ¾-mile from station.
Hotels. – *Rosemullion, Rolle, Southlands, Links-Pinewood, Park House, Long Range, Nattore Lodge.*
Hunting. – The East Devon Foxhounds meet in the district.
Library. – Branch of County Library in Station Road.
Population. – 4,360.
Post Office. – High Street. Sub-offices at Greenway and at Knowle.
Police Station. – Fore Street.
Tennis and Croquet. – Lawn Tennis and Croquet Club. Open tennis tournaments in August. Croquet tournaments in May and July. Tennis courts also at Games Club.

Budleigh Salterton is a holiday resort of comparatively recent birth, although it is recorded in 1210 as Saltre, and in 1405 as Salterne, the name being derived from the salt pans by the Otter, tended by the monks of Otterton Priory. A century ago it was merely one of many coves along the coast where smuggling was carried on, a cluster of less than a score of cottages. Today the resident population is more than four thousand. No town can develop without telling its story in new-looking shops and houses; but Budleigh Salterton retains much of its early simplicity, and can still claim to rank among the most pretty and secluded of Devon watering-places. It appeals especially to those who like a quiet seaside residence within easy access of other places. Exmouth is but a short westward run, Sidmouth is handy to the East, and Exeter is equally accessible.

Budleigh Salterton lies near the mouth of that sparkling trout stream, the *Otter*, in a charming valley, the hills of which protect it from all winds except the south-east, which is the aspect it turns towards the sea. Hence its climate is genial and warm in the winter months. As a holiday retreat, Budleigh Salterton has much to recommend it. It has a long stretch of beach, a charming typical Devonshire trout stream, and a countryside rich in historical interest and endowed with many natural beauties.

The beach of large oval pebbles, about two miles in extent, is open to the Channel.

The town consists mainly of a long street sloping gently from Knowle Hill down to the sea, but within recent years modern houses and villas have sprung up in every favourable situation. By the side of the street flows a small stream, which gives the town a quaint appearance, not lessened by the little bridges that span it to give access to the houses.

The **Parish Church** is a handsome building of Devon limestone with marble facings, dedicated to St. Peter. In Clinton Terrace is the **Roman Catholic Church** of St. Peter, with some interesting statues. Near the Station is the **Public Hall**, used for dramatic performances, concerts, films, etc.

But Budleigh Salterton is visited not for its features as a town, but for its sea air and glorious cliffs which rise gently from the little parade, which in turn gives access to the beach. On the east the Marine Parade slopes up to a little red sandstone bluff overlooking the saltings and the marshy vale of the Otter. In this conspicuous position, where the road turns inland, still on high ground, is the **War Memorial Cross**. From the car park, just beyond the Memorial, a footpath on the left leads up the valley and by bridge across the river to Otterton. The beach stretches away on the one hand as far as the mouth of the Otter, with a breezy walk along the pebble-ridge, and on the other for some distance under the cliff. From the Parade a broad path climbs the cliff westward, with seats at intervals, passing at the end of the houses the open space known as Jubilee Park. Rounding **Sherbrooke Chine**, a break in the cliffs, the path eventually reaches **Westdown Beacon**, one of the most delightful points of vantage for sea views in this part of Devon. From here **Littleham** (*see* p. 39) can be reached, or continuing by a steep, rough descent and across the neck of Straight Point, the path can be followed to Exmouth, with fine views most of the way from Salterton.

East Budleigh

Hayes Barton

Walks and Drives from Budleigh

East Budleigh

Some two miles north of Budleigh Salterton, is a typical, quaint Devon village, where thatched cottages abound and time seems to make the least possible change in its peaceful charms. The village is inextricably associated with Sir Walter Raleigh, and contains the mother church of the district, dedicated to All Saints.

The oldest part of the **Church** – the north side – is probably thirteenth century, the rest fifteenth century; its list of vicars goes back to "Stephen 1261" and the doors of the church are the original ones – about 500 years old. The first two pews on the left-hand side of the middle aisle are the Raleigh pews; the first bears the family arms, but those on the second (dated 1537) have been defaced, possibly at the time of Sir Walter Raleigh's execution. The church contains the tomb in which lie the remains of Sir Walter Raleigh's father's first wife.

The deeply carved pew-ends are very interesting; the subjects are all secular – a peculiarity shared by only one other church in England. They are over 400 years old and were probably all carved by local craftsmen. Other points of interest are the fifteenth-century font, and the double hagioscope on the south side of the chancel.

Sir Walter Raleigh's Birthplace

A mile westward from East Budleigh is **Hayes Barton**, the house in which Sir Walter Raleigh was born about 1552. It is now a farmhouse, nestling in a charming wooded dale. The house is E shaped, with projecting wings and pillared porch, its thatched roof broken by three gables. The reputed scene of his birth is a room in the west wing at the top of a dark winding staircase, and the interior retains many of its ancient features. *The house is open on week-day afternoons, admission fee, from June to mid-September or by appointment.*

Otterton

Eastward from East Budleigh is **Otterton**, a picturesque village, with many "cob" cottages and a fine chestnut grove.

The place belonged to Githa, mother of Harold, the last of the Saxon kings. The Conqueror gave it, with several adjacent manors, to the Abbey of Mont St. Michel, in Normandy. Stephen or John built a small Priory, capable of accommodating four monks, as a cell to that Abbey, bestowing on them a number of privileges and perquisites on condition of their distributing bread to the value of sixteen shillings a week to the poor. Henry V dispossessed the foreign abbey of the Priory and gave it to his then newly-founded monastery at Syon House, Isleworth.

An old writer states: "And after ye suppression it was purchased by Richard Duke, Esq., being a clarke in the coorte of augmentations. He bwilded a fayr howse in this place uppon an ascent over the river Other wch driveth his mylles underneath the howse". Remains of this house may still be seen, with traces of the Priory, near the **Church** (rebuilt 1871) and in the vestry are several memorial brasses to the family.

Otterton used to be a centre of the Honiton lace industry, and some years ago there was a lace club, the members of which walked round the village once a year with a large flag made entirely of Honiton lace.

The return to Budleigh Salterton may be made by road, or along the left bank of the river through Otterton Park. Most visitors, however, walk or ride out to the coast at **Ladram Bay**, little more than a mile from Otterton and linked with Salterton by bus. Ladram, with its interesting rocks, is described on p. 59.

Bicton

Bicton, a three-mile ride or walk from Salterton, is less than a mile north of East Budleigh. About half-way, at four cross-roads, is a square brick shaft, surmounted by a white stone cross, dated 1743. It serves a useful purpose as a guide-post, and its sides are inscribed with scriptural texts, perhaps the most appropriate being: "Oh, hold Thou up our goings in Thy paths that our footsteps slip not". A stone's throw from the stone obelisk is **Bicton Park**. On the confines of the park, in a grassed enclosure close to the road, is the beautiful modern **Church**, erected in 1851 by the last Lady Rolle (the title is extinct), and in the churchyard beside it are the ruins of its ancient predecessor, beside which is the base and stump of an old cross. Close to the ruins are some old stocks.

Bicton Gardens, forming part of Lord Clinton's estate and among the most beautiful in Britain, are open to the public from the week before Easter until mid-October. Teas available. Entrance about 200 yards from church. The gardens were laid out in 1735 to designs of Le Notre who planned the gardens at Versailles. In 1840 a Pinetum was added and now contains a fine collection of trees. An 18-inch narrow gauge railway runs through the grounds. A Countryside Museum contains many interesting exhibits relating to country life, including farm wagons, tools, cider-making apparatus, old tractors and traction engines.

Colaton Raleigh. The village, a mile north of Bicton, is attractive with a wealth of trees and cob and thatch cottages.

The Church has been rebuilt except for its fifteenth-century tower. It has a Norman font. Near it is an interesting building, Place Court, once known as the Dean's House. This manor once belonged to Sir Walter Raleigh's father, from whose family the last part of Colaton Raleigh is derived. The projecting porch has an upper chamber with a Gothic window and piscina, and was evidently at one time used as an oratory.

The return journey may be made across the Common by Yettington or by a much longer route taking in Woodbury Castle (p. 41).

Harpford

By road 5 miles north of Budleigh Salterton and 3 miles north-west of Sidmouth. On the east side of the bridge at Newton Poppleford take the turning for Harpford Church. In the churchyard is an old cross restored as a memorial to a former vicar, Augustus Toplady, author of the famous hymn, *Rock of Ages*. Turn left into the Tipton road at the corner of churchyard, where is a War Memorial Cross, and almost at once right, between houses. In a short distance turn right again down the lane, at the end of which is a gate and a stile on the right leading into **Harpford Wood.**

A favourite place for picnics is **Black Hill** (543 feet), reached by going up Knowle Hill and over the Common. The magnificent view well repays the climb.

To Sidmouth

It is a delightful walk of six and a half miles from Budleigh Salterton to **Sidmouth**, taking the path just beyond the Marine Parade up to the bridge across the Otter, then by path and drive to Otterton, and thence the reverse way to that described on p. 46, avoiding the turn to Ladram.

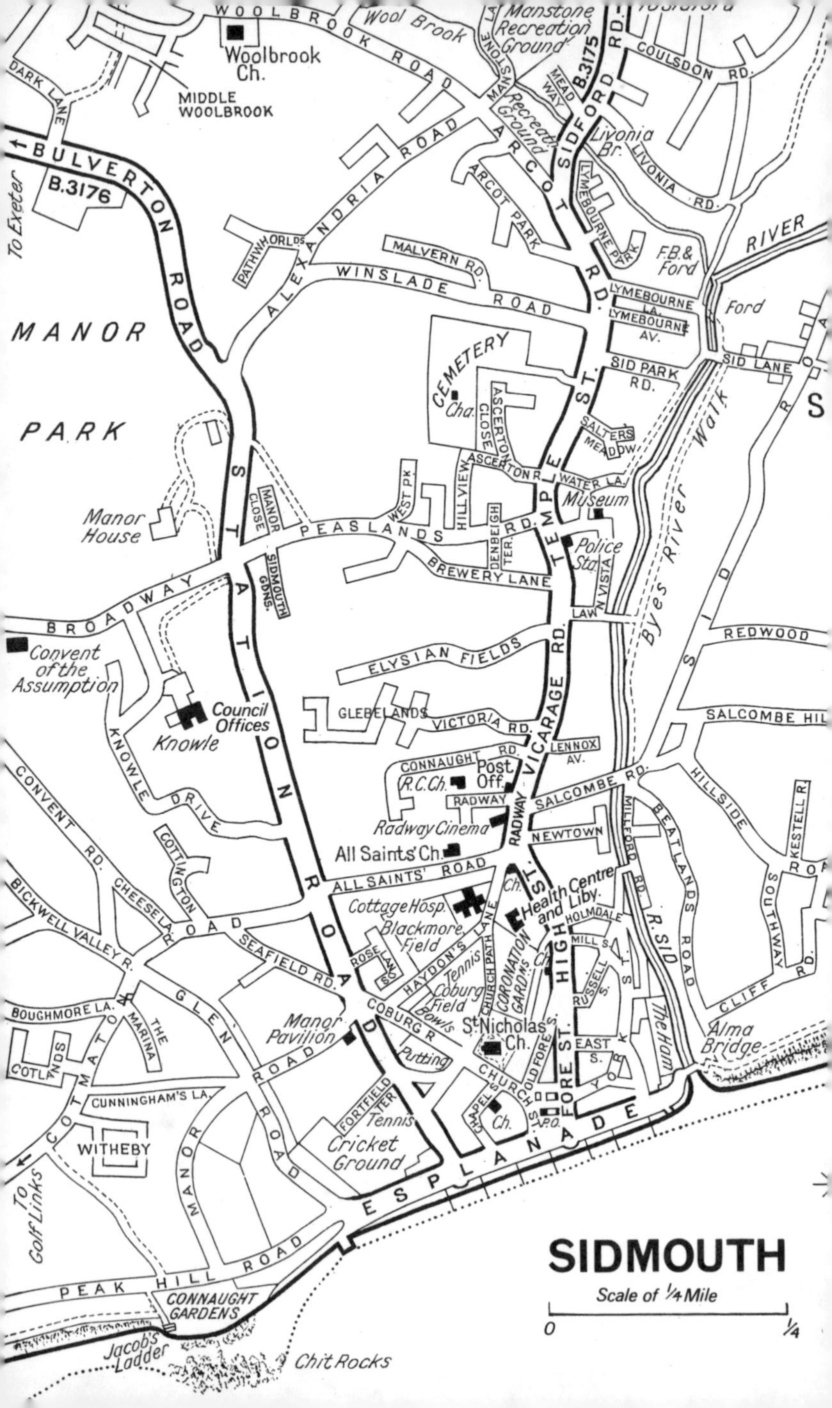

SIDMOUTH
Scale of 1/4 Mile
0
1/4
WOOLBROOK ROAD
Wool Brook
Woolbrook Ch.
MIDDLE WOOLBROOK
DARK LANE
BULVERTON ROAD
B.3176
To Exeter
MANOR PARK
Manor House
Manstone Recreation Ground
MANSTONE LA.
Recreatn Ground
MEAD WAY
B.3175
SIDFORD RD.
COULSDON RD.
Livonia Br.
LIVONIA RD.
LYMEBOURNE PARK
F.B. & Ford
RIVER
Ford
ALEXANDRIA ROAD
ARCOT RD.
ARCOT PARK
PATHWHORLDS
MALVERN RD.
WINSLADE ROAD
LYMEBOURNE LA.
LYMEBOURNE AV.
SID PARK RD.
SID LANE
CEMETERY
Cha.
ASCERTON CLOSE
ASCERTON R.
SALTERS MEADOW
WATER LA.
Museum
TEMPLE ST.
HILLVIEW
WEST PK.
MANOR CLOSE
PEASLANDS RD.
DENBEIGH TER.
Police Sta.
BREWERY LANE
STATION ROAD
SIDMOUTH GDNS.
BROADWAY
LAWN VISTA
Byes River Walk
SID ROAD
REDWOOD
Convent of the Assumption
Council Offices
Knowle
KNOWLE DRIVE
ELYSIAN FIELDS
GLEBELANDS
VICTORIA RD.
SALCOMBE HILL
CONNAUGHT RD.
Post Off.
R.C.Ch.
LENNOX AV.
VICARAGE RD.
SALCOMBE RD.
HILLSIDE
KESTELL R.
RADWAY
Radway Cinema
NEWTOWN
MILLFORD RD.
BEATLANDS ROAD
All Saints' Ch.
ALL SAINTS' ROAD
CONVENT RD.
COTTINGTON
CHEESE LA.
ROAD
Ch.
Health Centre and Liby.
HOLMDALE
SOUTHWAY
Cottage Hosp.
Blackmore Field
BICKWELL VALLEY R.
SEAFIELD RD.
ROSE LAWN SQ.
HAYDON'S LANE
Tennis
CHURCH PATH
CORONATION GARDNS.
HIGH ST.
MILL S.
RUSSELL S.
YORK ST.
R. SID
CLIFF RD.
BOUGHMORE LA.
COTMATON
THE MARINA
GLEN ROAD
Coburg Field
Bowls
COBURG R.
Manor Pavilion
St. Nicholas Ch.
OLD FORE S.
FORE ST.
EAST S.
The Ham
Alma Bridge
COTLANDS
Putting
CHURCH S.
CUNNINGHAM'S LA.
FORTFIELD TER.
CHAPEL S.
P.O.
WITHEBY
MANOR ROAD
Cricket Ground
ESPLANADE
To Golf Links
PEAK HILL ROAD
CONNAUGHT GARDENS
Jacob's Ladder
Chit Rocks

Sidmouth

Banks. – *Barclays, Lloyds, Midland, National Westminster, Devon and Exeter Savings Bank.*
Bathing. – Shingle beaches with sand at low tide. Good bathing.
Bowls. – Public greens and club at Coburg Field.
Buses. – To Exeter, Ottery St. Mary and Honiton. Budleigh Salterton and Exmouth, Beer. Seaton and Lyme Regis, Sidford and Sidbury.
Camping and Caravan Sites. – At Dunscombe Manor Farm and Thorn Farm, Salcombe Regis.
Car Parks. – Bedford Lawn, Ham, Esplanade, Manor Road (Jacob's Ladder Beach).
Cricket. – Frequent matches on beautiful ground adjoining sea front.
Early Closing Day. – Thursday.
Entertainments. – Cinema, band concerts, orchestral concerts, plays, dancing and shows in Manor Pavilion.
Fishing. – From beach and streams.
Golf. – Peak Hill (18 holes).
Hotels. – *Belmont, Victoria, Fortfield, Bedford, Royal York, Elizabeth, Woodlands, Riviera, Faulkner, Redlands, Royal Glen, Royal London, Westcliff, Kingswood, Sussex, Linstead, Devoran*, and many others.
Libraries. – County Library branch at Blackmore Drive. Church House Library at Coburg Road.
Museums. – Hope Cottage, Coburg Road; Woolacombe House, Woolacombe Lane.
Population. – 11,890.
Post Office. – Vicarage Road. Sub-offices at Market Place, and Woolbrook; Fore Street, Sidbury.
Sailing. – Sailing club with weekly races during season. Visitors welcomed.
Tennis. – Courts at Cricket Club ground. Courts also at Coburg Pleasure Grounds near St. Nicholas Church.

Midway between the estuary of the Exe and the mouth of the Axe the lofty cliffs drop suddenly to disclose a pretty valley through which the little river *Sid* runs gaily to the sea, and in which the town of Sidmouth spreads itself in the sun. The two enclosing heights are Peak Hill to the west, and Salcombe Hill to the east, and from either there is a grand view along the shores of the wide bay into which east Devon rivers debouch, and which extends from Start Point on the west to Portland Bill on the east.

Sidmouth is proud of its Regency history which still permeates the place. The town is one of the most delightful holiday haunts in the West and a favourite place of residence for retired folk. Its hilltops are still free from buildings. At the head of the valley is a famous Bronze Age burial ground and the town is encircled by sites of ancient forts. They were considered Iron Age but as the Devon Archaeological Society's research goes on, their history is shown to be far more complex and interesting. The mother of Harold possessed the manor, which was one of those which the Conqueror bestowed on the monks of Mont St. Michel as a thank-offering for the success which had attended his arms.

In olden times Sidmouth was quite an important port, mentioned in the same breath as Plymouth and Dartmouth. About 1450, owing to extreme storms and a simultaneous rise of the land, the harbour choked up, like those of Otter, Axe and those much farther east.

Jacob's Ladder Beach, Sidmouth

Sidmouth is an attractive and dignified town which has preserved much of its early nineteenth-century architecture. The sea front is bordered by comfortable friendly buildings – many of them Georgian or Regency "cottages". The beach is shingle, with sand at low tide and beyond Chit Rocks, the **Esplanade** is about a third of a mile in length and overlooks the bathing beach. Westward from the Esplanade are the **Connaught Gardens**, formally opened by H.R.H. the Duke of Connaught in 1934. The gardens cover 2½ acres, have sheltered walks, and provide views extending from Portland Bill in the east to Berry Head in the west. Band concerts, Folk and Old-Time Dancing take place here, and the gardens are floodlit. Adjoining them is **Jacob's Ladder bathing beach**, a sandy expanse where children may safely bathe and play. The coastal footpath leads to **Peak Hill**, and the open spaces of **Willoughby Field** and **Cliff Fields**. The height of **Peak Hill** shelters the Royal Glen, the former home of Queen Victoria. Glen Road leads past the **Convent of the Assumption** to the high ground of Muttersmoor; a left-hand turning leads to the **Golf Links** on the slopes of Peak Hill.

Abutting on the Esplanade is the **Cricket Ground**, one of the best pieces of turf in the West Country. Cricket is a prominent feature of Sidmouth life in the season, and the splendid croquet lawns and tennis courts also attract first-class players.

At the eastern end of the Esplanade is the ornamental **Alma Bridge**, beneath which the river Sid meanders down to the sea. In fact it only has a mouth for almost exactly half the days of the year. The sea has thrown up a pebble ridge across it, which needs considerable water to breach it. The medieval days when Sidmouth sent a little fleet to Calais are long over, and today the Sid is an insignificant stream that merely lends a picturesque charm to portions of the valley. Near the Bridge is a pleasant promenade and a car park at **The Ham**, where there is also a model boat lake and a playground for children.

From Alma Bridge, the lower slopes of **Salcombe Hill** are ascended by steps in the hillside, and there are seats at convenient intervals, from which charming views are gained. A short climb is well repaid by the sight of the town and beach – in summer always alive with holiday-makers. A zigzag path serves as an alternative to the steps ascent. Beyond the Alma Cliff there is a footpath up over Salcombe Hill some 500 feet above sea-level, from which very fine panoramic views can be obtained. A considerable area of land at the top of the hill is open to the public to enjoy.

Admirably situated on Salcombe Regis Hill is the **Norman Lockyer Observatory**, founded in 1912 by the late Sir Norman Lockyer and constituted as an independent corporation in 1916. It is now under the control of the University of Exeter and membership is open to any interested persons. It is occasionally open to view.

From the Esplanade, Station Road leads to the main Exeter Road. **Market Place** gives access to the main road through the centre of the town and to the Sidford road. To the left of the Market Place is the **Parish Church of St. Nicholas**. This was re-built in 1859–60, except for the fifteenth-century tower and the two arcades on either side of the nave. It is of some interest on account of its hexagonal pulpit of Devon marble, its handsome reredos, and panel of medieval glass. The window at the west end was erected by Queen Victoria in memory of her father. A building not far from the church that may attract attention is the **Old Chancel**, consisting largely of stonework taken from the church when the latter was re-built.

In Church House there is a library.

Sidmouth has an abundance of open spaces and pleasure grounds. Almost immediately adjoining the Parish Church is **Coburg Field**, where there are tennis courts and bowling greens. Opposite the Coburg Field Pavilion, Church Path leads to **Blackmore Hall Coronation Gardens**. Here are shady seats and lovely lawns and an atmosphere of peace and seclusion. **Barton Close** pleasure ground near-by has good putting greens. Knowle Grounds, Station Road are open to the public. At the northern end of the town are two more large recreation areas; at **Manstone** there are cricket and football fields extending 4½ acres; and at **Long Park** (at the junction of the Honiton and Exeter roads), is another large open space for public use. There is a pleasant footpath walk from Sidmouth to Sidford, which passes through fields called **The Byes**. Some of this area is in the care of the National Trust, and at Byes Lane is yet another recreation ground.

Branscombe and Beer

Between Sidmouth and Seaton, less than 10 miles apart, are sandwiched two of the most attractive of Devonshire villages – Beer and Branscombe. It is about five or six miles from Sidmouth to Branscombe, which may be reached mostly by the cliff, except for circling inland around Weston Mouth, but the path is steep and rough and *dangerous* in places owing to cliff-falls, while the route followed by vehicles is mostly dull.

Branscombe

is a scattered village of picturesque cottages and interesting houses, straggling from Weston through Street to the Square and the beach. It includes three groups known as Church Living, Hole and Edge – taking these names from the historic houses. Branscombe lies in a narrow valley, the houses nestling in several wooded combes, and sheltered to the east and west by towering chalk cliffs. Its beautiful situation, streams, trees and other natural charms attract many visitors. The upper village, with many old thatched cottages, slopes along the side of the winding valley towards the old Church, just below which is a picturesque smithy. Opposite the smithy is the Old Bakery, one of the oldest in the country and still using faggots to heat the oven. A quarter-mile lower down, the lower village lies where the valley curves seaward, and many visitors are drawn to the charming **Mason's Arms.**

The **Church**, dedicated to St. Winefreda, a little known Welsh saint who died *c.* 650, is of great age, and beloved by antiquaries. The building is cruciform, with a central tower and a circular turret. The earliest architecture is Norman, although the transepts are Early English. On an exterior corbel are the arms of George Neville, Bishop of Exeter (1455–65). In the north transept is a monument to Joan Tregarthin and her two husbands, John Kelleway and John Wadham of Meryfield. The monument exhibits small kneeling effigies of Joan, John the first, in academic dress, and John the second, in armour, with sword and ruff. Behind her on either side are the children of this "fruitful mother". (She is said to have had twenty, but in the monument only seventeen remain, twelve behind the former John, five behind the latter.) Nicholas Wadham, one of the sons, was the founder, in 1610, of Wadham College, Oxford. Among other features of interest are the Elizabethan gallery, the screen and altar rails, the sedilia, the low side windows, a three-decker pulpit and a portion of a fourteenth-century mural.

Not far from the Church, on the opposite side of the road is the medieval house called **Church Living**. It was probably used by the canons of Exeter as a summer residence. In the valley to the north is Edge Barton, known as **Edge**, or **Egge**, formerly the manor house of the Bronscombes and Wadhams, which still retains traces of medieval work. One fine gable still exists, with a large Tudor window,

Branscombe Church

also a few ancient chimneys and a circular stone stairway; the rest of the building has been modernized.

Other interesting houses are **Hole**, a late sixteenth-century house owned by the Holcombes for several generations until the seventeenth century – records show that a house existed on the site in 1249; and **Barnell**, formerly named Trafalgar House. It was built by Captain Yule who was on the *Victory* at Trafalgar.

On the edge of the cliff above the village is **Bury Camp**, a Roman earthwork, 952 feet long and 350 feet wide, and at Street, *Berry* (or *Bury*) *Barton Farmhouse*, said to be haunted. All the cliff area hereabouts is included in the South Coast Conservation Scheme and owned by the National Trust.

Branscombe to Beer. From Branscombe, Beer may be reached either by the rather devious road passing the quarries, by footpath across the common, which any native will point out, or by the cliff-path of about 3 miles from Branscombe Mouth beside the upland **Common**, where in its season the gold of the gorse and the blue of the sky and sea make a picture not easily forgotten. The feature of the cliff walk is **Beer Head** some 400 feet high. These towering cliffs – the most westerly chalk formation in England – and a real chalk-*rock*, not the crumbling chalk of the Home Counties – are pierced by numerous caverns, which, with the isolated rocks scattered about, are curious and picturesque. The head juts out for a considerable distance and is the most striking feature in all views of the bay.

The top of Beer Head is a wild common known as **South Down**. It commands extensive views, on the one side as far as Portland Bill, on the other to Start Point. There is a picturesque **Undercliff**, formed by a landslip.

The Beach and Cliffs, Beer

Beer

Access. – Train to Axminster, thence by bus.
Bank. – *Lloyds* (Monday, Wednesday and Friday).
Bathing. – The beach is shingly, but the bathing is excellent. Tents and huts may be hired at moderate rates.
Boating and **Fishing** are very popular.
Buses. – To Seaton; to Branscombe; in summer a service between Sidmouth and Lyme Regis passes; inquiries should be made as to a seasonal service to Lyme Regis, passing Dowlands for the Landslip and Rousdon P.O.
Hotels. – *Dolphin, Durham House, Anchor, The Bay, Hillside, Bovey House.*
Post Office. – Fore Street.

The village has greatly altered in recent years and the old picturesque cottages, long the joy of artists and photographers, have been almost entirely replaced by modern buildings, while new houses of all sizes are springing up in the combes at the back or high on the hillside, the latter commanding wide sweeps of sea. The straggling village street, a gurgling streamlet flowing down first one gutter, then the other, descends almost to the beach, terminating in a small open space where is a green enclosure containing a memorial to Hamilton Macallum, the artist, who died in 1896. At this point, on the right, is a *Car Park*.

On one side of the enclosure containing the memorial is a way to the beach with its nets and fishing-boats, and on the other a path curves round to the cliff and a miniature promenade overlooking the bathing-tents.

Here is a **Shelter**, more commodious than the look-out hut of the fishermen it has replaced, and the present light is more powerful than the old lantern which marked the haven. From this tiny promenade a steep path leads to the shingly beach. The path going upwards along the cliffs eastward can be followed most of the way to Seaton; for the final half-mile it joins the road, owing to landslips.

Above is the **Jubilee Garden**, delightfully placed on the higher cliff, and commanding fine views of the bay, one of the most picturesque on the coast. Views of the bay have an added interest from the contrast afforded between the white cliffs of Beer and the red cliffs of Seaton.

A mile north-west of the village is **Bovey House Hotel**. About the end of the thirteenth century the building belonged to the Walrond family, and subsequently to the Rolles. The house was at one time Royal property having been given to Catherine Parr as part of her wedding jointure by Henry VIII following the dissolution of the monasteries. The present house is mainly of sixteenth-century work with additions and changes made during the seventeenth and eighteenth centuries – notably two fine ceilings in what is now the Drawing Room and was once the great hall of the house. A rainpipe head at the roof bears the date 1592. An interesting feature is a well, 180 feet deep, that was at one time used as a hiding-place. About 30 feet down is a recess, or chamber, 10 feet square. Some years ago, while the roof of the house was being repaired, a secret chamber was discovered in one of the chimneys.

The house is now used as an hotel.

Fore Street, Beer

Seaton

Seaton

Access. – The nearest rail station is at Axminster from which there are connecting bus services. Coach services from London.
Banks. – *Lloyds and Midland*, The Square. *Devon and Exeter Savings Bank*.
Beach. – The beach is composed of pebbles, among which may be found good specimens of garnets, beryls and jaspers. A stretch of sand is exposed at low tide.
Bowls. – Public green at Seahill. Seaton Bowling Club.
Buses. – To Beer and Branscombe; to Axminster and Honiton; in summer to Lyme Regis and Sidmouth, connections for Exeter and for Budleigh Salterton and Exmouth. Bus depot in Station Road.
Early Closing Day. – Thursday.
Entertainment. – Cinema, shows at Town Hall, dancing. Various clubs.
Fishing. – Organised trips from the beach.
Golf. – Axe Cliff Golf Club, a mile eastward from Seaton. Miniature golf on ground between chine and Castle Hill overlooking the Bay. Two courses of 18 holes. Summer competitions. Putting course in Seahill adjoining bowling green.
Hunting. – The Axe Vale Hounds hunt fox and hare. Weekly gymkhanas during the summer.
Hotels. – *Bay, Esplanade, Golden Lion, Hawkshyde Motel, Pole Arms, Swallowcliffe.*
Library. – Branch Library, The Esplanade.
Parking Places. – Sea Front and East Walk, Sidmouth Street and Station Road.
Population. – 4,500.
Tennis. – Courts at Seahill and at the Cricket Club.

Seaton occupies a fine open situation, with steep hills at either side to mark off its sea-frontier. It is the nearest Devonshire watering-place to London, from which it is distant only 152 miles; it is 24 miles east of Exeter, and is just under 8 miles on the seaward side of Axminster. The place has long ceased to be the village of former days, when cob-walled and thatched cottages housed its few hundred inhabitants. Though some of the old buildings remain, others have been modernized, and many new houses have been built, both up the hills on the western border and on the levels of the Axe. There is a large licensed caravan park in Station Road.

The Esplanade extends from the pebble ridge that constricts the mouth of the Axe, close under the red Haven Cliff, to the foot of the White Cliff between Seaton and Beer. Along the eastern portion is a convenient *Car Park*. About midway along the Esplanade the word *MORIDUNUM* appears in large letters, an outward and visible form of the claim that Seaton is the descendant of a Roman settlement of that name. The claim has been disputed, but the word remains.

The western end of the Esplanade runs below rising cliffs on which is **Seahill**, a popular sports ground, with tennis courts, bowling greens and miniature golf courses.

At the western end of Seaton beach is **White Cliff**, a huge mass of whitish chalk, overgrown here and there by ivy. The cliff commands a fine panorama of sea and landscape – one's eyes travel across the valley of the Axe, and on the coast-line the cliffs near Bridport and solitary Portland Bill may be descried.

In the upper part of the town, in a typical tree-shaded country churchyard, stands–

St. Gregory's Church

It is Decorated in style, having been rebuilt in 1360, when a south tower was erected; but this was partly removed in the fifteenth century, and another built at the west end. Little of the original Early English church remains, and there are some late Perpendicular additions. There is an unusual form of hagioscope in the chancel, pierced with a two-light window, now opening into the vestry added in the early eighties. Another curious feature is that no two windows of the church are alike. The venerable appearance of the tower is marred by numerous rectangular holes which originated in the ancient custom of leaving the ends of the scaffolding in a completed building. In course of time the timber has disappeared, leaving the cavities.

Ladram Bay

Walks round Sidmouth, Seaton and Beer

To Ladram Bay

From the west end of the Esplanade at Sidmouth continue up Peak Hill almost to the top, turning left by the track to the gravel pits close beside the way. From this point there is a widespread land and seascape, the Big Picket Rock beneath High Peak to the right, and, close to Sidmouth and Jacob's Ladder, the **Chit Rocks**, known to all fishermen. This reef is all that remains of a pile which was washed down during a storm in 1824.

The cliffs can be followed most of the way to Ladram, but they are crumbling, and *care should be taken*, as the path in places may be unsafe. It should be followed through the pine wood around the shoulder of High Peak rather than close to the edge over the top. Once through the wood, the path follows the cliff-edge, with striking views both ways.

Ladram Bay is considered by many for grandeur of rock scenery and romantic shore-line unequalled on the south-east coast of Devon. The action of the waves on the red sandstone has detached enormous blocks from the cliffs; these stand out as sentinels, and are the homes of innumerable sea birds. Beyond Ladram is another bay with more isolated pillars of rock. The other – southern or western – end of Ladram is separated from the adjoining Chesilbury Bay by a headland. It is advisable to warn those who would explore the beach that *it is necessary to study the tide before going too far east or west, as there is no way of escape up the steep cliffs beyond this point*. The beach is mainly shingle, but there are some sandy patches and caves, large and small, which invite exploration. The bay is pleasantly sheltered by verdurous cliffs and is popular with picnic parties. Ladram Bay Caravan site is well placed.Caravans may be brought or hired or sites rented for caravans and camps. There is a restaurant. There are a few boats and a motor-boat puts in occasionally.

If, on returning to Sidmouth, an inland course be taken, the walk may be pleasantly extended along lanes, and visits made to Colaton Raleigh (p. 47) and Newton Poppleford – an extension of eight or nine miles, of which several may be accomplished by bus. There is little of note in **Newton Poppleford** other than the old thatched toll house at the top of the long street. After crossing the bridge that spans the Otter, there is a long hill to be climbed, skirting a portion of **Harpford Wood** (*see* p. 47).

By bearing to the right after reaching the top of the hill near Bowd, Sidmouth is regained in about four miles.

To Ottery St. Mary

Another favourite walk or ride from Sidmouth is to Ottery St. Mary and its famous church. It is about 6 miles along the road which, after passing Bowd, skirts Harpford Wood; by taking the Exeter bus to Bowd a good lift on the way may be obtained. A delightful alternative is to take the Sidbury bus and walk up the steep road through the woods over East Hill. A return route following East Hill most of the way gives very fine views; but close around Ottery itself a number of beautiful short walks can be made – inquiry locally for *Pixie's Parlour*, Knightstone, or the "Cleeve" above the river bank, will elicit adequate direction.

Ottery St. Mary is a pleasant town of approximately 4,500 inhabitants. In the late eighteenth century it was an important centre for the manufacture of wool. An old mill, now industrial premises, is probably the *Factory* alluded to in *Pendennis*, the birthplace of the poet Coleridge, whose father lived at Ottery as vicar and master of the King's Grammar School (founded 1545), it was also the headquarters of Fairfax for a short period, and in this quiet little town Thackeray spent his holidays while at school at the Charterhouse.

The **Church,** dedicated to SS. Mary and Edward, is the glory of the town and of the surrounding country. Indeed, architecturally it ranks next to the cathedral at Exeter, which in many respects – as in the possession of transeptal towers, of which these are the only two examples in this country, and the way in which part of the exterior is broken up by projecting chapels and porches – it very much resembles. The church was dedicated by Bishop Bronescombe in 1259, and made collegiate by Bishop Grandisson in 1337. The north, or Dorset aisle, was added in the sixteenth century. The church was badly damaged by Cromwell's soldiers. In 1850 it was restored, mainly at the expense of the Coleridge family. A plaque of S. T. Coleridge is on the south wall of the churchyard, with his lines "He prayeth best who loveth best . . ." The short spire on top of the northern tower is surmounted by a weathercock, six hundred years old, so constructed as to whistle when a strong wind is blowing. The roof – slabs of stone – is the only one of its kind in Devon.

The church consists of choir, nave, transepts (partially formed under the towers already referred to) and Lady Chapel. There are aisles to both nave and choir, these terminating in two chapels, dedicated to St. Stephen and St. Lawrence respectively. In the Lady Chapel are a few old stalls, and the wooden eagle and minstrel gallery will also be noticed.

Old Stocks, Ottery St. Mary

There are some pleasant Georgian houses east and north of the churchyard and several interesting houses in the neighbourhood. A mile northwest of Ottery is **Cadhay**, a fine specimen of Elizabethan domestic architecture. It has been carefully restored, much of the beautiful Tudor work of the interior having been cut away or plastered over in the early part of the eighteenth century. The quadrangle, named "The Court of the Kings" contains the figures of Henry VIII and his three children. *House and grounds (charge) are open Bank Holiday Sundays and Mondays, and on Wednesdays and Thursdays from mid-July to early September, fee.* A mile or so southeast is *Knightstone Farm* – a Tudor restoration of a medieval hall. *Bishop's Court,* due south, may have been the seat of Bishop Grandisson.

Sidford and Sidbury

In a beautiful amphitheatre of hills, not far from Sidmouth, as their names indicate, are the villages of Sidford and Sidbury. The combined parish is one of the largest in Devon.

Sidford has a modern church, but its most notable building is **Porch House**, dated 1574, at which, it is said, the fugitive Charles II found refuge after the battle of Worcester. Sidford Bridge, rebuilt and widened in 1930, has preserved the pleasing contour of the old high-backed pack-horse bridge, which dated from about 1100, without its danger; from it, the main road eastward up Trow Hill – formerly one of the road-terrors of the West – now rises by easy curves and a steady gradient.

North-westward from Sidford a good type of building development towards Core Hill is providing a new residential area with views down and across the valley to Sidmouth and the sea.

Sidbury, a mile northward, is a typical Devon village. The very interesting Church has a Norman tower, partly re-built in 1843, ornamented outside by two ancient stone figures. Inside the tower are four very early Norman carvings in the corners. A short spire was added in 1895. The old timbers of the roof, the carved arches of the aisles at the transepts, the squints, the wall paintings over the chancel arch and in the south-porch the central boss of the ceiling are notable. Below the choir stalls are the remains of one of the few Saxon crypts in England, *c.* A.D. 670; it can be seen only by appointment with the vicar.

West of the village are the remains of a British camp known as **Sidbury Castle**, about three miles from Sidmouth. Near by is a large cairn of dry flints called *The Treasury* or *The Money Heap*. There are many legends of buried treasure concealed near here, which give an added zest to the explorer of the woods and combes of the surrounding hills, with nooks and corners as beautiful as any Devon can show.

Colyford and Colyton

Two miles to the north of Seaton, on a sparkling tributary of the Axe from which it borrows its name, is the village of **Colyford**. It was created a borough *c.* 1231 and there was a bridge over the Coly here in 1254. The town of Colyford dwindled from the fifteenth century, and now it is a borough in name only, although it has retained its ancient ceremonies of "beating the hounds" and electing the mayor annually, and the old Manor House still stands. Modern buildings at Colyford house the Colyton Grammar School.

A mile farther north is **Colyton**, an even older foundation, for it is recorded as a Saxon settlement before A.D. 700. It stands by the Coly near its junction with the Axe, and is beautifully situated among wooded combes. The town clusters round the fine church of St. Andrew; the upper part of the tower is remarkable for its fifteenth-century octagonal lantern. The oldest part is the central Norman tower. There is some fourteenth-century work but the major part is of the following two centuries. There are several interesting memorials, especially of the Pole family in the south chancel aisle. A well-preserved Saxon cross stands in the south transept.

Among several interesting buildings in the town is the old Church House, the ground floor of which is fifteenth century, the two upper floors being added in 1612. The Vicarage was built in 1529. Above the porch is carved the coat of arms of Bishop Veysey (Exeter 1550) on either side of which is a Tudor rose of Henry VIII and the pomegranate of Catherine of Aragon.

About half a mile from the town is **Colcombe Farm**, incorporating the remains of Colcombe Castle, built by a Courtenay of the reign of Edward I. In 1644, Prince Maurice fixed his headquarters here, and a great deal of skirmishing between Roundheads and Cavaliers took place in the neighbourhood. There are several other sixteenth- and seventeenth-century houses in the neighbourhood – many of them built on the sites of medieval farms.

Colyton Church

Axminster

Axminster

Road Route. – From Sidmouth *via* Sidford and the main road eastward, turning left after crossing the Axe at Colyford.
Car Parking. – By Church, in centre of town, in Lyme Street and in Coombe Lane.
Rail. – Axminster is on the main London–Exeter line. Bus services connect with coastal towns.

Axminster is a household word and famous, of course, for the weave of carpets which bear its name. The first Axminster was woven in 1755 and the manufacture continued until 1835 when the looms were sold to another weaver of carpets at Wilton, nr. Salisbury. One hundred and one years passed before carpets were again manufactured in the town but the Company is now producing carpets which have become as well known as the original Axminsters. Several other industries thrive in the town.

Axminster is of great antiquity and today is a quiet town of a little over four thousand persons, and an important market town for a large rural area. It has an interesting church with a Norman doorway and much thirteenth-century work. Two miles south-west is Ashe House, once owned by the Drake family. The Duke of Marlborough was born in this house in 1650.

Honiton

Honiton is about nine miles from Sidmouth *via* Sidbury and Gittisham Hill. The road is hilly, but much of it runs through heathland, and walkers will find this an exhilarating tramp. A good alternative route is *via* East Hill, along the ridge above Ottery St. Mary. Steep hills exist on both routes.

Honiton (Hotels: *Angel; Dolphin*) consists mainly of one long street along which are a number of pleasant Georgian houses. A weekly market is held here and a Summer Fair, with peculiar privileges of sanctuary, on the Wednesday and Thursday after July 19. The old All Hallows' Chapel, for 300 years a schoolroom, is now a museum *(April–November, weekdays)*.

There is a shop where the famous lace is displayed and also a local pottery. Behind the War Memorial is St. Paul's Church, a late Georgian building.

The old **Church of St. Michael** stands on the hillside about half a mile from the centre of the town. It was destroyed by fire in 1911, little more than the tower escaping, so, although rebuilt, it is only the shell of its former self. It is, however, a very beautiful shell, especially within, the interior being flooded with white light through the clear-glass windows, which gives a wonderful quality to the greys of the old stone walls. Like some other churches hereabouts, this one slopes upward from the west to the east, the floor of the sacristy being quite 8 feet higher than the sill of the west door.

Just inside the north door is the tomb of Thomas Marwood, "who practised Physik and Chirurgery above 75 years", and died in 1617 at the ripe age of 105. Queen Elizabeth gave him an estate in the neighbourhood as a reward for his cure of the Earl of Essex.

On the Exeter road is the interesting **St. Margaret's Hospital**, founded for lepers in the fourteenth century. It was re-endowed by Thomas Chard, the last abbot of Forde Abbey (1520–39), who rebuilt the hospital chapel.

The Landslip

The Landslip lies between Seaton and Lyme Regis and consists of four miles of tumbled, broken ground of which the greater part is now covered with trees, bushes and turf. A path runs through it from end to end – now close down to the water; now high against the cliff which cuts the Landslip off from the neighbouring countryside and which is a feature to be remembered by indifferent walkers, since it bars all access to the neighbouring road. The only ways into and out of the Landslip are at the ends, a fact to be borne in mind by those who feel unable to walk the whole distance (Seaton to Lyme Regis is a good six miles of heavy walking).

Visitors are warned that at times the path becomes so overgrown as to be non-existent, and great care is necessary when negotiating obstructions.

Local enquiries should definitely be made before setting out with the full distance in mind.

Follow Station Road, Seaton, to the bridge over the Axe, and a few yards along the Axmouth road turn right up the wooded Squires' Lane that winds uphill to the golf links. When the lane ends at the Golf Club House keep straight ahead across the links, following the telegraph wires, to a continuing lane on the far side of the course. Ascend this lane for a few hundred yards, when a gate with a stile at the end of a narrow lane will be found on the right, a notice-board announcing that it is the public path to the Landslip. This comes out on the down at the end of the golf links, and, continuing downwards beside the hedge, another field is entered at the corner. The path slopes leftward, and continues not far from the edge of a cliff above broken ground. Where the ground begins to rise the entrance to the Landslip is reached; it lies in front, and the path through it will be seen just below.

The eccentricities of Nature in this stretch of coast were accentuated in 1839, when nearly a mile of land, seventy or eighty yards wide, sank from one to two hundred feet, at the same time thrusting forward the land that lay between it and the sea.

Time has spread a generous mantle of flowers and foliage over this former wilderness, and greenery now covers the huge rocks and softens the outlines of rents and fissures.

Exeter to Tiverton and Bampton

Access. – By road (15 miles to Tiverton) leaving Exeter by Queen Street and New North Road.

Some 2 miles north of Stoke Canon, between road and river, is the small church of **Nether Exe**. The present building is probably fifteenth century, but it has retained the Norman font of an earlier church on the site. Six miles (by road) from Exeter it is worth crossing the Exe to **Thorverton** village, which has a good (restored) church and some well-designed eighteenth- and nineteenth-century houses. From Thorverton is a pleasant walk or ride of 2¼ miles up a tributary valley to **Cadbury Castle**, an Iron Age earthwork on the hill from where are magnificent views, stretching to Dartmoor, Exmoor, Somerset and Cornwall. This was occupied by Fairfax in 1645. On the north side of the hill runs the road from Crediton to Tiverton, and by that it is 2½ miles north-east down to the Exe valley at Bickleigh.

Bickleigh

BICKLEIGH

Bickleigh "Castle" is about half-way between Tiverton and Exeter. It stands on the western bank of the Exe where the road crosses the river by a picturesque old bridge of five arches. The present late sixteenth- or early seventeenth-century construction replaced an earlier wooden one. Views up and down stream are particularly charming. The Castle (sometimes referred to as the "Court") was recorded as Alward's Castle in Domesday. A fortified Manor House belonging to the de Bickleigh family existed on the site in the twelfth century. Later the property was owned by the Earls of Devon and inherited by Thomas Carew who married into the Courtenay family. The Carews reconstructed the gatehouse which has a vaulted entry (*c.* 1400) and it is the Carew arms which can be seen about the arch. During the Civil War, it was "slighted" by Fairfax and was soon after abandoned by the last of the Bickleigh Carews. The Castle became a farm store; part of the early Norman chapel housed the farm animals and the estate decayed into a ruin.

Recently, the Castle, with the adjoining seventeenth-century farmhouse, and the lovely little chapel with its thatched roof and Norman double-arch doorway, has been restored. The moat has been cleared and the gardens beautifully laid out with trees, flower beds, water plants and a lawn. Above the gatehouse is a fine mullioned-windowed room with a minstrel's gallery. *The Castle and gardens are open April to September, Sunday, Wednesday and Bank Holiday Monday afternoons, also Tuesday and Thursday afternoons from June to August; fee.*

Bickleigh village is on the east bank of the Exe. In the churchyard is buried the "King of the Gipsies", Bamfylde Moore Carew (1693–1770), who was born at Bickleigh Court; but at the restoration of the church the foundations were carried over the spot. The parish church of St. Mary is a fourteenth-century building (restored) with a twelfth-century font and south doorway. Note the Carew monuments in the chancel, and old bench-ends. The neighbourhood of Bickleigh is very picturesque, and the valley of a small tributary – the Dart – which joins the Exe on the west bank about ½ mile below Bickleigh, is worth exploring. It is about 2½ miles up it to Worth Bridge, and thence 3 miles north-east by road to Tiverton.

North of Bickleigh the Exe valley, flanked by wooded and steep hills, is beautiful.

An alternative, or return, route for Tiverton may take in a trio of very fine churches, at **Broad Clyst** – with a fine sixteenth-century west tower and beautiful arcades and monuments; **Bradninch**, with an unusual screen the full width of the church and the rarely-seen dedication to St. Disen; and **Cullompton** – noted for its wonderful wagon-roof, richly carved and coloured. The Tudor buildings of the Walronds (1603–65) and the Manor House dating from 1603 are also noteworthy. This road is very hilly in parts, but commands a stretch of country from Haldon to beyond the Blackdown Hills.

By the Exe at Bickleigh

Tiverton

Fishing. – The River Exe and its tributary, the Culm, provide good sport. Salmon fishing is preserved but fly-fishing for trout is available.

Golf. – 18-hole course of Tiverton Golf Club by Wellington Road at Post Hill (2 miles).

Hotels. – *Boar's Head, Hartnall, Half Moon, Bridge, Tiverton Motel.*

Some 15 miles from Exeter, Tiverton is a pleasantly situated town of over 16,000 inhabitants, in a richly-wooded part of the Exe valley. The Church dates back to 1073 but was partly rebuilt in 1856. A Norman doorway survives in the north wall. The tower is early fifteenth century, and the south porch has a series of very interesting carvings. The Greenway Chapel, added in 1517, is also richly carved; it takes its name from its merchant-founder, John Greenway (*d.* 1529), to whom and his wife there are brasses. In the north aisle is an old chest, also an altar-piece, "St. Peter's Release from Prison", by Richard Cosway (*d.* 1821), the miniature painter who was a native of Tiverton.

Of the **Castle,** founded in 1105, the chief portion left – it was "slighted" by Fairfax, 1645 – is the fine gateway. The **Greenway Almshouses,** in Gold Street, were founded about the same date as the chapel *(above)*. **Blundell's School,** familiar to the readers of *Lorna Doone,* was founded by Peter Blundell (1604), a clothier. A new school, with large grounds, was built in 1882 at Horsdon, 1 mile from the town, and is a fine and complete institution. There are in Tiverton some technical science and art schools of importance, and also a huge *Lace Factory,* established 1816 by John Heathcoat, inventor of the bobbin-net machine. It still employs several hundred hands for the manufacture of lace, rayon, nylon and all types of textiles. At the north end of the Lowman bridge is a statue (by Hems) of Edward VII, this and a clock tower being given by a native, Thomas Ford, J.P., in 1907. In addition to textile manufacture, Tiverton is an important agricultural centre; agricultural and woodworking machinery is exported; there are also timber mills and flour mills.

North of Tiverton we still follow the Exe valley for 5 miles, then ascend the tributary valley of the Bathern to **Bampton,** a quiet little place, except during its famous pony fair, held on the last Thursday in October. The church has a fine screen and roof and in the churchyard some grand old yews. Bampton lies on the main Taunton–South Molton–Barnstaple road.

The Exeter–Barnstaple Road

Crediton

Access. – Rail from St. David's or Central Station. Road (7 m.) *via* Newton St. Cyres, leaving Exeter by Queen St. and New North Road.
Hotels. – *Ship, White Hart.*

Crediton is a busy country town of about 5,000 people. Although it is recorded as the birthplace of St. Boniface, *c.* 680, and a minster was established in 739, Crediton is likely to disappoint those who expect to find an ancient town. It is almost entirely modern, having suffered from several fires. "As fine as Kirton spinning" has lost its significance since cloth-making has passed away and sweet manufacture and other light industries taken its place.

Red is the earth of the fields surrounding it, and red is the colour of many of its buildings, including its fine heavy **Church,** built of red sandstone, some from local quarries still worked. Most of the present building is Perpendicular, but the base of the tower is Transitional Norman. The large clerestory windows are a notable feature, and the east and west windows are also fine, but during restoration the former, distinctive if not unique, was spoilt by being altered to conform with the other. The choir aisles lead through arches into the Lady Chapel, originally Early English in style, which served as the Grammar School from 1572 until 1860. In the south choir aisle is a fourteenth-century altar tomb, supposed to be that of Sir John Sully and his wife; he lived to a great age, fought at Crécy and Poictiers and in other battles. Near the Altar is the monument of Sir William Periam, an Elizabethan Chief Baron of the Exchequer, reclining in his robes, and next is one of the seventeenth century to members of the Tuckfield family. Over the tower arch at the east end of the nave is a memorial to General Buller. The mutilated stone sedilia, with what may be a tomb behind them, and the Norman font are worth noting. In the north aisle is a richly carved chest, *c.* 1420 in date, depicting on its panels, *The Adoration of the Shepherds.* When the bishopric was removed to Exeter the church was made collegiate and it remained so until the Dissolution. Edward VI sold it to twelve citizens for £200 and their successors are still called the Twelve Governors. In the Governors' Room, locked, are several relics of the Civil War.

Near St. Lawrence Green, at the top of the town, formerly the scene of fairs and bull-baiting, just off the main road is Lawrence Chapel, once a chantry but now used as a school chapel. About the middle of the long street is the *War Memorial,* distinctive in design, and just off the Tiverton road, in the new cemetery, is the ancient **Chapel of St. John the Baptist,** re-erected in 1925, when removed from an isolated site near Thorverton. Records show this was existing in 1425, and some thirty years ago was used as cottages, being then restored for sacred purposes by Sir John Shelley.

About 8 miles beyond Crediton a right turn leads to **Lapford**. The fifteenth-century church is outstanding for its beautifully carved screen and Tudor bench-ends.

Continue along the A377 for 5 miles when another right turn leads to **Chulmleigh** attractively set in the valley of the Little Dart. The church contains a magnificent rood-screen retaining some of its original colouring and stretching more than 50 feet across the nave and aisles. The wagon roof is adorned with angels and variously carved bosses.

For Umberleigh, *see* p. 204.

Exeter to Dawlish

The western bank of the Exe can be followed to **Dawlish,** past Powderham; it is pretty country that is traversed by good roads, well watered and wooded, and sprinkled with charming villages having associations with many a name great in English history. With the river-estuary close by, the beginning of the Haldon ridge on the right, and the first of the red cliffs by Lympstone or by Dawlish rising ahead, this forms an admirable approach to the South Devon seaboard. The trip can also be made by boat.

Exminster. Five miles from Exeter on the western side of the Exe and connected with Topsham by ferry is Exminster, a large village, the history of which goes back to Saxon times. The fourteenth-century Church of St. Martin was thoroughly "restored" in Victorian times, but has retained some interesting features, including the attractive tower, the ceiling of the Lady Chapel (1633, now restored) and some fine memorials. There are some interesting old houses in the neighbourhood. *Peamore* and *Matford* were originally Domesday manors. *Kenbury House* has a long history but the present building is mainly Georgian.

From Exminster it is an easy drive of 5 miles to Kenton (bus service) or Powderham.

Powderham Castle

Open mid-April to October, Sunday 2–6; *mid-May to mid-September, daily except Friday and Saturday* 2–6; *charge. Bus stop at gates.*

The beautiful country seat of the Earls of Devon is a little over a mile along the Exeter road. The Castle was built about the end of the fourteenth century by Sir Philip Courtenay, younger son of Sir Hugh Courtenay, and Margaret, daughter of Humphry de Bohun, his wife. The manor of Powderham was left by will to Sir Philip by his mother, who had it as a marriage portion from her father. Only four towers and the chapel of the old structure remain, the rest of the Castle having been built at various later periods.

The park is of great extent, and is only separated from the river by the railway, which runs along the eastern side. It is thickly planted with oaks, and on its highest ground is a tower, called the **Belvedere,** erected in 1773. The **Church** is entirely a fifteenth-century building with arcades of Beer stone; it contains an oak screen, reredos, and altar, besides several interesting memorials.

Powderham Castle

Kenton. A little south-west of Powderham is the village of Kenton which possesses a church described by Leland as "a right goodly church".

Built in the reign of Edward III, it is of Perpendicular architecture, with pinnacled buttresses to the south aisle, niched south porch, and tall red sandstone tower. The magnificent rood-screen believed to date from 1455 extending right across the east end of the church, is panelled and ornamented with carvings, and paintings of apostles, saints and prophets, on which are sentences from the Creed. The pulpit is coeval with the screen and at one time was broken up and destroyed, but it was possible to collect the fragments and restore it, the niches being filled with modern paintings. The capitals of the pillars merit attention and so does the south porch with its embattlements and parvise chamber. In the north chancel a memorial Lady Chapel has been constructed and was dedicated in 1954 to the memory of those who lost their lives in the Second World War. The Church is one of the most beautiful in Devonshire and an admirable example of the West Country Perpendicular style.

From Kenton it is a pleasant walk over the hill north-west of the church and up the valley to **Kenn,** where is an almost equally noteworthy church. From here it is only a step to the main road and bus for those wishing to return to–

Starcross. Two miles south-east of Kenton, Starcross is little more than a village though it is thronged with visitors during the season. A ferry crosses the Exe to Exmouth. The most prominent object in Starcross is a massive, red sandstone building with an equally massive tower. The part surmounted by the latter was once used as a Methodist Chapel, while the remainder served as stores; originally it was one of Brunel's pumping-stations in the early "atmospheric" days of the railway.

From Starcross the route may be continued by the main road direct to Dawlish, or a detour made via Cockwood and Dawlish Warren. Dawlish is described on p. 73.

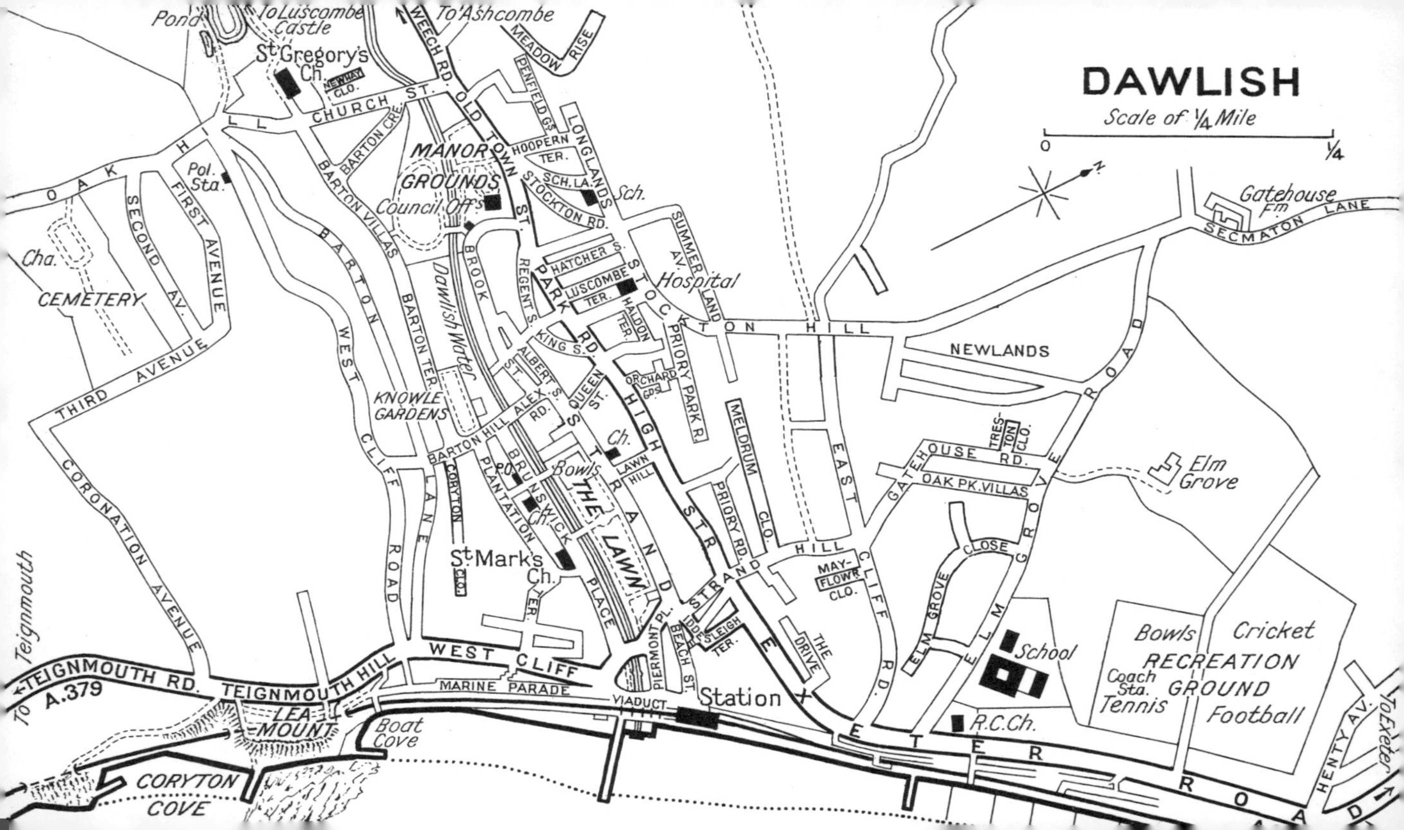

DAWLISH
Scale of 1/4 Mile
0
1/4
N
To Luscombe Castle
To Ashcombe
Pond
St Gregory's Ch.
NEWHAY CLO.
CHURCH ST.
WEECH RD.
OLD TOWN ST.
MEADOW RISE
PENFIELD GDS
HOOPERN TER.
LONGLANDS
SCH. LA.
Sch.
STOCKTON RD.
MANOR GROUNDS
Council Offs
BARTON CRE.
BARTON VILLAS
HILL
OAK HILL
Pol. Sta.
FIRST AVENUE
SECOND AV.
THIRD AVENUE
CEMETERY
Cha.
CORONATION AVENUE
BARTON
WEST CLIFF ROAD
BARTON TER.
Dawlish Water
BROOK ST.
REGENT S.
HATCHER S.
LUSCOMBE TER.
PARK RD.
STOCKTON HILL
SUMMER AV.
LAND
Hospital
HALDON TER.
KING S.
ALBERT S.
ST.
ALEX. RD.
QUEEN ST.
ORCHARD GDS
PRIORY PARK R.
HIGH ST.
KNOWLE GARDENS
BARTON HILL
BRUNSWICK PL.
PO.
Ch.
PLANTATION TER.
CORYTON
LANE
Bowls
THE LAWN
STRAND
LAWN HILL
St Mark's Ch.
CLO.
PLACE
MERIDRUM CLO.
PRIORY RD.
EAST CLIFF RD.
HILL
MAY-FLOWR CLO.
NEWLANDS
ROAD
TRES-TON CLO.
GATEHOUSE RD.
OAK PK. VILLAS
ELM GROVE
CLOSE
ELM GROVE
Elm Grove
Gatehouse Fm.
SECMATON LANE
IDDESLEIGH TER.
BEACH ST.
PIERMONT PL.
THE DRIVE
WEST CLIFF
MARINE PARADE
TEIGNMOUTH HILL
TEIGNMOUTH RD.
To Teignmouth
A.379
VIADUCT
Station
LEA MOUNT
Boat Cove
CORYTON COVE
EXETER ROAD
School
R.C.Ch.
Bowls
Cricket
RECREATION GROUND
Coach Sta.
Tennis
Football
HENTY AV.
To Exeter

Dawlish

Banks. – *Lloyds, Midland* and *National Westminster.*
Bathing. – Excellent from Main Beach and Coryton Cove. Swimming races and aquatic sports during the season.
Boating. – Rowing- and sailing-boats may be hired. Motor-boat trips in the bay.
Bowling Greens on the Lawn, and at the Recreation Grounds, Exeter Road.
Buses. – To Exeter; to Teignmouth, Newton Abbot and Torquay.
Car Parks. – Marine Parade, Barton Hill, The Strand and adjoining Recreation Ground, Dawlish Warren.
Cricket. – *Dawlish Cricket Club* play at the Playing Fields, Exeter Road. Visitors welcome.
Early Closing Day. – Thursday.
Entertainments. – Band on the Lawn. Shaftesbury Theatre.
Fishing and Angling. – Sea-fishing (dab, whiting, mackerel, etc.); local boatmen should be consulted. Coarse fishing in local rivers; good trout fishing at Chagford and Moretonhampstead.
Golf. – The *Warren Golf Club* on the Warren, north of the town. Also *Teignmouth Golf Club* links on Little Haldon.
Hotels. – *Charlton House, Brooklands, Elizabeth, Lisburne, Langstone Cliff, Rockstone, Westcliff, Great Cliff, Barton Grange, Mount Pleasant Inn, Tropicana, Oak Park, High Trees, St. David's,* and many others.
Information Bureau. – The Strand.
Library. – Old Town Street.
Population. – About 10,000.
Post Office. – Brunswick Place. Sub-offices, Exeter Road, Holcombe Village and Dawlish Warren.
Putting Green. – York Gardens, near station; and Dawlish Warren.
Tennis. – Public courts (4 hard and 6 grass) at the Recreation Grounds, Exeter Road.

Dawlish and Teignmouth are neighbouring resorts on the coast between the mouth of the Exe and the sandy Teign estuary, and are only three and a half miles apart. Though so close, they bear little resemblance. Dawlish is essentially pretty and *petite* – a gem among seaside resorts; the view obtained from the railway line of the Lawn with houses on either side of its green expanse, and divided down its centre by the docile Dawlish Water, suggests a dolls'-house scene. The stream flows on its way to the sea without any vulgar gurgling or broiling, its water dotted with proud swans and spanned at intervals by lightly-made bridges.

There is no prettier place in its own particular style on the South Devon coast. North and south, towering red cliffs sentinel the town, and between them for a mile and a half stretches the parade, provided with seats, and pleasant in almost any weather and at any season, for Dawlish claims an equable climate – eight degrees cooler in summer and to a like extent warmer in winter than London.

On the sunny hillsides violets bloom from September to early April and flower-growing, particularly the fragrant *Princess of Wales Violet*, is one of the chief industries of Dawlish. Boxes of flowers are sent to all parts of Britain and to the Continent.

Happy the town that has no history. We read of no exploits of Romans and Danes here. The deed of gift executed by Edward the Confessor, presenting the estate of *Doflisc,* as Dawlish was then spelt, to the Bishop (Leofric) of Crediton, is still in the possession of the Dean and Chapter of Exeter. In Domesday it appears as *Douelis;* and it is spelt by various authorities as *Doules, Doeles, Dalditch,* and *Dulishe.*

At the beginning of the nineteenth century the inhabitants of Dawlish occupied thatched cottages on the banks of the stream round their parish church half a mile from the sea (some of these still stand in the "old town"); the pretty valley in which the modern watering-place stands was neglected, and its mouth used only as a place for fishermen to dry their nets and beach their boats. Later the stream was broken by artificially constructed waterfalls, and the area of the Strand and the Lawn developed into its present attractive form. With the coming of the railway in 1846 it was found necessary to carry the line along the sea front, but this was done in a manner which allows free access to the beach.

The Lawn. A feature of Dawlish is the neatly kept Lawn, with its trim gardens, between the Strand and the "Brook" – as the Dawlish Water is locally called. On the Lawn there is a bowling green which is the scene of first-class tournaments. Among the water birds on the brook may be seen black swans – rare in this country – the progeny of parents imported from Australia.

Proceeding inland from the Lawn one comes to **Manor Grounds.** This site, in the centre of the old town, is now a public park, and the Manor House (*c.* 1800) occupied by the offices of the Dawlish U.D.C. Nearby is the ancient **Parish Church of St. Gregory,** whose first recorded vicar was Capelanus in 1272. It is charmingly situated at the back of the town, about ten minutes' walk from the station. The tower and pillars are all that remain of an older foundation. The nave was rebuilt in 1823, and a new chancel and transepts added in 1875. Among the monuments are two by Flaxman. Outside the church is the stump of the old cross, with the **War Memorial Cross** in an enclosure opposite. There is a Chapel-of-Ease, **St. Mark's Church,** facing the Lawn. On the opposite side of the Lawn is the **United Reformed Church,** surmounted by a spire. On the East Cliff is the **Roman Catholic Church,** dedicated to St. Agatha.

Not only is the town itself pleasant, but the sands are extensive and firm, and they slope so gradually that bathing may be enjoyed without risk; while there are walks in the neighbourhood extensive enough to satisfy the desire of the most ardent pedestrian. Bounded by a sea-wall –

The Beach extends northwards from the Marine Parade for a mile and a half to **Langstone Cliffs.**

At the southern end of the beach is **Boat Cove,** where rowing-, sailing- and motor-boats can be hired. If one follows the sea-wall southwards, past the detached red sandstone rock, and mounts the zigzag path, one reaches the seats and shelters of **Lea Mount** (a breezy but shady pleasure ground presented to the town by Sir Thomas Lea). From here fine views can be obtained of the coastline, extending beyond Exmouth and Straight Point to Beer Head, and on occasion as far as Portland.

The sea wall has been continued beyond Lea Mount to **Coryton Cove,** a sheltered beach much favoured by bathers and sun-bathers. Beyond this is **Shell Cove,** popular for picnics; this cove is usually reached by boat, being accessible by land only at the lowest tide. Still farther southwards

The Sands, Dawlish

is the curious rock formation known as the **Parson and Clerk,** the subject of local legend.

Northwards from Lea Mount, the best route to Langstone Cliffs is to follow the sea-wall, except at high tide, when it may be necessary to follow the Exeter Road until the footpath to **Ladies' Mile** is reached. Langstone Cliffs contain several little caves that can be explored at low water. Above the beach is **Mount Pleasant,** a wooded height on which is an hotel. An arch in the sea-face of the rocks, and a curiously shaped rock known as the **Elephant** are among the other natural attractions of the spot.

Beyond Lanstone is –

The Warren, a low, sandy bar almost blocking the mouth of the Exe. It is a breezy walk across the Warren to the end of it facing Exmouth, but full of interest, for Dawlish Warren is noted for its wild bird life and for certain rare flowers. The Warren is a playground for young and old alike for it is an area which caters for most tastes. Facilities include a large car park with a capacity of 2,000 cars. A mile and a half-long stretch of fine, sandy beach, washed by the tide, offers safe bathing, boating and relaxation. Near at hand is an amusement centre, children's railway, putting and obstacle golf and also an 18-hole golf course. Beach huts are available for renting. Immediately inland from the Warren are numerous well-laid-out caravan and chalet parks and a holiday camp offering facilities for those preferring a self-catering holiday. There is also an interesting railway museum with model railway.

Walks and Drives round Dawlish

Dawlish is an excellent centre for walks and drives. One walk is suggested by the view from the Lawn of the wooded heights of **Luscombe Park.** The Castle, built 1800–1804, stands in a delightfully wooded combe and was designed by Nash; it is not a show place, but the park is opened to the public on special occasions.

Proceeding by way of Luscombe Lane in a westerly direction, one may reach the moorland stretch known as **Little Haldon,** where are the links of the *Teignmouth Golf Club.*

Great Haldon is in the background, a mile or so north-west. On one side of Little Haldon are the remains of a circular encampment, known as **Castle Dyke.** It is about a hundred and twenty-four yards in diameter, and encloses an acre and a half within the vallum. This is about eighteen feet high; and there are faint traces of a second vallum outside it.

Ashcombe. About two miles northward by the Exeter road from Little Haldon is a turning leading to Ashcombe, a village in a sheltered combe. Ashcombe Church is in the midst of sylvan scenery. It is of Decorated and Perpendicular architecture (tower *c.* Norman), and was consecrated in 1259, the capitals of the columns being ornamented by the peculiar Devon wreaths and by shields containing the arms of the Kirkhams, lords of the manor in the reign of Henry III, the Newmans of Mamhead, and others. The bench-ends are quaintly carved.

From Ashcombe it is five miles back to Dawlish down the beautiful valley of the *Dawlish Water.*

Mamhead House. Two miles east of Ashcombe is Mamhead House, built by Robert Newman, M.P. for Exeter from 1818 to 1826, to the design of Anthony Salvin. It is now Dawlish College, a boarding school for senior boys. The house is one of the best examples of early Victorian architecture in the country. The magnificent grounds of some 350 acres *(open to the public)* contain extensive lawns and gardens, and a fine collection of trees. In the Kenton Drive is the famous Turkey Oak said to be the largest tree in Europe. Within the grounds is the little Perpendicular red sandstone **Church** used by the school, but also serving as parish church and open to the public. In it are some memorials to former owners of Mamhead; and under the churchyard yew, said to be over nine hundred and fifty years old, Boswell is said to have registered one of his oft-repeated and as often broken vows, "never to get drunk any more".

The plantations in the neighbourhood are very fine. The summit of a lofty hill, **Mamhead Point,** is surmounted by a stone obelisk, a hundred feet high, built in 1742, a well-known landmark.

Cofton is reached by a lane on the right of the Exeter road, at about three miles from Dawlish. It has a small thirteenth-century church, consisting of a nave 50 feet long, with a north aisle added in recent times. It is mentioned in a deed of 1270, and in 1384 Bishop Brantyngham authorised the vicar of Dawlish to perform divine service. After the Reformation, the chapel was disused until Dr. Kendall, a native of the village, officiated in it after being ejected from the living of Kenton. He died in 1663; and the neighbouring clergy continued to conduct service in the chapel until 1760, when its use was discontinued owing to the unsafe condition of the roof. Remaining in a ruinous state for nearly eighty years, it was in 1839 restored by the Earl of Devon; and in 1864 a district was assigned to it including the whole of Dawlish Warren, and a vicar appointed. This little church possesses a remarkable chalice, made of mother-of-pearl, said to have been taken from a Spanish ship.

Lidwell. Another walk of two and a half miles from Dawlish is westward, taking the path from the far side of the parish church and turning left along the course of the Aller to the ruins of **Lidwell.** There is a tradition to the effect that a villainous priest dwelt here, who was accustomed to rob and murder travellers, and throw their bodies into a deep well (Lady Well). One day he met his match and now his wraith is supposed to haunt the spot. All that remains of the chapel are an archway and window, in a crumbling ivy-mantled wall.

The view from it, however, is not to be compared with that obtained by scrambling up the steep side of **Haldon** behind it.

Holcombe Down. There is another walk that both Dawlish and Teignmouth can claim, that between the two towns by way of **Holcombe Down,** a stroll of three and a half miles by the steep but pleasant old high road. The route to the Down is a steady climb by way of Dawlish Church and Oak Hill. The Down lies stretched out in front, with a view of the coast-line to Berry Head in the south-west and eastward as far as Portland Bill. There is a maze of lanes round Holcombe, and the best view is from a track across fields leading into a road on the high ground north of Teignmouth.

Holcombe is midway between the two towns in a hollow nearer to the sea. It was the subject of one of the oldest known grants of land, a document in the Cathedral at Exeter showing that William the Conqueror, in 1069, gave an estate here to Leofric, Bishop of Exeter. The hamlet is at the head of a beautiful fern-clad Devonshire lane, known as **Smugglers' Lane.** Passing down this and under the arch that carries the railway, access is gained to the beach at the extreme end of the terraced walk that runs on the seaward side of the railway to Teignmouth.

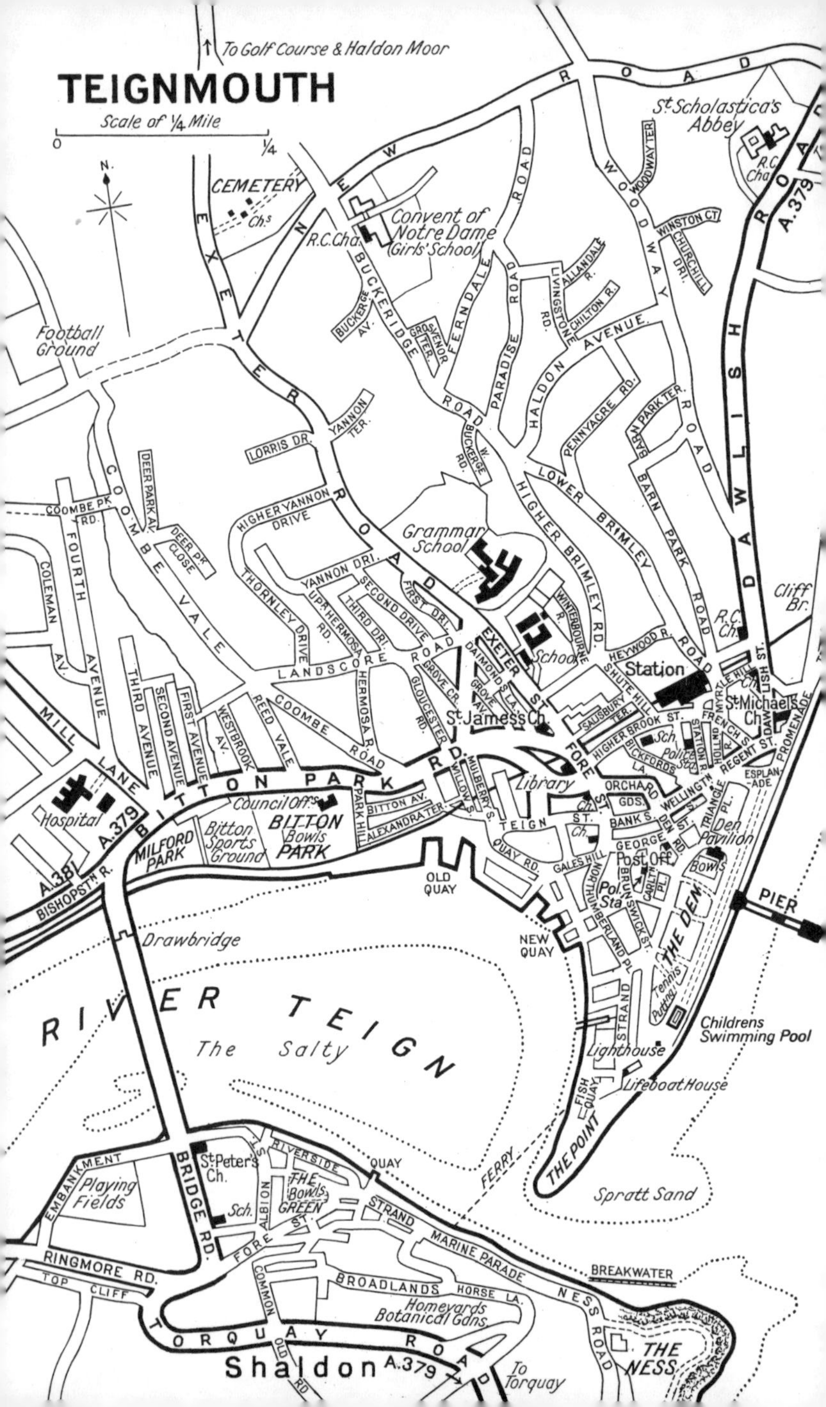

TEIGNMOUTH
Scale of 1/4 Mile
0
1/4
N.
To Golf Course & Haldon Moor
NEW ROAD
St. Scholastica's Abbey
R.C. Cha.
A.379
CEMETERY
Chs.
Convent of Notre Dame (Girls' School)
R.C.Cha.
EXETER
BUCKERIDGE
BUCKERGE AV.
GROSVENOR TER.
FERNDALE
PARADISE ROAD
LIVINGSTONE RD.
ALLANDALE R.
CHILTON R.
WOODWAY TER.
WOODWAY
WINSTON CT.
CHURCHILL DRI.
HALDON AVENUE
PENNYACRE RD.
BARN PARK TER.
ROAD
DAWLISH ROAD
Football Ground
YANNON TER.
LORRIS DR.
W. BUCKERGE RD.
LOWER BRIMLEY
HIGHER BRIMLEY RD.
BARN PARK ROAD
COOMBE PK. RD.
DEER PARK AV.
DEER PK. CLOSE
COOMBE VALE
HIGHER YANNON DRIVE
Grammar School
FOURTH AVENUE
COLEMAN AV.
THORNLEY DRIVE
YANNON DRI.
UP. HERMOSA RD.
SECOND DRIVE
THIRD DRI.
FIRST DRI.
EXETER ROAD
WINTERBOURNE R.
R.C. Ch.
Cliff Br.
MILL LANE
THIRD AVENUE
SECOND AVENUE
FIRST AVENUE
WESTBROOK AV.
REED VALE
LANDSCORE ROAD
HERMOSA R.
GLOUCESTER RD.
GROVE CR.
DAIMOND S. LA.
GROVE AV.
EXETER ST.
School
HEYWOOD R.
Station
SHUTE HILL
MYRTLE HILL
DAWLISH ST.
St. Michael's Ch.
SALISBURY TER.
HIGHER BROOK ST.
Sch.
STATION R.
HOLLAND R.
FRENCH S.
COOMBE ROAD
St. James Ch.
FORE ST.
Police Sta.
BICKFORDS LA.
REGENT ST.
PROMENADE
ESPLANADE
Hospital
A.379
BITTON PARK RD.
MULBERRY S.
WILLOW S.
Library
ORCHARD GDS.
WELLINGTN. ST.
TRIANGLE PL.
Council Offs.
PARK HILL
BITTON AV.
ALEXANDRA TER.
TEIGN ST.
Ch.
BANK S.
DEN RD.
Den Pavilion
MILFORD PARK
Bitton Sports Ground
BITTON Bowls PARK
QUAY RD.
GALES HILL
GEORGE S.
Post Off.
Bowls
A.38
BISHOPSTN. R.
OLD QUAY
NORTHUMBERLAND PL.
Pol. Sta.
BRUNSWICK ST.
CARLTN. PL.
THE DEN
PIER
Drawbridge
NEW QUAY
Tennis
Putting
STRAND
RIVER TEIGN
The Salty
Childrens Swimming Pool
Lighthouse
Lifeboat House
FISH QUAY
THE POINT
FERRY
Spratt Sand
BRIDGE RD.
St. Peter's Ch.
Sch.
EMBANKMENT
Playing Fields
RIVERSIDE
QUAY
ALBION
THE Bowls GREEN
STRAND
FORE ST.
MARINE PARADE
BREAKWATER
RINGMORE RD.
TOP CLIFF
COMMON
BROADLANDS
HORSE LA.
Homeyards Botanical Gdns.
NESS ROAD
TORQUAY ROAD
THE NESS
Shaldon
A.379
OLD RD.
To Torquay

Teignmouth

Banks. – *Barclays, Lloyds, Midland, National Westminster, Devon and Exeter Savings.*
Bathing. – Excellent. The vicinity of the estuary should be avoided by swimmers.
Boating. – Rowing- and sailing-boats may be hired. Motor-boats ply along the coast and up the river to Coombe Cellars.
Bowls. – Public greens on the Den, Bitton Park, and on Shaldon Green.
Buses. – To Bishopsteignton; to Torquay *via* Newton Abbot; to Torbay *via* Shaldon; to Exeter *via* Dawlish and Kenton.
Car Parking Places at the southern end of the Den; Eastcliff, Brunswick Street; the Ness, Shaldon; and various free parking places.
Cinema. – *Riviera,* Den Crescent.
Clubs. – *Unionist,* Somerset Place; *British Legion; Teign Corinthian Yacht Club,* Powderham Terrace.
Concerts and Dances. – At the Carlton Theatre.
Cricket. – Club Cricket, Bitton Park; visitors welcome. Weekly matches.
Early Closing Day. – Thursday.
Ferry. – Motor ferry to Shaldon, starting from near the Lifeboat House, frequent service.
Fishing. – Bass, pollack, etc., and in the season good mackerel fishing in the bay. A sea-angling festival is held in August each year. Salmon and trout in the Teign; but the angling is strictly preserved and confined to members of local associations and friends, although members of other associations may become honorary members.
Golf. – *Teignmouth Golf Club,* 18-hole course on Little Haldon. Professional available. Miniature putting course on the Den and at Shaldon.
Hotels. – *Royal,* Sea Front; *Dunmore,* Shaldon; *Beach,* Sea Front; *Lugano,* Sea Front; *London,* Bank Street; *Glendaragh,* Barnpark Road; *New Quay; Bella Vista,* Sea Front; *Portland,* Sea Front; *Seacroft,* Sea Front; *Bay,* Sea Front; *Seymour House,* Dawlish Road; and many others.
Hunting. – The South Devon Hounds meet within easy reach during the season, also the Haldon Harriers.
Model Yacht Pond. – West Promenade, near Lighthouse.
Population. – 13,220.
Post Office. – Den Road. Sub-offices in Bitton Street, Coombe Vale, Lower Coombe and Shaldon.
Putting Greens. – At the Den, and at the Ness, Shaldon.
Sailing. – During the season a programme of regattas and sailing events is arranged by the *Teign Corinthian Yacht Club* and the *Shaldon Sailing Club.*
Sea Excursions. – Regular sailings from Beach, etc.
Tennis. – Public courts on the Den.
Theatre. – Carlton Theatre (summer show).
Zoo. – Children's Zoo and Pet's Corner at the Ness, Shaldon.

Situated on a triangular plateau under the lee of one of the spurs of Haldon, Teignmouth is bounded on the south-east by the English Channel, while on the south-west is the broad, sandy estuary of the river Teign. Where one's eye, in glancing round the town, does not rest on water there are wooded hills, which effectually shelter it from the north and north-east. Indeed, the inhabitants set great store by the situation of their town and its climate. Teignmouth is pleasant at most times of the year, and is usually warm in the winter. In summer the mean minimum temperature is 57 degrees and the mean maximum 68 degrees. The resident population is just over 13,000 and is gradually increasing.

TEIGNMOUTH

An Eventful History

Teignmouth has a long and not always peaceful history. Its manor of old belonged to the Bishop of Exeter, who, in the reign of Henry III, obtained a charter for its inhabitants, giving them the right to hold a weekly market and a fair on September 28, 29 and 30. Worth says it sent representatives to a shipping council in the reign of Edward I, and it had members in at least one Parliament of Edward III. When the latter monarch set out on his expedition to Calais, the port supplied him with seven ships and a hundred and twenty men; and it took its proper share in all similar expeditions during the centuries which preceded the establishment of the regular navy, and, in return, had to bear its share of the not always delicate attentions which the French were in the habit of bestowing on south coast towns and villages.

Teignmouth became popular as a seaside resort from the beginning of the nineteenth century, and still shows a considerable amount of pleasing Georgian architecture. The poet Keats resided here for a short time, and a tablet at 20 Northumberland Place marks the house where he stayed. *Endymion* was finished here, and its introduction is dated "Teignmouth, 1818". Another poet, but of lighter verse, connected with Teignmouth was Winthrop Mackworth Praed, M.P., who lived at Bitton. His rhyming descriptions of the town show that, after all, life in a holiday resort has not changed so very much in a century.

In the Second World War, Teignmouth suffered severely from "tip and run" air-raids, which caused 79 deaths and destroyed 228 buildings. The war damaged area has now been re-developed with five new roads and excellent blocks of flats.

The Sea-Front and Den

The chief attractions of Teignmouth are its sea front, the River Teign, and the varied beauties of the surrounding country. Facing the sea is the **Den,** six acres of green turf forming a delightful marine promenade, and laid out with flower beds, rockeries, paths and shelters. On the Den, too, is the **War Memorial,** an obelisk of granite. At the northern end is the *Carlton Theatre* and a public bowling green, and towards the southern end a putting course and tennis courts. A well-stocked Aquarium is a further attraction.

Why this pleasant stretch of greensward is called the Den is not very certain. One theory is that the word is derived from the familiar *dune,* a hill, on the ground that the Den was once a barren stretch of sand hills or dunes.

Teignmouth has for long been famous for its bathing. The sand is coarse but firm and shelves gradually.

The Sea-Wall Promenade

The seaward front of Teignmouth offers the attraction of a well-surfaced sea-walk of two miles. From where the Den at its southern end is washed by the waters of the Teign as they flow under the Ness (the great red sandstone headland on the fringe of which Shaldon has been built) to Hole Head on the north, is a dry, level walk. Where the Den ends at the north-east, there begins almost immediately a terraced walk under the shadow of the cliffs, at the base of which tamarisk and other shrubs have been planted to lend additional shelter to the seats. Beyond the point where the railway runs from the town to the edge of the sea under the **Cliff Bridge,** leading to Holcombe and Dawlish, there is a sea-wall, the trains being on one side and the sea on the other. The sea-walk terminates at **Hole Head,** where the railway leaps the little cove at the foot of Smugglers' Lane. Walkers can vary the return route by proceeding up this pretty lane to the Dawlish and Teignmouth road, and thence (by taking Cliff Road to the left) returning to Teignmouth along a narrow lane and over the Cliff Bridge.

The Town

At the southern end of the Den are the ferry to Shaldon and boats for fishing, rowing or sailing. Near the extreme point is the **Lighthouse,** the red lamp of which operates in connection with a similar one on the front of Powderham Terrace. Here, too, is the principal public car park.

Proceeding inland *via* the Strand, Northumberland Place, and Fore Street, one arrives at the parish church of West Teignmouth, **St. James's Church,** a heavy, battlemented octagonal building, its interior presenting a peculiar appearance on account of the slender pillars supporting the roof, in the centre of which is an octagonal lantern. The reredos is a beautiful specimen of fourteenth-century stone carving. It is Perpendicular in style, with exquisite little figures of saints under canopies surmounted by delicate pinnacles and finials. The Commandments were painted later. The tower on the western side of the octagon is all that remains of the structure mentioned in Bishop Bronescombe's Register, dated 1275. The bells in it are said to have been rung after the battle of Crécy, 1346; but they were recast in 1879.

A quarter of a mile west of the church is the pleasant open space of **Bitton Park.** This consists of five acres of well-kept and sheltered gardens at the west end of the town, a little short of the bridge, and overlooking the river. The Park formed part of the old Bitton estate, once the seat of that Lord Exmouth famed in connection with the bombardment of Algiers, then a stronghold of the Barbary pirates.

Teignmouth consists of two parishes, divided by a stream called the **Tame,** now covered in and almost forgotten. The parish church of West Teignmouth has already been described; that of East Teignmouth is **St. Michael's Church,** near the sea front. This is a modern church, though an ancient foundation. The tower, 87½ feet high, is constructed of limestone, with a plinth of dark red Kingsteignton stone and dressings of Doulton stone, a figure of the patron saint being above the west door. The tower contains eight bells and a clock with four dials.

On the Dawlish Road are the **United Reformed Church** and the **Church of Our Lady and St. Patrick,** the latter belonging to the Roman Catholics, who have a considerable settlement in this district. On a commanding position is the enclosed **Convent of St. Scholastica,** belonging to the Benedictine sisterhood, with a chapel attached. **Notre Dame Convent,** a

Shaldon, Teignmouth

boarding school for girls, occupies a site in Buckeridge Road commanding a splendid sea view.

The River Teign and Shaldon

The navigation of the Teign calls for considerable skill. Outside the harbour is a shifting bar of sand, and within is more sand. At low water the channels down which the river flows are so comparatively unnoticeable that a stranger might think he could wade across from the quays to Shaldon. Large quantities of china or ball clay, dug and mined so extensively round Newton Abbot, are exported from Teignmouth; and a certain amount of wood-pulp for paper-making is imported.

Shaldon *(Dunmore, Ness House)*, across the sandy estuary of the Teign, is reached either by the ferry from the Point or by the **Bridge** beyond Bitton Park. Any point on the bridge is a pleasant spot from which to admire adjoining scenery, and especially the wooded banks of the Teign, the entire course of which is of great beauty.

Shaldon, for all practical purposes a part of Teignmouth, has a shelving beach and pleasantly situated houses. The village is cosily sheltered; yet its inhabitants have all the advantages of the sea quite close at hand. Close to the bridge is **St. Peter's Church,** a modern building, displaying great originality of style. Its ornamentation is remarkably beautiful, and it is quite one of the show-places of the district. Overlooking the estuary are the Homeyards Botanical Gardens, containing many sub-tropical plants.

Above Shaldon is the twin village of **Ringmore.**

Ness Point and Labrador

The **Ness Headland,** in the Shaldon parish, is a well-known landmark, and with it the surrounding land has been purchased by the Teignmouth Council and opened to the public. In summer, the headland is floodlit as a background to the illuminations of Teignmouth. The area commands the entrance of the Teign and there are extensive views. This delightful spot is easily approached either by ferry or by Shaldon Bridge. A tunnel through the cliff leads to **Ness Cove,** a secluded spot for bathing. Farther south is **Labrador,** said to have taken its name from a certain Captain Trapp who resided here in the seventeenth century, and traded between Teignmouth and Labrador.

Stoke-in-Teignhead

Excursions from Teignmouth

From Shaldon or Teignmouth many pleasant excursions may be made up the river Teign. A favourite walk or drive is to–

Coombe Cellars

On the Torquay side of the river, so-called from the salt-pans *(salaria)* which existed here in medieval times, Coombe Cellars was formerly the unloading point for waterborne freight to the neighbourhood, and was also a notorious smuggling centre. The pleasant riverside inn is accessible by road or river from Shaldon (3 miles) or Teignmouth (4 miles), and the stretch of water here is a popular venue for sailing and boating. The late S. Baring-Gould made Coombe Cellars the scene of his novel *Kitty Alone*. The nearby village of **Coombeinteignhead,** set in a lovely valley running down to the river, can be reached by field path or by road (½ mile). Its church is mainly Perpendicular in style but retains Decorated transepts and nave arcade. There is a Norman font, a rood-screen of *c.* 1450, and in the north transept some sixteenth-century benches richly carved with grotesque animals and figures. Also in the north transept is the fine altar-tomb to Gregory Hockmore of Buckland Baron (*d.* 1571) and his wife Alice (*d.* 1613), whose epitaph on a heraldic brass tells us that she bore him 15 children. In the village street is the old Church House, a picturesque Tudor building donated to the parish in 1620 by the third Earl of Bath to provide profits for maintaining the church.

A mile south of Coombeinteignhead is the diminutive church of **Haccombe** (p. 91).

On the by-road to Torquay, turning up the hill near Ringmore Church, midway between the coast and the river, and not far from Coombeinteignhead, is the village of–

Stoke-in-Teignhead

which is within easy reach of Teignmouth and also of Newton Abbot and St. Marychurch. The village, purely agricultural, with some delightful thatched cottages, is very picturesque, lying in a valley formed by several hills. The **Church** (dedicated to St. Andrew) dates from the fourteenth century, and has many objects of interest, including a remarkably fine oak rood-screen, dating from Richard II. The arcades are Perpendicular, with carved capitals of great beauty. The transepts retain a piscina, a stopped squint and rood-stairs. A palimpsest brass in the sanctuary is one of the only two fourteenth-century brasses in Devon. Another in the floor, of 1641, in the shape of a heart, is inscribed in old French. In the porch are preserved the parish stocks. The registers start at 1538.

Stoke-in-Teignhead is only a mile west of the main road to Torquay, and buses are available for either out or home journey.

On the northern or Teignmouth side of the Teign is–

Bishopsteignton

a walk or car ride of a little over two miles from Teignmouth, or four from Newton Abbot. The village is on the hillside opposite Coombe Cellars and under the height of **Haldon** (800 ft.). There are buses from Teignmouth.

Bishopsteignton owes the "teignton" (which it shares with Kingsteignton, some three miles to the west) to its position on the banks of the river; while the prefix distinguishing it from the other village is believed to have been bestowed because Bishop Bronescombe of Exeter, lord of the manor from 1258 to 1280, erected a palace here, portions of the walls of the chapel attached to which are still in existence – in the lane leading from Ash Hill to the Teignmouth–Exeter high road on Haldon.

Bishopsteignton Church is an old foundation, largely rebuilt in 1815. The western doorway and font are Norman, and good specimens of that style. Outside, on the south wall, is a carving of very early design and considered unique, representing the Adoration of the Magi. In the churchyard are ruins of a sanctuary chapel built by Bishop Grandisson (1327–1369).

Kingsteignton, three miles west of Bishopsteignton, was indebted for its distinguishing prefix to the fact that the manor belonged of old to the Crown. The village is on the Teignmouth–Newton Abbot bus route, and its Perpendicular Church *(St. Michael's),* portions of which are very old, forms an attractive feature of the landscape. Signs of the outline of a former Saxon village may be traced in Berry Lane, Fore Street and Church Street.

The Teign Valley and Haldon Country

Kingsteignton may be regarded as the beginning of the beautiful Teign Valley, though the first sight of its broad expanse hereabouts is not inviting, dotted as it is with the stagings and white heaps of the ball clay workings, and the refuse dumps, mingled with poor lignite, often take fire and emit sulphurous fumes. At Kingsteignton, too, the bus for **Chudleigh** may be joined. A favourite short circular coach tour from Teignmouth includes a stop at Chudleigh, so that its Rocks and Glen may be visited, the return or outward journey being over Haldon, with its fine views of Dartmoor and the sea.

Chudleigh has lost its one-time importance and is now simply a small town. It was rebuilt after having been nearly destroyed by fire in 1807. The Church, dedicated to St. Martin and St. Mary, was consecrated by Bishop Bronescombe in 1259.

The very scanty remains of an old palace of the Bishops of Exeter are on the land of Palace Farm, on the way to the **Glen** and **Chudleigh Rocks,** an imposing mass of limestone, several hundred feet high, almost perpendicular on one side. It should be stated that the quarry at the head of the Glen is not the Rock. To reach the latter turn down by a garage on the outskirts of the town. Where this lane forks, a path on the right leads above the Glen, with a steep descent to the brook and its little waterfall, round to the Rock, almost lost amid the trees which encompass it. On the eastern side is a ledge known as the **Golden Chair,** but beware the slippery turf and uneven ridges. From the south-west side the view is extensive and beautiful. There are two caves on the rock-side; one, the **Pixie's Cave,** in the Glen, has two entrances. At the turn in the middle is a rock, the

Pope's Head by name, in which those who observe the proper rites stick a pin and wish; but if the pin falls the wish is futile – as the majority seem to be! A light should be carried, as the passage is very low, with holes that invite a nasty fall. On the other side of the rock is **Chudleigh Cavern,** long since closed to visitors, as falls of rock render it dangerous.

It is a pleasant walk to **Ugbrooke Park,** the seat of Lord Clifford. *Admission is by written permit and is confined to the rides (no dogs).* The park is nearly six miles round. Within the park is *Castle Dyke,* an ancient earthwork. Ugbrooke has been in the possession of the Clifford family for some three centuries, but at one time was part of the estate of the see of Exeter, supplying much of the timber used in the Cathedral.

Haldon Lanes and By-ways

The hardy walker fond of quiet lanes and fine views can be recommended to walk to Chudleigh, returning by coach or bus. The Exeter road is followed for a little over two miles to the ridge of Little Haldon, near the golf course, when a lane left for Luton, Ideford, and Chudleigh must be taken. This drops steeply to the first-named – where the road forks a little short of Luton keep left. Passing through, avoiding turnings in the valley, a crossing road is reached where a road left and then down right, leads to the larger village of **Ideford** (pronounced Idford). Chudleigh Arch – where the by-road passes under the Exeter-Kingsteignton highway – comes next, the way then skirting Ugbrooke on the left and over the hill to Chudleigh.

A more sequestered route, and one more difficult to find, avoids both villages, coming out close to Chudleigh Arch. Turn up the steep Mill Lane opposite the Milford Park at Bitton, at the crossway passing the site of the old toll-house (left Bishopsteignton, right for Coombe and back to Teignmouth), the way growing steeper and stonier until it meets a cross road – left for remains of Bishop's palace, Bishopsteignton; right, back to the main road and first route. Continue ahead, bearing slightly left, when across the common another road is reached. Here the toils of the ascent are forgotten, for this ridge of **Little Haldon,** offers one of the finest views in South Devon. A path across the common somewhat to the left leads to a plantation and a steep lane down to the confines of **Lindridge.** Keep right, past the lodge and turning, then left to a cross-roads, where turn up left and immediately right by a fir plantation, down to a brook, and up steeply, eventually coming out close to the Arch.

Ramblers will find these lanes and by-ways of the Haldon range full of unsuspected delights, and tea-houses may be found in unexpected places, while roads with their bus routes encircle it.

Newton Abbot

Access. – Newton Abbot is a major railway junction and is on the direct route from Paddington to the Torquay area, and from Liverpool and Manchester. Excellent bus services serve all parts of the area. The local bus station for the "Devon General" services is near the market. Long-distance coaches stop outside the railway station.
Bowls. – Public green in Courtenay Park.
Camping. – Numerous good sites in the district.
Car Parks.–Recreation Ground, Victoria Place, Penn Inn, Newfoundland Way, Bradley Meadow, Cattle Market.
Cinemas. – *Alexandra* and *Odeon*.
Cricket. – South Devon Cricket Club. Saturday matches in Marsh Road. Special holiday subscriptions per match for visitors.
Early Closing Day. – Thursday.
Fishing. – Salmon and trout; *Teign* and *Dart:* also coarse fishing in the five ponds of Rackerhayes and in Stover Park Lane. Licences from Messrs. Percy Hodge Ltd., 104 Queen Street, Newton Abbot, and Drum Sports, 47 Courtenay Street, Newton Abbot.
Golf. – Stover Golf Club (18 holes) is 2½ miles from the town on the Bovey Tracey Road. There is a putting green at Forde Park.
Hotels. – *Globe,* Courtenay Street; *Queen's,* Queen Street; *Bradley,* Market Street; *Sandford Orleigh; White Hart; Courtenay Arms; The Drive Inn*.i
Hunting. – Dart Vale Harriers, Haldon Harriers, South Devon Foxhounds.
Information Bureau. – Town Hall, Courtenay Street.]
Library. – At junction of Bank, Highweek and Market Streets.
Market Day. – Cattle and Pannier, Wednesday; Pannier, Saturday.
Parks. – Courtenay, Forde, Baker's, Osborne, Penn Inn.
Population. – 19,940.
Post Office. – Bank Street.
Racing. – Under National Hunt rules. Meetings from April to September, and on Boxing Day.
Railway. – Newton Abbot station, Western Region line. Motorail terminal.
Sailing and Canoeing. – Decoy Lake.
Swimming. – Up-to-date open-air, heated, bathing pool with diving boards, etc., at Penn Inn Park.
Tennis. – Hard courts at Baker's Park and Forde Park.
Woods. – Bradley, Milber, Decoy.

Newton Abbot is a thriving market town, and busy centre of a large agricultural area. The town stands in a beautiful vale, watered by the river Lemon, which flows into the Teign, a short distance below the spot where that river changes its character as a boisterous moorland stream for that of a placid estuary. The little river Lemon forms the boundary between two parishes; but within the limits of the town it is mostly arched over, and the continuity of the streets and houses is unbroken.

The pleasure-seeker is well catered for at Newton Abbot. There is a good cricket ground in Marsh Road belonging to the South Devon C.C., where are also tennis courts; there are public hard courts in Baker's Park, and hard courts in Forde Park, the Bowling Club's green in Courtenay Park, a Greyhound track at Kingskerswell with twice weekly meetings, the Racecourse just across the Teign, and close to the Bovey Tracey road is the beautifully situated course of the Newton Abbot (Stover) Golf Club, 2½ miles from the town (frequent bus service) and the same distance from Bovey Tracey. In the opposite direction is the Little Halden course, above Teignmouth. Hunting takes place during the season.

The **Penn Inn Swimming Bath,** opened in 1935, is situated by the Torquay road. The swimming-pool is an open-air one, 120 feet by 40 feet, with diving platform, and has a Pavilion well provided with dressing-rooms.
Adjoining is **Penn Inn Park** with a number of amusement facilities for children and a café. There is a Model Railway track with station, Penn Inn Halt, used at week-ends by Newton Abbot and District Model Engineering Society. Operation is voluntary.

The town originated in a small settlement called **Nova Villa** on the south side of the river *Lemon* about the end of the twelfth century. It passed into the possession of Torre Abbey as part of the manor of Wolborough, and so the name became Newton Abbot. Fifty years later, another settlement was established north of the river, called **Newton Bushel,** after the manorial Bushels of Bradley. Gradually the two markets merged into one, and the whole borough was named Newton Abbot. From the seventeenth to nineteenth centuries, wool and leather trades flourished. Now the main activities are pottery, clay pit workings, and various light industries.

The most interesting incidents in the history of the town are associated with **Forde House,** a pleasing Tudor manor-house, to the east of the railway, built by Sir Richard Reynell in the early days of the eventful seventeenth century. It is now a residence (antiques for sale). Its plaster ceilings and panellings are admirable.
The house has been visited by two sovereigns. Charles I came in 1625 (accompanied by the Duke of Buckingham), soon after his accession to the throne; and William of Orange made it his first, or second, sleeping-place (some ascribe priority to Paignton, and others assert that priority goes to Brixham itself) after leaving Brixham, when on his way to London to assume the government of the kingdom. The bedroom he occupied at Forde is still pointed out. His army was encamped on Milber Down, close by; and his first proclamation was read by the rector of Wolborough, the Rev. John Reynell, from the stump of the old market cross – according to the inscription on it – at the east end of Wolborough Street, in front of St. Leonards's Tower. The date is given as November 5th, but it should be the 6th or 7th. Fairfax apparently passed one night at Forde, and it is more than possible that Cromwell was with him.

Newton has some interesting buildings. **Wolborough Church** is prettily situated on a slope, from which may be seen some of the tors of Dartmoor. It is in the Perpendicular style, with a fine rood-screen, a noteworthy Reynell tomb, and a fireplace in the south porch; the font is Norman. The decay of the ancient framework prevented the bells from being rung, and in 1926, through the munificence of several Newtonians, the three old bells were recast with their old inscriptions and a full peal of eight completed. One of the old bells, weighing 15¾ cwts., is exhibited in the church. The rarest possession of the church is the old brass eagle lectern, one of fifty such left in the churches of England. Opposite the lych gate is a good path which, passing the Mackrell Almshouses, leads to Wolborough Street and the centre of the town, conspicuous objects of which are the **Market Place** and **St. Leonard's Tower,** about 60 feet high, all that was spared in the demolition of the old church of St. Leonard in 1834. The new church stands about 300 yards away.

At the end of Wolborough Street is **Baker's Park,** where are tennis courts. Close to the station is **Courtenay Park,** with a bowling green, and, almost adjoining, **Forde Park,** with hard tennis courts and a pavilion, and a putting course.

Highweek Church, on a commanding site, is a Perpendicular building dating from early in the fifteenth century, but it was sadly mutilated during alterations in 1786 and now shows little of interest save one memorial to the Yardes, a few fragments of old glass, and an old wagon-roof. From the churchyard a wide-spreading view up the Teign Valley towards Haldon is obtained.

The Newton Abbot **College of Art** and the **Public Library** form a fine block at the corner of Highweek and Market Streets. Passmore Edwards defrayed the cost of the Library as a memorial to his mother, a native of Newton Abbot. The **Hospital** in East Street may be mentioned as being originally the scene of early researches into the cure of cancer by means of radium.

There is a Grammar School, and a short distance from Highweek is the **Seale-Hayne Agricultural College,** a beautifully situated and well-equipped centre for agricultural education and research.

Forde House

Excursions round Newton Abbot

Newton is in the midst of scenery of diversified beauty and can be heartily recommended as headquarters for daily excursions.

Bradley, Ogwell, Denbury

Bradley Woods present one of the finest sylvan scenes in the country. It is a pleasant walk of half a mile along the bank of the river Lemon to –

Bradley Manor House, one of the oldest inhabited houses in Devonshire and now owned by the National Trust *(open Wednesdays in summer* 2–5 *p.m., fee, and at other times on written application)*. Mostly fifteenth century, and incorporating an earlier house of the thirteenth century, this home is a good specimen of a small manor-house of the West Country type. It has a chapel of Perpendicular architecture. The house was originally quadrangular, but two sides were pulled down in the eighteenth century. Some of the rooms contain good plaster work, and over the fireplace of the old guest chamber are the arms of the Yarde family, one of whom obtained, in 1428, a licence for the chapel, which possesses a wagon-roof with carved bosses. In the porch is the wheel of the ill-fated *Herzogin Cecilie,* wrecked on the Ham Stone near Bolt Head in 1936.

Continuing, the path leads across the stream to the ruins of **Ogwell Mill,** picturesquely situated with a bungalow beside it, and by turning to the left to a rising track, **East Ogwell** (with an interesting church containing a Reynell tomb, a fine fourteenth-century font and some ancient windows in the vestry) will be reached.

About a mile to the west is the church and manor of **West Ogwell.** The house is now the convent of an Anglican religious order and is not open to the public, but the charming small church with its box pews is worth a visit.

(An alternative way is to take a path to the left not long after passing Bradley Manor House; cross the stream by a footbridge, follow the path, right, through the wood and over the down to a stile, then down through fields.) Hidden in the Woods on the south bank of the Lemon is a rough overgrown hollow known as the **Puritans' Pit,** where seventeenth-century Nonconformists held secret services under the ejected minister of Wolborough. From time to time commemorative services are held on the spot. The Pit was bought in 1953 by a local benefactor and the deeds presented to the Congregational Church, which arranges the services. The woods at this point are private property, and it is only by the courtesy of the land-owners that the Pit, an impressive sight, may be visited. The best approach is by a path up from Ogwell Mill.

By crossing the stream at the mill and continuing along the north bank, a charming woodland walk to Chercombe Bridge may be enjoyed. Here by turning to the right the Newton road may be gained, or to the left, after 2 miles, the ancient village of Denbury. Close to the latter is **Denbury Down,** thickly wooded, on which is a large oval entrenchment, 250 yards long and 200 broad, with nearly circular mounds in the centre – one of the many Iron Age hill-earthworks in this district. This may be gained by going west through the village along the Ashburton Road, until in half a mile there is a path (L.) opposite a road coming in. This path is frequently almost a waterway and leads through a gate at the top immediately into the wood. Here is a double rampart with deep ditch between, which may be followed round three sides of the wood to an exit path going down over a pasture to the road again. **Denbury** is very ancient, and the old manor-house, of which it is possible to obtain a glimpse, is said to occupy the site of a still older building belonging to Tavistock Abbey. The **Church of St. Mary** is a fourteenth-century structure; it contains a twelfth-century font.

Ipplepen and Torbryan

On an elevated site, less than 2 miles from Denbury, about 3 miles from Newton and 6 from Torquay, is the village of **Ipplepen.** In the centre stands a cross 11 feet high, a restoration as a War Memorial of the old Market Cross, of which only some 5 feet 6 inches remained. A market was granted by Royal licence in 1318.

The Church, of Perpendicular architecture, is worth visiting, its eastern flamboyant window being particularly fine. It has a well-preserved tower erected about 1400; a well-restored screen, carved pulpit and font of the same date; a restored cross in the churchyard; the stocks; and among its plate is a magnificent chalice of 1627, possibly the stirrup-cup of a local family.

But, to the walker from Denbury, Torbryan comes first on the road, and Ipplepen next. Leaving Denbury village, he should go south beside the high manor wall, past the green, leaving the *Union Inn* on the left. Later there is a path across a sports field to a finger post. Torbryan is less than a mile ahead with Ipplepen Church coming into view over the trees on the left.

Soon, at the bottom of a hill, is **Torbryan** almost hidden among trees. The village is well situated in the midst of picturesque scenery, dotted with outcropping rocks, with a stream beside the road. The *Church House Inn,* built about 1400, was formerly the Church House; it has retained its old panelling and fireplace. Visitors are welcome to view. The Church is worth close examination. The altar front was formed out of the pulpit, which now consists mainly of its old base; the screen is fifteenth century, the central gates depicting the Virgin Mary being crowned and on the lower panels, a series of unusual figure paintings. A good deal of old glass will be noticed in the upper windows.

In **Dyer's Wood** (½ mile) are some caves which have yielded specimens for the Natural History Museum, South Kensington, and in recent years a beginning has been made to explore more thoroughly those less disturbed. A little pottery was found, but hyæna remains constituted the chief discovery.

The return walk to Newton is through Ipplepen and along the Newton–Totnes road.

Haccombe

one of the smallest parishes in England. It is reached from Newton Abbot by taking the Torquay road to the Penguin Hotel. Here bear left along the Shaldon road, up hill and then down until a cider factory is seen on the right. Here a right turn leads to Haccombe House and nearby Haccombe Church. The manor belonged to the Haccombe family in the twelfth century. The medieval mansion has been replaced by a pleasant Georgian house built in 1778 and now converted to use as a holiday centre. During conversion two panels with signatures of the Carew family were discovered.

The tiny Church, consecrated in 1328 and dedicated to St. Blaise, is well worth inspection. On the church door are nailed a horseshoe and part of another, all that remains, according to the story, to record a famous wager between a Carew and a Champernowne, both members of ancient Devon families. Inside, the little church is full of memorials to one-time owners of Haccombe. The big altar-tomb is that of Sir Hugh Courtenay and Philippa, his wife, and close by is the miniature memorial to Edward, their son. His sister brought Haccombe to the Carews by her marriage to Sir Nicholas Carew, a brass to whom will be found in the chancel. The effigy of a knight (Crusader) represents Sir Stephen de Haccombe, and near him, in a niche in the north wall, is that of his wife Margaret. The numerous brasses are of great interest, and the ancient encaustic tiles should be noted, as also the stone arms designed for candle-holders. Note the ancient cross outside the church.

Between Haccombe and Newton Abbot rises **Milber Down.** Leaving Haccombe the walker should go west by the climbing road until he joins the St. Marychurch road, when the way is sharp right down past the Milber reservoir (L.) concealed by cypresses, to the ancient camp.

On this Down, the army of William III encamped after he landed at Brixham, and there are the remains of an ancient hill-fort, strongly fortified with a triple entrenchment. In 1937–1938 excavations yielded ancient pottery and some Gallo-Roman bronzes. This hill-fort is the largest of its kind in Devon and its ramparts make three concentric sides. Unfortunately the Newton Abbot–Maidencombe road runs through them, but the portion south of this road is well preserved and from its highest vallum there is an uninterrupted view across to Denbury Camp (p. 90), 4 miles to the west.

The walker returning to Newton Abbot should continue downhill to a path through the Milber Woods (Pine Walk) and so into the town by the Torquay road.

Bradley Manor

Newton Abbot to Chagford

Bovey Tracey lies north-west of Newton Abbot. It is a small but rapidly growing town and is a good centre for excursions in the eastern bounds of Dartmoor. It lies beside the little river Bovey which flows into the Teign lower down. From it there are beautiful views of Haytor and the Moor. The church was burned down and the present building is early Perpendicular with a Decorated tower. There is a richly-carved rood-screen.

For a note on **Moretonhampstead** *see* p. 96.

Chagford. "Chaggyford", as the natives call it, is an old market town, and was formerly one of the Stannary towns, the special places where tin had to be weighed and stamped. It is a favourite headquarters for Dartmoor visitors, for here all tastes can be gratified, anglers being provided with good fishing in the Teign, antiquaries with a boundless field for their inspection and investigation, lovers of scenery with the glorious Teign Gorge, and the lover of the Moor with access to some of the wildest as well as to most of the more familiar parts of it.

The town consists of a few irregularly-built streets that branch off from a Square, in the centre of which is the **Market House.** The **Church** is well situated, and is an Early Perpendicular building of Dartmoor granite. It contains a monument of Sir John Whyddon, who died in 1575, a member of an ancient family now extinct, whose name survives in Whiddon Park and Whiddon Down.

For riding on the Moor, Chagford is well placed, a minimum of road having to be traversed before reaching the turf of the open moor (good selection of mounts locally); while among the short–

Walks from Chagford

is one to **Gidleigh Church** and **Castle** (2½ miles away by measurement, but 5 by its alternate ascents and descents). Descending the hill from Chagford Square, turn right over the bridge and ascend (left) Walland Hill to Murchington (a better way for walkers is to take the path, entered by a stile next to a gate, on the left a short distance beyond the bridge. This slopes up to the road close to the village), where keep left and descend to Highbury Bridge and cross the brook, mounting the hill in front and turning to the right to Gidleigh village. The Perpendicular Church is built almost entirely of granite–pulpit, reading-desk, reredos and all. The building, as also its fine rood-screen, dates from the fifteenth century. The ruins of **Gidleigh Castle** with its fourteenth-century dungeon and tower are close by, while opposite is the old **Manor Pound.**

A fine tramp in the Chagford region, and one which also introduces the visitor to many of the finest of the peculiar features of the Moor, begins along the road leading west-south-westward from the town. Towards the outskirts of the town turn left, cross a stream at the foot of the hill and then mount to *Waye Barton.* Here at the fork we can turn immediately to the left, or take the lane a little farther on at **Thorn.** Either will lead us to **Metherall** (3¾ miles out). Beyond are

Typical Dartmoor

plantations of the Forestry Commission and on the South Teign is the **Fernworthy Reservoir,** completed in 1942. In its construction several Hut Circles were sacrificed, though they were first excavated with some interesting success. At the north-end of the reservoir is a *kistvaen.* The cairn enclosing it was opened in 1879, and a fine flint implement and other flint remains were found.

The stream is crossed at **Fernworthy Bridge,** near to which is a very good specimen of a one-slab **Clapper Bridge,** the slab being some 10 feet by 4 and quite a foot thick.

To reach the **Fernworthy Circle,** a small though well-preserved example, it is necessary to go round the head of the reservoir into the lane which runs west of the remains of *Fernworthy Farm.* The stones range from 1 to 3½ feet high, and there are twenty-seven of them, the diameter of the circle being 63 feet. A row of smaller stones is found a short distance away in a north-easterly direction, and another to the south.

To return by a different route we can make our way back towards Thornworthy Tor, and, leaving that on our right, make for Shovel Down and Batworthy and then on to Gidleigh Common, passing on our way the **Three Boys,** only one of which is left, a stone some 5 feet high that once formed one of the supports of a dolmen, of which it is the only surviving portion. There are signs between here and the **Longstone** of a continuation of the avenue, or stone row, which may have connected the Scorhill and Fernworthy Circles and have had a continuation in the direction of the Grey Wethers, a little to the south-west of the latter; but the stones themselves are mostly lacking. The Longstone, 10 feet high, is a monolith of great antiquity that for many centuries marked the "Forest" boundary and the dividing point of the Chagford and Gidleigh Common lands.

Remains of the stone avenues are again in evidence as we pass an old cairn which once no doubt housed a kistvaen; but more notable is the **Triple Circle,** or what remains of three concentric stone circles, interesting particularly in connection with the stone rows, the cairn and the longstone menhir; while the rock basins on the adjacent **Kes Tor,** under whose shadow we are, one of which is the largest on the Moor (7¾ feet in diameter and 2½ feet in depth), remind us that by climbing to the top we shall be rewarded by an exceedingly fine view of the northern half of the Moor, as well as of the Teign gorge and valley. The tor is really nearly 1,500 feet above sea-level, but of course we are already on high ground. We have now to make for the **Round Pound,** an enclosure of triangular, "with a tendency to circular", form with an entrance of sorts from one of the ancient roads or trackways; it is below Kes Tor at the edge of the steep drop to the river. There are other hut circles and a rectangular enclosure known as the **Square Pound** in the immediate neighbourhood.

Returning up the road, we turn right at the end of the Batworthy enclosures and descending parallel with the wall make for the two-slab bridge a little to the west, near where the **Walla Brook** joins the Teign. The Walla Brook itself is crossed by a single-slab clapper bridge, and a track indicates the approach to the well-known **Scorhill Circle,** sometimes called the Gidleigh Circle, from its situation on **Gidleigh Common,** of which Scorhill Down may be said to form part. It consists of twenty-three upstanding stones, one of which is over 8 feet high, and seven fallen ones. The enclosed area, the diameter of which is 88 feet, is perfectly level.

At the foot of the down, a little below the bridge, and opposite the corner of the Batworthy enclosures, is the **Tolmen Stone,** only, however, entitled to that appellation as being a *Tol-maen,* or Holed Stone. It is a great granite block, resting in the bed of the Teign, well above the water except at such times as the river is flooded. Making our way in a north-easterly direction, we quickly reach the path, or "stroll", between enclosures leading to Berry Down, or Berridon Farm, and thence to Highbury Bridge, Murchington and Chagford.

For tramps farther into the centre of Dartmoor, experienced company and a reliable map and compass are strongly advisable; bogs and mists are real dangers at certain seasons, but with reasonable care few tracts of country can provide more exhilarating walks.

Exeter to Plymouth via Princetown

Dartmoor is almost bisected by the B3212 running across it from north-east to south-west, and forming an alternative route to the A30 main road through Ashburton and Ivybridge. Running from Exeter by way of Pocombe Bridge and Longdown, this road begins to traverse the Moor not far beyond Moretonhampstead.

About 7 miles from Exeter take a left turn along the B3193 and in 2 miles turn left again to **Doddiscombsleigh** where the church is famous for its medieval stained glass. It fills five windows in the north aisle, the finest perhaps being the most easterly, depicting the seven sacraments. To the south lies the village of **Higher Ashton** whose church has a richly carved fifteenth-century screen with a number of painted panels.

Return to the main road and continue towards Dartmoor.

Moretonhampstead is a favourite centre for Dartmoor. A former market town of some importance, it is prettily placed on sloping ground. The impressive Perpendicular church of granite has a fine tower. Of interest are the former **Almshouses** built of granite in 1637, the Bowring Library and the Smethhurst Hall.

There is a fine view from the Blackingstone Rock to the south-east.

From the town a southward turning leads to the peaceful and pretty old-world village of **North Bovey,** a place that should certainly be visited. The unpretentious village cross at one time served as a footbridge across the Bovey, but is now restored to a more dignified position. In the church are carved roof-bosses representing Edward I and his queens; the bench-ends are rather poor, and the rood-screen has been sadly mutilated.

Some six miles from Moretonhampstead the Princetown road reaches *Warren House Inn,* near which are many interesting antiquities.

Grimspound. A road striking southward from the Princetown road gives vehicular approach to Grimspound. Here massive granite blocks form an irregular wall, some 150 yards long by 120 broad, around an area of about four acres. The height of the wall now is only some 3 or 4 feet, but there are indications that this was probably more than double originally, and that the walls were in addition surmounted by a sort of turf parapet. There are entrances south, east and west, the former, paved, being the oldest, and a pathway or track passes through, leading from Manaton to Headland Warren. The ruins of some twenty-four hut-circles within the enclosure, one of which has been restored, and most of which were undoubtedly at one time inhabited, prove the existence here of a prehistoric village, probably of the Early Bronze period, fortified, for protection against foes, wild beasts or human, or both, and a place of safety for flocks and herds.

From Warren House the road continues south-westward to–

Postbridge, one of the most perfect existing specimens of the old clapper bridges. Here we have four piers supporting four great slabs, one at each end and two side by side in the centre. The bridge, which stands some 7 feet above the river, is 42 feet 8 inches long.

The old clapper at Postbridge has withstood the fury of the East Dart for centuries, and may still be used without the slightest risk. The ancient paved trackway, which is distinct from the pack-horse road, can be traced for some distance to the west of the Dart, and there are many interesting remains in the neighbourhood. A footpath along Lakehead Hill leads to *Bellever Farm* where there is a *Youth Hostel.*

Just before reaching **Two Bridges,** where we cross the highway connecting Ashburton and Tavistock, the Princetown road passes on the right **Crockern Tor** (1,391 ft.), sometimes called the Parliament Rock. This tor is quite historical. There is venerable authority for the statement that from the reign of Edward I until the middle of the eighteenth century the Stannary Court – the parliament of the tinners – was held here. Tavistock, Plympton, Ashburton and Chagford each sent to it twenty-four burgesses, whose duty it was to enact laws and regulations, which, when ratified by the Lord Warden of the Stannaries, were binding. The privileges accorded to the tinners, and the arbitrary character of many of their acts, are proverbial in Devon and Cornwall. In later times, it became the custom of the court to meet here and go through the preliminary forms; and then, owing to the bleak and exposed situation, to adjourn for the transaction of business to one of the Stannary towns, generally Tavistock.

Wistman's Wood, a little to the north of Crockern Tor, is equally interesting. It occupies the side of a hill overlooking the *West Dart,* and covers an area about 700 yards long by a hundred wide. The wood consists of a few clumps of stunted oaks, which have existed for centuries with but little change, though they are gradually decaying owing to the close embraces of the ivy and other parasitic plants that entwine them.

Princetown (at which most motor-coaches make a stop sufficient for lunch or tea and an examination of the place and its immediate surroundings) is so called in honour of the Prince of Wales, afterwards George IV, because it and the whole of Dartmoor form part of the estates of the Duchy of Cornwall. It owes its origin to the persistent efforts of an eighteenth-century worthy who imagined that a fortune was to be won by the exploitation of Dartmoor. This gentleman, Sir Thomas Tyrwhitt, was secretary to the Council of the Prince of Wales, and Member of Parliament successively for Okehampton and Plymouth. It was at his suggestion that the locality was selected in 1806 as the site of a prison for the army of Frenchmen who had been captured in the wars. Later it was used for Americans taken during the war of 1812–14. A stained-glass east window in memory of American prisoners who died was presented to the church in 1910 by the National Society of United States Daughters of 1812. The church was built by French and American prisoners, and is not far from the prison.

The high boundary wall of the present establishment encloses an area of nearly thirty acres and surrounds the buildings in which the prisoners of war were lodged, the inscription over the gateway, *Parcere subjectis* ("spare the vanquished"), being more appropriate to the prison's original purpose than to its later use. By the time the prison was built and occupied Princetown had grown into a hamlet of considerable size. When a few years later peace was proclaimed, the place fell into decay. In spite of the efforts of Tyrwhitt, it remained a deserted village until 1850, when, probably at the suggestion of the Prince Consort, who had visited it a few years before, the old war prison was used for convicts.

From the front there is little to be seen of the Prison. By far the best viewpoint is a spot on the Two Bridges road just beyond the Princetown 30 mile speed limit sign.

Yelverton. From Princetown the road continues south-westward over the high Moor and descends to Yelverton, on the Plymouth-Tavistock road. Yelverton and its neighbour, **Dousland,** make a good centre for exploration in the Meavy and Plym valleys. Trout and the occasional salmon may be hooked in four rivers nearby – Meavy, Cad (Plym), the Walkham and the Tavy. There is a golf course. The church, though in fourteenth-century style, is modern.

Postbridge

Torquay

Banks. – *Barclays,* Fleet Street and Lower Union Lane; *Devon and Exeter Savings,* Fleet Street; *Lloyds,* Vaughan Parade (facing the Strand), and Union Street; *Midland,* Strand; *National Westminster,* Strand and .Union Street.

Buses. – In addition to the regular local services, there is a limited stop service to Exeter, extending to Sidmouth, Seaton and Lyme Regis by some buses, and another to Plymouth *via* South Brent, Ivybridge and Plympton. The regular services are to Newton Abbot; to Totnes; to Ashburton and Buckfastleigh; to Bovey Tracey, Moretonhampstead, Chagford and Okehampton; to Exeter *via* Chudleigh, Haldon and Kennford, and *via* Teignmouth, Dawlish and Starcross; to Shaldon, *via* Watcombe, Maidencombe and Labrador; to Paignton, Churston, Brixham and Kingswear.

Paignton, Brixham and Kingswear buses start from outside the Pavilion and Newton Abbot buses from Marine Square opposite the Pavilion. Plymouth buses from behind the Town Hall; all the others from the Strand. During the summer some of these services connect with seasonal trips or services starting from Exeter or elsewhere, particulars of which will be found in the time-tables. Current issues should always be consulted. Tickets can be obtained to some places from which return can be made by rail, or *vice versa.*

Car Parks. – *Lymington Road,* near Town Hall; *North Quay,* near Pavilion; *Beacon Quay; Lower Union Lane; Meadfoot Road; Sheddon Hill; Wall's Hill.* Street parking where indicated.

Clubs and Societies. – There are over 30 sports clubs and 40 social, cultural societies, etc. The complete list may be obtained from the Information Bureau.

Coach Trips. – During the greater part of the year, morning, afternoon, evening and whole day coach trips are run to all the famous places of interest, in Devon and adjoining counties. For routes, see bills and local papers. Coach station at Lymington Road.

Early Closing. – Shops: Wednesday, higher part of town; Saturday, lower part of town. Offices: Saturday.

Hospitals. – *Torbay,* Lawes Bridge; *Rosehill* (children), Warberry Road; *Shrublands* (maternity), Morgan Avenue.

Hotels. – *Grand, Palace, Cavendish, Devonshire, Rosetor, Victoria, Queen's, Abbey Lawn, Livermead House, Lincombe Hall, San Remo, Imperial, Palm Court, Royal, Osborne, Toorak, Kistor, Sherwood, Roslin Hall, Princes, Torbay, Belgrave, Vernon Court, Ashley Court, Bute Court, Beach Spa,* and a great many others of all grades.

Information Centre. – At 9 Vaughan Parade.

Libraries, Museum, Aquarium and Picture Gallery. – The Public Library *(Reference Library open* 10 *a.m. to* 8 *p.m.; Thursday,* 10 *a.m. to* 6 *p.m.)* in Lymington Road, a few yards from Castle Circus, contains excellently equipped lending and reference departments as well as a reading-room. The lending library is available to visitors presenting home library tickets; the Reading and Reference Rooms are also open to visitors, and the latter contains a fine collection of books dealing with local history and topography. The Natural History Society's Library in Torwood Street possesses some 30,000 volumes; temporary membership and use of reading-room available.

The **Museum** is in the Babbacombe Road (opposite Torwood Garden), and the municipal **Art Gallery** at Torre Abbey.

The **Marine Aqualand** is on Beacon Quay.

Local Government. – From 1 April 1968 a new authority, the County Borough of Torbay, came into being. It comprises almost all the former municipal borough of Torquay and the urban district of Paignton; the built-up part of the urban district of Brixham; parts of the parishes of Coffinswell and Kerswells in the Newton Abbot rural area; and parts of the parishes of Churston Ferrers and Marldon in the rural district of Totnes. The total area is 15,500 acres.

Places of Worship. – (with hours of service on Sundays). *(These times should be verified, as they vary with the season: some of the Sunday evening services start at* 8 *p.m. during the summer.)*

St. Saviour's Parish Church of Tormohun. – 8.15, 11 and 6.30.

All Saints', top of Belgrave Road. – 7.30, 10.

St. John's, Montpelier Place. – 8, 10.15, 11 and 8.15.

St. John the Baptist, Cadewell Lane. – 8, 9, 11 and 6.30.

St. Mary Magdalene, Union Street. – 8, 11, 12 and 6.30.

St. Luke's, St. Luke's Road. – 8, 11 and 6.30.

Christ Church, Ellacombe. – 8, 10, 11.15 and 6.30.

St. Matthias', Babbacombe Road, Ilsham. – 8, 11, 12 and 6.30.

St. Mark's, St. Mark's Road, Torwood. – 8, 11, 12.15 and 6.30.

St. Peter's, Queensway, Chelston. – 7, 9 and 6.30.

Holy Trinity, Torwood Gardens. – 8, 11 and 6.30.

St. George and St. Mary, Cockington. – 8 (last Sunday in month), 11, 8 (during summer months only; for times at other seasons, see notices).

St. Matthew's, Chelston. – 8, 10, 11 and 6.30.

Good Shepherd (Mission Church), Hele.–6.30 p.m.
All Saints', St. Alban's Road, Babbacombe.–7, 8, 9.30, 11 and 6.30.
St. Mary the Virgin, Fore Street, St. Marychurch.–7, 8 and 10 (11.15 and 6.30 June, July, August).
St. Martin's, Barton.–8, 10.30 and 6.30.
Roman Catholic Church of the Assumption, Abbey Road.–7, 8, 10, 11, 5 and 6.30.
Roman Catholic Church of Our Lady the Help of Christians and St. Denis, Priory Road, St. Marychurch.–7.30, 9, 11 and 6.30.
Roman Catholic Church of Holy Angels, Chelston; and *SS. John Fisher and Thomas More,* Hele Road.
Methodist, Union Street, Market Street, Babbacombe Road, and Old Mill Road, Chelston; Barton; Victoria Park; and at Shiphay.–All at 11 and 6.30.
Baptist, Upton Vale, St. Marychurch Road, Hele Road, and Barton.–11 and 6.30.
United Reformed, Abbey Road, Furrough Cross, St. Marychurch.–11 and 6.30.
Belgrave United Reformed Church, Tor Hill Road.–11 and 6.30.
Society of Friends, 48 Tor Hill Road.–11 and (first Sunday in month), 6.30.
Unitarian Free Christian (Unity Church), Montpelier Terrace.–11.
Brethren, Warren Road; Gospel Hall, Torre Hill; Fore Street, St. Marychurch; and Fore Street, Babbacombe.–11 and 6.30.
Christadelphian Hall, Higher Union Street.–11 and 6.30.
First Church of Christ Scientist, Torwood Gardens.–11 and 6.30. Reading Room at Torwood Street.
Hebrew, Synagogue Chambers, Abbey Road.
Salvation Army, Market Street.

Police.–South Street, Torquay. Tel. 22293.
Population.–109,800 (whole of Torbay).
Postal.–The General Post Office, Fleet Street. There are sub-offices in all districts.
Railway Stations.–There are two stations, both on the Western Region Line, **Torquay** (Tel. Torquay 25227) and **Torre** (Tel. Torquay 3206). The latter is the more convenient for Shiphay, Torre and Upton.

Entertainments and Pastimes

Since Torquay is a popular resort at all seasons, entertainment is provided throughout the year.

Bridge.–Torquay Bridge Club, 60 Torwood Street; Devonshire Bridge Club, Roselea Hotel; and Torwood Bridge Club, 56 The Terrace.
Cinemas.–*A.B.C.,* Castle Circus; *Odeon,* off Union Street; *Colony,* off Union Street.
Concerts.–Celebrity concerts at Pavilion and in Town Hall.
Dancing.–The Town Hall (as advertised); Torbay Hotel; Walnut Grove Club; and at many hotels. Open-air dancing at the Roughwood Hotel, Babbacombe.
Illuminations.–Central Sea Front and Babbacombe Downs nightly from June to October. Also at Christmas, Easter and on special occasions.
Regattas.–In July and August.
Theatres.–*The Pavilion,* Drama, Comedy, Revue, Variety, Repertory (summer only). *Princess Theatre,* Revue, Opera, Ballet, Variety, Plays, Pantomime throughout the year. *Babbacombe Theatre,* Summer Revue.

Sports

Athletics.–Meetings at Wall's Hill, Babbacombe.
Badminton.–St. Marychurch Town Hall. Several clubs.
Bathing and Swimming.–Torre Abbey Sands, Beacon Cove, Corbyn Beach, Meadfoot Beach, Anstey's Cove, Redgate Beach, Babbacombe Beach, Oddicombe Beach, Maidencombe Beach, Livermead Beach, Watcombe Beach, and at numerous coves and sandy inlets.

Enquiries regarding the hire of chalets and beach tents should be addressed to the Manager (Outdoor Amenities), Resort Services Department, Lymington Road.

Boating.–Speedboats, sailing- and rowing-boats for hire from harbour and principal beaches. Details of mooring and facilities for all types of craft from Harbour Master, Beacon Quay. Tel. 22429.
Bowls.–Public greens at the King's Gardens, Upton Park, Cary Park, Ellacombe Green. The Torquay Bowling Club is in Belgrave Road.

Ten-pin Bowling.–Union Street.

Cricket.–Torquay Cricket Club, Recreation ground opposite Torquay Station; Babbacombe Cricket Club, Wall's Hill; Corinthian Club, Cockington Court.
Fishing.–Sea fishing from the Piers and from rocks and boats. Freshwater fishing from Corporation Reservoirs. Fly-fishing for salmon and trout from the Dart and Teign Rivers.
Golf.–Torquay Golf Club, Petitor (18 holes); Churston Golf Club (18 holes).
Putting.–Courses at Cary Park (Babbacombe) and in Abbey Gardens.
Riding and Hunting.–Shiphay Manor Riding School, Shiphay; Tel. 63362. Sladnor Park Riding School (88928). Lowes Bridge Riding School (3756).

Hunting.–The South Devon Foxhounds and the Dart Vale and Haldon Harriers meet during the season.

Ski-ing.–There is a plastic ski run at Barton Hall Chalet Hotel.
Squash.–Courts at Grand Hotel, and Palace Hotel.
Tennis.–Hard and grass courts at Abbey Gardens, Upton Park, Cary Park. Torquay Lawn Tennis Club in Belgrave Road welcomes residents and visitors. Covered courts at Palace Hotel–open lawn tennis championships in November.
Water Ski-ing.–Dart Marina Cruising and Water Sports Club; South Devon Water Sports Club.
Yachting.–Royal Torbay Yacht Club. Regattas held in July and August.

In and About Torquay

Charles Kingsley maintained that rough English weather made tough English people, but we cannot all be tough, and for many people, the problem, when autumn sets in, is: Where can we find sunshine and shelter within the limits of these islands? Anything like a certainty of prolonged sunshine in mid-winter is, of course, impossible, but though the golden days of an English winter must inevitably be interspersed with many grey ones, there are places along the south coast where soft airs are to be found with a complete freedom from the fogs which render the Midland and Home Counties, and especially the neighbourhood of great cities, so trying in November and December. In looking for the best the British climate can provide, we naturally turn to the coast facing the distant shores of Spain, the Gulf Stream touching its beaches and its cliffs open to every warm breath that chance may send up from the Azores. In this respect no place in Great Britain is more favourably situated than Torquay, for it not only faces south but occupies a position which is largely sheltered by the hills and headlands forming Torbay.

Torquay has always been famed as a place of winter residence, but, since it enjoys an equable climate, with mild winters and cool summers, it is popular in all months of the year.

A First View of Torquay. Built on a cluster of hills which jut into the sea, the town has the advantage of conditions which, if not insular, are at least peninsular. The rugged, rocky cliffs, often over 200 feet in height; the deep quiet coves which lie at their feet; the long perspective of old red sandstone coast, glowing as the sun sinks like a dying flame; the bay and harbour; and the deep inlets on all sides of this pleasant promontory, form a region on which much that is beautiful has been well and wisely reared.

From the Marine Drive skirting the waters of Torbay the scene presented on a fine day cannot fail to win admiration, and "lovely" is the adjective naturally suggested by the first glimpse of this terraced town, set, like Rome, on seven hills (Braddon, Warberry, Waldon, Lincombe, Park, the Beacon Hills, and Peaked Tor). From the sea-girt road one sees all of Torquay that turns its face to the sea; the succession of hills, with the cleft in the middle where gently rising roads lead by circuitous ways to the tops of hills that, seen from below, suggest mountain-climbing and scaling ladders. At first glance it is difficult to believe one is looking at an English scene. The profusion of sub-tropical trees, luxuriant flowers and flowering shrubs against a background of terraced hills, with here and there an unusual style of architecture, give a Continental appearance to Torquay. The Torquay authorities have learnt the art of conquering a hill without levelling it by bad planning to the monotony of a plain.

Harbour and Vane Hill, Torquay

Torquay is at the northern end of **Torbay,** on which Paignton and Brixham are also situated – a place of shelter long-famed among sailors. From Berry Head on the south-east to Hope's Nose on the north-east – the extreme ends of the two arms of land that protect the bay – is a distance over the water of rather more than 4 miles, and the town of Torquay, facing due south, is sheltered from the east by the very hills on which a greater part of it is built.

The Seafront. The **Seafront** sweeps northwards from **Corbyn Head,** a charming viewpoint. Below the Head is one of the fine bathing beaches, to the confines of which the Torre Abbey Bathing Platform has been extended. South of Corbyn Head is the most southerly of Torquay's beaches, **Livermead Sands** and **Institute Beach,** the nearest bathing point to Paignton.

Inland are the **King's Gardens,** with a bowling green and a large pond, less than a foot in depth, where during the summer hundreds of children pass happy hours sailing their little craft. Its continuation as a stream is crossed by rustic bridges, and its ducks are an additional attraction to the youngsters.

The **Recreation Ground** is near at hand. Here the Rugby football club plays in winter, and the cricket club in summer.

Eastward a short distance farther along the coastal road are the beautiful grounds in which is situated –

Torre Abbey. Dedicated to St. Saviour, or Holy Trinity, the Abbey was founded in 1196 (*temp.* Richard I) by Lord Brewere, a powerful baron of the day, who owned the barony of Tor among other possessions. He richly endowed the Abbey, and bestowed it on monks of the Præmonstratensian order, founded by St. Norbert in 1120. That it was a magnificent edifice the remains show. Leland tells of "three fair gatehouses", and the one still standing proves that the adjective was deserved. The bulk of the buildings have been transformed into the present mansion.

In the grounds are still to be seen the ruins of the church tower, the arches which formed the entrance to the chapter house, and some fragments of the chancel archway. There are also remnants of the monastery itself – the Abbot's tower, the converted refectory, and the Tithe Barn, the last-named generally known as the **Spanish Barn,** because the captured crew of the *Nuestra Senora del Rosario,* flagship of Don Pedro de Valdez, a commander of the Armada of 1588, were for a time confined in it.

The present mansion, now the property of Torbay Corporation, is the result, first, of conversion by the Ridgeways, owners of the property at the end of the sixteenth century; secondly, of additions by the Carys, owners from 1662 right up to 1930. The Ridgeways had turned the Refectory, internally, into a house; the Carys gave it a top floor, a terrace and wings, one of which is connected with the venerable gateway to which we have referred. During renovation in 1874, two ancient crypts were brought to light beneath the Chapel and what was once the Abbot's apartments. In the Chapel, originally the Guest Hall of the monastery, four of the bosses of the ancient roof are still preserved. The lavatorium near the refectory is still perfect, and is of great interest. On the top of Chapel Hill (p. 110) is St. Michael's Chapel, no longer thought to be connected with the Abbey. At Ilsham, two or three miles distant, the monks had a grange. The late Hugh R. Watkin explored the Abbey and threw much new light upon its early history. Quite recently he discovered a document of 1300, which is Bishop Bitton's confirmation of the possession by the Abbey of seven churches in Devon.

The Abbey now contains the municipal **Art Gallery,** and exhibitions are held from time to time.

Torre Abbey Meadows

The grounds surrounding the Abbey cover an area of approximately 8 acres. Here are exquisitely designed Italian, Rock and Water Gardens, flower beds displaying a magnificent wealth of colour, exotic shrubs, and Palm and Cacti Houses.

Within the grounds are tennis courts, bowling greens, an approach golf course, and putting greens.

On the opposite side of the Promenade are the **Torre Abbey Sands,** one of the most popular beaches for children. Just above a shelter overlooking the Abbey Sands is the **Professor Summers' Memorial Clock.**

Now we approach **Waldon Hill;** on the seaward face is –

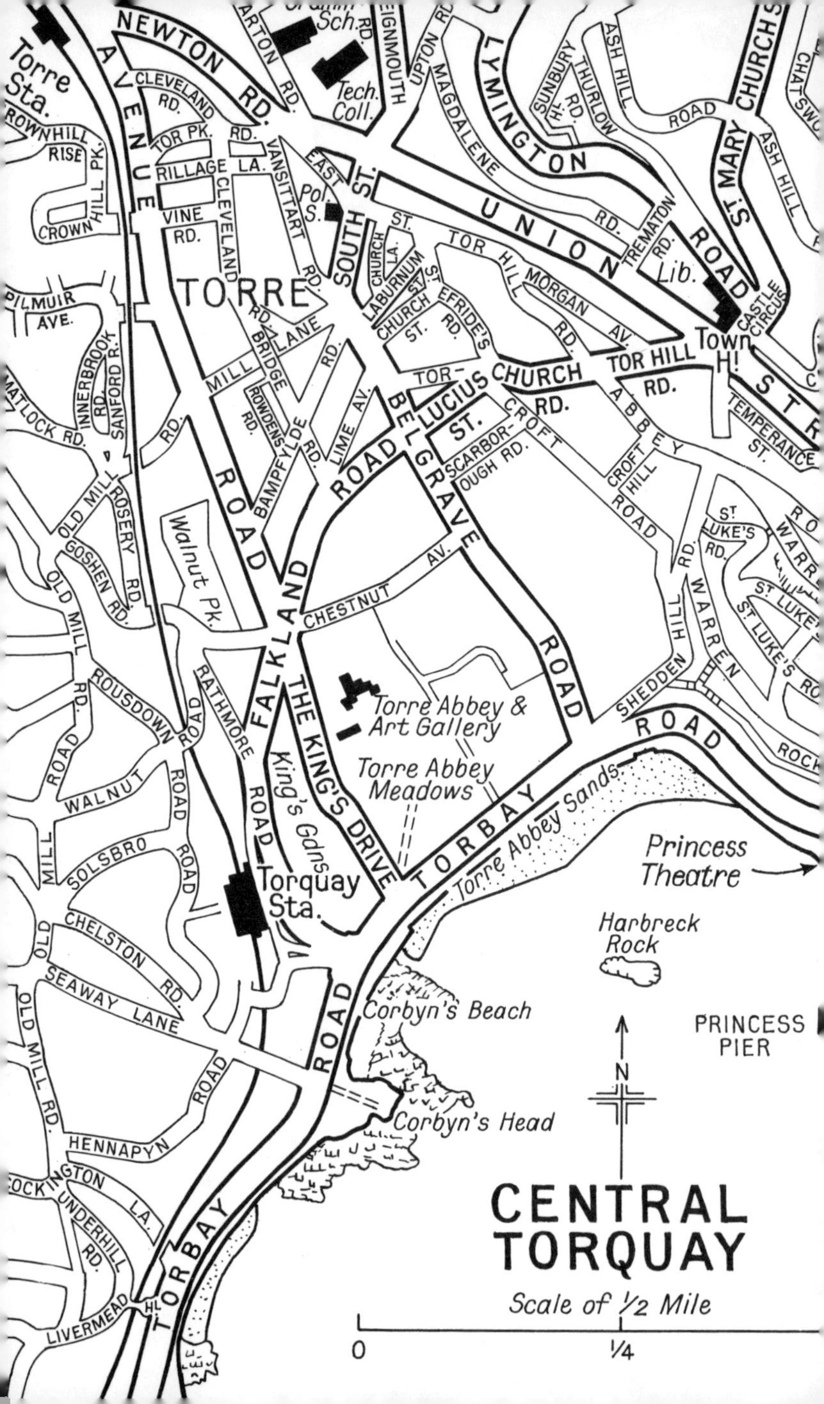
CENTRAL TORQUAY
Scale of 1/2 Mile
0
1/4
N
Torre Sta.
Torquay Sta.
TORRE
Tech. Coll.
Sch.
Pol. S.
Lib.
Town Hl.
Walnut Pk.
Torre Abbey & Art Gallery
Torre Abbey Meadows
King's Gdns
Torre Abbey Sands
Princess Theatre
Harbreck Rock
Corbyn's Beach
Corbyn's Head
PRINCESS PIER
NEWTON RD.
AVENUE
UNION ST.
LYMINGTON RD.
ST MARY CHURCH RD.
TOR HILL RD.
CHURCH ST.
LUCIUS ST.
BELGRAVE ROAD
FALKLAND ROAD
THE KING'S DRIVE
TORBAY ROAD
SHEDDEN HILL RD.
ABBEY ROAD
CROFT ROAD
AVENUE ROAD
RATHMORE ROAD
CHESTNUT AV.
WALNUT ROAD
MILL LANE
CHELSTON RD.
SEAWAY LANE
HENNAPYN ROAD
OLD MILL RD.
COCKINGTON LA.
UNDERHILL RD.
LIVERMEAD HL
TEMPERANCE ST.
CASTLE CIRCUS
ST LUKE'S RD.
WARREN RD.
ROCK RD.

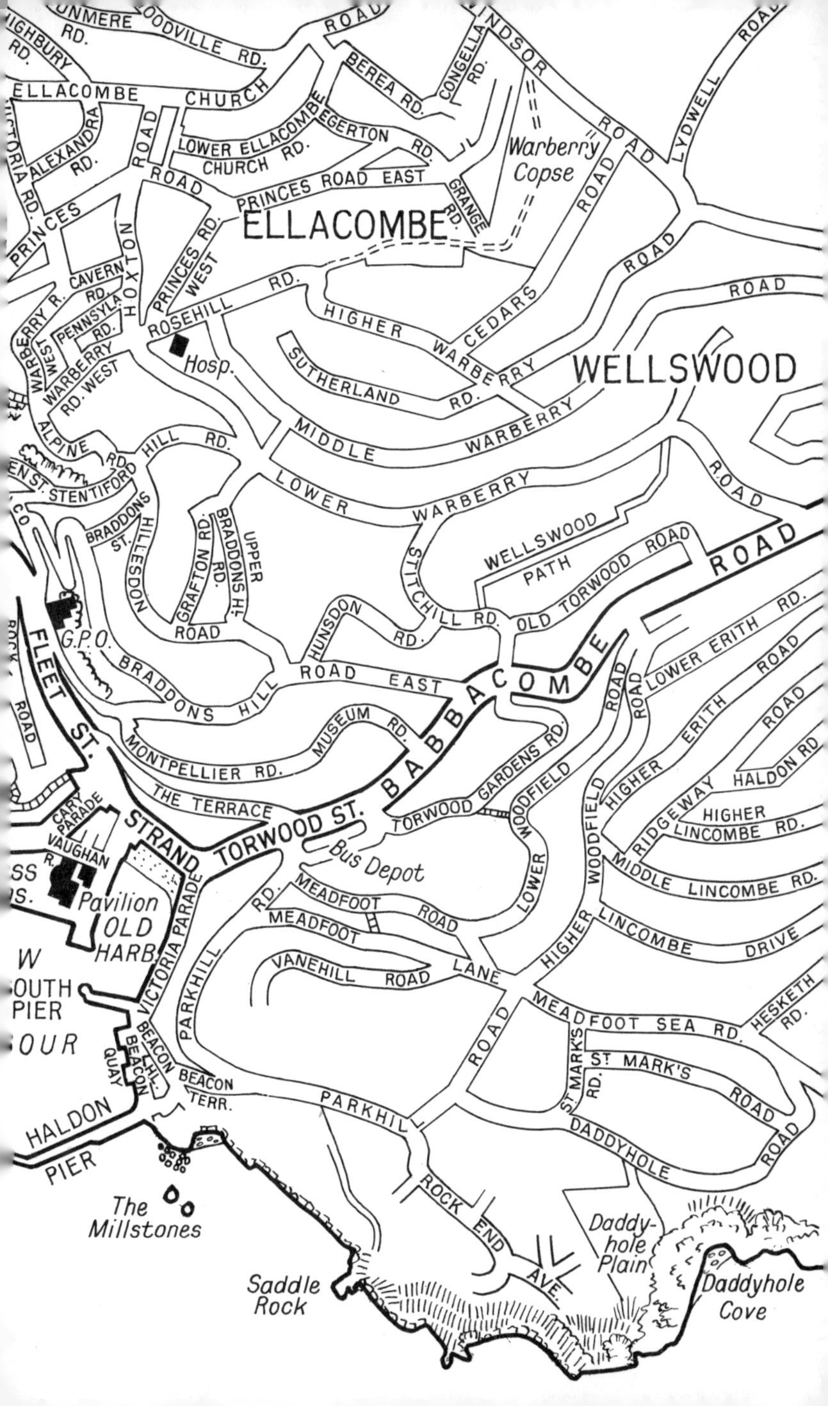

ELLACOMBE
WELLSWOOD
BABBACOMBE ROAD
TORWOOD ST.
STRAND
FLEET ST.
Warberry Copse
Hosp.
G.P.O.
Bus Depot
Pavilion
OLD HARB.
SOUTH PIER
HALDON PIER
The Millstones
Saddle Rock
Daddyhole Plain
Daddyhole Cove
ELLACOMBE CHURCH ROAD
LOWER ELLACOMBE CHURCH RD.
PRINCES ROAD EAST
PRINCES RD. WEST
HIGHER WARBERRY RD.
MIDDLE WARBERRY
LOWER WARBERRY
SUTHERLAND RD.
CEDARS ROAD
LYDWELL ROAD
WELLSWOOD PATH
OLD TORWOOD ROAD
STITCHILL RD.
HUNSDON RD.
BRADDONS HILL ROAD EAST
MUSEUM RD.
MONTPELLIER RD.
THE TERRACE
TORWOOD GARDENS RD.
WOODFIELD ROAD
LOWER ERITH RD.
HIGHER ERITH ROAD
HALDON RD
RIDGEWAY
HIGHER LINCOMBE RD.
MIDDLE LINCOMBE RD.
LINCOMBE DRIVE
MEADFOOT ROAD
MEADFOOT LANE
VANEHILL ROAD
PARKHILL RD.
MEADFOOT SEA RD.
HESKETH RD.
ST. MARK'S ROAD
DADDYHOLE ROAD
ROCK END AVE.
VICTORIA PARADE
CARY PARADE
VAUGHAN R.
BEACON QUAY
BEACON TERR.
ROSEHILL RD.
ALPINE RD.
STENTIFORD
HILLESDON ROAD
GRAFTON RD.
UPPER BRADDONS HL.
BRADDONS ST.
HOXTON
CAVERN RD.
PENNSYLVA RD.
WARBERRY RD. WEST
ALEXANDRA RD.
VICTORIA RD.
WOODVILLE RD.
HIGHBURY RD.
BEREA RD.
CONGELLA RD.
EGERTON RD.
WINDSOR ROAD
GRANGE RD.

The Rock Walk. The Rock Walk is a raised esplanade above the Torbay Road, overlooking the sea. With its abundance of sub-tropical foliage, palm groves, slopes, and sheltered seats, this is the most picturesque promenade of Torquay, and the most popular.

A terrace garden runs along the foot of the cliffs; other walks wind in and out up the face of the rocks, from which a beautiful panoramic view of the harbour and bay is obtained.

The cliffs are covered with wild and cultivated shrubs and climbing plants. Cacti, aloes, and many rare trees from foreign countries are planted here.

The **Princess Pier** runs out into the sea from the western end of the Princess Gardens, directly opposite the Terrace Walk. It extends more than 1,500 feet, just stopping short of joining with the **Haldon Pier,** which has been thrown out westward from the base of Beacon Hill.

The Princess Gardens. These gardens owe much of their charm to their situation between the foliage-covered cliff of Waldon Hill and the sparkling waters of Torbay. The fascination of the Gardens rests in the fact that, while they are at the water's edge, flowers and shrubs flourish and trees afford shelter from the sun all the year round as in hardly any other resort in England. A *Cenotaph,* designed by Sir Reginald Blomfield (the architect in his younger days of St. Luke's Church in the town), stands in the Gardens in memory of those who fell in the two World Wars.

The Princess Theatre forms the main feature in recent development of the gardens. It is one of the most modern theatres on the south coast, has seating for 1,500 people, and two sun lounges overlooking the harbour. On the esplanade fronting the gardens is a popular two-tier elliptical deck.

At the eastern end of the Princess Garden is the **Pavilion.** This is open for the summer only for the presentation of shows by professional and amateur companies on the fine stage. There are musical and variety shows throughout the summer. Sunday evening concerts are given from June until the end of September.

Adjoining the theatre is a fully licensed restaurant.

The Strand. At the head of the Inner Harbour is the **Strand,** a genuine strand or sea-margin bordered by shops and with bus shelter and numerous seats facing the Harbour, convenient for those waiting for motor-coaches and buses which make this their starting point. In the season the Strand is a busy spot, for it is the hub of Torquay's holiday road traffic, and there is generally a certain liveliness in connection with the yachts and other craft using the Harbour. The Harbour occupies the site of the old quay used by the fishermen of the little village which sprang up under the protection of Torre Abbey and was connected with Torre by a narrow lane, where are now the shops of Fleet Street. **Victoria Parade,** leading to Haldon Pier, obtains its name from the fact that Queen Victoria landed here on one of her visits to the town.

High on the hillside above the Strand is the tower of **St. John's Church.** This spacious and impressive modern church was designed by G. E. Street, the architect of the Royal Courts of Justice. The large illuminated cross, which at night shines out to sea, was given as a memorial to the eminent actor Cyril Maude by his widow. Within the church, the reredos,

Torquay Harbour

carved in Caen stone, should be noted. There are Venetian mosaics by Salvatti on the north wall. The great west window, and paintings on either side of the altar, are by Burne-Jones.

The Harbours. Halden and **Princess Piers** form the great **Outer Harbour,** within which is the Inner Harbour, with an area of about 6 acres, while the Outer Harbour encloses a water surface of fully 35 acres. These harbours provide safe shelter, and in the yachting season the Outer Harbour is filled with pleasure craft of all sizes and descriptions while in the Inner Harbour there is a variety of small rowing and other boats. With such advantages it is not surprising that the town should be thronged at times with yachtsmen, for whom there are excellent clubs. At the **Annual Regatta** many visiting yachts take part, and splendid sport is witnessed in the Bay. There is a lively fair ashore each day, with fireworks in the evening.

The walk may be continued by way of Victoria Parade, where note outside the *Regina Hotel,* formerly the old Bath House, the plaque in memory of Elizabeth Barrett Browning who lived there from 1838–1841. Victoria Parade merges into Beacon Terrace, where is the home of the **Royal Torbay Yacht Club** and **Beacon Quay.**

On Beacon Quay is **Aqualand,** a fine modern marine aquarium *(open daily, charge)*. The cold water sea collection features the marine life of Torbay. There are Tropical Marine Fish and Reptile collections, the latter centring on the rare and grotesque. There are 45 tanks of great interest.

The Town. Radiating in all directions from **Castle Circus,** its centre, are thronged business streets and quiet residential roads, the counterpart of many others in provincial England.

Castle Circus is dominated by the **Town Hall,** an English Renaissance block occupying the whole of its northern side. The hall has an excellent dance floor, and the clock tower is 100 feet high. Local materials were used almost entirely in its construction, the quarries at Barton, Ipplepen, Ashburton, and Beer being freely drawn on, while local marbles figure largely in the interior decorations. There is a tablet in honour of Prof. Oliver Heaviside (1850–1925), the scientist, who lived and worked in Torquay. The Public Library is round the corner in Lymington Road.

Some of the town's bus services start from, and all north-bound district services, the Circus, while round the corner, beyond the Library, is the Town Hall car park.

From the Circus, Union Street, converging into Fleet Street near the **General Post Office,** leads to the **Harbour.** This is the principal shopping street and business thoroughfare. Facing the harbour is the **Strand,** a starting place for many of the local bus services. (Note that a few services start from the bus park in front of the Pavilion.)

Bordering the eastern side of the harbour is **Victoria Parade.** On the opposite side of the harbour is **Vaughan Parade;** here are the **Information Centres** and many of the booking offices for coach and sea trips.

In Babbacombe Road (opposite Torwood Gardens) is the **Museum of the Torquay Natural History Society** *(open each weekday* 10 *a.m.* to 5 *p.m.; admission charge; temporary membership* 75*p.),* best known for its systematically arranged collection of prehistoric remains from Kent's Cavern. A notable exhibit is a human skull which the late Sir Arthur Keith stated to be that of a woman about 25 years of age, living some 15,000 years ago. Including specimens from local caves, the contents of the museum illustrate the geology of Devon and show its animals and birds. The carved wooden figures on the staircase wall, which came from Waddeton Court, Stoke Gabriel, and are supposed to be Flemish work of the fifteenth century, attract attention, while those contemplating a voyage of archæological discovery on Dartmoor may note the kistvaens in the hall and second floor. During the summer months a pleasant feature is the wild-flower collection set out in the Entrance Hall, and visitors are willingly given assistance in identifying their finds. In the Laycock Gallery, opened in 1955, will be found a comprehensive display of Devon cottage and farmhouse furniture, as well as agricultural implements of bygone days.

109 *The Harbour, Torquay*

Excursions from Torquay

Distances. – By road from Torquay (approximate).

	Miles		Miles		Miles
Ashburton	14	Dawlish	12	Moretonhampstead	19
Becky Falls	16	Dittisham (ferry)	9	Newton Abbot	6½
Berry Head	10	Exeter	23	Paignton	3
Berry Pomeroy	7½	Fingle Bridge	22	Plymouth	32
Bishopsteignton	10	Hennock	15	Powderham Castle	16
Bovey Tracey	12	Hay Tor Rock	15	Princetown	29
Bradley Woods	7	Holne Chase	17	Slapton Sands	17
Brixham	8½	Ivybridge	22	South Brent	17
Broadhempston	11	Kenton	16	Starcross	15
Buckfastleigh	15	Kingsbridge	22	Staverton	12
Buckland Beacon	16	Kingskerswell	4	Stoke Gabriel	7
Chagford	22	Kingsteignton	9	Tavistock	37
Chudleigh	12	Kingswear	11	Teigngrace	9
Churston	6	Lustleigh	16	Teignmouth	8½
Cockington	1	Mamhead	15	Totnes	9
Compton Castle	4	Manaton	16	Ugbrooke Park	12
Dartmouth (ferry)	11	Milber Down	6	Widecombe-in-the-Moor	19

Chapel Hill

One of the most popular short strolls is to **Chapel Hill,** separated from Torre railway station by the roadway only, and a mile north-west of the centre of the town, from which it is easily reached by bus.

From the sea front, a pleasant walking route is through Torre Abbey Gardens, then, at the exit, **Avenue Road** leads to the approach to Chapel Hill. Winding paths through the woods give access to the summit where is **St. Michael's Chapel.** Little is known of its origin and history, but it was probably built in the twelfth century. As it is dedicated to St. Michael, the patron saint of mariners, tradition ascribes its erection to the gratitude of a sailor for deliverance from drowning. The chapel has walls 4 feet thick, a rough rock floor, and a pointed barrel roof. The Bath stone cross was erected some years ago by the Marchioness of Bute. There are fine views embracing Torquay and Torbay and the Dartmoor Tors.

From Chapel Hill a footpath leads eastwards past two of the Corporation reservoirs (247 feet above the sea) to Barton Road along which the walk may be continued (L.) past the Cemetery and the high ground round Hele, thence regaining the centre of the town by way of Teignmouth Road and Upton Vale; or by turning right along Barton Road at the end of the reservoir path the town may be reached in a few minutes.

Kent's Cavern

Bus from the Strand to Wellswood, or by same service in reverse direction from St. Marychurch to Wellswood.
Admission. – Fee. Free car park.

Kent's Cavern, one of the oldest recognizable human dwellings in our country (another is the Pin Hole in Derbyshire), is of extraordinary interest and should not be missed. The most direct road is by way of the Babbacombe Road and Ilsham Road, the Cavern being about a mile and a quarter from the Strand. Visitors may be recommended to preface their visit to the Cavern by a visit to the Natural History Society's Museum (see p. 108) and a detailed examination of the specimens which have been excavated. The skull of the Great Cave Bear, discovered in 1948, is exhibited in the entrance hall to the Cavern.

The Cavern is about half a mile from the shore, and 200 feet above sea-level. It consists of two parallel caves, connected in one place, and divided into chambers, varying in breadth from under a yard to over 20 yards, and nowhere more than 30 feet high. The natural ventilation of the cave is remarkably good, and the temperature remains constant at 52 F. The Cavern is now provided with flood-lights; this enhances the beauty of the colouring, and has led to the development of small ferns, which contrive to exist on the limestone wall. Stalactites of all sizes, and delicately coloured, hang from the roof, and the floor was, before it was broken up for examination, entirely covered with stalagmites. But it was the destruction of the floor which revealed the features which impart the principal interest to the Cavern. Its existence has been known from ante-Roman ages; and names and dates written on portions show that it was a "show place" in 1571, 1615 and 1688. But it was not until 1824 that Northmoore found a number of fossil bones in the cavern and prepared the way for the interesting discoveries which have since been made. His researches were supplemented by those of the Rev. J. McEnery, chaplain at Torre Abbey, who between 1825 and 1841 brought many bones and a number of flint implements to light. In 1846 the Torquay Natural History Society took the matter up, and in 1864, under the auspices of a committee of the British Association, of which Lyell, Lubbock, Boyd-Dawkins, Edward Vivian and William Pengelly were members, the cave was thoroughly and scientifically explored.

Anstey's Cove, Torquay

Cockington

Cockington. Cockington is the western portion of Greater Torquay, and Torquay Station is in the parish.

Cockington village, long beloved by artists and photographers, is still quite unspoilt by the modern builder and retains its old-world air. The best approach is along **Cockington Lane,** which branches at right-angles from the main road to Paignton, about 300 yards beyond Corbyn Head. This is a typical Devon byway, and may be followed all the way; or from the first road junction one may take the footpath which runs parallel to Cockington Lane. The path rejoins the Lane short of the Forge, or a little earlier at one of the entrances to Cockington Court. The visitor should continue the walk until he reaches the **Forge** at the corner – a quaint old building which has been committed to canvas times without number and might well have been the home of "The Village Blacksmith" of the famous song.

From the Forge it is only a stone's throw to the picturesque thatched and timber-fronted lodge from which a drive leads to **Cockington Court,** the gracious sixteenth-century manor-house owned formerly by the Cary family, and then for nearly 300 years by the Mallock family. It is now the property of the Torbay Corporation, and part of the old house is used as a restaurant.

The lovely grounds, with lakes, lawns, trees, and gardens, prove a beautiful setting for the thatched village, the old Manor House, and the charming fifteenth-century **Church of St. George and St. Mary.** The nave of the church dates from *c.* 1075, but the present building is mainly fourteenth and fifteenth century, with a thirteenth-century tower. The Tudor pulpit came from Tormohun (Torre) church. Among the many other items worthy of note are a fine fifteenth-century font, a restored fourteenth-century rood-screen and the carved bench-ends below the tower.

Leading from the manor-house is a long avenue planted in 1951 to commemorate the holding in Torquay of the International Conference on Tariffs and Trade. Thirty-nine nations were represented, each planting a tree in the avenue.

A large and attractive modern inn, *The Drum,* designed by Sir E. Lutyens, has been set up near the Forge.

From Cockington, Torquay may be reached by Chelston or Seaway Lane. If a longer route is required, a pleasant walk may be obtained by following the road uphill from the Forge for about 2 miles, turning left at Five Lanes to **Churscombe,** and bearing left again to **Shorton Valley,** whence a bus returns to Torquay.

Anstey's Cove and the Bishop's Walk

The walk over **Warberry Hill** (448 feet above sea-level and the apex of Torquay) involves a preliminary clamber, but gives grand views of Torquay and its surroundings, and towards Dartmoor one sees Rippon Tor and the rocks of Haytor.

From half-way up Union Street turn right up Market Street and after proceeding 200 yards, mount a long steep flight of steps (R.) leading to Warberry Road West. Continue uphill to **Warberry Wood,** and entering the wood follow the main path. This emerges at the end of Quinta Road, and immediately opposite is a footpath marked "To Babbacombe Road". A few yards farther on, some steps on the left give access to a seat with a fine view of the coast line. The footpath presently drops steeply in the open and enters Babbacombe Road *(bus route)* opposite Wall's Hill Quarry, and a short distance to the right is a lane leading to Anstey's Cove leaving the *Palace Hotel* on the right.

(Those who wish to see Warberry Hill but do not like the steep approach from the Town should start from the Babbacombe Road end *(bus to Quarry)* and make a gentle start by footpath up to Windsor Road and enjoy the final step down into Market Street, which provides a bird's eye view of clustered houses and busy streets.)

Anstey's Cove

Bus from the Strand *via* Babbacombe Road, alighting at Anstey's Cove Road.

Situated at the end of a deep ferny combe, Anstey's Cove is sheltered from unpleasant gusts by lofty cliffs, of brilliant colour and satin-like glossiness, some of the masses of limestone rock bearing a resemblance to the ruins of a feudal keep. No spot near Torquay is more popular with visitors.

From Anstey's Cove a footbridge leads round **Devil's Point** to **Redgate Beach,** where there is a fine shingle slope with good bathing facilities and a refreshment pavilion. Boats go from here to Torquay and Babbacombe.

Walkers can continue the stroll northwards to Babbacombe, about half a mile distant, by way of **Wall's Hill,** the stepped path starting just beyond the

Thatcher Rock

entrance to the Cove. This path skirts the cliffs above Redgate Beach and Long Quarry Point and may be reached by a zigzag climbing path from Redgate Beach itself up the face of the old (Comfort's) Quarry. Continuing across the Down an easy road leads down to **Babbacombe Beach.** Note on the way the faint remains of the old Rifle-range butts and, nearer the small pavilion, part of an ancient British earthwork.

The return to Torquay from Babbacombe can be made by way of a footpath through the Warberry district, or from the Cove southward through the beautiful Bishop's Walk (see below); but the easiest route is by bus from the end of St. Anne's Road. There is a car park near the entrance to Anstey's Cove and another in Wall's Hill Road.

Returning to the car park above the Cove, we find on the left the entrance to the **Bishop's Walk.** This is so named because it was the favourite walk of the famous Henry Phillpotts, who, although Bishop of Exeter, preferred to establish his palace near Torquay; the palace has now become the *Palace Hotel.*

The path is well-marked, threading the trees on the cliff or skirting small fields, with fine views to the Parson and Clerk Rocks and the East Devon coast. When the Ilsham Marine Drive is reached (R. at finger-post) cross the Drive and take the path which runs at a higher level, giving a wide outlook, especially when the ridge is crossed and a glorious view of Torbay obtained. Descending, the path soon rejoins the Drive and so to Sea Road at Meadfoot, though the **Thatcher Pines** path past the shelter (to the left after passing Thatcher Avenue) offers a further escape from the roadway until Kilmorie is reached. The return routes from Meadfoot to Torquay, see p. 117.

Daddy Hole Plain – Meadfoot – Hope's Nose

This walk reveals the charms of the northern arm of Torbay. Apart from its natural beauty, it has a distinct advantage in that it is capable of many variations, so that, as a glance at our plan of the town will show, the walk can be lengthened or shortened. No one should leave Torquay without going at least as far as Daddy Hole Plain.

From the Victoria Parade, at the eastern side of the Harbour, there is a variety of routes, but none better than to follow the road uphill past Beacon Terrace. A short distance up on the right, by the *Imperial Hotel,* is the lane to **Land's End.** This lane is marked "Footpath to *Peaked Tor Cove"* and presently steps go down, through a garden with seats, to a terrace and small bathing cove. The lane, now a path, goes on to a walled finish above Land's End where, close in, is the *Saddle Rock*. A close view is obtained of **London Bridge,** a natural arch of limestone which has been partially worn away by the waves.

To reach **Daddy Hole Plain** we take an attractive path which climbs through ilex oak trees, passing an old martello tower. Immediately below us lie Torbay and the glinting waters of the English Channel. Four miles distant is Berry Head, the limestone bluff above Brixham, and probably some of the motor trawlers that make Brixham their home will be seen or yachts racing in the bay below, adding life and interest to a scene full of beauty. Due east are three rocky islets like ships in line: nearest is **Shag Rock** and farthest off is the **Oarstone,** beyond Hope's Nose. Between them is the largest, **Thatcher Stone,** with a thatch of green. **Leadstone,** a fourth, is farther north, near in to Hope's Nose. This elevated limestone plateau on which we stand has some points of resemblance to Plymouth Hoe before the latter was levelled, rolled and asphalted into a civilized appearance, but Torquay's Hoe is smaller and has no great historic memories. Where the Plain fronts the sea is a great chasm in the cliff, occasioned by a landslip which occurred more than a century ago. It is attributed to "Daddy", otherwise the Devil. Cars may be parked on the Plain.

By following the protecting fence at the cliff edge and descending some steps to the continuing path, the spur of land on the east may be gained. A rough scramble leads to a seat on the slope. From this point a view is gained of the Sea Road and of **Meadfoot Beach** (p. 116), with well-equipped bathing station, moored raft and diving steps, the sands shining white against the green of the trees and shrubs of Lincombe Hill and its Gardens; while beyond the road may be discerned the **Marine Drive,** passing above **Hope's Nose.** Close by the eastern side of Daddy's Hole is the Torquay "gold mine", where gold is said to have been discovered, a discovery that had almost passed out of remembrance until recently, when traces of gold were again found.

Bordering Meadfoot Beach is the Sea Road which leads eastward to the junction of Ilsham Road and **Ilsham Marine Drive,** perhaps the finest marine drive in South Devon, giving grand views of Torbay and the open sea. After climbing the southern slopes of the peninsula, of which Hope's Nose forms the extreme point, it runs along the sloping cliff above the sea, and then turns inland near the beginning of the Bishop's Walk, rejoining Ilsham Road. For part of the way, from Thatcher Avenue, walkers can take the old and higher path, affording even better views to the north and east. Those who are interested will find their way down the sloping plain to the southern end of the Nose where, covered with cemented sand, is the famous raised beach beloved of geologists.

Meadfoot. To drop down from Daddy Hole Plain to Meadfoot is the task of a few minutes. With verdure-covered headlands on either side, the sandy beach of Meadfoot is all the more noticeable from above, and the temptation to bathe is perhaps greater here than at any other spot in Torquay, because the sands look so inviting and the beach is so sheltered. Way out in the bay are the familiar small islets already mentioned (p. 115).

From this point there is a choice of route. One may ramble about the Meadfoot district and explore the beach and **Manor Gardens;** or take an easterly course and stroll to **Hope's Nose** by way of the Marine Drive, and then, continuing along the Drive past Hope Cove, return to Torquay through Wellswood. The Drive may be left by a path leading off to the right which winds delightfully round to the famous Thatcher Pines (the Thatcher itself is only 200 yards away) and so rejoins the Drive above Hope's Nose, just past a shelter with good views on three sides. Notice

Oddicombe Beach, Babbacombe

Ilsham Grange (part of which is a fifteenth-century building that once belonged to Torre Abbey) reached by a curving lane (R.) at the end of the Marine Drive just before the road to Anstey's Cove. The medieval tower-like chapel is said to have been built in 1251 by Reginald de Mohun; it is not open to the public. Continuing towards Wellswood, we pass near Kent's Cavern (pp. 110–111).

Or from Meadfoot one may walk through Manor Gardens, bearing left to the beautiful **Lincombe Drive,** which twists and turns until the town is reached at Wellswood, not far from Kent's Cavern. Just at its final turn (L.) is a swing gate (R.) with a path down, winding over a green to a post marked "Kent's Cavern". A second post directs down a dark path to the lawn in front of the Cavern. The return to the town may be made by the Babbacombe Road.

The most direct route back to central Torquay from Meadfoot is to follow Sea Road westwards, past Hesketh Crescent (1846), "the most ambitious of Torquay's terraces", and a landmark from the sea. A pleasant alternative is to turn right at Hesketh Road, from which stepped paths mount to Lincombe Drive, and then to Middle Lincombe Road. Here keep to the left, but bear right until opposite the end of Higher Erith Road, when a descending turning (L.) marked "Town and Harbour" will be noticed; go down this turning, cross another road and steps lead to **Torwood Gardens** close to the Christian Science Church with Babbacombe Road, not far from the Strand, a short distance farther on.

Babbacombe, Watcombe and Maidencombe

The Cliff Path, or New Coastal Walk, links up Babbacombe, Watcombe, and Maidencombe, and continues northward to Labrador. Thus walks of any length may be planned, starting and finishing at selected points.

Babbacombe may be reached by bus from the Strand to St. Anne's Road, or from Castle Circus to All Saints' Church (1867). Or one may walk from Torquay over Warberry Hill as described on p. 114, turning left when Babbacombe Road is reached.

Few spots charm a visitor more than Babbacombe Downs, a breezy plateau perched so high that on a clear day Portland Bill – full 40 miles away – may be seen. Nearer at hand one sees Teignmouth, with the red cliffs of Dawlish beyond, and the white bulk of Beer Head in the distance. The Downs are now laid out with public gardens, promenade, shelters, and concert hall; the beach far below can be reached by the steep descent of Beach Road, at the foot of which is a stone jetty where boats from Torquay and Teignmouth call. From here one may take a pleasant cliff walk over Wall's Hill to Anstey's Cove (p. 113).

From the other end of the Downs, Babbacombe Beach may be reached more easily by the **Cliff Railway** *(daily* 10 *to* 6 *or later)*. Besides the Cliff Railway is a road with hairpin bends which also descends to **Oddicombe Beach,** the beach which adjoins Babbacombe Beach on the north side. A zigzag path leads from Oddicombe Beach up to **Petitor Cliffs,** the grassy slopes below the tor, dotted with seats, forming an ideal lounging place. From the end of the little peninsula a path of sorts gives access to the strip of beach below Petitor, but the cliffs are unstable, and slips on both this and the Oddicombe side occur from time to time. The links of the Torquay Golf Club are just beyond, on the farther side of the Petitor Road which leads inland to the bus route and–

St. Marychurch. The **Church,** now rebuilt after war damage, deserves a visit, if only to see the Saxon font, with a chain of ovals round the bowl, in which are depicted a number of strange figures–man on horseback with bugle, man with falling sword, boar and dog, harp player, etc. Henry Phillpots, Bishop of Exeter 1837–1869, is buried in the churchyard. The tower commemorates him. The inscription over the door of the rebuilt Saxon aisle reads: "The enemy razed this church, 30th May 1943, killing 26 children and teachers."

Close at hand is the **Roman Catholic Church,** dominated by a very graceful spire and containing a beautiful west window.

Watcombe may be reached by bus from the Strand or Castle Circus to Easterfield Lane with a half-mile walk to the cliff path. Or by bus to St. Marychurch, and thence by Petitor Road and the Cliff Path.

Watcombe Beach, pretty and secluded, is at the foot of the **Valley of Rocks,** with the famous **Giant Rock** towering at the head of the combe. Here the rocks rise in disordered grandeur to a considerable height above the valley, and suggest the great cliff castles to be seen on the Cornish coasts. Obvious signs of frequent falls of rock do not invite undue loitering beneath them, but one may spend several hours exploring this broken undergrowth-covered combe or descend to Whatsand Beach by means of roughly cut steps in the soft stone. For those who wish to see the New Red Sandstone in all its naked glory there is no better place than this Valley of Rocks.

Watcombe Park, now renamed **Brunel Manor,** has associations with the Brunels, father and son, who, apart from their individual work, together planned and built the Thames Tunnel. Isambard Kingdom Brunel (1806–1859) constructed the Great Western Railway, its bridges including the Saltash bridge, viaducts and tunnels. The Manor is now owned by the Woodlands House of Prayer, a Christian Charity, and used as a family guest house and conference centre. The magnificent grounds may be glimpsed from Hele and Barton (Brunel Manor is a useful bus-stop on the Torquay–Teignmouth route).

Maidencombe. By bus from the Strand to Maidencombe Cross, then turn right down Steep Hill to the secluded hamlet nestling at the foot of this fine unspoilt valley or combe. The hamlet contains a fine old specimen of the rare Judas tree. A very steep footpath leads down to the attractive and sheltered beach with rocks, sand and safe swimming.

From Maidencombe the coastal walk may be followed northwards to Labrador (see p. 83), or southwards to Watcombe *via* the steep descent of the Goats Path, and the Valley of Rocks.

Marldon, Compton and Kingskerswell

From Cockington (reached by Seaway Lane, Cockington Lane, or bus to Chelston) a road runs uphill from the Forge leaving the church and manor-house on the right. In about $1\frac{1}{2}$ miles a road junction known as **Five Lanes** is reached, and from there the road on the right leads to the village of–

Marldon

Marldon, anciently Marldone or Meagheldon, from *meargelle* meaning gentian, and *don*, a hill.

The earliest reference to the **Church** dates back to 1348, in which it is described as a chapel dependent on the church at Paignton. The oldest part today is the massive and embattled tower added in about 1440 to an earlier building. The rest dates mainly from about 1460 and it contains a number of items connected with the family of Gilbert of Compton in this parish, and original tracery in three of the windows. The capitals of the pillars of the arcades are wreathed with carved foliage of the type peculiar to Devon churches.

Compton Castle

From the church the road northwards leads, in less than a mile, to–

Compton Castle

Open to visitors Mondays, Wednesdays, Thursdays, April–October, 10 *to* 12*;* 2 *to* 5. *Admission fee.*

Compton Castle, one of the finest remaining examples of a fortified manor-house, was built about 1329 by Geoffrey Gilbert who married Joan, daughter and co-heir of William de Compton.

In 1440–50 it was converted from an undefended to a defended house by the addition of the high curtain wall containing two portcullis entrances; and by the construction of a number of loopholes in the bases of the defensive towers, of which there are five remaining, and of the machicolations, the projecting slots high upon the walls which enabled the defenders to pour missiles upon anyone attempting either to scale or undermine them. At that period the French had attacked Teignmouth and Plymouth and Fowey, and the defences of Compton were no doubt designed to counter such raids.

In Queen Elizabeth's time it was the home of Sir Humphrey Gilbert, half-brother of Sir Walter Raleigh, and for this reason is of special interest in connection with the Empire, Sir Humphrey having taken possession of Newfoundland in 1583, England's first Colony. In 1584 Sir Walter Raleigh sent the first of several expeditions to Roanoke Island in what is now North Carolina, to be followed in 1607 by the establishment of the colony of Virginia. In 1607, also, Raleigh Gilbert, the son of Sir Humphrey, was one of the eight grantees of King James's charter for the settlement of America, and himself led the Plymouth Colony that year to the Sagadahoc river in what is now the State of Maine.

In the private chapel of the Castle can be seen the commemorative carved oak tablet sent by the Sir Humphrey Gilbert Chapter of the Imperial Order Daughters of the Empire of St. John's, Newfoundland, where he is also commemorated on the site of his landing.

Compton was abandoned by the family in 1880 but repurchased, in an almost ruinous condition, in 1930 by Commander Walter Raleigh Gilbert, and it has since by him and Mrs. Gilbert been fully restored and given with the surrounding farmland to the National Trust, the family remaining in residence.

Continue past the castle to a cross-roads, where turn right and, in a few minutes at a fork near the stream, left down a wooded valley. Proceeding, with the stream on one side, past turnings (on both sides) and houses, the **Stonycombe** quarries and limeworks come into sight near the railway. Those who venture into the quarry workings (whence concrete aggregate – coral limestone in this case – is obtained and used among other things to lend colour to flooring) should be careful to keep from the quarry face. At the crossway just beyond the railway turn right and under the railway again to **Kingskerswell,** where there are a few remains of a fortified manor-house. The church with three effigies in stone, monuments to Dinhams, will interest the ecclesiologist. Kingskerswell is gradually becoming a settlement of bungalows and villas. A good bus service makes the return to Torquay easy.

If, instead of turning right for Kingskerswell where indicated above, one continues straight on, one soon reaches **Abbotskerswell.** Here the village church is over 500 years old, and possesses a medieval statue of the Virgin Mary.

Alternatively, those desiring a long tramp can continue ahead at the cross-roads near Compton Castle along the main road to the Newton Abbot–Totnes highway and on to Ipplepen, almost adjoining it, with Torbryan just beyond (see p. 91), returning to Torquay by bus from Ipplepen, *via* Newton Abbot.

Barton, Great Hill, Daccombe and Coffinswell

Take a bus to Jack's Lane, Barton. From here the road slants upward to **Barton Cross** signpost, at the end of a triangular bit of green with seats. For **Great Hill** swing right up Great Hill Road and keeping right again at the fork there will be reached the entrance-gate to the track leading by a hedge and a sturdy line of *macrocarpa* conifers up to the reservoir, whose embanked sides attract the eye on the hill-top to the right. There is no entrance for cars at the iron gate but there is limited parking space. (A longer way is to take the Shaldon bus from Castle Circus to Solomon's Post and turn left along Claddon Lane which sweeps down and up under Great Hill to the black iron exit gate of the Reservoir Drive.) A drive or broad pathway with a few seats has been constructed round three sides of the Reservoir, giving one of the most extensive and breezy views round Torquay. The town and Torbay lie below to the south, and away to the west the eastern escarpment of Dartmoor can be traced. Nearly 600 feet high, there is an uninterrupted view from the south-west corner of the terrace, and no one eager for an extensive land-and-sea-scape should miss a visit to Great Hill. Less than 1½ miles away are prominent the two neighbouring churches of St. Marychurch and by a coincidence these two buildings are seen as one, with a tower (C. of E.) at one end and a spire (R.C.) at the other. Note survey-post at top of reservoir.

Returning from Great Hill to Barton Cross, turn right through **Daccombe,** and almost at the end of the hamlet take the left-hand road. **Coffinswell Church,** its tower easily recognizable by a pronounced batter or tapering, comes into sight in about a mile. The tower, nave and chancel of the church date from the thirteenth century.

From Coffinswell, **Kingskerswell** can be reached in about half an hour by a lane over a hill, or a slightly longer route round it, and thence the return may be made by bus to Torquay.

Or by keeping through Coffinswell and going left at the fork at the end of the village, the road to Newton Abbot will be gained at **Aller.**

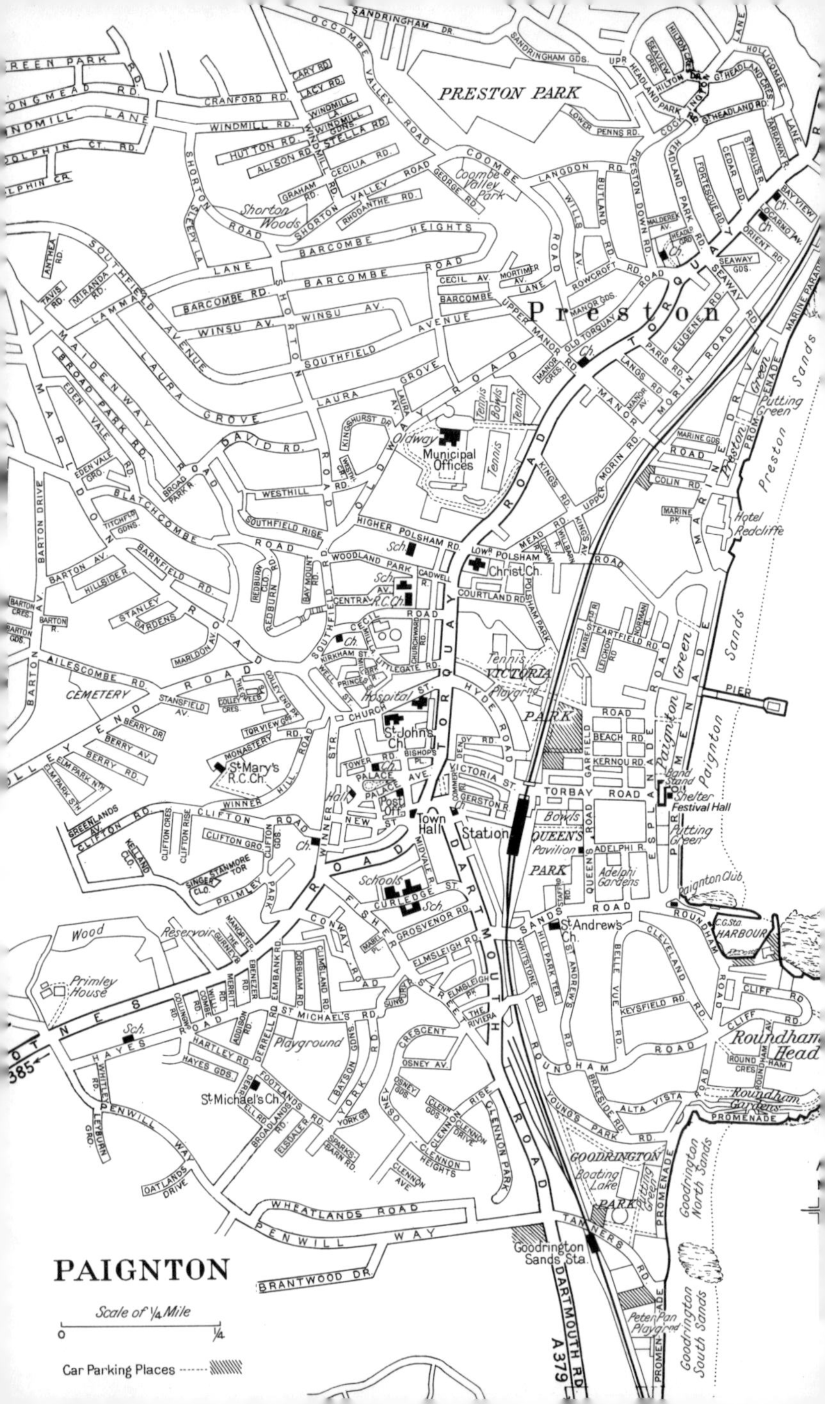
PAIGNTON
Scale of 1/4 Mile
0
1/4
Car Parking Places
PRESTON PARK
Preston
Sandringham Dr.
Occombe Valley Road
Sandringham Gds.
Green Park Rd.
Longmead Rd.
Windmill Lane
Dolphin Ct. Rd.
Dolphin Cr.
Cranford Rd.
Windmill Rd.
Cary Rd.
Lacy Rd.
Stella Rd.
Hutton Rd.
Alison Rd.
Cecilia Rd.
Graham Rd.
Shorton Road
Shorton Woods
Shorton Valley Road
Rhodanthe Rd.
Coombe Road
Coombe Valley Park
George Rd.
Lower Penns Rd.
Langdon Rd.
Wills Av.
Butland Rd.
Preston Down Rd.
Headland Park Rd.
Upr. Headland Park Rd.
Seaview Cres.
Hilton Cres.
Hilton Rd.
Cook Rd.
Gt. Headland Rd.
Gt. Headland Cres.
Hollicombe Lane
Cedar Rd.
St. Paul's Rd.
Fortescue Rd.
Tarraway Rd.
Bay View
Locarno Av.
Orient Rd.
Seaway Gds.
Seaway
Malderek Av.
Headland Gro.
Torquay Road
Barcombe Heights
Barcombe Lane
Barcombe Road
Barcombe Rd.
Sleepy La.
Anthea Rd.
Tavis Rd.
Miranda Rd.
Southfield Avenue
Lammas
Cecil Av.
Mortimer Av.
Rowcroft Rd.
Manor Gds.
Winsu Av.
Southfield Avenue
Upper Manor Road
Old Torquay Rd.
Manor Cres.
Eugene Rd.
Paris Rd.
Langs Rd.
Manor Av.
Morin Road
Marine Parade
Preston Green
Putting Green
Preston Sands
Promenade
Marine Drive
Marine Gds.
Colin Rd.
Marine Pk.
Hotel Redcliffe
Maidenway Road
Broad Park Rd.
Eden Vale Rd.
Eden Vale Gro.
Laura Grove
Laura Av.
Kingshurst Dr.
Oldway Road
Oldway
Municipal Offices
Tennis
Bowls
David Rd.
Westhill Rd.
Westhill
Southfield Rise
Blatchcombe Road
Titchfield Gdns.
Marldon Road
Barton Drive
Barton Av.
Barton Cres.
Barton Gds.
Barton R.
Hillside R.
Barnfield Rd.
Stanley Gardens
Marldon Av.
Higher Polsham Rd.
Lowr. Polsham Road
Kings Rd.
Upper Morin Rd.
Mead Rd.
Logan Rd.
Wilbarn Rd.
Kings Av.
Woodland Park
Cadwell R.
Christ Ch.
Courtland Rd.
Polsham Park
Redburn Rd.
Redburn Clo.
Bay Mount Rd.
Central Av.
R.C. Ch.
Sch.
Cecil Road
Churchward Rd.
Kirkham St.
Littlegate Rd.
Well St.
Princes St.
Hospital
Steartfield Rd.
Ware Cross Rd.
Norman Rd.
Leighon Rd.
Paignton Green
Esplanade
Paignton Sands
Pier
Victoria Playground
Victoria Park
Tennis
Aylescombe Rd.
Cemetery
Colley End Road
Colley End Pk.
Colley Cres.
Stansfield Av.
Berry Dr.
Berry Av.
Berry Rd.
Elm Park
Torview Gds.
Monastery Rd.
St. Mary's R.C. Ch.
Winner Hill Road
Church St.
St. John's Ch.
Tower Rd.
Palace Ave.
Bishops Pl.
Hyde Road
Torquay Road
Victoria St.
Gerston R.
Beach Rd.
Garfield Road
Kernou Rd.
Torbay Road
Bandstand
Shelter
Festival Hall
Putting Green
Greenlands Av.
Clifton Rd.
Clifton Road
Clifton Cres.
Clifton Rise
Clifton Gro.
Clifton Gds.
Kelland Clo.
Singer Clo.
Stanmore Tor
Primley Park
Winner St.
New St.
Post Off.
Town Hall
Station
Bowls
Queen's Park
Pavilion
Queen's Road
Adelphi R.
Adelphi Gardens
Paignton Club
Schools
Curledge St.
Dartmouth Road
Midvale R.
Fisher St.
Sch.
Grosvenor Rd.
Sands Road
St. Andrew's Ch.
Stafford Rd.
Roundham Rd.
C.G. Sta.
Harbour
Cleveland Road
Cliff Rd.
Wood
Reservoir
Manor Ter.
Conway Road
Mabel Pl.
Elmsleigh Rd.
Elmsleigh Pk.
Hill Park Ter.
Whitstone Rd.
St. Andrew's Rd.
Belle Vue Rd.
Keysfield Rd.
Roundham Head
Primley House
Totnes Road
A385
Collingwood Rd.
Combe Rd.
Merritt Rd.
Ebenezer Rd.
Elmbank Rd.
Corsham Rd.
Cumberland Rd.
Addison Rd.
Derrell Rd.
St. Michael's Rd.
The Riviera
Crescent
Hayes Road
Sch.
Hartley Rd.
Hayes Gds.
Playground
Footlands Rd.
St. Michael's Ch.
Batson Gds.
York Road
Osney Av.
Osney Gds.
Clennon Rise
Clennon Park
Clennon Drive
Clennon Heights
Clennon Ave.
Whitley Rd.
Leyburn Gro.
Penwill Way
Oatlands Drive
Broadlands Rd.
Elsdale Rd.
York Gds.
Sparks Barn Rd.
Young's Park Rd.
Braeside Rd.
Alta Vista Road
Round Ham Cres.
Roundham Gardens
Promenade
Goodrington Park
Boating Lake
Putting Green
Goodrington North Sands
Wheatlands Road
Penwill Way
Brantwood Dr.
Tanners Rd.
Goodrington Sands Sta.
Dartmouth Rd.
A379
Peter Pan Playground
Goodrington South Sands

Paignton

Approach. – By rail to Paignton Station on the Western Region Line, 201 miles from London (Paddington). There is a halt at Goodrington Sands. Frequent fast trains daily from all parts.

By Coach. – Express services from all parts. Coach station at Garfield Road.

Banks. – *Barclays, Devon and Exeter Savings, Lloyds* (and at Preston), *Midland* (and at Preston), *National Westminster* (and at Preston), all in Palace Avenue.

Bathing. – At Paignton, Preston, Goodrington, Broadsands, Saltern Cove, Elberry Cove.

Boating. – Motor- and rowing-boats from Paignton Harbour and Beaches. Motor-boats at Goodrington Park.

Bowling. – Oldway Grounds and Queen's Park; open tournament in July.

Bingo. – *Odeon,* Preston.

Buses. – From Bus Station (adjoins Railway Station) to Torquay, Newton Abbot, Brixham and Kingswear, Greenway Ferry (for Dittisham), Stoke Gabriel, Totnes (direct and *via* Berry Pomeroy), Buckfastleigh, Plymouth (*via* Totnes, South Brent and Ivybridge), and local services (Goodrington, Kings Ash, Compton).

Camping and Caravanning. – There are numerous camping, caravan and holiday camps in the area. Details from Information Centre.

Car Parks. – Colin Road (for Preston sea front), Goodrington South Sands, Goodrington Park, The Harbour, Victoria Park, and Oldway.

Cinemas. – *Regent,* Station Square; *Torbay,* Torbay Road.

Cricket. – Queen's Park; where Rugby is also played.

Civic Centre. – Oldway houses Education and Community Service departments. Other services at Torquay Town Hall.

Dancing. – Oldway and Badminton Hall; Casino; and at many of the hotels and night clubs.

Early Closing Day. – Wednesday.

Ferry. – From Promenade (Goodrington Cliff Gardens) to Brixham and Torquay (summer only).

Fishing. – In Torbay, for whiting, pollock, mackerel, etc. Freshwater fishing in the rivers Dart, Teign, etc. Sea Anglers' Club at harbour.

Horse Riding. – Stables in Dartmouth Road; and at Churston.

Hotels. – *Redcliffe, Palace, Benfield and Bonair, Harwin, Grosvenor, Coverdale, Hunter's Lodge, Oldway Links, Broads and Links, Queen's, Hydro, Marina, Ocean, Middlepark, Alta Vista, Ebor Towers, St. Ann's, Sunhill,* and many others.

Information. – Information Centre, Festival Hall, Esplanade Road.

Library. – County Borough Library, Courtland Road.

Population. – 109,800 (whole of Torbay).

Post Office. – Head Office, Palace Avenue. Sub-offices at Preston, Goodrington, The Harbour, Collaton St. Mary, and elsewhere.

Putting. – Oldway Grounds; Paignton Green; Preston Green; Goodrington Park; Roundham Head.

Sea Trips. – Motor launches run trips to Brixham, Torquay, Teignmouth, River Dart, etc. Start from beach, opposite the Festival Hall, and from the Harbour.

Tennis. – Nine hard courts in Victoria Park and nine grass and six hard courts in Oldway. Lawn Tennis Championship in June.

Theatre. – Palace Avenue Theatre, and at Festival Hall.

Yachting. – Torbay Sailing Club has its headquarters in Paignton Harbour. Regular weekly races. Regattas in July and August.

Zoo and Botanical Gardens. – Totnes Road. Open daily.

Paignton is a flourishing seaside resort with a resident population of over 35,000. During July and August, when the summer season is at its height, this population is almost doubled, and there is also an increasing number of winter visitors. Possessing fine stretches of golden sands, where children may safely play and bathe, and an extensive area of grassland between the beach and the road, it is an ideal resort for family holidays.

History

Paignton is recorded in Domesday Book in 1086 as Peintone. This spelling is derived from the Saxon form of *Paegintun* – meaning Paega's farmstead; the village was probably founded in the eighth century by Saxon colonists. They built their church on the site of a Bronze Age burial mound, half a mile from the sea, since between the barrow and the shore the ground was marshy and much of it covered by lakes. About 1100 a Norman Church replaced the Saxon building and the Bishop of Exeter built a summer palace nearby(see p. 125). A causeway connected the village with its church and manor-house to the small quay under the shelter of Roundham Head. This causeway, originally called Fisher Streete, is now the modern thoroughfare, Sands Road. Fishing was an important industry for many centuries. Coastal shipping also made use of the quay. During the nineteenth century there was a great impetus in building. The harbour was rebuilt in 1832 and rows of houses filled the gap between the village of Paignton Well inland and Paignton quay. Gradually as road transport developed, the harbour trade and commercial fishing declined. In 1936 the harbour was bought by the Paignton U.D.C., who made it more accessible and enjoyable to the visitor for pleasure fishing and boating.

At Preston, Paignton, Goodrington, and Broadsands, are wide expanses of firm, gently sloping sands, providing safe bathing and playgrounds, and there are numerous rock pools and bathing coves along the coastline. The broad promenade is closed to all vehicles during the summer, making it an excellent strolling place. Separated from the sea only by the promenade is Paignton Green, a fine stretch of grass – ideal as a children's playground for cricket and other games. Here, too, in the Festival Hall, on the Green, seasonal shows are performed.

Beach tents and chalets are available for hire at Goodrington, Preston, Paignton and Broadsands. The Pier, projecting 800 feet out to sea, is the starting point of the motor-boat trips. Fishing boats go out in the bay for dab, whiting and mackerel. There are special events throughout the year – swimming, rowing, and sailing matches, athletic sports, sheepdog trials, car rallies, cycle races, etc. The numerous sports clubs include Cricket, Rugby, Hockey, Bowling, Amateur Athletics, and Badminton.

Those fond of club life are provided for in the **Paignton Club,** at the southern end of the Promenade. The **Constitutional Club** is in Palace Avenue.

From the Esplanade, Torbay Road leads to the Railway Station and Bus Station, beyond which is the centre of the town. Near the station is **Queen's Park** with cricket and football pitches and bowling greens. The Park is used for gymkhanas and is also the venue for the Annual Dog Show. The charming **Victoria Park,** bordering the railway on both sides near the station, is a favourite resort, comprising pretty flower-beds, walks and ornamental waters, the last named used for model yacht sailing, and as a children's boating lake. Here also are grass and hard lawn tennis courts and a pavilion and changing-rooms provided with shower-baths.

In the centre of the town are the **Palace Avenue Gardens,** in which is the **War Memorial.** In the Assembly Room, once the Royal Bijou Theatre, at the rear of the Gerston Hotel, *The Pirates of Penzance,* Gilbert and Sullivan's popular opera, was first staged only a few hours before its première in New York. Church Street adjoins, in which is –

The Harbour, Paignton

The Parish Church

The present building is mainly early fifteenth century. Foundations of a Saxon church have been discovered under the chancel and nave. Bishop Osbern built a Norman church on the site about 1100, and of this building a few relics have survived. Among the many features of interest are the magnificent Norman west door, with its curious blend of red sandstone and white Beer stone, the eleventh-century font, the skeleton monument in the south aisle, the fifteenth-century pulpit of Beer stone, and the exquisite Kirkham chantry, which, in spite of mutilations, still possesses a wealth of intricate carving. Note the little dog-door in the north doorway and the remains of two holy water stoups. The Rood, together with an illuminated Book of Remembrance, forms the War Memorial. The reredos was given in 1927 by the Chaplin family of Detroit, U.S.A., in memory of their ancestor, Samuel Chaplin, baptized (1598), married (1623) in the church and sailed for America (1638).

Near the Church are the ruins of the **Palace,** of the early Bishops of Exeter, the last episcopal occupant having been Miles Coverdale, who visited Devon as a kind of army chaplain to Lord Russell while engaged in quelling the Western rebellion in 1549. Two years later, Coverdale was appointed coadjutor Bishop of Exeter, and it was then that he occupied the Paignton Palace. The tower still standing in Vicarage Garden has been called "The Bible Tower", owing to a local tradition that it was during his residence here that Coverdale carried out his translation of the Bible, but as this work had been published in 1535, some years earlier, the story must be set aside. On the confines of the churchyard, near the Tower, are some remains supposed to be part of the undercroft of St. Mary's Chapel, belonging to the palace.

In nearby Kirkham Street is **Kirkham House** *(open daily, except Sunday mornings),* a rare and interesting example of west country medieval domestic town architecture.

Oldway, long the residence of the Singer family, is a handsome and imposing mansion, first built in 1874 by Isaac Merritt Singer, the sewing machine millionaire, then completed in 1907 by his son Paris Singer whose designs were inspired by memories of Versailles and Paris. Only the west elevation remains unchanged from the building of 1874. It is ideally situated in 22 acres of well-wooded grounds with luxurious gardens. Today it is owned by the local authority. There are first-class tennis courts, bowling greens, and other sports facilities. Tennis Championships and Bowling Tournaments are held, in addition to civic and social functions. An excellent restaurant and also tea gardens are open to the public. Notice the two brass signal cannons from *H.M.S. Victory* at the foot of the stairs.

Preston lies north of the pier and its seaside green (on which is a putting course, with space for other games) is already challenging the popularity of its larger and older rival. Now, except for the short break at the Redcliffe Hotel, Paignton's front extends from the headland near the Torquay gasworks to Roundham Head. (The *Redcliffe Hotel* occupies what was known as Redcliffe Tower, on the sea-front – a faintly Mogul-like building said to have been built by a retired Nabob.)

Southwards from the harbour and separated from Paignton sands by Roundham Head, is **Goodrington,** which can be reached *via* Roundham Road, or there is a pleasant cliff footpath (¾ mile) which leads through cliff gardens to Goodrington Bay. This is a most attractive and well-equipped bathing station. There is a large park, terraced walks, lawns, gardens and a promenade. Children have a variety of amusements – a Peter Pan playground has been laid out, with model yacht pools, boating lake, miniature railway, swings, and toy cars. A children's week is held in August, when there are competitions, races and firework displays.

Buses run frequently to Goodrington and there is a rail halt. There are two large car parks and a large camping ground.

A mile or two beyond Goodrington is Galmpton Warboro, on the confines of which is the **Churston Golf Club.** The course is but two minutes' walk from Churston Station and adjoins the main road (frequent bus service).

Several cups are played for annually, and there are monthly medal and bogey competitions. There is a good club-house and the total length of the round is 6,213 yards.

Paignton Zoological and Botanical Gardens are entered from Totnes Road. There is a frequent bus service from Paignton station. The Zoo is a very popular centre of attraction to both young and old at all times of the year. There is an excellent collection of animals and birds from all parts of the world, together with a Tropical House, Aquarium, Parrot and Palm House, Monkey House, and a Pets' Corner, the whole situated in Botanical Gardens of great beauty and interest occupying 75 acres. During the season a Miniature Railway runs through the grounds. Refreshments are available, and there are licensed bars, and picnic lawns.

Excursions from Paignton

Compton Castle, a fine old fortified manor-house, the ancient seat of the Gilberts, is rather more than 3 miles distant by way of Marldon village (see p. 119); *good bus service.* Closer to the town are the lanes round **Shorton,** some of which afford fine views over land and sea, though this district is rapidly becoming suburbanized. On the south side Clennon Park, turning out of Dartmouth Road, leads to **Clennon Hill** (240 feet), with Old Quarry, giving wide-spreading views. Many will find a ramble along the coast to the south of the Goodrington Beaches more inviting, and some of the other coves and beaches, including Broadsands, may be visited. From Cliff Park Road, near Goodrington Sands Halt, a footpath runs parallel to the railway as far as Broadsands Park Viaduct, then takes a left turn to **Broadsands.** From here the path follows the coast line over the headland, then descends to **Elberry Cove** which can also be approached by boat. Only those familiar with this coast and having knowledge of the tides should attempt to visit the beaches by walking along the shore round the cliffs that separate them. From Elberry Cove the walk may be extended to Brixham by way of a path going inland at the *north* end of the Cove to a footpath leading to Churston Church. After passing the church, a turn to the left a short distance beyond leads to Fishcombe Beach where there are bathing facilities and a café. From Fishcombe, the Marine Walk, affording splendid views, leads to Brixham. (*Note:* There is no coast way between Elberry Cove and Fishcombe Beach.)

This walk takes one from the red sandstone of Torbay to the limestone and slate of Berry Head.

One of the most enjoyable rambles or drives from Paignton is that along the Totnes Road to –

Berry Pomeroy Castle

(Admission charge. Open to view from 10 to 6 daily. Teas.)

rather more than 4 miles distant. It is most easily reached by motor coach, or the Totnes bus may be taken, alighting at True Street, unless it is the service which goes to Totnes *via* Bladgon and Berry Pomeroy, when it will be necessary to alight at the fork just before entering Berry.

The remains of this ancient fortress – the most picturesque ruin in Devon – stand on a limestone rock at the head of a lovely glen, down which the Gatcombe brook flows to join the Dart below Little Hempston. The original castle is said to have been built by Ralph de Pomerai, a knight who came over with the Conqueror, and who received, among other possessions, the lordships of Berry, or Biri, as it was then spelt, in return for his services. The older portion of the ruin seen now – the Gatehouse with guard-room, and Lady Margaret Tower – seems to have been mainly erected towards the end of the thirteenth century. The

Berry Pomeroy Castle

other and more beautiful portion, which was never completed, was the work of the Seymours, to whom the property passed in the reign of Edward VI. Sir Edward Seymour, M.P. for Exeter, Speaker of the Long Parliament, and head of the "western alliance" in the reign of James II, was the last occupant of the castle.

A ramble round the castle may be made to include a visit to the adjacent **Castle Hill.**

The village of **Berry Pomeroy** contains a Church of some interest, built by the Old Pomeroy family. It is mainly in the Perpendicular style, with remains of Early English and Decorated work. It contains a remarkably fine screen, some painted glass, mostly representing the arms of the Pomeroy family and their connections, and several interesting monuments, among which is that of Lord Edward Seymour, son of the Protector. The Rev. John Prince, author of the *Worthies of Devon,* who was vicar of the parish for forty-two years, was buried in the chancel, and there is a tablet to his memory in the north wall.

The return to Paignton may be made from Totnes (described on p. 151) by bus, or directly from Berry Pomeroy *via* Blagdon (limited service).

To Parliament House and Berry Pomeroy

Take the Totnes bus as far as Longcombe Cross. Turn down the Stoke Gabriel road, left, and there just past the turning on the right is seen the modest but picturesque group of cottages formerly known as **Parliament House,** where William III is said to have held his first parliament after landing at Brixham on November 5, 1688. This is recorded on a stone in the garden.

Those who prefer to walk from Paignton should bear left at Collaton St. Mary and follow the road towards Stoke Gabriel, leaving this by bearing right until they reach the hamlet of **Aish.** Beyond Aish, fork right to Parliament Cottages and Longcombe cross-roads. Or, taking a slightly longer route, fork left descending to a picturesque creek of the Dart, where stands a mill; then turn right and continue until the previous road is rejoined just beyond Parliament Cottages.

The road opposite leads to **Berry Pomeroy Church.** For **Berry Castle** lodge leave the Church (L.) and continue past the re-roofed tithe-barn to the cross-roads higher up, where turn right and at the next fork left. Past the lodge the way skirts Berry Woods, and at the road which comes up through the trees turn right to a cross-roads. (If the Castle is not visited the walker need not go so far as the Castle lodge, but turn right instead of left at the fork after the Berry village cross-roads, and again right at the next cross, when the routes join.)

Continue ahead, over the cross and, in about half a mile, just above the hamlet of **Blagdon,** a road goes off left to a meeting of five lanes below the summit of Beacon Hill (these lanes are not to be confused with the more familiar Five Lanes on the other side of Beacon Hill).

A return to Paignton may be made by taking the first lane to the right, which leads past the Reservoirs to Kings Ash Cross.

A more direct route is to return *via* Blagdon and Collaton to the Totnes-Paignton road and bus route.

Brixham and the Harbour

Brixham

Access. – By rail to Churston, thence by bus. By bus from Torquay, Paignton and Kingswear, and by motor-coach from over a wide area. By steamer and motor-boat from various South Devon coast resorts.

Brixham is about 30 miles by road from Exeter, 8 miles by road and 4½ by sea from Torquay, 5 miles by road and 10 miles by sea from Dartmouth, and 9 miles by road from Totnes.

Banks. – *Lloyds, Midland, Barclays* and *National Westminster.*

Bathing. – At Shoalstone (Bathing Pool), Mansands, St. Mary's Bay, Fishcombe, Breakwater Beach, etc.

Bowls. – Furzeham Recreation Ground and St. Mary's Park.

Buses. – Frequent services to Paignton, Torquay, Newton Abbot and Kingswear. Good internal services. Bus station in Middle Street.

Camping. – Brixham is well provided with sites for visitors' own caravans or tents and also with up-to-date "Holiday Chalets" camps with board and accommodation and all conveniences.

Car Parks. – Central, Southern Quay, Freshwater Quarry, at Breakwater and Shoalstone Beaches, and at Berry Head.

Concerts. – Band concerts at the Harbour on Saturdays and Wednesdays during the summer. Bingo or Revues, Town Hall Theatre.

Cricket. – Brixham Cricket Club, Northfield Lane.

Early Closing Day. – Wednesday.

Fishing. – Excellent facilities for bass, pollock, mackerel, conger, etc., at numerous points. Shark fishing is a speciality.

Golf and Putting. – At Churston. Miniature courses at Furzeham and St. Mary's Park; all 18 holes.

Hotels. – *Northcliffe, Quayside, Berry Head House, Bolton, Parkway House, Parkham, Beverley Court, Cottage, Brioc.*

Information Centre. – Market Street.

Library. – Near Town Hall.

Museum. – Off Middle Street.

Population. – 109,800 (whole of Torbay).

Post Office. – Bolton Cross, opposite Town Hall. Sub-offices at Ranscombe, Furzeham and Higher Brixham.

Regatta. – Usually towards end of August for three days, and including yacht racing, fishing contest and athletic sports and fireworks. Speedboat racing.

Sea and River Trips. – Motor-launches to Paignton and Torquay. Also a regular daily service to Goodrington, Paignton and Torquay, with half-hourly ferry between Brixham and Torquay (Princess Pier). Fishing trips from Pier. Rowing-boats at Inner Harbour and St. Mary's Bay. River trips to Dittisham and Totnes.

Tennis. – Furzeham Recreation Ground, and at St. Mary's Park.

Brixham is situated, facing north-east, about a mile and a half west of Berry Head, the southern horn of Torbay. It is easily accessible by rail and road, but the best approach is by sea from Torquay. The view of several hundred houses huddled in the valley running down to the sea, and terraced irregularly on the sides of the hills, is quaint and picturesque. The hills rise so steeply on either side of the harbour that steps are mostly used instead of lanes to connect each terrace with that above or below. On the beautiful skyline of irregular shapes can be discerned the turret of All Saints' Church, overlooking the town. Eastward, the dark mass of Berry Head thrusts into the sea, and curving north-westward are the golden sands of Goodrington and Paignton.

Brixham has a long history. Brixham Cavern, accidentally discovered in 1858, yielded evidence of contemporaneous existence of ancient man and prehistoric animals. Romans knew the neighbourhood, for large numbers of their coins and remains of pottery have been found at Berry Head. The Parish Church of Higher

BRIXHAM

Brixham is on the site of the original seventh-century Saxon settlement. In Domesday Book, Brixham is recorded as Briseham and, in 1525, Leland described in his survey "a praty towne of fischar men called Brixham". But the town's chief claim to historical fame is that William of Orange landed on Brixham Quay when he came to England to receive the crown. A stone, averred to be the identical one on which William first set foot, is set in the base of an obelisk on the harbour pier, with the following inscription:

"On this stone, and near this spot, William, Prince of Orange, first set foot on landing in England, the 5th of November, 1688."

Brixham has retained its essential character of a working harbour of fishing people. In spite of its increasing popularity as a holiday and artistic centre, it has not commercialized its beautiful setting. The simplicity and charm of Brixham lie in its marine associations. Brixham trawlers and their crews were long famous but the red and brown-sailed smacks have now gone. Trawl fishing is carried on by diesel-driven craft.

The Harbour and Breakwater

The Brixham roadstead is well known owing to its accessibility in every state of weather, wind and tide, and for its deep water and the excellence of its anchorage. The Breakwater is 3,000 feet in length and protects an area of over 140 acres, providing anchorage for a large fleet of vessels. The stroll along the breakwaters to the lighthouse is a favourite walk with many visitors – both for its exhiliarating breeziness and for the fine views obtained in all directions. The Torbay Lifeboat is moored in the harbour.

On the strand of the inner harbour, is a **Statue of William III.** It was unveiled on November 5, 1889, the foundation-stone having been laid on the bicentenary of the landing a year previously. The statue represents the Prince standing bareheaded with his right foot on a piece of rock in the act of making the memorable announcement recorded on the pedestal:

"WILLIAM, PRINCE OF ORANGE, afterwards William III, King of Great Britain and Ireland, landed near this spot, 5th November, 1688, and issued his famous declaration, 'The Liberties of England and the Protestant Religion I will maintain'."

The **Cavern** *(admission charge; open from* 10 *a.m. daily; Saturdays,* 10 *to* 1*)*, in Mount Pleasant Road (at top of Cavern Steps, leading up from Fore Street, turn right), was accidentally discovered in 1858. The Cavern is more than 600 feet long and contained bones of animals not now found in Great Britain, mingled with flint implements and other evidences of the presence of "cave men". It was evidently at one time the bed of a mountain stream. Many fine stalactites and stalagmites are very much in evidence. It is one of the most perfect caves in the country, and is electrically lit throughout.

The Town

From the harbour, **Middle Street** and **Fore Street,** in which are the principal shops, run to **Bolton Cross.** Near the cross-roads are the old **Town Hall** buildings, the **Library,** and the **General Post Office.** Two centuries or so ago, the sea came inland up the long natural estuary which stretched beyond Bolton Cross. Now the stream runs underground and houses stand where once wharves bordered the inlet. Overlooking them is–

All Saints' Church. Special interest attaches to All Saints', the parish church of Lower Brixham, from the fact that its first incumbent was the Rev. Henry Lyte, who wrote the beautiful hymns "Praise, my soul, the King of Heaven" and "Abide with me", so popular with Christian communities in all parts of the world. The church, originally erected in 1816, was rebuilt in 1907 as a memorial to its gifted first vicar, hardly anything pre-Victorian being left. There is a carillon of ten chimes which play verses from Lyte's hymns.

From Bolton Cross, Bolton Street leads to **St. Mary's Church,** the Parish Church of Higher Brixham. It is a large fifteenth-century building of Perpendicular architecture, built over and outside an earlier structure, and surmounted by an embattled tower, 103 feet high. Notable features are the interesting monuments, the fourteenth-century font, and the fifteenth-century altar-tombs.

In the other direction, at **Furzeham,** is a **Recreation Ground** containing putting and bowling greens and hard tennis courts. This ground commands a fine view of Torbay, and it is worth while to continue by road and path leading to **Fishcombe Beach** and **Churston Quay Cove.** Those fond of boating, sailing and fishing are well catered for. Safe sea-bathing may be enjoyed at eight beaches and coves all within 3 miles from the town centre. The Brixham Yacht Club at the harbour welcomes visitors. Races are held twice weekly in the summer and regattas in August. There are excellent facilities for angling–especially for bass and pollock, and trawling and mackerel fishing trips can be arranged. **The Brixham Sea Anglers' Association** and the **Brixham Sea Anglers' Club** will be pleased to give information. There is a fully licensed Club House in Caster Road and a headquarters at Breakwater Hard. Shark angling is also available for a moderate fee.

At Freshwater Quarry *(car park and café),* I.C.I. have established a Marine Research Station.

Overlooking the sea near the Breakwater is Brixham's *War Memorial,* a Celtic cross of granite.

Shoalstone Beach

Shoalstone Beach and swimming pool are situated to the north-east of the harbour breakwater and comprise a small promenade with seats and shelters just above the rocks with steps leading to a small grassy slope. The open-air seawater pool is available irrespective of the tide. Adjoining is a small café and car park. From the end of the promenade the road is rejoined where it enters the land attached to the *Berry Head House Hotel,* formerly Berry House. Not far beyond this gate is the beginning of the somewhat rough path that leads through the bracken and over the common to the Head. From the town right away to the edge of the head-

At Brixham

land, there is a wonderful series of seascapes, ample compensation for the climb.

Berry Head forms the southern extremity of Torbay. It is a favourite "grandstand" from which to enjoy the magnificent views in all directions. The summit is nearly 200 feet above the sea, and consequently it is a good place from which to enjoy a "blow" should the weather be sultry. Refreshment facilities.

The 85 acres of Berry Head are available to the public, with few restrictions. Some say this is the spot where Vespasian and Titus landed in Britain. There is no doubt, however, that it was once the site of a Roman encampment, and close by, at the entrance to the *Berry Head House Hotel,* is the **Ash Hole,** a cavern in which many Roman remains have been found, and which was evidently used by the soldiers for the deposit of refuse.

It was off Berry Head here and within range of the guns once mounted in these old forts that Napoleon, aboard the *Bellerophon,* awaited the result of his appeal to the most generous of his enemies. A week later he was transferred to the *Northumberland* and sailed to St. Helena.

The **Lighthouse** on the Head is 191 feet above sea-level, and is interesting on account of its short stature, the lantern being quite near the ground. The lighthouse gives a double flash, visible 20 miles, every 15 seconds. Behind and dominating the lighthouse is an important Coastguard station.

Seats are dotted about the furzy common, and even on a windy day shelter can be obtained in the hollows or under the lee of the **Fort.** These forts are impressive works, polygonal in shape with their embrasures pointing landward as though to cover any attempt to destroy the Brixham harbourage. Each of the forts has a deep moat. Just beyond them a stile marks the beginning of the path by which **St. Mary's Bay** (formerly Mudstone Sands), a beach shut in by cliffs, is reached. The beach is a very safe one and is composed of half shingle and half sand. St. Mary's Bay can be reached more quickly and directly by way of Ranscombe Road from the harbour, or Bolton Street and Rea Barn Road from the centre of the town.

Farther south and approached by lane and path from Higher Brixham or from the hamlet of Boohay off the Kingswear Road from Hillhead are the more secluded **Mansands.** This is a delightful unspoilt beach of sand and pebble. From Higher Brixham, St. Mary's Road gives access to a footpath leading to the coast and bearing right to Mansands to give a coast walk of extreme loveliness.

At Higher Brixham, behind the church, is St. Mary's Park, an 8-acre recreation ground with hard tennis courts, bowling greens, putting, pavilion and grounds for cricket and football.

Brixham to Kingswear by the Coast

This walk of about 12 miles passes some charming coves and splendid cliff scenery and from time to time unexpectedly fine views of the colourful and undulating countryside open up; but it must be understood that the going is very hilly and at least four hours should be allowed.

In any case, difficulties of right-of-way may make it necessary to turn aside, but if these can be overcome by courteous inquiry and regard for crops and gates, the walk is worth while.

From Brixham the route is as outlined above to St. Mary's Bay and Mansands. Next come **Scabbacombe Sands** from which those who turn inland in a westward direction will come to **Mill Bay Cove,** nearly opposite St. Petrox Church at the mouth of the Dart, and connected by road with Kingswear. Those who follow the coast more closely beyond Scabbacombe will come in turn to Ivy Cove, Pudcombe (Dead Donkey) Cove and Mill Bay Cove – any one of which is worth a special visit. Care should be taken not to confuse the Downend Point which is just south of Scabbacombe and the Downend which is 3 miles walking distance away, near Mill Bay.

Royal Naval College
Sandquay
Dartmouth Rowing Club
FERRY
A379
COLLEGE WAY
MT BOONE
RIDGE HILL
CORONATION PARK
Tennis & Putting
CLARENCE HILL
CLARENCE ST.
VICARAGE HILL
MAYOR'S AV.
Car Park
ROSEVILLE ST.
MARKET SQ.
Ch.
Bowls
VICTORIA ROAD
LAKE ST.
DUKE ST.
The Butterwalk
GARDENS
THE QUAY
Boat Float
EMBANKMENT
SOUTH FORD RD.
Guildhall
CROWTHER'S HILL
SMITH ST.
Post Off.
Hosp.
Steamer Quay
Sch.
Cha.
ROAD
DART
Yacht Moorings
RAILWAY FERRY
JAWBONES LANE
Dartmouth Sailing Club
NEWCOMEN
Castle
Waterhead Creek
B32
Station
Royal Dart Yacht Club
Kingswear
Kingswear Woods
The Redoubt
DYER'S HILL PARK
SOUTH TOWN
RIVER
Half Tide Rock
Warfleet Creek
SWANNATON LANE
One Gun Point
N.
Warfleet
B3205
CASTLE ESTATE
St. Petrox Ch.
Dartmouth Castle
Car Park
Castle Cove (Bathing)
Brookhi
Gomero
Kingswear Castle
DARTMOUTH
Scale of 1/4 Mile
0
1/4

Dartmouth

Angling. – In River Dart for salmon, sea-trout. bass, pollock, whiting, mackerel, etc. Sea-fishing for bass, pollock, whiting, skate, conger, mackerel, etc.
Band Performances. – In Royal Avenue Gardens, Sundays, in summer.
Banks. – *Lloyds, Midland, National Westminster.*
Bathing. – At Castle Cove and Sugary Cove.
Boating. – Boats may be hired at the landing stage. Sea and river trips.
Bowls. – *Dartmouth Bowling Club,* Victoria Road.
Buses. – To Blackpool Sands, Strete, Torcross, Kingsbridge and Plymouth; Dittisham, Halwell and Totnes. Boats to Dartmouth Castle by arrangement.
Car Parks. – The Market Square; The New Ground, Mayor's Avenue; The Quay; Blackpool Sands.
Carnival Week. – Competitions. shows, balls, fetes, processions at end of June or early July.
Cinema. – Mayor's Avenue.
Dacing. – Royal Avenue Gardens and at the Guildhall.
Early Closing Day. – Wednesday and/or Saturday.
Ferries. – Ferry from the Landing Stage on the Quay to Kingswear Station jetty to connect with service to Paignton run in the summer by the Dart Valley Light Railway.
Lower Ferry for passengers and vehicles, 7 a.m. (Sundays 8 a.m.) to 11.30 p.m. (10.45 p.m. in winter). Just beyond the southern end of the Embankment.
Higher Ferry for passengers and vehicles, 6.30 a.m. (Sundays 9 a.m.) to 10.45 p.m. Floating bridge from the northern end of the Embankment.
Golf. – *Churston Golf Club,* 18 holes, 4 miles by rail or bus; 18-hole putting course at Coronation Park.
Hotels. – *Royal Castle, Queens, Commercial, Manor House, Raleigh, Gramercy Tower, Townstal House, Royal Oak Inn, Yacht, Dart Marina.*
Library. – Newcomen Road (branch of the Devon County Library).
Museums. – The Borough Museum (historical and maritime) is in the Butterwalk, Duke Street. Henley Museum (etchings, books) is in Anzac Street. Newcomen Engine House is in Royal Avenue Gardens.
Population. – 6,720.
Post Office. – South Embankment. Sub-office at Townstal.
Regatta. – Dartmouth Royal Regatta, part of the Torbay Fortnight, is held on the last Thursday, Friday and Saturday in August.
Tennis. – 4 hard courts in Coronation Park.
Yachting. – *Royal Dart Yacht Club,* headquarters at Kingswear. Seasonal races. *Dartmouth Sailing Club,* headquarters 22 South Embankment. *Dart Marina* and *Dartmouth Boatel,* North Embankment.

Dartmouth is one of the most picturesque and interesting old towns in the country. Snugly situated on the hillside, just within the mouth of the Dart, it is beautiful at all seasons; the deep sheltered harbour provides magnificent anchorage, the surrounding hills guard the town, and the river frontage is fringed with gardens, rocky coves and churches and castles.

On the western side of the harbour is the town of Dartmouth, and on the eastern side is **Kingswear.** From Kingswear jetty passengers cross the river by ferry to Dartmouth. (There are also two car ferries.) Kingswear is supposed to be older even than Dartmouth. The **Church** (dedicated to St. Thomas à Becket) stands on an elevated spot overlooking the estuary of the Dart, and was rebuilt in 1847, the tower of the older structure (originally built about 1170) being preserved.

On **Mount Ridley,** above the church, are the remains of the fort which Sir Henry Cary surrendered after all Dartmouth, except the Castle and its surroundings, had fallen to the assault of the Parliamentary forces under Fairfax. Following the road past the church, we easily reach **Brookhill,** an early nineteenth-century mansion, in the dining-room of which is an ingenious arrangement of the arms of the principal county families. Below the house are the ruins of **Gommerock,** a fortified medieval house.

Below the building is a slate platform, which was intended to bear the strong tower of **Kingswear Castle,** eventually erected farther down the river in 1480, though the round tower was added many years later. Both house and castle were ruined in the Civil War, but the Castle has been restored as a private residence. The great harbour chain seems to have been secured on the Kingswear side by passing it round a slanting pillar of rock formed by a double entrance cave at the water's edge.

Dartmouth's History

Though Dartmouth may have been "a fuzzy down" when Kingswear was a market town, Dartmouth has a history. It is a municipal – and was for centuries prior to 1868 a parliamentary – borough, containing over 6,000 inhabitants. As late as Domesday (1086) the shores of the Dart as far as the open sea were under the authority of the lord of Totnes, but when decked sailing ships came in, the town at the mouth of the river sprang up. Rufus sailed for Normandy from Dartmouth in 1099, and in 1147 the fleets of northern Europe gathered there for the Second Crusade. Another great fleet sailed in 1190 to join Richard Cœur de Lion in his voyage to the Holy Land.

During the Second World War (1939–45) the harbour of Dartmouth proved of first-class importance to the Allies.

The forces of the United States set up a great training base for their landing craft, using Slapton beach and the country behind it for their exercises. Finally, on June 4, 1944, a great armada of 485 British and American craft conveyed and convoyed the left wing of the U.S.A. forces to the beaches of Normandy. A Corporation memorial tablet on the North Embankment commemorates this great event.

Old Houses. Along the quay are the gables and buttresses of several of the handsome and roomy houses built between 1585 and 1640. The front part of the *Royal Castle Hotel* consists of two such houses (with a fine plaster ceiling in the dining room), though altered in Pickwickian times to make an interesting example of a coaching inn. Apart from the Butterwalk, the finest example of these old houses is 5 Higher Street, now restored. Another is the fifteenth-century house (Cherub Club) with rare Gothic wooden windows.

The roomy old houses which still remain give an air of dignity to the town, and as one wanders the streets there are in carved doorways, heavily-timbered fronts and mullioned windows, frequent reminders of Dartmouth's important past. In the Mansion House, built about 1750, are some beautifully carved ceilings.

West of the Quay is what is known as –

The Lower Dart Ferry

The Butterwalk, Duke Street, a row of houses built in 1635–1640. After long years of neglect and a very near escape from total destruction by a bomb, these houses have been restored in a very handsome manner, and now stand as a splendid example of the style of domestic architecture evolved in the reign of Elizabeth I and her Stuart successors.

The western pair were built by a prosperous merchant, Mark Hawkings (initials on the frieze) in 1635 and he extended the row five years later. The ground floor of each house was used for business purposes, and the covered walk eventually became the haunt of the farmers' wives with their baskets of produce on market days. The upper part of the building bears much vigorous and skilful carving, and the whole effect is decidedly romantic.

At Number 12 Duke Street, the first-floor parlour has a superb plaster ceiling, moulded in deep relief to depict the descent of Our Lord through 28 generations of kings and prophets from Jesse. Number 10, now a restaurant, has a magnificent ten-light window, good panelling and a plaster overmantel showing figures of Moses and David as well as the scene at Pentecost (Acts 2, vv. 1–4).

The first floor of Number 6 Duke Street is now used as the **Borough Museum** – Historic and Maritime *(admission each weekday, small fee)*. Approached by the original newel stair the front room has splendid panelling, a good plaster ceiling and a superbly carved and coloured display of the Royal Arms, placed here after the visit of Charles II in 1671. The suite of rooms display many objects and pictures of local interest, with a collection of ships models of various periods.

Near the bottom of Ridge Hill is the private residence known as Newcomen Lodge, incorporating parts of Newcomen's old house and of several other houses demolished when the Newcomen road was constructed in 1864. Newcomen may well be termed "The Father of the Steam engine", as he developed his atmospheric steam engine in 1712, and there were over 200 of these in use in England, Europe and America before Watt introduced his improved design sixty years later (see also below).

St. Saviour's Church. Dartmouth has four churches. That of St. Saviour, in the centre of the town, near the river, with houses built close round it, is thoroughly characteristic of the Dartmouth of the fourteenth century, from which it dates, though it was partially rebuilt in the seventeenth century. It is partly of Decorated architecture, with a plain embattled tower. The *South Door* (which is now to be seen on its old hinges inside the church) is covered with curious iron ornaments, which represent a tree, showing its root, with vine-like branches radiating from the trunk and a leafy top. Across it are two figures of the lion (the supporters of the town arms) and the date 1631. The chancel was restored, the whole edifice re-roofed, and the vestry and organ enlarged in 1887–1888. The altar is built up by incorporating the four carved legs of the old communion table (perhaps 1588). The rood-screen, dating from the fifteenth century, is exquisitely carved; the rood itself is a nineteenth-century addition. The screen is surmounted by a double cornice, and the tracery has ogee canopies, with carved crockets and finials over each pair of lights under the arcaded heads. The stone pulpit is divided into panels, each elaborately carved and coloured, the figures of saints, said to have been destroyed at the Puritan revival, having been replaced by national symbols; rose, harp, fleur-de-lys, etc. The front of the gallery is painted with coats-of-arms of local families. The carved bench-ends include one of the Royal Standard.

St. Clement's Church. The Parish Church of Dartmouth and the mother-church of the town is about a mile to the north-west of the town. Being on Boone Hill, it forms a prominent landmark. It is an Early English structure of little interest apart from its thirteenth-century font and the monuments to the Boones and Roopes.

The **Church of St. Petrox** is close to the castle and is used only in the summer. It may be viewed when service is not taking place, and its interesting interior is worth examination. A church has stood upon the site since early in the sixth century, and a booklet draws the attention of visitors to the chief points of interest: the east window is a memorial to the famous mathematician and engineer of Stoke Fleming, George Parker Bidder. A brass of John Roope, a leading merchant of the town, who died in 1609, bears a quaint inscription.

The fourth church is that to **St. Barnabas,** a mock Gothic edifice.

Adjoining the boat harbour in the centre of the town front is the bandstand and the beautifully laid-out **Royal Avenue Gardens.** In these are the **War Memorial,** a granite cross, and two memorials to Thomas Newcomen. On one of these his first engine is depicted on a bronze plate, and on the other is an ancient engine with cylinder and other metal parts dating back to 1725. The latter is housed in a building erected by the Newcomen Society, owners of the engine.

North of the Gardens the Embankment leads to the Higher Ferry and to **Coronation Park,** which has hard tennis courts and a putting green.

Moving inland from the Boat Harbour past Butterwalk, one passes on the left Anzac Street where there is a small **Museum,** mainly devoted to etchings and books, and maintained as a memorial to a singularly gifted and versatile tradesman, the late William Henly. A little farther inland is the quaint **Market** and still farther the Guildhall on the left and a bowling green on the right.

The Britannia Royal Naval College. Dartmouth is the cradle of the Navy. Up to 1905 all cadets for the Navy were trained in the cadet training-ship *Britannia,* which, after being stationed in the harbour for upwards of sixty years, has been broken up. Its work is now carried on in an extensive range of buildings finely situated on the slope of the hill above the town. *Special permission is always required to visit the College, and applications should be made in writing to the Commanding Officer.*

The foundation stone of the College was laid by King Edward VII in 1902 – one of the proudest days in Dartmouth's history – and in 1905 the College opened its doors to the cadets. Designed by Sir Aston Webb, it occupies a magnificent position overlooking the town and harbour. From the terrace are obtained grand views of the harbour and Channel. Beyond are the extensive playing-fields and down at Sandquay are the Engineering shops. The College has always had strong associations with Royalty.

With such a splendid harbour, Dartmouth is naturally famous for its yachting. The **Royal Dart Yacht Club** (founded 1866) has its club-house at Kingswear. There is also the **Dartmouth Sailing Club** which welcomes visitors. These two clubs provide capital sport for decked yachts and dinghies during the season which culminates in the three-day Royal Regatta at the end of August. There are also rowing races and swimming and dancing.

Although the central and northern parts of the Embankment have many attractions, the walk by the harbour side to the Castle and the river mouth is probably the most interesting. At the end of the Embankment is the **Lower Ferry** and, beyond, the medieval quay known as **Bayard's Cove.** The Pilgrim Fathers' ships, *Speedwell* and *Mayflower,* anchored off here in 1620 before the latter sailed for America. Here are attractive old houses with the **Customs House** (1739) fronting the cobbled pavement boldly marked 1665. At the end of the quay is the primitive artillery work of 1537 known as **Bearscove Castle.** Then along South Town to the river mouth there are splendid views towards the charming inlet of **Warfleet Creek.** Beyond the creek leafy walks of the Castle Estate on the flanks of Gallants Bower lead to the Castle at the river mouth with densely wooded hills either side.

Dartmouth Castle

Dartmouth Castle

It was the great John Hawley who first fortified the mouth of the river in 1388. This work is represented by the stone cut ditch and curtain wall on the landward side, enclosing the courtyard where he could mount his engines of war to hurl bolts and stones at the enemy ships. The courtyard (now a car park) was later occupied by the manor house of the Carews of Stoke Fleming. In the reign of Edward IV there was an agreement between the King and the Dartmouth burgesses, the King undertaking to pay the latter £30 per annum "for ever", on condition that they built and maintained there a "strong and mighty defensyve newe Towre," with "a cheyne sufficient in length and strength to streche and be laide overthwarte or a travers the mouthe of the haven of Dartmouth." The Dartmouth people kept their part of the bargain by building a fortress. Its remains consist of a round and a square tower, with elementary embrasures for cannon. The tower was completed in 1493 and the great chain, supported by six boats (cobles), was put across the harbour in times of trouble until 1643, which is the last we hear of it. Leland says that the Dartmouth men got their chain from Fowey, when they went to help subdue the unruly Cornishmen in 1475. The strong tower is flanked by batteries repeatedly modernized, the main work being a two-storey battery for 64-pounder guns in 1862. Thus the castle reveals the whole history of coast defence, from the day of the bow to those of the bomb.

A very pleasant hour can be spent in strolling about the enclosure, with its enchanting sea and river views. There is an attractive restaurant known as the

Old Battery. The river below the Castle is full of fish. At the proper times mackerel and whiting come in shoals, and dolphins are frequently seen. On the opposite side of the river is the twin stronghold of Kingswear Castle, now privately owned.

Close at hand is **Castle Cove,** and a little farther off are **Sugary Cove** and **Compass Cove**–all suitable for bathing. The hillside forming the **Castle Estate** has been laid out as a pleasure ground, with many paths and seats in shady nooks, which afford glorious views of the harbour mouth and the Kingswear side. Some of these paths descend to rocky tree-shaded coves, and the higher one can be followed until it becomes a lane leading past Little Dartmouth to **Stoke Fleming.** Landing steps (known as "Stumpy Steps") near the castle are used by the motor-launch services from Dartmouth quay.

From Stoke Fleming a good motor road, at times running very close to the cliff edge, and offering grand views, continues through **Strete** to **Torcross** (8 miles) or to **Slapton.** Here lived Sir Richard Hawkins, and according to the story, his wife had two black boys to place a carpet for her to walk upon on her way to church. Here, too, are the remains of a Chantry.

Some delightful walks may be had in the immediate vicinity of Dartmouth, the steep climb out of which is more than repaid by the views obtained, the bus being used on the return. Thus one can follow the bus route from Townstal, turning off on the high ground down to Riversbridge behind Stoke Fleming and along the lane beside the brook which enters the sea at **Blackpool,** or reach it more directly by proceeding up the steep Swannaton Road from South Town with splendid backward views of the harbour. From about opposite Townstal Church and just at the side of the entrance to the Britannia Royal Naval College, a steep lane (Old Mill Lane) leads down to the charming **Old Mill Creek,** and continues past the sixteenth-century house of Bosomzeal over Fire Beacon Hill, where bonfires once blazed to give warning of the coming of the Armada, to **Dittisham,** noted for its thatched cottages and plum orchards. Dittisham Church is worth a visit, if only on account of its screen, font, pulpit and stoups, which are said to be relics of the Saxon church.

No visitor omits a trip up the river, but the wise ones also take the journey by road to **Kingsbridge** which, as far as **Torcross** and **Stokenham,** is one of the most entrancing drives in the country and not on any account to be missed.

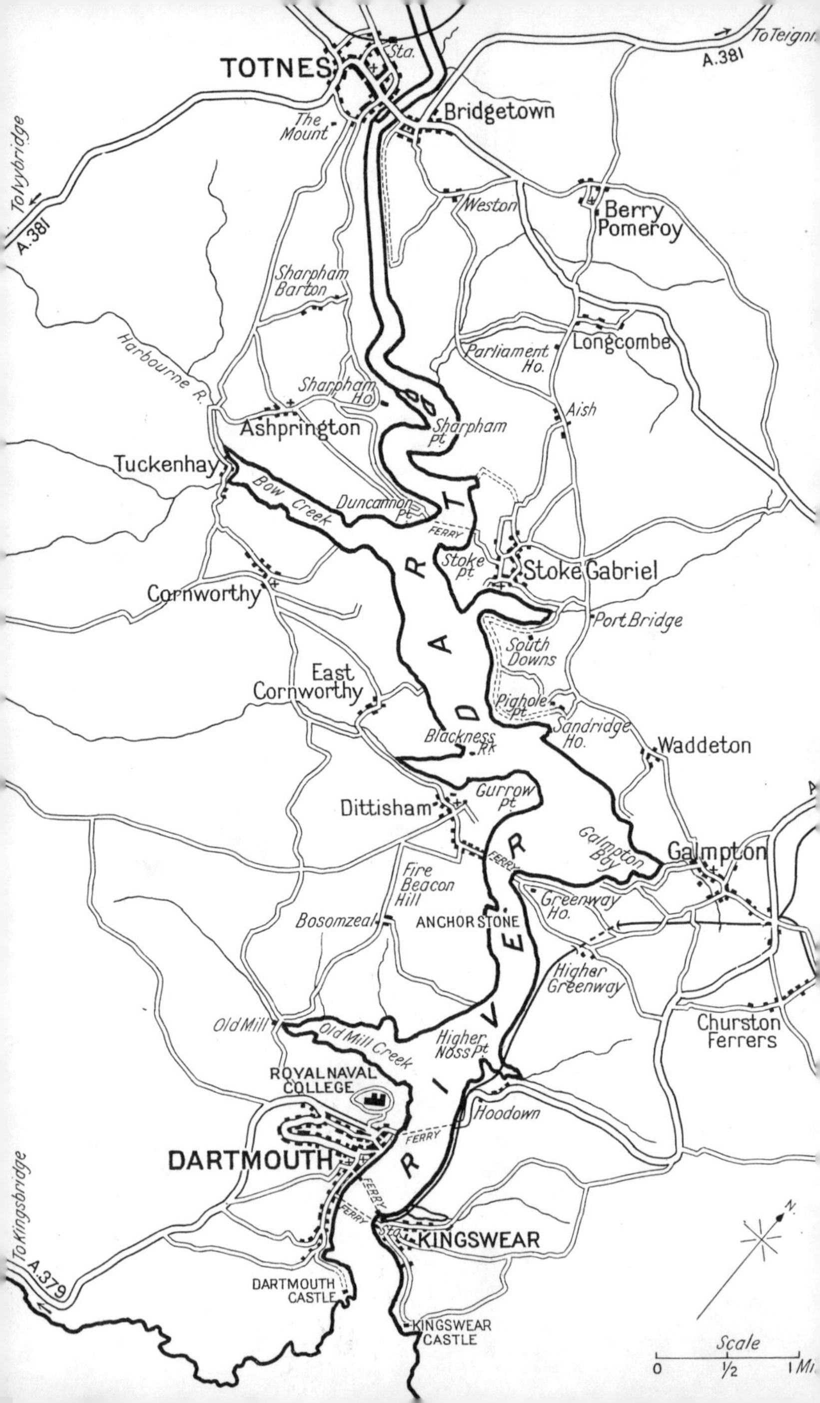

TOTNES
Sta.
To Teignm
A.381
Bridgetown
The Mount
To Ivybridge
A.381
Weston
Berry Pomeroy
Sharpham Barton
Harbourne R.
Longcombe
Parliament Ho.
Sharpham Ho.
Aish
Ashprington
Sharpham Pt.
Tuckenhay
Bow Creek
Duncannon Pt.
FERRY
Stoke Pt.
Stoke Gabriel
Cornworthy
Port Bridge
South Downs
East Cornworthy
Pighole Pt.
Sandridge Ho.
Blackness Rk
Waddeton
RIVER DART
Gurrow Pt.
Dittisham
Galmpton Bay
Galmpton
FERRY
Fire Beacon Hill
Greenway Ho.
Bosomzeal
ANCHOR STONE
Higher Greenway
Old Mill
Old Mill Creek
Churston Ferrers
Higher Noss Pt.
ROYAL NAVAL COLLEGE
Hoodown
FERRY
DARTMOUTH
FERRY
FERRY
To Kingsbridge
Sta.
KINGSWEAR
A.379
DARTMOUTH CASTLE
KINGSWEAR CASTLE
N.
Scale
0
½
1 Mi

A Trip up the Dart

Steamer, Launches, Motor-boats. – Dartmouth to Totnes or *vice versa* (11 miles by water). The journey takes about an hour and a half. In summer there are three or four boat services daily each way, according to tide.

Devon and Cornwall have three rivers of exceptional beauty – the Dart, the Tamar and the Fal – but the Dart is the stream that is best known, though there are many champions of the Tamar and the Fal. It would be impossible to exaggerate the charms of the Dart between Totnes and the sea. It sweeps along in leisurely fashion; here broadening into a veritable lake and sparing some water to an inlet running far inland, right or left; at another point becoming narrow. But, narrow or broad, it is hedged with hills and with trees that creep down to the very water's edge and cluster so closely that the actual cliffs are seldom seen; there is only a succession of densely foliaged trees – hanging woods mirrored in the stream – with here and there the chimneys of a mansion rearing their heads among the greenery, and at several points villages snugly ensconced in some leafy valley.

Proceeding up the Harbour, an excellent view is obtained on the left of the **Britannia Royal Naval College,** reached by a winding path leading from the small boat dock, gymnasium and fives courts. At Sandquay on the left the old shipyards have been reconstructed as a hotel and a marina for yachtsmen. On the opposite bank are shipbuilding works where many light ships, pilot boats, minesweepers, and other craft are constructed.

Beyond the college the boat passes the beautiful **Old Mill Creek** and soon skirts the estate of **Greenway House** on the right which occupies the site of Greenway Court in which Sir Humphrey Gilbert, the colonizer of Newfoundland, was born, and which is also associated with his half-brother, Sir Walter Raleigh. Almost opposite Greenway House is a rock known as the **Anchor Stone,** now marked as a danger spot for ships. Passing the rock, the boat reaches the broader part of the river, with **Galmpton Bay** stretching away to the right. On the left is the village of **Lower Dittisham** (famous for its fine plums and its gardens). **Sandridge House,** built by John Nash in 1805, next comes into view. In an older house on this site, the sixteenth-century Arctic navigator, John Davis, was born. In the opposite direction a glimpse is obtained of **Higher Dittisham.**

On the approach to **Duncannon Point,** a creek may be seen running to the right. This is **Stokemouth,** halfway between Dartmouth and Totnes. A quarter of a mile inland is the village of **Stoke Gabriel,** the square tower of its fifteenth-century church conspicuous. At this point the river resembles a great lake, with only one apparent outlet on the left. But this arm is in reality **Bow Creek,** formed by the **Harbourne,** a tributary stream. About 2 miles up this stream is the village of **Tuckenhay,** famous for its hand-made paper. After passing Stoke Gabriel the Dart itself wriggles round to the right to **Duncannon,** where nets and other fishing gear give evidence of the occupation of the villagers.

Following the river as it twists and turns, the vessel continues past the famous woods of **Sharpham,** once well known for an extensive heronry. After rounding Sharpham Point the stream is more confined, and the long reach to Totnes is entered. Totnes's old red sandstone church tower appears prominently on the horizon.

The Dart at Dittisham

Totnes

Access. – *By rail:* on main Western Region Line. Totnes is 203 miles from London. Holiday Runabout tickets are issued at Totnes Station.
By road: Western National and *Devon General* bus companies connect Totnes with all parts of Devon.
By river: Daily sailings from Dartmouth and Totnes from beginning of May to end of September.

Banks. – *Barclays, Lloyds, National Westminster, Midland.*

Bowls. – In the Borough Park.

Car Parking Places. – The Plains, North Street, Coronation Road, Leechwell Street, Leechwell Lane, and by Civic Hall.

Early Closing Day. – Thursday.

Fishing. – Rod and line fishing for salmon and trout from February 15 to September 30. Licences and information from the *Clerk to the Dart District Fishery Board, Totnes.* For fishing between Totnes and Buckfastleigh, the Dart Angling Association licence must be obtained.

Hotels. – *Royal Seven Stars,* The Plains; *Fairseat,* The Quay; *Seymour Lodge,* Bridgetown; *Dart Vale Manor,* Bridgetown; *Chateau Bellevue.*

Library. – Branch of the Devon County Library.

Market Day. – Friday (Pannier Market). Cattle markets every Tuesday.

Museum. – In Fore Street.

Population. – 5,830.

Post Office. – Bottom of Fore Street. Sub-offices: High Street and Bridgetown.

Tennis. – Grass and hard courts in the Borough Park opposite the station.

The Story of Totnes

Totnes is one of the most charming of old towns. Legend dates its history from 1170 B.C., for a tradition repeated by Geoffrey of Monmouth assures us that Brutus the Trojan, the reputed colonizer of Britain, landed at this spot, when the Dart was an inlet of the Channel and its waters laved the hill on which the old town stood; and the inhabitants point with pride to the **Brutus Stone,** a granite block sunk into the pavement just above No. 51 Fore Street (a sign is placed in the wall above it), as proving the truth of this assertion. The name "Brutus", however, is probably a corruption of Bruiter's or Town Crier's Stone. The stone at one time projected 18 inches above the pavement, but was levelled in the interests of traffic. The Mayor still stands upon it on the proclamation of a new sovereign.

Totnes claims to be one of the oldest boroughs in the kingdom. Saxon coins minted at Totnes were found during excavations at the castle. As coins were only minted in fortified towns, Totnes, in the tenth century, was probably a small settlement covering about 10 acres, and surrounded by earthen ramparts, which were replaced later by stone walls. In the eleventh century, William the Conqueror bestowed this royal *burh* on Judhael – the reputed founder of Totnes Castle (see p. 150).

Totnes was an important town when the Normans subjugated England, for we find from Domesday Book that it was held by Judhael direct from the King; that there were "within the borough one hundred burgesses, less five, and fifteen without the borough, working the land" and that it was only taxed when Exeter was taxed. "If an expedition sets out by land or by sea," the entry goes on, "Totenais, Barnestaple, and Lideford (Lydford) render between them as much service as Exeter renders." In 1206, King John granted the town its first charter and it possesses the original roll of the Guild merchants, said to be the oldest in existence. The list of mayors dates from 1331; the public ceremony of swearing in the mayor is held annually at the Guildhall.

Totnes quay has been in use for nearly a thousand years. The Saxons used the port, and there was probably some overseas trade. The height of its importance was between the fourteenth and seventeenth centuries, when large quantities of wool and cloth were exported and Totnes merchants grew very wealthy. Trade declined, and the harbour silted up. Constant dredging is now necessary to enable the chief industry of the town – the importation of timber from Northern Europe – to be carried on.

Totnes Grammar School was founded in 1553 by Edward VI and has produced many notable men. Among them may be mentioned Benjamin Kennicott, whose Hebrew Bible was published in 1776; Sir William Whiteway, who became a Premier of Newfoundland; and Charles Babbage, the mathematician. Other eminent men born in Totnes are Edward Lye, the Saxon grammarian and compiler of the dictionary of that language; William Brockedon, author, painter, and Alpine traveller; and the Earl of Totnes, who made his mark in the Irish wars of Queen Elizabeth I's time. On a granite **Obelisk,** in front of the *Royal Seven Stars Hotel,* in the Plains, is recorded that it was erected "In honour of William John Wills, native of Totnes, the first, with Burke to cross the Australian continent; he perished in returning, 28 June, 1861." Among the names of distinguished freemen is that of the well-known soldier Lord Birdwood of Anzac and Totnes.

The best approach for the visitor to the town is from the bridge which spans the river, a short distance from the spot where the steamer lands passengers from Dartmouth. The landing-place is very near to what is known as the **Island,** reached from the bridge, a delightfully shady riverside pleasure-ground, laid out for the enjoyment of the townspeople by a former Duke of Somerset. The bridge is the boundary between the parishes of Totnes and **Bridgetown,** its less important neighbour. The view from this point, up the steep hill which the town's chief thoroughfare climbs laboriously – passing beneath the quaint old **East Gates** which spans the roadway – suggests something of the antiquarian and historical interest which this old town excites.

Totnes is one of the few places in the kingdom where the curfew bell is still rung and where, in addition, a day bell is rung early every morning – an ancient call to prayers.

The town is one of the chief gateways to the South Hams. It was spoken of by Camden as a "little town hanging from east to west on the side of a hill" – a description which still holds good. Of old, it was defended by a strong castle, and was surrounded by walls which may still be traced, and which show that it was then much smaller, so tiny that it must have been one of the smallest walled towns in the kingdom. There were in the wall four gates, opening to the cardinal points of the compass. Of these, two remain, the **North** and **East Gates.** In Fore Street, not far above the Brutus Stone, is an Elizabethan house in which is the **Totnes Museum** *(April–September, weekdays)*. Nearby is the **East Gate** which spans the roadway and divides Fore Street from High Street. It has been greatly altered of late years; but of old it consisted of two arched portals, one for carriages, which was enclosed with gates, and a smaller one, "a needle's eye," for foot passengers. The clock, with a face for each side of the arch, was added in 1878. On the east side is an oriel window.

Stone steps lead from the East Gate to Rampart Walk, a narrow road which follows the line of the old walls past the church and Guildhall to the stone arched North Gate.

The **Parish Church of St. Mary's** is a grand and impressive red sandstone edifice of the fifteenth century, in the Perpendicular style, with a massive square tower surmounted by crocketed pinnacles. Halfway up are three niches containing statuettes. It is known from a charter of Judhael de Totenaes in 1088 that there was a church here, and from the deeds of Totnes Priory it is evident that soon after that date a Priory Church was built to the north-east of the present church, and other buildings erected in connection with the Benedictine Priory, the only remains of which are now the Guildhall and, in part, a private house called "The Priory". The Priory Church and the parish church were united in 1259, and in the first half of the fifteenth century the parish church was rebuilt. The church was restored (1867–1879) by Sir G. G. Scott. The rood-screen, with two parclose screens of Beer stone, is one of the finest stone screens in England, but the loft was removed at the restoration. Other objects of interest are the Corporation seats bearing the town arms, a Bible and Prayer Book (both at the west end of the north aisle), presented to the church for the use of the mayor by Lady Ann Seymour, in 1690, together with the Indulgence granted by Bishop Lacy mentioned above, and an altar cloth of 1682; two handsome candelabras, dated 1701 and 1732; and some interesting tombs.

Opposite the church, Barclays Bank is housed in an old building (No. 16) bearing the date 1585, and lower down the initials N.B., standing for Nicholas Ball, one time mayor and M.P. Thomas Bodley, the founder of the famous Library at Oxford, married the rich widow of Ball in 1586.

The **Guildhall** stands to the north of the church and is one of the most interesting municipal buildings in the west of England. When not in use, it is daily open to the public. The Guildhall occupied part of the site of St. Mary's Priory, founded about 1088 by Judhael. After the dissolution of the monasteries, the land was granted to the Corporation, and the present Guildhall, which is of sixteenth- and seventeenth-century date, was built on the site.

In the main hall will be seen the old stocks, a man-trap, and the old bull ring; a large oil painting, depicting a scene from Ossian, painted by William Brockedon, a native of the town; a portrait of Brockedon, by himself; and portraits of Mayors and Members of Parliament. At one side is the doorway of the old lock-up. The Council Chamber is a low room, the ceiling sloping up to a large skylight, and with old oaken stalls for the Mayor and Corporation, and a fine plaster frieze, with the town arms and date, 1624, over the fireplace. In the Guildhall are kept many of the valuable records of Totnes. Adjoining the Guildhall is the original site of the Grammar School, which is now in Fore Street.

A few steps from the church, and near the North Gate of the town, are the well-preserved ruins of **Totnes Castle,** of red sandstone *(admission fee, from* 9.30 *a.m. to* 7 *p.m., winter* 5.30 *p.m.)*. The circular keep with 15 feet walls, occupies a lofty mound, from the top of which are extensive views.

The Castle is generally believed to have been founded by Judheal de Totenais, the Norman knight to whom the Conqueror gave the manor; but this is uncertain, and Hooker inclines to the belief that "it was buylded either by the inhabitants of the same for the defence of theymselffes and of their towne when before the Conquest the Danes and fforeyn enemyes used invasions and exercysed great cruelties as well in this west countrie as yn other places of the lande, or by someone of the lordes, and for their command of the towne did buyld the same."

Near the Castle, at the bend in the High Street, is the site of the **West Gate,** demolished at the beginning of the nineteenth century. Just beyond are two colonnades known as **Butterwalk** and **Poultry Walk.** The upper storeys of the buildings project over the pavement, and are supported by pillars, thus providing a picturesque covered walk. Before the market was built, poultry and farm products were displayed and sold in the sheltered *piazzas*–hence the names. In High Street and Fore Street are several sixteenth- and seventeenth-century houses, many of them possessing richly decorated plaster ceilings. Others have the typical Devon slate-hung fronts. In byways and lanes are other reminders of Totnes's antiquity. A Leper House once stood in Maudlin Road and the narrow footpath connecting it with Leechwell Lane is still referred to as "Leper's Way". Yet, steeped in history and tradition as it is, Totnes does not rest on past achievements. It is a thriving centre with excellent shops and a busy market. It is an attractive holiday resort, and is rapidly developing light industries.

Totnes Motor Museum *(Easter to October, daily* 10–6*)* is a private collection of cars many of which are in everyday use for both travel and racing. It specializes in vintage, sports and racing cars.

Excursions from Totnes

Totnes is the centre of a lovely district (with good bus services in all directions), 6 miles from Paignton, between 8 and 10 miles from Newton Abbot, Torquay and Brixham, and on the threshold of the Dartmoor National Park.

Of walks in the immediate neighbourhood, that past the Landing Stage on the banks of the river can be recommended, while of longer walks none is more popular than that to **Berry Pomeroy Castle,** about 3 miles distant. After crossing the Dart, the suburb of **Bridgetown** is traversed, and the steep hill to True Street climbed; then to the left along the main road to Berry Pomeroy. From Bridgetown there is a walk *via* Bourton to **Littlehempston** (2 miles) where there is a fourteenth-century manor-house and 12 acres, sealed by covenants to the National Trust.

Dartington Hall. The Dartington Hall estate lies in a large bend of the River Dart. The fourteenth-century manor-house, built by John Holland, half-brother of Richard II, is an interesting example of careful restoration. The estate is now a Trust with agricultural and commercial enterprises formed into several companies. Endowed departments are Dartington College of Arts (including the Devon Centre for Further Education sponsored by the Devon Education Authority), a co-educational boarding school and the Adult Education Centre. In the garden the fine trees and flowering shrubs, and the terraces overlooking the old tiltyard are of particular interest. The estate is private property, but the gardens and Hall (if not in use) may be visited without appointment (no coaches).

The walk may be extended by following the Ashburton road from Dartington Church to Huxham's Cross. From here a descent through the woods emerges by the lovely old bridge which spans the Dart at Staverton. The return may be made by the Totnes bus.

Another delightful walk from Dartington Church is to the beautiful old village of **Rattery,** reached by turning left at Huxham Cross. The church is a thirteenth-century building with fifteenth-century additions; it has a fine Norman font and fifteenth-century screens. Adjoining the church is one of England's oldest inns, the eleventh-century *Church House Inn.*

Totnes is a convenient centre for **Buckfastleigh,** a small town with a thirteenth-century church, standing high up away from the town. The ruins of an old chapel adjoining this church are still visible, and the view from the site extends far and wide, especially towards –

Buckfast Abbey

a Saxon abbey founded in 1018 by Ethelward, an ealdorman of King Canute, and generously endowed by the king himself. The tradition that a Celtic foundation had existed on the spot before Canute's time is no longer admitted. In 1147 Buckfast Abbey was affiliated to the Cistercian Order, to which it remained attached until the Dissolution under Henry VIII in 1539. From that time onwards

Buckfast Abbey

the buildings were gradually dismantled. A modern house built on the site in 1806 completed the destruction of the old abbey, but in 1882 a group of French Benedictine monks bought the place with a view to its complete restoration. The Abbey church was rebuilt by the monks themselves, to the plans and under the direction of the late Fred A. Walters, a London architect. This rebuilding, started in 1906 by Abbot Anscar Vonier and a few Brothers, was completed in December 1938. Only the structural work was carried out by the monks themselves; the altars, stalls, windows, etc., being the part of secular professionals. Splendid examples of metal work, executed at Aix-la-Chapelle by the world's leading goldsmiths, are to be seen on the high altar, the font and Stations of the Cross. The Memorial plaque to Abbot Vonier, who was buried in the church by special privilege, was the work of the late Benno Elkan. In 1960 Buckfast Abbey was affiliated to the English Benedictine Congregation, to which Downside, Ampleforth, etc., also belong. In 1965 a new Blessed Sacrament Chapel was added. The stained glass, a conspicuous feature, was carried out by the monks. In 1967 a small preparatory school was inaugurated, the teaching staff being made up of the Abbey monks.

The Dart Valley Railway (privately owned) from Totnes to Buckfastleigh and Ashburton and the main road from Exeter to Plymouth pass, at Dart Bridge, within sight of the Abbey, and secondary roads lead to Dartmoor, a couple of miles away.

Holiday-makers spending a long day at Buckfastleigh should, if they are walkers, have a ramble on the confines of Dartmoor, quickly reached from the town. For instance, take the road to Wallaford Down on the south side as far as or short of Cross Furzes, descend to the Holy Brook Valley on the other side for the return, or proceed to Ashburton by way of Holne, a long tramp that presents typical Dartmoor border scenery.

Set in the midst of 327 acres of National Trust property is **Hembury Castle,** an Iron Age hill-fort known locally as Danes' Camp. It stands above Holy Brook, 2 miles north of Buckfastleigh.

About 2 miles south-west of Buckfastleigh is the parish of **Dean Prior,** of which the poet Herrick was vicar. He was presented to the living in 1629, and held it for eighteen years, when he was ejected by the Puritan supremacy. He returned to Dean Prior at the Restoration in 1662 and lived here until his death at eighty-three. The registers contain a record of the burial of "Robert Herrick vicker," October 15, 1674. There is a modern brass tablet to his memory in the church, and in 1926 there was unveiled in the chancel a very beautiful window dedicated to his memory.

Dean Court – passed *en route* to Dean Prior – now a farmhouse, was the Tudor mansion of the Giles family, and was built in Edward VI's reign. It has an interesting old hall, decorated with trophies of the chase. Sir Edward Giles (*d.* 1642) and family have an interesting monument in Dean Prior church.

Ashburton

beautifully situated in very lovely country, has some of the most attractive portions of Dartmoor within comparatively easy reach. The town stands on a small tributary of the Dart, the *Ashburn.*

The town has a number of typical Devon gabled-styled houses and a Late Decorated and Perpendicular church with a fine west tower decorated with niches for statues. North of the town is **Terrace Walk** giving some splendid views.

From Ashburton a road runs right across the heart of Dartmoor *via* **Dartmeet,** where the East and West Dart streams merge, and Two Bridges to Tavistock. Two miles to the north of this road is **Buckland-in-the-Moor** with some picturesque sheltered farms and cottages and a low-towered church possessing a fine screen and a Norman font.

Three miles farther north is the village of **Widecombe-in-the-Moor,** beautifully situated on the East Webburn which rises near Hameldown Tor two or three miles to the north. Widecombe has long been known for its church and fair, the latter made famous by the song "Uncle Tom Cobleigh". The church is spacious and is notable for its 120-feet high tower. Church House in the village (National Trust) is a fifteenth-century building part used as a cottage and part as parish hall.

Hameldown Tor, 1,737 feet, rises three miles to the north of Widecombe. Some wonderful views of the surrounding tors are to be enjoyed here.

For **Grimspound,** see page 96.

About 2 miles south-east of Totnes off the Kingsbridge road is–

Harberton

This village is notable for its church whose outstanding feature is the great fifteenth-century rood-screen. Partly restored in the Victorian period, it stretches across the church resplendent with carvings and coloured in gold, blue, green and red. The fine stone pulpit is adorned with carvings of the apostles executed in the seventeenth century.

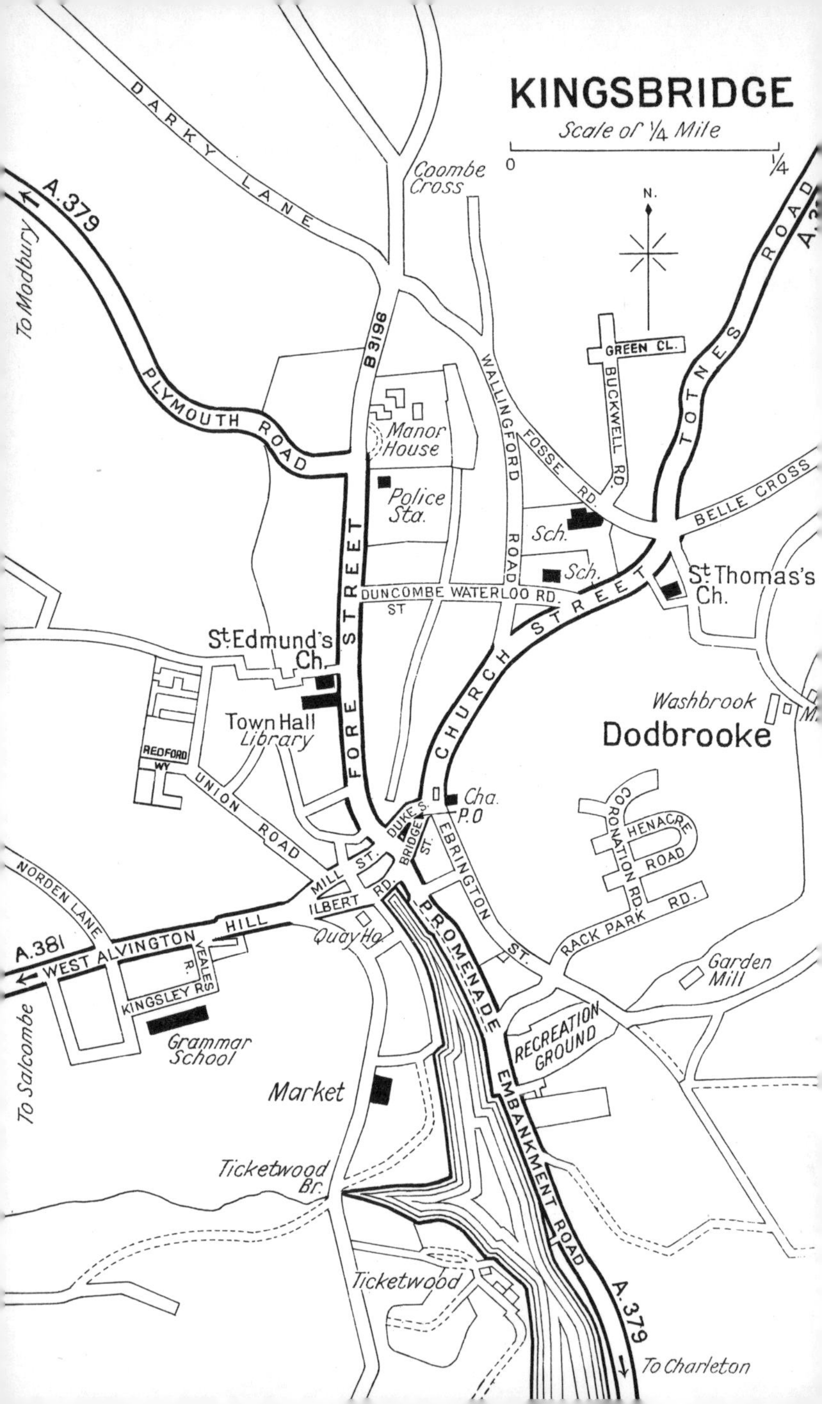
KINGSBRIDGE
Scale of 1/4 Mile
0
1/4
N.
DARKY LANE
Coombe Cross
A.379
To Modbury
PLYMOUTH ROAD
B3196
Manor House
Police Sta.
FORE STREET
WALLINGFORD ROAD
FOSSE RD.
GREEN CL.
BUCKWELL RD.
TOTNES ROAD
BELLE CROSS
Sch.
Sch.
St. Thomas's Ch.
DUNCOMBE ST
WATERLOO RD.
CHURCH STREET
St. Edmund's Ch.
Town Hall
Library
REDFORD WY
UNION ROAD
Washbrook
Dodbrooke
Cha.
P.O
DUKES
BRIDGE ST.
EBRINGTON ST.
CORONATION RD.
HENACRE ROAD
RACK PARK RD.
NORDEN LANE
MILL ST.
ILBERT RD.
HILL
A.381
WEST ALVINGTON
VEALES R.
KINGSLEY RD.
Quay Ho.
PROMENADE
Garden Mill
Grammar School
RECREATION GROUND
To Salcombe
Market
EMBANKMENT ROAD
Ticketwood Br.
Ticketwood
A.379
To Charleton

Slapton Sands

In the South Hams

If a line be drawn from Plymouth to Totnes, following more or less the road and the Western Region main line, all the country lying to the south is the **South Hams,** a district famous in the West Country for the soft beauty of its landscapes, the varied charms of its indented coast line, and for its rivers, which drain the watershed of south-western Dartmoor and give to the district its fertile character.

Kingsbridge is no longer served by rail, but bus services connect with Totnes, Kingswear and other stations on the main line.

The road services also connect Kingsbridge with Dartmouth on one side, and Modbury, Yealmpton and Plymouth on the other. These services are constantly increased, now connecting Kingsbridge and Salcombe several times a day with Hope, Thurlestone, Bigbury, Loddiswell, etc., while at intervals during the day the Totnes bus gives a through service from Salcombe. The service from Stokenham to East Prawle and East Portlemouth provides an alternative route to Salcombe. There is also the motor ferry which runs between Kingsbridge and Salcombe during the summer months.

Kingsbridge

Banks. – *Barclays, Lloyds, Midland* and *National Westminster*.
Bowls. – Public Bowling Green in the Recreation Ground, The Quay, and at Thurlestone.
Buses. – To Salcombe; to Hope; to Thurlestone; to Totnes; and to Stokenham and East Portlemouth; to Torcross and Dartmouth; to Modbury, Yealmpton, Plymstock and Plymouth; to Frogmore and South Pool; to Loddiswell; to Bantham (Wednesdays only).
Car Parking Places. – The Quay, charge; Fore Street, charge.
Cinema. – Church Street.
Early Closing Day. – Thursday.
Fishing. – See under Salcombe.
Golf. – *Thurlstone Golf Club* (18 holes), on the cliffs overlooking Bigbury Bay. Sunday play. There is also a course at Bigbury (18 holes).
Hotels. – *King's Arms, Buttville, Happy Return Motel, Anchor, Buckland-tout-Saints.*
Information. – Urban District Council, Kingsbridge; or The Chamber of Trade, Kingsbridge and District.
Market Day. – Wednesday.
Population. – 3,660.
Post Office. – Bridge Street.
Tennis. – Public courts (hard) at the Recreation Ground, Embankment Road. Sixteen grass tennis courts in addition to hard courts are available for play at Thurlestone Golf Club; others at Hope Cove.

The little town of Kingsbridge lies in the extreme southern part of Devon, within 4 miles of the open sea and amongst magnificent scenery. It owes its prosperity to its situation in the centre of the South Hams, where agriculture has always held up its head, and is a very ancient market town retaining many of its old customs. It is regarded as the "capital" of the South Hams and, although small, is of some administrative and commercial importance. It still possesses a town-crier. The town, consisting of one main street and several by-ways, dates back many centuries, and a tale is related to explain its name. A Saxon king on one of his progresses is said to have come to the Dod brook. There was no bridge near, and a loyal subject carried the king across the stream on his back; but more probably the name refers to an actual bridge – mentioned in a charter of the year 962 – linking two royal estates.

The town is built on a hill rising steeply from the water's edge, with the tower and spire of its **Church** overtopping all other buildings.

This church is dedicated to St. Edmund, king and martyr, a quite usual dedication in East Anglia, but somewhat surprising in Devon. It is a large cruciform structure, thirteenth century in part, containing several stained windows and monuments of departed worthies – one, notably, by Flaxman. In the porch are the old stocks. Cut on a headstone by the chancel door is to be found the well-known epitaph:

"Here lie I at the Chancel Door;
Here lie I because I'm poor;
The farther in the more you'll pay;
Here lie I as warm as they."

The visitor should note the unusual lectern, a brass eagle mounted on a granite rock. Some ancient documents found in the church are now preserved in Exeter.

In Fore Street, near the Church, is a short arcade, somewhat similar to that at Totnes. It is known as the **Shambles,** or Butterwalk, and was built about 1586. The supporting granite pillars are undoubtedly of earlier date, while the upper storey was altered in 1796. The **Town Hall** is in the main street (note four-sided clock) and the **Cattle Market** just outside the town. In Mill Street the now disused Town Mill stands on the site of the old mill of the Buckfast Abbots, which was in use in the fourteenth century. The Old Grammar School houses the **Cookworthy Museum** *(Easter to October, weekdays)* with exhibits illustrating local history and trade, particularly the china clay industry. There is a pleasant **Promenade** on the quay. At the end of this promenade, on the opposite side of the road, is a small Recreation Ground, with a bowling green, a putting course, and hard tennis courts. Golf, tennis and bowls may also be enjoyed at Thurlestone.

Dodbrooke

Kingsbridge's twin town, stands on the other side of the valley through which the Dod flows. It has a venerable Perpendicular **Church,** dedicated to St. Thomas à Becket, whose statuette is seen over the south porch. The north aisle, restored in 1887, has a window formerly the east window of South Pool Church. It has a good screen, with a restored cornice and modern rood, and the panels show paintings of apostles, saints and bishops. By turning right just beyond the church along the old pack-horse road to Charleton and down past **Washbrook Mill,** another right turn near the hilltop allows the town to be reached at the end of the promenade. Those with time to spare can be recommended to continue another half-mile and descend to the head of Bowcombe Creek, then, going right, return to Kingsbridge (2 miles) by the road beside the estuary, remembering its attractions are not so great at low tide though the old bridge on the Kingsbridge–Charleton road is a source of pleasure at any time. It once had a swing-bridge section at the eastern end to allow vessels to pass up to the mill.

Kingsbridge

Excursions from Kingsbridge

To Portlemouth – Prawle Point – The Start

This is a delightful 11-mile walk. **East Portlemouth** is Salcombe's *vis-à-vis* on the banks of the Salcombe inlet and is reached by ferry. The tower of the **Church,** like so many in this part of Devon, is a landmark on account of its elevated position. The structure, dedicated to St. Onolaus (Winwalloe), contains a richly-carved screen and an interesting fifteenth-century font.

From the church the most picturesque route is by the road overlooking the Harbour to **Rickham,** proceeding along the coast-watchers' path to **Prawle Point,** which may also be approached by road. The bus between Portlemouth and Kingsbridge (*via* Stokenham) makes readily accessible the fine coast near the typical cliff village of **East Prawle,** close to the point. If the climb from the Portlemouth ferry up to the church is not made then the path (R.) from the ferry may be taken past Mill Bay Cove to the wood where the National Trust takes over. The path goes through the wood and follows the coast line keeping to the edge of the old golf-links till it joins a lower path and proceeds to Prawle Point.

Against Prawle Point, the most southerly point of the Devon coast, the waves in stormy weather beat with all their fury, and it has been chiselled and chipped most fantastically. From the village steep and stony lanes wind past fields and rock-strewn waste land to a little beach where it is sometimes possible to bathe.

It is 4 miles along the coast from Prawle Point to Start Point, a rough walk, passing the little opening and beach at **Lannacombe** (with good sand and bathing) and **Pear Tree Point,** the twin promontory of Start Point, from which it is about three-quarters of a mile distant. Pear Tree Point commands an excellent view of its neighbour. Composed of the dark Devonian rock –

Start Point stands some 146 feet above sea-level and has a strangely gloomy and impressive appearance. It is generally spoken of as "the Start". Remarkable quartz veins descend vertically to the sea.

The name Start is derived from the Saxon *steort,* a "tail" or promontory. The Point stretches boldly out to sea, its rocky sides sloping off like the roof of a house. The area is a designated Nature Reserve and popular with bird-watchers.

The two wireless masts to be seen are a prominent feature for some miles around. Each 450 feet high, they form the aerial system of the **B.B.C. Start Point Transmitting Station.**

The **Lighthouse,** on the extreme point of the cliff, is about 94 feet high and exhibits two lights – a brilliant revolving one, giving three flashes every ten seconds, to guide ships bound up Channel; and a fixed red light to warn those running in-shore they are near the Skerries, a dangerous bank off the coast. The lighthouse may be visited on weekdays from 1 p.m. to one hour before sunset at the discretion of the keeper in charge.

A footpath from the car park leads to the small sandy cove of **Mattiscombe,** situated between Lannacombe and Pear Tree Point. The cove is increasingly popular and offers safe bathing.

Torcross is on the margin of Start Bay, 4 miles north of Start Point. It has become popular on account of its bathing and its salt and freshwater fishing. North and south of the village are leys (or lakes), **Slapton Ley** and **Widecombe Ley,** well stocked with pike, perch and roach.

Slapton Ley, the larger, to the north, is about 2 miles long. It is divided into the Higher Ley, largely overgrown, and Lower Ley by the road to Slapton village, and is separated from the sea by a bank of shingle, over which vehicles pass on their way to Dartmouth. This freshwater lake is formed by three small streams which here unite their waters, but have not sufficient force to remove the bank of shingle. The Ley water percolates through the sands in the summer and so reaches the sea, in the winter it overflows through a culvert at Torcross. The sands are the home of sea-kale, which grows wild here, and was first cultivated for kitchen use in the garden of Mr. Southcote, of Stoke Fleming, about 1775. Roots were then sold in Exeter market at half-a-crown each.

A mile or so south of Torcross is the popular beach and fishing hamlet of **Beesands,** sheltering under low cliffs to the south of Widecombe Ley, which is quite small compared with that at Slapton. The direct approach from the cliff path to Beesands is something of a scramble, but the picturesque village possesses an inn and a café, and is renowned for its crabs and lobsters.

Slapton lies about half a mile inland from the Ley to which it gives its name, has a Decorated and Perpendicular **Church,** with low tower and spire, a screen, a sanctuary ring, and notable remains of a chantry (tall tower and walls beside the *Tower Inn*) founded by Sir Guy de Brian, who bore the standard of Edward III at the siege of Calais, and is described as "one of the prime founders of the Order of the Garter". The parish is historically interesting because Sir John Hawkins resided at Pool, about a quarter of a mile from the village; and John Flavel, the celebrated Nonconformist divine, found refuge at Hudscott on the passing of the Five Mile Act.

Slapton Sands comprise the northern portion of the sandy beach which extends for about 7 miles to Start Point. The beach consists mainly of coarse sand mixed with shingle, and is becoming increasingly popular as a picnic resort during summer. Caution is necessary when bathing here as storms sometimes cause such a steep shelving of the beach that a bather may be out of his or her depth after taking only one or two steps into the sea.

Half way along the Sands at a point almost opposite the Slapton road is the granite pillar set up by the United States Army authorities and "presented to the people of the South Hams who generously left their homes and their lands to provide a battle practice area for the successful assault in Normandy in June, 1944". The area included the villages of Blackawton, Chillington, East Allington, Slapton, Stokenham, Strete and Torcross. Upwards of 200 farms were evacuated.

Northward of the Ley our road begins its climb to higher ground by a loop inland at Strete Gate, and on looking back picturesque views may be gained of the coast line and sands, bounded on the south by Start Point and the Lighthouse. It is not far to the hamlet of **Strete,** and then once more the road dips down a steep hill to **Blackpool.** There is nothing to recall the Blackpool of the North; a quieter, more out-of-the-world place it would be difficult to imagine. There are the shingle beach, a car park, some picturesque private houses, and a prettily wooded valley stretching inland. It suffers from gales from time to time and during recent winters its very existence seemed threatened.

From Blackpool the road ascends again to **Stoke Fleming,** with an imposing thirteenth-century church tower erected as a landmark for ships making for Dartmouth. The church contains several objects of interest, notably a fine fourteenth-century brass of John Corp and his granddaughter, the oldest dated brass in the West. The War Memorial was originally a fine fifteenth-century wayside cross, which, after a chequered history, was restored and placed in its present position in 1920. The modern pulpit (1891) carries some exquisite carving by Miss Violet Pinwill. After passing Stoke Fleming, in which there are some quaint corners that can be investigated by the curious, the buses follow the road

Bantham on the Avon

to Townstal parallel to the Dart and along the Ridges. But those who desire a walk cannot go wrong if they alight at Pinhey's Cross (Recreation Ground), the toll-house, or at Deadman's Cross for descent down into Dartmouth.

Kingsbridge to Salcombe

Salcombe, like Dartmouth and Fowey, is situated just inside the mouth of the harbour. It stands on the west side of the inlet which runs from Kingsbridge to the Channel, but a new settlement is springing up along the eastern side, though, thanks to private munificence, a considerable stretch of coast has been leased to the National Trust at a purely nominal rent in order to preserve it from development.

Salcombe is best approached from Kingsbridge by water, and the journey of about 4 miles will leave pleasant memories of the hills that hem in the river on either side, of the numerous creeks with their wooded banks, and of the air of content and prosperity under which the countryside appears to slumber.

Leaving the Quay, we pass on the right the remains of **Ticket** (or **Tacket**) **Wood,** said to be so called from the fact that Nonconformists who assembled here in days when it was a crime to worship God in any other way than that prescribed by the State, issued tickets to those entitled to attend their meetings, and so nonplussed the spies who sought to betray them. After passing Highhouse Point the inlet widens, a creek branching off north-east past **Charleton,** a long straggling village with a quaint old church. About a mile farther comes **Wide Gates,** where creeks eating far into the hillside cause the estuary to widen. In the centre of this expanse is an islet, the **Saltstone,** upon which, as it was a sort of no-man's-land, belonging to none of the surrounding parishes, and therefore out of the jurisdiction of all the justices of the neighbourhood, the persecuted Nonconformists were accustomed to hold their meetings. On the east the lake-like expanse runs up a little over 2 miles to the village of **Frogmore,** known for its slate quarries, which were worked as far back as the reign of Henry VIII. Then, after narrowing, the waters broaden again off Ilbertstow Point, where a double-headed creek runs up to **South Pool** and **Waterhead,** not far from **Chivelstone,** villages small in size but of some interest on account of their churches. That of South Pool has an Easter sepulchre with a carving of Roman soldiers, a beautiful screen and an imposing tower. Chivelstone Church possesses a splendid tower, a beautifully coloured and carved screen, a Sanctuary ring on the south door, and a pulpit hollowed out of a solid block of oak. This is the only church in the country dedicated to St. Sylvester, a Spanish saint. Under **Ilbertstow Point** – on rounding which the tourist gains his first view of Salcombe, embowered amid its trees and apparently guarded seawards by a huge spiky dragon crawling down Bolt Head – the waters of a shallow creek run up to **Batson,** which can be reached by a field-path beginning at the end of a turning just beyond the Salcombe gasworks.

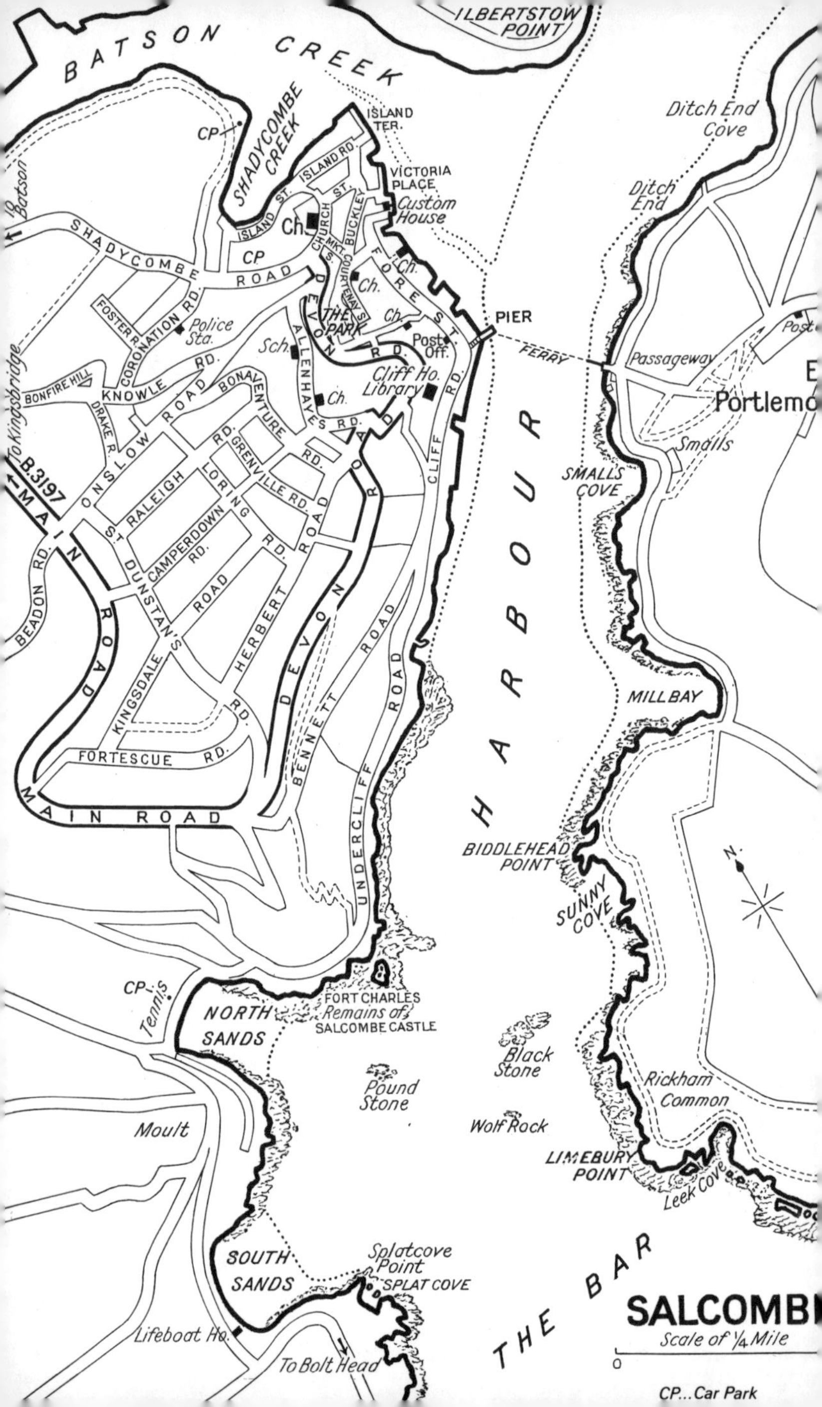
BATSON CREEK
ILBERTSTOW POINT
SHADYCOMBE CREEK
ISLAND TER.
ISLAND RD.
ISLAND ST.
VICTORIA PLACE
Custom House
Ch.
CHURCH ST.
BUCKLEY ST.
MKT. S.
COURTENAY S.
FORE ST.
CP
To Batson
SHADYCOMBE ROAD
DEVON RD.
THE PARK
Post Off.
PIER
FERRY
FOSTER R.
CORONATION RD.
Police Sta.
Sch.
ALLENHAYES RD.
Cliff Ho. Library
CLIFF RD.
To Kingsbridge
BONFIRE HILL
KNOWLE RD.
DRAKE R.
BONAVENTURE RD.
ONSLOW ROAD
GRENVILLE RD.
LORING RD.
RALEIGH RD.
B.3197
MAIN ROAD
ST DUNSTAN'S RD.
CAMPERDOWN RD.
BEADON RD.
HERBERT ROAD
DEVON ROAD
KINGSDALE
BENNETT ROAD
UNDERCLIFF ROAD
FORTESCUE RD.
MAIN ROAD
HARBOUR
Ditch End Cove
Ditch End
Passageway
Post
Portlemo
Smalls
SMALLS COVE
MILLBAY
BIDDLEHEAD POINT
SUNNY COVE
N.
CP
Tennis
NORTH SANDS
FORT CHARLES
Remains of SALCOMBE CASTLE
Black Stone
Pound Stone
Wolf Rock
Moult
Rickham Common
LIMEBURY POINT
Leek Cove
SOUTH SANDS
Splatcove Point
SPLAT COVE
THE BAR
Lifeboat Ho.
To Bolt Head
SALCOMB
Scale of 1/4 Mile
0
CP...Car Park

Salcombe

Access. – By bus from Kingsbridge. Ferry motor-boat from Kingsbridge, and from East Portlemouth. Long distance coach services connect at Exeter for Salcombe.
Banks. – *Lloyds* and *Midland*.
Bathing. – Good and safe on sandy beaches, especially on Portlemouth side.
Boats. – Rowing, sailing and motor, can be hired at moderate charges by the hour, day or week.
Bus to Kingsbridge; from East Portlemouth to Torcross.
Car Parks. – North Sands, Shadycombe, Shadycombe Creek, Whitestrand.
Early Closing Day. – Thursday, though few shops close.
Ferries. – (From the Pier.) Across the harbour to Portlemouth. To Bolt Head (South Sands).
Fishing. – Good for bass, pollock and mackerel just outside, especially off Prawle Point. Restricted trout fishing in the Avon.
Hotels. – *Bolt Head, Tides Reach, South Sands, Beadon Prior, Grafton Towers, The Wells, Knowle, Allenhayes, St. Elmo, Castle Point, Bay View, Carberry, Sunny Cliff.*
Library. – Devon County Library, Cliff House.
Population. – 2,370.
Post Office. – Fore Street.
Tennis. – Grass and hard courts available at North Sands and Onslow Road. (*Salcombe Tennis Club,* visitors welcome.)
Youth Hostel. – "Overbecks," Sharpitor.

To the east of Salcombe Harbour towers the church-crowned hill of **Portlemouth** (a ferry plies across the harbour from 7 a.m. to 9 p.m., and 8 a.m. to 8 p.m., Sundays), whilst on the other side of the water is **Salcombe,** built under the lee of a hill clothed in foliage, through which are seen the villas of the many who have settled in this favoured spot. Beneath these houses is the town itself, consisting of one long street together with the parallel Devon Road which follows the windings of the shore, and from which newer thoroughfares branch out – architecturally a not very interesting town, but containing sufficient shops to meet the wants of visitors.

Originally a fishing village, Salcombe later achieved fame for its fruit clippers and its shipbuilding yards. Now it is a quiet fishing and yachting centre, attracting an increasing number of residents and visitors by virtue of its climate and magnificent position.

The **Harbour,** the glory of Salcombe, is safe, but the bar and the sunken rocks at its mouth make it somewhat dangerous and difficult to enter at night.

Just beyond the *Salcombe Hotel* is the **Jetty,** reached by a flight of steps, and lighted by a double lamp; but it is not carried far enough out into the harbour for vessels to approach at all states of the tide. For all that, the jetty is very useful. It is the starting-point of the ferries to Portlemouth and Kingsbridge and the motor-boats which run down the harbour to Bolt Head, disembarking their passengers at South Sands. (A pontoon landing stage at Whitestrand is accessible at almost any state of the tide.)

On the summit of Church Hill stands the **Parish Church** (modern Gothic), built in 1843 – Salcombe having been in West Alvington parish before that time. It was enlarged in 1889. The chancel window is a memorial of

At Salcombe

the eleventh Earl of Devon, who contributed liberally to the fund for its erection and endowed the vicarage.

Close to the *Marine Hotel,* on a slope whose foot is washed by the inlet, are the **Cliff House Gardens,** an attractive viewpoint. At the top beside the road is the *Memorial* to the men of Salcombe who fell in two World Wars and those who lost their lives in the lifeboat disaster of October 27, 1916. On the opposite side of the road is **Cliff House,** with County Library and Reading Room, and next door the headquarters of the *Salcombe Yacht Club*. Another public garden in Courtenay Street, in the residential part of the town, is called **The Park.**

Most of the usual holiday amusements are available although Salcombe's surroundings are so beautiful that the strenuous life receives little encouragement. Good and safe bathing on sandy beaches may be had in Mill Bay and Sunny Cove on the Portlemouth side and at North and South Sands when the tide serves, and there are one or two tiny rock-sheltered inlets suitable for a dip if not a swim. On the Salcombe side the sands remain wet owing to freshwater springs running down to the sea, but below Portlemouth the beaches dry quickly and make ideal playgrounds for children of all ages. Bathing under the cliffs facing the open sea is dangerous in most places, and should be avoided except when local opinion declares it safe.

Excursions from Salcombe

Chief among excursions is the 3-mile walk to Bolt Head. The road skirts the cliffs for most of the way, giving a view of the ruins of **Salcombe Castle,** part of Henry VIII's fortifications of the South Coast, on a rock surrounded by the sea.

It descends to **North Sands,** a little bay with an open front to the sea, where the sand is said to hide the remains of a submerged forest.

Then, after a steep clamber over the intervening peninsula, comes **South Sands,** a favourite picnicking and bathing spot. From here it is only a short distance to the beginning of **Courtenay Walk,** a pathway cut in the cliff slopes and affording magnificent views after it emerges from the woodland. Passing through the crags and two swing gates, it becomes a narrow path on the steep slope down to the old cable hut at Starehole Valley, where paths lead to the sea. Winding through the bracken above the little bay the path climbs again through the rock piles of–

Bolt Head

which rises 420 feet above the level of the sea. Those unable to stand heights may find part of the way trying, and most will notice some uncomfortable peeps down the steep slopes to the rocks far below. From the breezy headland itself, the view, owing to the configuration of the land, is disappointing after those enjoyed on the way, and the walk must be continued past the peninsula, of which it is the farthest point, before the coast westward opens up.

The cliff walk may be continued, with some rather rough going, for another 5 miles north-westward by way of the little cove of Soar (Sewer) Mill Sands and **Bolberry Down** to **Bolt Tail.**

It was on the **Ham Stone,** seen off Soar Mill Cove, that the famous windjammer, the *Herzogin Cecilie,* was wrecked in 1936. At Bradley Manor, near Newton Abbot, one may see the wheel of the vessel hung in the porch. In the *Cottage Hotel,* Hope, is a miniature cabin made entirely of material from the wreck.

Much of the land hereabouts is now National Trust property. Also held by the Trust is **Overbecks** in its gardens at Sharpitor. The museum here is open from April to October, 11–6; Botanical Garden all the year.

At the beginning of Courtenay Walk a rough road to the right leads to **Sharpitor** as a signpost directs. The way winds round through the wood on the hillside above South Sands, past *Overbecks* (see above) until it reaches the ground of the National Trust. Where cultivated ground meets the brambles, a steep path leftwards practically forms the boundary between them. This soon leads to the sloping cliff-top with a magnificent view over the coast eastwards, Salcombe Inlet, and inland towards Malborough, a far finer view than that from Bolt Head proper. Crags and boulders rise above the bracken, bramble and gorse, and near at hand is the pile of Sharpitor, the cap of the crags pouring down the cliff which make such a striking impression when first seen on entering from the sea or rounding Ilbertstow Point when coming down from Kingsbridge. Here at the summit (429 feet) is a toposcope (horizon disc) erected in 1934 in memory of Walter Newton Drew. Unfortunately most of the places indicated on the disc are completely obscured either by distance or intervening heights.

Aveton Gifford – Modbury – Bigbury

The high road from Kingsbridge to Plymouth – that followed by the buses – passes through Aveton Gifford, the town of Modbury, and Yealmpton. The distance to Plymouth is about 20 miles; to Modbury it is about 8 miles.

It is a steep ascent from Kingsbridge to **Churchstow,** with its conspicuous church tower; then it is a drop to **Averton Gifford** at the head of the estuary of the Avon. The Early English church here was considered one of the oldest and finest in Devon. The east end and tower and rectory were badly damaged by bombs in 1943. Restoration began in 1948 and reconsecration by the Bishop of Exeter took place on 12 October 1957. Continuing for some three miles and a half, up hill and down dale, **Modbury** is reached. Down to the early years of the nineteenth century it was a place of considerable importance as one of the smaller centres of the Devon woollen industry; its cattle market continued until recent years. Now mainly a residential town and a small shopping centre, it still retains the visible character of a town rather than a village, with much good building of eighteenth-and early nineteenth-century date, including many slate-hung houses of characteristic South Hams type. The church, of early fourteenth-century date, but enlarged in the fifteenth century, has a medieval spire (unusual in Devon), which makes a permanent landmark.

South of Modbury is the village of Bigbury, set well back from the coast, and **Bigbury-on-Sea,** on Bigbury Bay (see p. 167) to which buses run from Plymouth. From Kingsbridge connection is made with this service at Harraton Cross on the Kingsbridge–Plymouth route.

Malborough – Hope – Thurlestone

This excursion will introduce the visitor to the coast line between Bolt Head and the mouth of the Avon. Whether a start is made from Salcombe or Kingsbridge is immaterial; in the former case, the walk can be shortened by making use of the Salcombe–Kingsbridge service which passes through the village of Malborough, as does also the direct Hope bus from Kingsbridge. If the entire walk from Salcombe is intended, the delightful route by way of Bolt Head and Bolt Tail to Hope should be followed (see p. 165), a distance of about 8 miles; this walk can be extended to Kingsbridge, another 5 miles, thence taking bus or boat back to Salcombe. This is not particularly interesting, but a route through the village of **South Milton** – rather picturesque, with an interesting church – and on to the Kingsbridge–Salcombe road to pick up the bus is not unattractive. If the excursion is commenced from Kingsbridge, walkers cannot do better than take the bus to **Malborough,** thus covering an uninteresting piece of road. The village has an old Perpendicular church *(All Saints'),* with a tower and broach spire.

Three miles west of Malborough – passing through the hamlet of **Galmpton** – is the little village of **Hope,** famous for crabs. Years ago, the fisherfolk gained considerable notoriety as smugglers, the village being particularly well situated for contraband trade. Hotel and farmhouse accommodation is available, and some of the cottagers take boarders. Every summer now Hope is visited by admirers of the rugged coast scenery in the vicinity, and good walkers find it an excellent holiday centre. A breakwater has been built for the benefit of the fishermen. The view seaward is very lovely on a clear summer morning. Many

Burgh Island

parts of Devon are famed for the redness of the soil, but at few places is it so gorgeously purple as in the vicinity of Hope.

Hope possesses a variety of coast line, Bolt Tail protecting it from the south and south-west, and from the inn *(car park)* one ascends the crumbling cliffs northwards and down again to the dunes and rock-strewn sands where is the **Thurlestone,** an arched rock of red conglomerate which stands solitary in the centre of the small bay.

From the beach, a sandy paradise for children, one returns to the road leading to the village of **Thurlestone.** Above the village is the 18-hole course of the *Thurlestone Golf Club,* 6,000 yards in length. There is a good club-house with a practice putting green close by. There are also hard and grass tennis courts, with a lawn that is available for bowls or croquet.

From Thurlestone visitors may be recommended to pay a visit to the hamlets of **Buckland** and **Bantham,** at the mouth of the Avon, or the latter may be reached by path along the cliffs or by a path over the intervening down which crosses a small marsh by stepping stones and arrives at the *Sloop Inn* in the village. Bantham Ham protects the mouth of the Avon and has become very popular among motorists. Bathing is popular, but can be very dangerous if warning notices are disregarded. Sailing matches frequently take place in the estuary of the Avon, almost a landlocked lake at high tide, a trickle among the sands at low. Here is a ferry, allowing one either to climb up to the course of the Bigbury-on-Sea Golf Club or continue round to the developing resort of **Bigbury-on-Sea,** if the tide allows, visiting Burgh Island *en route.* The 18-hole course above Bigbury has a pavilion where luncheons and teas may be obtained.

The principal feature of **Burgh Island** is the large modern hotel. A novel feature is the tractor-driven "bus on stilts" by which visitors are conveyed to and from the mainland. *The Pilchards,* an old smugglers' inn, is said to date from the fourteenth century, and is well worth a visit.

Plymouth

Banks. – *Barclays,* Princess Street; *Midland,* Old Town Street; *Lloyds,* Royal Parade; *National Westminster,* St. Andrew's Cross; *Trustee Savings,* Derry's Cross. All have branch offices in various parts of the city.

Beach Huts for hire at Tinside and Pebbleside, Hoe Foreshore and Devil's Point.

Bowls. – Greens at The Hoe, Tothill Park, Central Park, North Down, St. Budeaux, Devonport Park, Victoria Park, Plympton and Dean Cross, Plymstock.

Car Parking. – Meter controlled zone in city centre. Numerous car parks. Certain street parking available in Citadel Road, Hoe Road, Madiera Road, Grand Parade, Radford Road, Pier Street.

Distances. – Bodmin, 30; Dartmouth, 30; Exeter, 42; Kingsbridge, 21; Looe, 19; Torquay, 32; London, 211.

Early Closing Day. – Wednesday.

Fishing. – Excellent sea fishing both from the shore and from boats readily available for hire, the deep-water marks of Eddystone and Hand Deeps being famous. Sea Anglers Club. Open Fishing Festival in August.

Permits for brown trout angling in Burrator Reservoir from Water Department, Municipal Offices.

Golf. – 18-hole courses at Yelverton and Stadden Heights. 9-hole course at Elfordleigh, Plympton. Miniature golf course in Central Park.

Greyhound Racing. – Pennycross Stadium.

Hotels. – *Continental, Mayflower Post House, Duke of Cornwall, Grand, Holiday Inn, San Remo,* and many others of all grades.

Information Centre. – Municipal Offices.

Museum – Art Gallery – Library. – Drake Circus.

Population. – 249,800.

Post Office. – Head Office at St. Andrew's Cross. Branch Offices at Devonport, Derry's Cross, Mutley, Plympton, Plymstock, St. Budeaux, Stonehouse and West Park.

Swimming Pools. – Tinside Open Air Pool, Hoe Road, Mount Wise Pools, Mutton Road, Devonport. Heated indoor pool in Central Park.

Tennis. – Courts at West Hoe Recreation Ground, Freedom Park, Tothill Recreation Ground, Hartley Recreation Ground, Central Park, Devonport Park, Plympton and Plymstock.

The city of Plymouth lies at the mouth of the River Tamar which here forms the boundary between Devon and Cornwall. It faces on to Plymouth Sound, a great expanse of water almost 3 miles square. The city incorporates the formerly separate townships of Devonport, Stonehouse and old Plymouth and with a population of 250,000 is the largest centre in the West Country.

The foreshore is shaped like a great bow and extends for a distance of 7 miles from the point where the river Plym becomes the Cattewater, the old commercial harbour, round the shore of Plymouth Sound and up the Hamoaze, the great naval anchorage, to beyond the fine road bridge across the Tamar.

The Hoe, 120 feet above sea-level, is one of the finest promenades in Europe. The broad asphalted plateau is about a quarter of a mile in length. On the seaward side it slopes down to the rocks which form the barrier of the waters of the Sound, while townwards it drops gently through lawns and gardens fringed with trees. The Sound, as seen from the Hoe, is a constant theatre of maritime activity with all manner of vessels from giant naval warships to tiny rowboats gracefully pursuing their ways. The Hoe is, of course, famous in history for it was here that Drake finished his game of bowls despite the approach of the Spanish Armada.

The **Armada Memorial** is only one of several on the Hoe. The statue of Sir Francis Drake is by Boehm – there is a duplicate at Tavistock. The **Naval War Memorial,** a lofty obelisk designed by Sir Robert Lorimer,

Royal Parade, Plymouth

serves also as a sea mark for ships entering the Sound. On the townward slope is Hoe Park with bowling greens, putting and a teahouse and at the entrance the Town War Memorial.

Smeaton's Lighthouse stands boldly on the grassy slopes. It first stood on the Eddystone rock for a hundred and twenty years before being replaced by the present structure on an adjacent rock. The old lighthouse was taken down and re-erected here. Eastward in a railed enclosure is a beautifully-kept little garden and nearby the **Hoe Theatre,** built in 1962.

The **Citadel** *(open certain times)* is a picturesque fortification built in the time of Charles II. The gateway on the inland side is beautified with fine carving. Much of the original buildings has been replaced and additions made. In front is the **Aquarium** *(weekdays, fee)* of the Marine Biological Association.

Sutton Pool is the ancient harbour of Plymouth, lined with quays and stores. Beyond Phoenix Wharf (ferry to Turnchapel) is the old Barbican, a point of great historic interest. On the West Pier is the famous **Mayflower Stone** commemorating the departure from this spot of the Pilgrim Fathers on 6 September, 1620. There are many quaint old buildings nearby.

In New Street is an interesting **Elizabethan House,** a survival of the sixteenth century which has been restored and furnished according to the period *(weekdays, and Sunday afternoons in summer).*

From the Barbican, Southside Street and High Street lead to Whimple Street and so to **St. Andrew's Church,** the parish church, rebuilt in 1957 after almost total destruction in the war. It has a Piper window of interest.

Of great moment to Plymouth has been the rebuilding of the city centre, wiped out by the devastating air raids of 1941. An ambitious and farseeing plan was evolved and has been carried out speedily and with commendable success. It involved a shopping community surrounded by an inner ring road, well landscaped with gardens and floral displays and permitting a direct pedestrian route, now Armada Way, from the rail centre to the sea. Several traffic-free precincts have been included.

The fine **Guildhall** was badly damaged but a new complex has been built within the old walls, whilst close by are the new Law Courts and the Police Station. Opposite rises the new **Civic Centre,** a mammoth modern building from the roof of which *(daily, fee)* there is a wonderful prospect over the city and water.

Plymouth to Ivybridge and South Brent

The A38 Ashburton road runs eastward from Plymouth via Plympton, Ivybridge and South Brent, skirting the southern borders of Dartmoor.

To the south of the road 2 miles out of the city is–

Saltram House (National Trust: *April–mid October, daily, fee*) standing in a splendidly well-landscaped park with views extending over Plymouth Sound. The Classical façades added in the middle of the eighteenth century hide the remains of a large Tudor house. Within is fine plasterwork and woodwork. Among the contents are fine period furniture, pictures and china.

Plympton, once a village, and now contiguous with the city, is famous as the birthplace of Sir Joshua Reynolds. The old Grammar School where he was educated along with companion artists Northcote, Haydon and Eastlake, is a seventeenth-century building with a fine cloister. The old church is mainly Perpendicular but shows some traces of Early English work and has a fine lofty tower.

Ivybridge lies 6 miles to the west in a beautiful situation and is a good centre from which to make various excursions on to southern Dartmoor.

Ermington, 2 miles to the south above the River Erme, has a church with a thirteenth-century crooked spire and a fine Elizabethan brass.

Harford lies 2½ miles to the north of the village. Here was born John Prideaux, Bishop of Worcester, and in the little Perpendicular church (St. Petrock's) is a memorial erected by him to his parents and family.

Seventeen miles from Plymouth, on the banks of the river Avon, which flows picturesquely over a rocky bed in its short course to the sea in Bigbury Bay, is–

South Brent, a typical moorland town, though its Spring Fair and pony market are of much less importance than formerly. The old weather-beaten church is in the Perpendicular and Decorated styles, with a low Norman tower. There is a fine Norman font, and there are piscinae in the chancel and south transept. Fragments of a former screen are incorporated in the altar rails and form the base of a war memorial.

Plymouth to Tavistock and the North Coast

The A386 Tavistock road leaves Plymouth on the north from its suburb Crownhill, running past Roborough, the Plymouth airfield, and Bickleigh. In 10 miles from the city is **Yelverton** (*see* page 98) where the moorland road strikes north-eastward across to Princetown and Two Bridges.

Two miles to the west of Yelverton is –

Buckland Abbey (National Trust: *Easter to September, daily; in winter on Wednesdays, Saturdays and Sundays, fee*), a thirteenth-century monastic foundation subsequently given by Henry VIII to Sir Richard Grenville, grandfather of Richard Grenville of the "Revenge" and later bought by Sir Francis Drake. It is now a naval and Devon folk museum with Grenville and Drake relics.

Bere Ferrers, a remote village to the south-west on the Tavy estuary, has a beautiful fourteenth-century church with some interesting monuments.

Tavistock

Banks. – *Barclays, Lloyds, Midland, National Westminster, Devon and Exeter Savings.*
Early Closing Day. – Wednesday.
Hotels. – *Bedford, Newmarket, Queen's Head. Cornish Arms.*
Library. – County Library, Bedford Square.
Market Days. – *Cattle,* Wednesdays; *Pannier,* Fridays.
Post Office. – Abbey Place. Sub-office, Ford Street.

Tavistock, with a population of just under 7,000 people, is an ancient market town set astride the River Tavy. At one time it was a stannary town and a seat of the woollen industry. Of its ancient abbey founded in the late tenth century there are few remains. In the town centre buildings of interest include the pinnacled Town Hall, 1860, with some interesting portraits, and the Church, dedicated to St. Eustachius, dating mostly from the fifteenth century. Behind the Town Hall is the market, busy on a Friday. Tavistock's ancient Goose Fair, held on the second Wednesday of October, attracts visitors from many miles around.

North of Tavistock on a by road is the village of **Peter Tavy,** picturesque with a Perpendicular church surrounded by lime trees and with weather-worn embattled western tower. Back on the main road is the sister village of **Mary Tavy** with a similar church with fifteenth-century wagon roof.

Lydford, to the west of the Okehampton road, is well known for its castle, gorge and waterfall, while it also possesses a church of some interest. The castle, of which only the keep remains on an artificial mound, was built about 1150 and as a prison had an unsavoury reputation. The church close by, mainly Perpendicular with traces of Early English work, has a Saxon granite font and a beautiful piscina.

Lydford Gorge (National Trust), a mile west of the main road, lies in a beautifully wooded ravine where the Lyd frets and fumes among great black boulders. The White Lady waterfall has a drop of some 90 feet.

Okehampton

Banks. – *Lloyds, Midland, National Westminster, Devon and Exeter Savings.*
Early Closing Day. – Wednesday.
Fishing. – Trout fishing in East and West Ockment rivers.
Golf. – 18-hole course in Okehampton Park.
Hotels. – *Plume of Feathers, White Hart, Okehampton Motel, Brandize Park.*
Library. – Branch of County Library, Fore Street.
Post Office. – George Street.

Okehampton is situated between the East and West Ockment rivers which unite just below the town. It is the most northerly of the Dart towns and is a good centre for tours and trips in beautiful scenery.

The **Castle** *(open daily, fee)* was dismantled in the time of Henry VIII. It stands on the summit of a rock near the Launceston road, close to the left bank of the West Ockment, about half a mile south-west of the town. The site commands a wide view of the valley. The ruins include a small rectangular keep, part of the outer gate near the river, portions of the great hall with its huge chimney and old baking ovens at the back, and the chapel.

To the south of Okehampton across Okehampton Common are **Yes Tor,** 2,027 feet, and **High Willhays,** which, at 2,038 feet, is the highest peak on Dartmoor.

The A386 continues northward to **Hatherleigh,** where the church has splendid wagon roofs adorned with angels, and on to Great Torrington (page 194) and Bideford (page 183).

Clovelly

Clovelly

Access. – Clovelly is served by buses on the Bideford (11 miles)–Bude route. Services daily throughout the year. The village is also much visited by motor-coaches and, when available, steamers provide a popular service from Ilfracombe and the Bristol Channel ports.

Bank. – *National Westminster,* Mount Pleasant Cottages at the top of the street, the first Thursday in each month, 12–2 p.m. and from July 16 to September 11 every Thursday.

Boating. – Rowing-boats may be hired and motor-launches make trips in the bay.

Car Park. – Near the top of the precipitous street is an extensive public Car Park, including a number of private lock-ups.

Donkeys available for children's rides on the quay only.

Hotels. – *New Inn,* near the top of High Street; *Red Lion,* on the Quay. There are refreshment places which provide tea and light luncheons. Café at top car park. *Other Accommodation:* At farms and cottages in Higher Clovelly and at cottages in Clovelly village. There are three camping and caravan sites in Higher Clovelly.

Population. – 434.

Post Office. – About half-way down the street.

The road from Bideford is along the summit of a ridge sufficiently high to command a succession of extensive views, with the sea away on the right, and on the left the church towers of Parkham and Buckland Brewer. The entrance to the famous Hobby Drive is passed before the steep descent to Clovelly begins. Cars stop on level ground, where an extensive car and coach park has been constructed.

Clovelly has only one street, a steep winding path culminating in a series of wide cobble-paved steps. It was first climbed by car in 1920, but except for a special shuttle service, is now closed to vehicles.

Clovelly, "a village like a waterfall", as Edward Capern called it, has been truly described as a place unlike any other in the country, and this is the secret of its popularity with many visitors. The one street is often so crowded with visitors, in the summer season, as to resemble a queue awaiting entrance at a theatre. Looking down, a narrow torrent of flower-decked cottages is seen, no two exactly alike, either in design or colouring. Flowers bloom everywhere. Giant fuchsias, almost wild, quite cover the fronts of some of the tiny cottages, and the air is so mild that later than at almost any other place in Devon may be seen in flower honeysuckle, hydrangeas, jasmine, camellia, japonica and rhododendrons.

The descent is at times so steep that the base of one cottage is on a level with the roof of its neighbour.

Far below is the strongly built stone **quay,** constructed by George Cary, whose family held the manor as far back as the reign of Richard II. At the harbour is a Lifeboat House. Boating may be enjoyed from the sheltered harbour. The water is exceptionally clear.

Back on the cliff-top, at what may be called the entrance to Clovelly, is **Clovelly Church.** Dedicated to All Saints, it is an ancient structure of mixed architecture. There is a lych gate, a rebuilt Norman porch, and a low embattled west tower. While Rectors of Clovelly cannot be traced further back than the thirteenth century, an ancient font of Saxon design, and other marks, suggest that a church has stood here for a thousand years. A sundial is dated 1678, but the register dates from a few years later, 1686. Within the Communion rails is a brass, dated 1540, representing a knight of the period, with the request, "Praye for the soule of Walter Robert Cary, Esquire".

A curious Cary memorial is to be seen on the window sill in the north side of the chancel, a square brass, depicting a skeleton holding a spade, commemorating the young daughter of Dr. George Cary who died in 1655. A brass on the left of the little chancel commemorates Charles Kingsley's association with Clovelly. The old peal of four bells was increased to five in 1900, and in 1905 a sixth was added. The latest bell bears the inscription: "Ring out, ye bells of Clovelly". A fine avenue of yews leads to the porch.

Close to the church is **Clovelly Court,** a former mansion on the site having been occupied by the Carys. At the lodge entrance is an inscription, "Go North, Go South, Go East, Go West; Home's Best".

The **Hobby Drive.** On weekdays only during the season, cars are allowed to proceed through the Drive, one way only, entering from the Bideford–Bude road. The fee charged includes parking at the end of the Drive near the top of Clovelly village.

The Hobby Drive is so named because its construction was the hobby of its projector, Sir J. H. Williams. The entrance from the Clovelly road is on the right, at Hobby Lodge, a mile beyond Bucks Cross, or eight miles from Bideford, and Clovelly itself can be reached by this route. The three-mile drive winds through the thickly wooded combes to the east of Clovelly, and presents a succession of exquisite views between trees.

Mount Pleasant is the open space at the top of the street, opposite the entrance to the Hobby Drive on one side and the Yellery Gate entrance to the grounds of Clovelly Court on the other. It was presented to the National Trust for the use of the public. From it are fine views over the Bay.

Clovelly Dykes are three ancient encampments, each with its own vallum and ditch, close to the junction of the Bideford–Hartland road and the road to Clovelly village. The outer embankment surrounds an area of some 30 acres. There is a splendid view from the highest point.

Bucks Mills

Bucks Mills is the collection of little white houses which may be seen from the Clovelly Quay, 3 miles to the east, perched in a seemingly precarious position on the cliffs. It is an increasingly popular but secluded seaside resort, of somewhat the same type as Clovelly, but has a small sandy beach, safe bathing and cars can go down to the village. At low tide Bucks Mills may be reached by walking along the shore, from which can be seen tumbling from cliff to beach the **Freshwater Cascade** which originally flowed through Clovelly, but now adds to the countless attractions of the Hobby Drive.

175 *Clovelly Cove*

Clovelly main street

Bucks Mills is 7 miles from Bideford, and is reached via Bucks Cross from the main road by delightfully wooded road.

The church is beautifully placed in the wooded valley, a hundred yards or so below the cross-roads at Bucks Cross in a position almost carved out of the rock. Although Victorian in origin it contains some fine furnishings and fittings.

About a mile and a half south-west of Bucks Cross is the village of Woolsery, or **Woolfardisworthy West,** to give it its correct name. There is an inn, and set at 600 feet above sea-level the village provides some extensive views, particularly in the direction of Dartmoor. Its church (All Hallows'), originally Norman, has a fine Norman porch and font, and some interesting bench-ends, including an unmutilated crucifixion. On its Cole memorial some of the original colouring is still to be seen.

Gallantry Bower and Mouth Mill

The walk here is again through private property. The entrance, called the *Yellery Gate,* is at the top of Clovelly village, on the right. The footpath passes in sight of Clovelly Court. Or from the harbour the turning by the *Red Lion Hotel* leads up to Clovelly Park Gates. A two-mile walk from here leads to the bower.

Gallantry Bower is the inappropriate name bestowed on a huge cliff of 400 feet, almost perpendicular and wonderfully smooth. Peeps at the cliff are easily obtainable by following the right path to one or two view-points at the side. The path continues across a common-like expanse and by a zig-zag descends to the entrance gate to **The Wilderness,** affording fine views of Gallantry Bower. Then it ascends to a cliff nearly as high and just as perpendicular, overlooking the little bay at **Mouth Mill,** a charming dell opening on to the sea, with a gorgeous background of sloping hills clothed with semi-tropical luxuriance. It can be reached by the road just below the entrance gate of The Wilderness. Of course, there is a stream, which bubbles a noisy course through the wood, races joyfully through the open vale, and is quietly swallowed by the ocean. The rocks at Mouth Mill are stupendous. The walk up the combe, through a fairyland of ferns, trees and stream, is recommended, and a more lovely place for walk or picnic it would be hard to find.

Mouth Mill to Hartland Point

The distances are: Hartland Point and the Lighthouse, 4 miles from Mouth Mill, with a return road to Clovelly of about 7 or 8 miles.

After mounting, by a very stiff climb, the cliff on the west side corresponding to the cliff descended from Gallantry Bower, another ravine must be crossed. Next comes **Windbury Head,** on which are some earthworks. Then **Exmansworthy Cliff,** 100 feet higher than Gallantry Bower, is crossed. The **Chapman Rocks** are next passed, then **Fatacott Cliff** – the highest point on this part of the coast. A mile beyond Chapman Rocks is **Shipload Bay,** the only place hereabouts where it is possible to descend to the shore. It is sheltered and bathing is possible. On the right, when looking towards the sea, will be seen the peculiarly contorted rocks of **Eldern Point.** Further progress along the cliff path is prevented by a Services station on Titchberry Cliff and it is necessary to turn inland through **Titchberry Farm** (National Trust) by the road which leads in 3 miles to Hartland Town. Turn right shortly after the farm and the way is clear for a mile to **Hartland Point** (325 feet high) and the Lighthouse. On the way to the Point turn right through a gate for *Blagdon Farm,* a few yards beyond which is a car park. The Lighthouse is about 500 yards on from the gates.

From the Lighthouse the road inland leads to Hartland Town, whence the return to Clovelly can be made or the cliff path continued to Hartland Quay, 3 miles, the direction being due south, passing Blackmouth.

Hartland

The parish of Hartland, extending over a considerable area, is the second largest in the county. The small town is 14 miles from Bideford and 3½ miles from Clovelly. As the western limit of Devon is approached the coast-line assumes a rougher and bolder character. The scenery is indeed magnificent and the district is very popular for walking and camping.

Hartland Town

Access. – By the Bideford and Bude bus service. By coaches from Bideford, Bude, etc.
Banks. – *Lloyds, Barclays.*
Hotels. – *King's Arms; Hartland Quay.*
Inns. – *Anchor* and *New Inn.*

Hartland Town, or Harton, was once an important borough larger than the Bideford of Elizabeth's time, but the railways which brought trade to the others did not reach Hartland, and the sweeping away of its harbour in 1870 was a final blow. Its charter, dated 1285, has lapsed, and the port reeve and burgesses no longer exist, but the Town Trust holds the property of the defunct corporation. The Town Hall has vanished and on its site was built, in 1839, St. John's Chapel-of-Ease. In the tower is the Town Clock removed here from the Town Hall. It is the oldest clock in North Devon and one of the earliest pendulum clocks in the country. It was made by John Morcombe of Barnstaple in 1622.

Westwards, midway between Hartland Town and the Church of St. Nectan's, and situated in a romantic valley, is little **Bow Bridge.** It affords a most pleasing view of the Abbey, with its surrounding woodland.

Those visiting the church from Hartland Town can make a part of their trip circular by including this bridge in the walk.

Hartland Abbey *(the occasional open days are announced in the local press)* is a mansion built on the site and incorporating the cloisters of an abbey bounded as a house of Austin Canons in the reign of Henry II (1154–89), by Geoffrey de Dinham. This in turn had replaced a college of secular canons established here in the eleventh century, in connection with the Church of St. Nectan, by Gytha, wife of Earl Godwin, and the mother of Harold, as a thankoffering to St. Nectan for the preservation of her husband from shipwreck.

Hartland

St. Nectan's Church lies 2 miles west of Hartland Town at **Stoke,** a part of Hartland parish between the town and the Quay, which is about a mile farther. The church replaced, about 1350, an early eleventh-century building. It was restored in 1848, and further extensively repaired in the period 1925–35. The tower, 128 feet high, including pinnacles, contains six bells. From many a long mile away it is seen on the skyline in spite of high hills around; consequently the view from the top (not a difficult ascent) is extensive. On the east wall is a large figure representing St. Nectan, and near the church is a well bearing his name. The most treasured possession of the church is its nobly proportioned fifteenth-century screen, lavish and ornate, and displaying fine workmanship.

Just beyond the lych gate is the old Church House, a fine fifteenth-century building granted by Henry VIII to Sir William Abbot in 1545.

Hartland Quay is about a mile westward of Stoke Church. The few buildings are not seen until one is almost at the cliff edge. A road and pathway descend steeply to the rocks below. There is a small beach for bathing. But for the hotel (*Hartland Quay* with its swimming pool) and a few houses, the Quay would be more name than reality.

Hartland Quay to Hartland Point (3 miles). At the top of the steep hill behind the hotel is a building containing lifesaving rocket apparatus. Beside this is a stile which cross and proceed along the cliffs, passing the ruins of a stone-built summer house. **Blackpool Mill** *(Beachmouth)* soon comes in sight. The mill has vanished, but the Mouth at all seasons is a place of wonder. In rough weather the scene is one of wild grandeur; in calm, of quiet loveliness. A little bridge crosses

Hartland Quay

the stream which flows from the valley down through the Mouth. About a hundred yards below the bridge is a cascade.

The path to Hartland Point will be seen creeping up the steep north side of the Mouth. The path continues along the cliff top, passing **Damehole Point.** The **Cow and Calf** rocks jutting out to sea and the rocks nearer the Point are a magnificent sight.

Hartland Point, a fine, bold headland, 325 feet high, forms the north-western extremity of the county and affords the finest coast view–both ways–in North Devon. On a clear day it is possible to see eastward to Morte Point, 20 miles, and to the west as far as Trevose Head, 40 miles. Lundy lies off shore 10 miles to the north-west, and the coast of Wales is discernible 40 miles to the north. The cliff scenery is very grand.

At the top of the headland is a coastguard station which keeps a 24-hour watch on the coast and may be visited. The station maintains radio contact with Lundy and lifeboats when in operation. It is also a meteorological recording and observation station and Lloyds Signal station.

On a plateau below, but 120 feet above sea-level, stands the **Lighthouse** *(Open to visitors daily, except Sundays, from* 1 *p.m.)*. Every 15 seconds the lantern gives six flashes, visible nearly 20 miles. Beside the lighthouse gates is a curious cemented slope. Until quite recently this served, as a rain water catchment, as the sole water supply for the lighthouse.

Hartland Bay to Bude by the Cliffs. This is a favourite route for enthusiastic walkers, for the scenery is magnificent and the travelling not really difficult when one gets used to the deep combes intersecting the coastline. As the crow flies Bude is some 12 miles from Hartland, but the numerous indentations of the cliffs and the diversions necessary in getting into and out of combes increase the walking distance to close on 30 miles; the going is hard (especially in windy weather) so that only really hardy walkers should aim to cover the whole distance in a day. Hartland to Morwenstow is a very good day's work for those to whom walking is less a business than a pleasure.

A little south of Hartland Quay is St. Catherine Tor (locally Cattern Tor) on which are fragments of the foundations of a fourteenth-century chapel. Farther south is **Speke's Mouth Waterfall,** where a good trout stream ends in a fine waterfall over the cliff. From Speke's Mouth it is a good 3 miles to **Welcombe,** a parish of hamlets most appropriately named, as it is the first the visitor reaches on entering Devon from the Cornish side. The surrounding scenery is very attractive, and those seeking a restful holiday with the best of sea and country air, would do well to make a note of this hospitable spot. Several farmhouses offer good accommodation. Close by may be found the source of the rivers Torridge and Tamar. They rise about 5 miles from the sea and flow nearly 50 miles before reaching the ocean on opposite sides of the county.

The valley south of Welcombe ends in **Marshland Mouth,** a beautiful combe which with its stream helps to divide Cornwall from Devon.

The Quay, Bideford

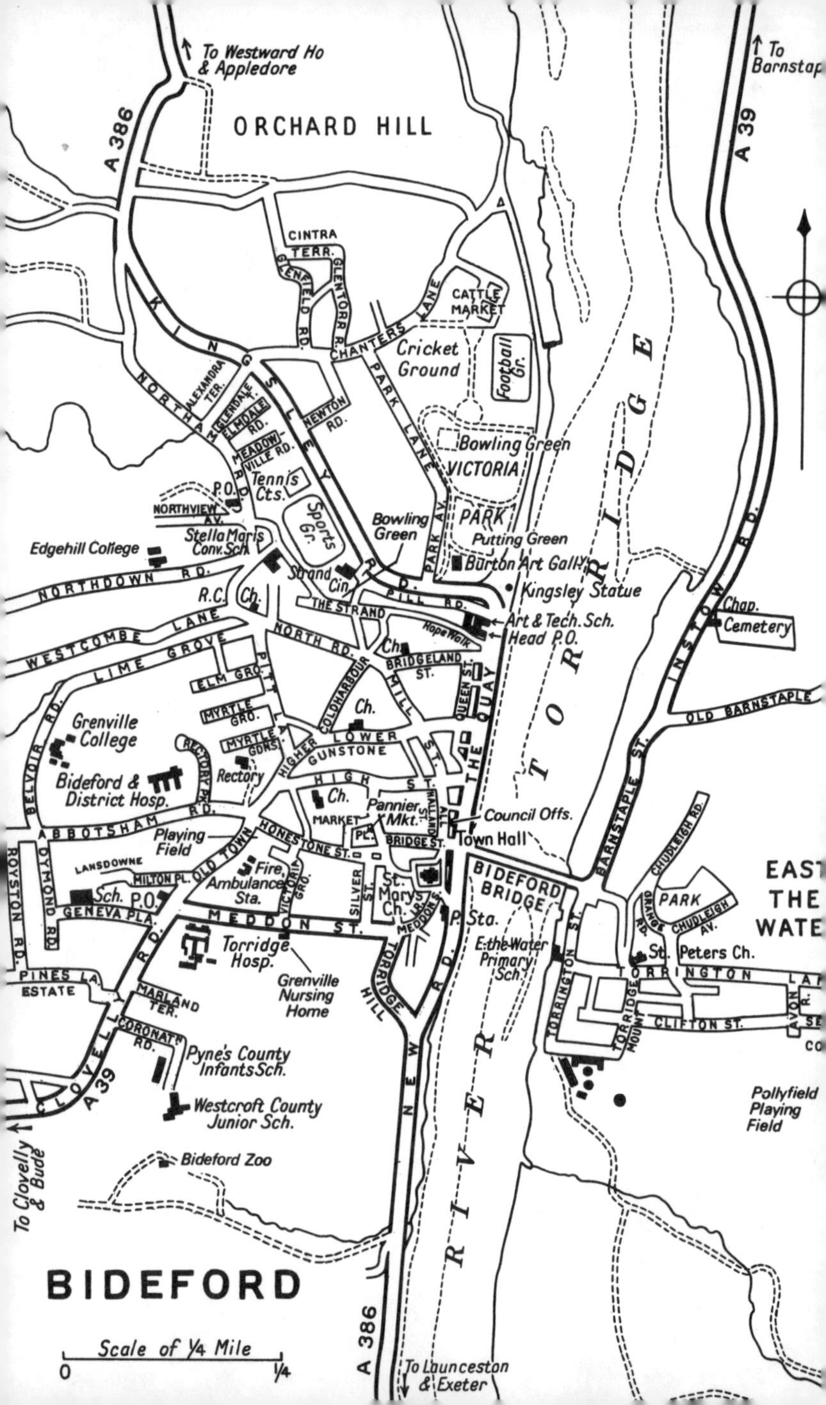
BIDEFORD
Scale of 1/4 Mile
0
1/4
To Westward Ho & Appledore
To Barnstaple
ORCHARD HILL
A 386
A 39
CINTRA TERR.
GLENFIELD RD.
GLENTORR RD.
CHANTERS LANE
CATTLE MARKET
Cricket Ground
Football Gr.
PARK LANE
KINGSLEY RD.
NORTHAM RD.
ALEXANDRA TER.
GLENDALE TER.
ELMDALE RD.
MEADOW VILLE RD.
NEWTON RD.
Bowling Green
VICTORIA PARK
Tennis Cts.
Sports Gr.
P.O.
NORTHVIEW AV.
Stella Maris Conv. Sch.
Edgehill College
PARK AV.
Putting Green
Burton Art Gall'y
Kingsley Statue
Strand Cin.
NORTHDOWN RD.
R.C. Ch.
THE STRAND
PILL RD.
Art & Tech. Sch.
Head P.O.
Hope Walk
WESTCOMBE LANE
NORTH RD.
Ch.
BRIDGELAND ST.
LIME GROVE
PITT LA.
ELM GRO.
MYRTLE GRO.
MYRTLE GDNS.
COLDHARBOUR
MILL ST.
QUEEN ST.
THE QUAY
RIVER TORRIDGE
Grenville College
Bideford & District Hosp.
RECTORY PK.
Rectory
HIGHER GUNSTONE
LOWER GUNSTONE
HIGH ST.
BELVOIR RD.
ABBOTSHAM RD.
Playing Field
MARKET
Pannier Mkt.
MALLAND ST.
ALL
PL.
BRIDGE ST.
Council Offs.
Town Hall
HONESTONE ST.
OLD TOWN
Fire, Ambulance Sta.
VICTORIA GRO.
SILVER ST.
St. Marys Ch.
BIDEFORD BRIDGE
LANSDOWNE
MILTON PL.
Sch.
P.O.
GENEVA PLA.
DYMOND RD.
ROYSTON RD.
MEDDON ST.
MEDDON ST.
P. Sta.
Torridge Hosp.
Grenville Nursing Home
TORRIDGE HILL
NEW RD.
E. the Water Primary Sch.
PINES LA. ESTATE
MARLAND TER.
CORONAT'N RD.
CLOVELLY RD.
Pyne's County Infants Sch.
Westcroft County Junior Sch.
Bideford Zoo
To Clovelly & Bude
To Launceston & Exeter
INSTOW RD.
Chap.
Cemetery
OLD BARNSTAPLE
BARNSTAPLE ST.
CHUDLEIGH RD.
PARK
GRANGE RD.
CHUDLEIGH AV.
EAST THE WATE
St. Peters Ch.
TORRINGTON ST.
TORRINGTON LA
TORRIDGE MOUNT
CLIFTON ST.
AVON R.
Pollyfield Playing Field

Bideford

Banks. – *Lloyds, Midland, National Westminster, Barclays,* in High Street; *Devon and Exeter.* Grenville Street.
Boating. – Rowing- and sailing-boats for hire. The pull up-river to Weare Giffard with the tide is recommended. The river is wide enough to sail without difficulty. Two rowing clubs. Annual regatta first week in September.
Bowls. – Bowling Club with excellent green in the Strand. Annual Open Tournament commencing first Monday in August. Municipal green in Victoria Park.
Buses. – To Barnstaple, Instow, Ilfracombe, Northam, Westward Ho!, Appledore, Clovelly, Hartland, Bude, Torrington, Okehampton, Plymouth, Exeter, etc. Services start at The Quay.
Cinema. – Kingsley Road.
Distances. – Barnstaple, 9; Bude, 26; Clovelly, 12; Hartland Town, 14; Ilfracombe, 20; London, 204; Torrington, 7.
Early Closing. – Wednesday.
Fishing. – Trout fishing in the Gammaton and Jennetts reservoirs.
Both Taw and Torridge are good for trout and occasional salmon (Devon River Authority licence required).
Below the bridge large mullet can be taken and at Appledore there is good sea fishing. Bass are plentiful.
Hotels. – *Royal, Fisherman's Cot, Durrant House, New Inn, Ring O'Bells, Kingsley, Edelweiss, Yeoldon House.*
Library, Museum, etc. – Public Library at Municipal Buildings. Burton Art Gallery, Victoria Park.
Market Days. – Tuesday and Saturday. Cattle market on Tuesdays.
Parking Places. – On the Quay, north of bridge, and adjoining Kingsley Road, charge. Free parking at Riverbank and south of bridge.
Population. – 12.610.
Tennis. – Municipal hard courts at Kingsley Road.

Bideford's lovely position on the Torridge is one of its chief glories. It derives its name from "Byda's ford" (Byda, or Bidna was a landowner here in Anglo-Saxon times), on what was then a very important highway along the coast from Cornwall through Devon into Somerset. During excavations on the eastern side of Bideford, a paved footway, 12 feet in width, presumed to be part of the old Roman fosseway, was discovered.

For those who love a town possessing a real life of its own instead of existing merely as a show place, Bideford has a wonderful attraction. It seems to be an epitome of English history. Quay and Bridge, and the ford it replaced, have seen the development of transport from dugouts through the brave little ships that harried the Armada to modern steamers and lovely yachts – from pack animals to stream-lined cars. But Bideford does not live on its memories – market, bridge and river are still busy. Indeed, the bridge, which one almost feels is a sentient being with its long history and manifold possessions, must be faintly surprised at traffic lights and the constant roll of wheels. The river, too, in which almost free anchorage was granted as a reward for the provision of Armada boats, has generally plenty of shipping lying in its hospitable harbours.

Bideford Bridge. The bridge across the Torridge is one of Bideford's proudest possessions. The picturesque structure is 677 feet long and consists of 24 arches of differing widths. It connects East-the-Water and Bideford proper. As a promenade it is very popular for, from it, there is a fine view towards Instow at high tide on a summer's day, especially when some shipping is using the fairway. A ford here was first replaced by a bridge near the end of the thirteenth century. It was, of course, of wood and had two chapels upon it with a large cross in the centre. It was superseded by a stone bridge about two hundred years later. Originally very narrow, it has been widened several times and was virtually reconstructed in 1923–5. In 1969 two arches collapsed but the damage has been made good.

At the west end of the Bridge and facing it on the right is the **Bridge Hall,** which in 1882 supplanted a hall built in 1757. On the left are the **Municipal Buildings,** comprising the Town Hall, the Public Library and Museum. The Court Room is embellished with the Granville Arms, whilst the Council Chamber exhibits the Borough Arms executed in beautiful tapestry. In the Chamber is a valuable silver ship presented by Sir Basil Peto, Bart., in commemoration of the restoration to Bideford of the title and dignity of Port in August 1928. Adjoining the Town Hall is the **Library** and **Museum.** Bideford was one of the first towns in the west to adopt the Public Library system, a proportion of the necessary funds having been given by the late Andrew Carnegie. Among the objects of local interest in the Museum are an Armada chest, the old parish stocks and some good examples of Bideford pottery.

The Parish Church (St. Mary's) stands on the site of a Saxon church replaced by a Norman structure (in 1259) which, with the exception of the tower, the font, the tomb of Sir Thomas Grenville and the monument to John Strange, a notable mayor of Bideford, gave place to the present modern Gothic building in 1865. The font, of late Norman work, is a circular bowl divided into eight panels framed in cable twist. The Grenville chantry, with the tomb of the founder, Sir Thomas Graynfyld (Grenville), died 1513, is in the south transept. Very interesting is the representation of medieval armour. In the south aisle, at its eastern end, is a brass erected by the Rev. Roger Granville, one-time rector, in memory of the gallant Sir Richard Grenville, who commanded the little *Revenge.* On it is inscribed the great sailor's memorable farewell.

The **Quay** runs northward from the bridge and the municipal buildings. It has been several times widened, and a broadening of the road on the south side of the bridge and building of a promenade on the bank provides with the quay a good half mile of riverside parade. It is a broad promenade, tree-sheltered on one side, shops and private residences lining the other. On the upper wall of the former *Ship Inn* is painted an inscription marking the building as "Where the Brotherhood of the Rose was founded". At different times the inn bore the names of *The Blue Anchor* and the *Newfoundland Inn* but the whole building has long since been put to other uses. Part is now in use as a restaurant. There is provision for car parking and buses and coaches start from here. At the north end is a *Statue of Charles Kingsley* and nearby a large **car park.**

In Kingsley Road and backing on to Victoria Park is the **Burton Art Gallery**. The building was gifted to the Corporation for housing the pic-

The Torridge and Bridge, Bideford

tures and art treasures given to the town by the late H. Coop R.B.A., but the collections have since been added to. Temporary exhibitions are held under the auspices of the Arts Council of Great Britain.

Between Kingsley Road and the river is **Victoria Park** a pleasant recreation ground converted out of many acres of marshland. A section is attractively laid out as a park, and there is a large open space for sport. There are an 18-hole putting course, bowling green, swings and other playground equipment. The whole is bounded by a pleasant riverside walk, provided with seats, along a beautiful avenue. The view from this walk embraces the river and the hills as far down as Instow; on the other hand is the ancient bridge.

By the bandstand in the park are eight ancient guns, commonly called the **Armada Guns**. At one time they were used as mooring posts but were removed here when the quay was widened in 1889. Though their origin is not known with certainty, they are unquestionably very old and of foreign make.

From Kingsley's Statue, three thoroughfares connected with him run inland, **Kingsley Road**, part of a useful by-pass for Northam, Appledore and Westward Ho!, the **Strand**, and **Bridgeland Street**. In the Strand is the **Stella Maris Convent School**. The older part of the school, Kingsley Hall, then known as North Down House, was at one time Sir Charles Kingsley's home, and where he wrote part of *Westward Ho!*

The broad **Bridgeland Street** was the site of tobacco warehouses when Bideford merchants were engaged in prosperous trading with Virginia. Many of their fine houses remain unspoiled. It is in this street that Kingsley places the home of Rose Salterne.

The **Masonic Hall**, adjoining the United Reformed Church, is said to occupy the site of the house, if it is not the house itself, in which Rose's father entertained Don Guzman and reminded Amyas of the oath taken when the Brotherhood of the Rose was founded. There is a fine old brick-fronted house with the original lead gutter-pipes dated 1685.

From the upper end of Bridgeland Street **Mill Street** goes southwards. At No. 28, opposite the line of Bridgeland Street, lived Edward Capern, the postman-poet, and in an upper room Charles Kingsley conducted for some time an Art Class for young men.

Mill Street runs into the lower end of High Street, across which is the short and narrow **Allhalland Street** named after the thirteenth-century chapel of Allhallows which once stood at the west end of the bridge. At its end, a house now the Headquarters of the Church Lad's Brigade, and formerly the *Castle Inn*, is said to have been for some time the residence of Sir Richard Grenville. Allhalland Street leads to the foot of **Bridge Street**. At its upper end is the **Market House**, which, like that at Barnstaple, accommodates a Pannier Market and has butchers' shops alongside it on each side of a covered way.

On the other side of the river, opposite the bridge, is that part of Bideford known as **East-the-Water**. Crowning the hill behind the *Royal Hotel* is **Chudleigh Fort**, a small castellated erection which, when of service, commanded the river approaches to the town. It was one of two forts built by Major-General Chudleigh, when Barnstaple and Bideford declared for the Parliament against the King. In 1919 it was purchased by public subscription as a site for the **War Memorial**, and the ground was laid out as a public park, affording beautiful and extensive views. The other fort was built on the opposite side of the river. It has always been referred to as the Appledore Fort, but its site is conjectural.

The River Torridge,

one of Bideford's chief attractions, with its beautiful curves between wooded cliffs, rises a few miles only from the sea, close to the source of the Tamar, near Hartland. At Hatherleigh it receives the waters of the *Okement*, and in the form of a large loop it wanders for 53 miles, until at Appledore it joins the *Taw*, which flows from Dartmoor to Barnstaple and enters the sea at Barnstaple Bar. The great width of the Torridge, except at low water, renders sailing most enjoyable. Rowing also is very popular. By carefully watching the tide and selecting the right time, excursions can be made with the current each way. The trip to Weare Giffard and back is about 10 miles, with the perfection of river scenery. There is no great depth of water at Weare Giffard, but enough for ordinary requirements. Care should be taken to avoid shoals. Down-stream, Appledore and Instow may be visited.

The Bideford District

Bideford is excellent as a centre for exploring North-west Devon. There are charming walks in the vicinity, numerous boat trips, and the larger resorts farther afield including Ilfracombe, Lynton, Exmoor, Exeter and Dartmoor are easily reached.

Of the walks the shortest is that to –

Northam

Centre of an urban district which embraces Appledore and Westward Ho!, Northam is situated 1¾ miles north of Bideford. The **Kingsley Road** from the north end of Bideford Quay is part of the by-pass which rejoins the old road about midway between Bideford and Northam.

The little town has a few quaint old houses. One medieval building in the Square was in use as an Infants School for over a hundred years. At the cross-roads is the *War Memorial* and near it is a drinking trough in memory of fallen war horses. The **Church**, a very fine stone building in the Decorated and Early Perpendicular styles, was completely restored between 1849 and 1865. On one of the pillars is the inscription, "This Yele (aisle) was made Anno 1593". The tower, 109 feet high, has a peal of eight bells cast 1553, recast in 1770 and again in 1920. The register of baptisms dates from 1538, of marriages from 1606, and of burials from 1541.

Close to the church is **Bone Hill**, a public space affording fine views and crowned by a cairn of Westward Ho! pebbles and inscribed to naval men. A covered shelter has been erected here in memory of the late Mr. Strachan Carnegie, a local resident and cousin of the late Andrew Carnegie.

Appledore

Access. – Via Northam. Or by a pleasant riverside walk of 3½ miles from Bideford Quay. By boat from Bideford or by ferry from Instow.

Hotels. – *Royal, Grand, Bradbourne House, Rising Sun, Seagate, Prince of Wales.*

One of the most beautiful walks in the district is that by the river bank from Bideford to Appledore (3½ miles). The way from the Quay is past Victoria Park and continues by the waterside to Cleavehouses, where the path, after turning up a narrow lane, winds through lovely woods, enchanting glimpses of the river being obtained through the trees. In places

Appledore

the path reaches a considerable height, with fine views of Westleigh nestling among the trees on the other bank and Instow close to the water's edge.

Appledore, called by Kingsley the "little white fishing village", is a delightful unspoilt natural village situated at the junction of the beautiful Taw and Torridge estuaries. The views from the Quay and from West Appledore take in the North Devon cliffs extending to Hartland point in the west, the beautiful solitary Braunton Burrows to the north-east and the delightful, friendly village of Instow just across the estuary (ferry available).

The village has narrow streets with many picturesque old houses and cottages, some of which date from Elizabethan times and some having sail lofts reminding us of Appledore's maritime and essential fishing village origin.

The cottages are everywhere colour washed in a variety of colours and form a picturesque whole. The Quay itself has been widened and forms the centre of the village. Salmon fishing has been carried on in the estuary since Saxon days and provides great interest for visitors. Fishing for bass between Appledore "Pool" and the Bar is also popular.

Car parking is permitted along the Quay and a public car park is also available.

Visitors bringing dinghies and small craft can leave them on the public Boat Park (free) situated right on the Quay and convenient free slipways are close at hand. Appledore is a wonderful place in which to spend a boating holiday and trips can be taken out to sea and up towards Bideford. Water skiing is also engaged in by its devotees. A regatta is held in August.

Westward Ho!

Access. – By road *via* Northam, 3 miles from Bideford (bus). By road and footpath about 2 miles. Signposts point the way. The path starts on Raleigh Hill.
Distances. – Bideford, 3; London, 207.
Golf. – *Royal North Devon Golf Club*, 18 holes.
Hotels. – *Youngaton, Grenville Arms, Belle Vue, Aguella* (guest), *Eastburrow Lodge* (guest), *Sea View* (guest), *Dunnington* (guest).
Population. – 2,192.
Putting. – Two 18-hole greens adjoining tennis courts and on Promenade.
Tennis. – Three hard courts on Golf Links Road. Also courts available to public at Golden Bay Hotel.

With its natural advantages, it is remarkable that Westward Ho!, except for its well-deserved reputation in golfing circles, remained so long in the background. It has now become much more popular, the provision of additional accommodation, a rising interest in golf, and magnificent sands being contributory factors. There is fine surf bathing from the superb sands which stretch for 3 miles, or one may take a dip in the Pools, natural places in the rocks which have been adapted for swimming. A suntrap swimming bath is open to the public. A café adjoins.

A protective sea wall has been built and stone breakwaters erected. The Recreation Ground overlooking the beach has a putting green, tennis courts and cricket ground. There is ample parking for cars and full facilities for camping are provided, while bungalows and holiday chalets may be hired furnished. A large holiday centre has been established, its 12-acre site affording ample space for tennis, putting and children's playgrounds, dance hall and indoor amusements.

The name, Westward Ho! was given, after Charles Kingsley's famous novel, in 1863, when the Countess of Portsmouth attended a foundation-stone laying ceremony and much was hoped of the "settlement". However, things seemed to go contrary. The Kingsley Memorial College did not last; the tide washed away the pier and some houses as well; and many years ago the United Services College was removed nearer London. It was in this college when on its original site that Rudyard Kipling was educated, and he rendered it famous by the exploits of *Stalky & Co*. In 1927 the cliffs which he explored as a boy were named in his honour the **Kipling Tors**. In 1937 they were passed to the National Trust. The College buildings are let as flats and now bear the name of Kipling Terrace. The gymnasium has been converted into a Badminton and Dance Hall. At No. 1 is the *Kipling Guest House*.

The **Pebble Ridge**, the most distinctive feature of Westward Ho!, is the great ridge about 2 miles long, 50 feet wide, and 20 feet high, composed of smooth, oval, grey stones, varying from 2 feet to a few inches in diameter.

It is supposed that each of these pebbles was once a piece of rock torn from the Hartland cliffs by the waves, worn smooth in transit, and finally deposited, after miles of wandering, on the beach of Westward Ho! On one side it slopes steeply to the turf of the Burrows; on the other at a less inclination to a broad area of sand. In this form it stretches from the cliffs to a point opposite the bar of the rivers, but once within the influence of this obstruction it loses its character as a ridge and the pebbles lie heaped upon sloping sandhills. It is not safe to walk on the sandbank leading out to the Bar, nor to bathe in the estuary.

Protected by the Pebble Ridge are the famous golf links of the **Royal North Devon Golf Club**. These links are the chief glory of Westward Ho! and many players, amateur and professional, maintain that they are unexcelled in the south or west of England.

Abbotsham Cliffs

The cliffs are about 4 miles westward of Bideford and 1½ miles south-west from Westward Ho! It is an enjoyable walk from Bideford; the bus can be taken to Abbotsham cross-roads, some half a mile south of the village of **Abbotsham** (Abbot's Ham – the ham or homestead of the Abbot of Tavistock in 1086).

The **Parish Church** (St. Helen's), an ancient structure in the Early English style, was restored in 1870. It was built between 1250 and 1275 and contains the Norman font from the original church which was sited on Puse Hill in a field still named Chapel Field. The principal features of the interior of the church are a monument to Anthony Hony dated 1639 and Latin inscribed to the effect that he was "sweet by nature as also by name", beautifully carved bench-ends, and a screen, constructed in 1912 from oak taken from the belfry. An unbroken list of Vicars from 1285 appears on a board in the chancel wall.

The **Cliffs** can be reached by going through the village, taking the lane on the right past the Post Office, taking the first turn to the right in this lane, joining a road coming in on the right and going left soon after, continuing to the lodge of Abbotsham Court, close to which a gate gives access to a narrow lane eventually leading to the cliffs. A very beautiful view is obtained.

Instow

Access. – By road, or river from Bideford, from which it is 3 miles north-east, or by ferry from Appledore.

Hotels. – *Marine, Commodore.*
Youth Hostel. – Worlington House.

A splendid stretch of firm sand makes Instow an ideal place for children. The bathing from the beach is quite safe. Bass fishing is popular. Sailing is delightful in the wide reaches of the breezy Torridge, and boats, with experienced men in charge, may be hired. The North Devon Yacht Club has its headquarters in a picturesque house on the quay, adjoining which is the Marine Hotel. Water ski-ing is popular off the beach.

For years Instow has been popular with artists, because of its abundance of subjects on land and sea. There are picturesque vessels lying in the Pool or on the foreshore at Appledore; there is the wide Torridge with green banks and Bideford in the distance. In the early morning sun particularly the grey-roofed white houses of Appledore in the middle distance contrasting with green background and the occasional red tiles and the red hulls of boats at the quayside is a charming sight.

The Sands, Instow

The effect of solitude in the north, with the mouth of the Taw and lowlands of Braunton, and the lovely stretch of Instow sands in the foreground, is heightened by the lonely Braunton Lighthouse. Beyond the confluence of the two rivers the great waves of the Atlantic roll over the bar, and in the far distance mysterious Lundy, over 20 miles away, lies like a huge flat tableland against the horizon. Over Appledore the eye follows the dim, dark blue line of coast past Clovelly and Gallantry Bower to Hartland Point, with the Lighthouse, like a dot, at the foot. On a clear evening the lights of Lundy and Hartland are well seen.

Instow Quay, though not large, is substantially built. Dating from about 1620, it was erected by Sir John Speccot, then Lord of the Manor. It makes a convenient landing for ferry passengers from Appledore, but, except at high tide, a long stretch of sand must be crossed. This ferry is most useful for anyone staying at Instow, as it brings Westward Ho! and the Pebble Ridge within easy reach.

At intervals along the front are sedate rows of green-shuttered white houses with pleasant gardens.

Instow is the headquarters of the North Devon Cricket Club, with an attractive pavilion and finely situated ground.

The name Instow signifies John's Place (In or Jn = John and "stow" = place).

The **Church**, dedicated to St. John the Baptist, is an ancient Gothic structure, restored in 1875. It has an embattled west tower, and contains some interesting memorials. It stands at the approach to **Instow Town**, inland from the main road. Its direction is indicated by a finger-post, about three-quarters of a mile north of the quay and 5¾ miles south-west of Barnstaple.

The view from the churchyard is superb.

A still more extensive view is obtained from Worlington, a hamlet perched on the hill, reached by taking the lane almost opposite the church. From here a magnificent panorama is unfolded, over miles of hill, river, dunes and sea.

On the inner road at Instow is the small All Saints' Chapel, a delightful building in the Italian style, built by Mr. N. Orphoot, a local architect, in memory of his wife.

Less than a mile south of the quay is Tapeley Park set in 300 acres of lovely grounds and woodlands which are occasionally open to the public in connection with the Gardens of England scheme.

Littleham, Buckland Brewer and Parkham

Distances from Bideford. – Nearly 3 miles. A bus goes to Littleham cross-roads and the village is 1½ miles from that point.

This walk southward involves a stiff climb but there is the reward of fine scenery and views. There is a view of surrounding villages dotted over the landscape, and of several church towers while Bideford and its bridge are well seen.

Littleham Church (St. Swithin), of Early English and Perpendicular work, has an embattled west tower and six bells. The building was restored and lavishly decorated in 1892. Some fine workmanship is to be seen in the white marble altar-tomb, 5 feet high, of Lieut.-General Crealock. During the restoration a fresco representing St. Swithin and other murals were discovered on the north wall under plaster. Portions of a fine old rood-screen were also met with and the screen was restored. The rood-loft stairs remain. The seating incorporates some old carved bench-ends.

About 2 miles southward from Littleham cross-roads is **Buckland Brewer**, where in the re-built church is a fine Norman doorway with beaked heads. It was between Bideford and Buckland Brewer that Edward Capern, poet as well as postman, was the letter-carrier for many years.

Buckland is a common place name in Devon. Buckland is really "book-land", land held by book, by a royal and ecclesiastical privilegium, implying settled law and order accompanied by payment of taxes. Brewer is the surname of the lord of the manor.

The former manor-house, *Orleigh Court*, a mile north of Buckland Brewer, built by a merchant of Bideford, was the birthplace of Speke, the discoverer of the source of the Nile.

Parkham is 2½ miles to the west. The Earl of Halsbury derives his title from the ancient Barton of Halsbury (in Parkham parish) which came into the Giffard family by marriage, in the reign of Edward I.

Hembury Castle or Camp, 2 miles south of Buckland Brewer, marks the first permanent settlement of the Saxons in the neighbourhood.

Monkleigh

Distance from Bideford. – 4 miles. Plymouth buses pass through several times daily.

Monkleigh, once a manor held by the monks of Montacute in Stephen's reign, is a charming village high among the hills, south of Bideford on the western side of the river, on the Holsworthy–Plymouth road which branches from the Torrington road at Landcross. Included in the parish are some fine houses. There was once one called Annery (now pulled down) which was the home of Lord Chief Justice Hankford, who, in 1422, gave court judgement against the son of Henry V (*see* below).

On reaching the village go to the left. At the fork take the left branch and then the first turn on the right for the church.

The **Church**, dedicated to St. George, is an ancient building in the Perpendicular style. It was restored in 1862. An embattled west tower contains six bells, of which the two oldest date from 1711.

A canopied altar-tomb in the south aisle, with a cusped arch and rich cornice, commemorates Sir William Hankford, the Lord Chief Justice. Noteworthy are the carved bench-ends, the pew doors in which ancient carving has been incorporated, the western screen (sixteenth century), and several brasses.

Weare Giffard

Distance from Bideford. – 3½ miles by road (bus services).

Hotels. – *Weare Giffard, Southcott House.*

The straggling village, 2 miles in length, is situated in an idyllic spot, very similar to many in the Wye Valley. It takes its name from the Giffard family, now Earls of Halsbury, who once held the manor.

The ancient **Hall,** with embattled gatehouse, makes a striking picture, in a little amphitheatre of cliffs and hills, with the Torridge sweeping round it. The house is considered a very fine example of medieval architecture and is noted for its ornate hammer-beam roof. During the Civil War it was unsuccessfully defended against the forces of Parliament. A couple of centuries later it was used as a farmhouse. It is now a guest house and restaurant.

The adjoining **Church** (Holy Trinity) was built in the twelfth century. In the embattled western tower are six bells. On the tenor is inscribed, "Religion, death and pleasure make me ring". Within recessed arches in the north wall of the nave are recumbent effigies of a cross-legged knight and a lady. They may represent Sir Walter Giffard, lord of the manor in 1243, and his wife. Modern benches have fine old carved ends, probably preserved when the church was restored in 1869.

The chancel has a fine fifteenth-century timbered roof. Over the chancel door in the south wall is a mural painting in good preservation representing the martyrdom of St. Edmund.

The Lady Chapel contains memorials of the Fortescue family. In the upper lights of its east window is some old glass. The window was originally a Jesse window.

The return to Bideford could well be made by **Landcross**, midway between the two places, and situated in a loop of the river. It is the smallest parish in the county, and interesting houses include *Pillmouth*, a very old farm, the finely thatched *Grange* and *Monk's Cottage*, which tradition maintains was the birthplace of George Monk, later to become General Monk of Commonwealth and Restoration fame. The tiny church, which stands slightly east of the Bideford-Torrington road, was built in 1435 upon foundations of a very early church. It has some good carving on the bench-ends, pulpit and reading desk.

Great Torrington

Acess from Bideford. – 7 miles. By road (bus service), through some charming scenery. Great Torrington is 3 miles beyond Weare Giffard. A pleasant circular run is to take the river road for the forward journey, returning *via* Frithelstock (ruins of ancient Prior, *c.* 1220) and Monkleigh. This will only add about 2 to 3 miles to the distance.

Banks. – *Barclays, Lloyds, Midland, National Westminster* – all near one another in High Street and Fore Street.

Bowls. – On the Castle Mound is the oldest bowling green in North Devon.

Car Park. – South Street and Barley Grove.

Distances. – London, 199; Barnstaple, 12; Bideford, 7; Exeter, 36.

Early Closing. – Wednesday.

Fishing. – Excellent fishing may be had free by residents. Devon River Board licences available from Black Horse Inn, The Square, and at Council Offices.

Golf. – 9-hole course at Furzebeam.

Hotels. – *Black Horse Inn, Globe, Hunter's Inn, Newmarket, New Inn, Torridge Inn, Castle Hill.*

Hunting. – Cheriton Otter Hounds; Stevenstone Foxhounds; Torrington Farmers Hunt; Hatherleigh Harriers. Regular hunts.

Library. – Branch of County Library, South Street.

Markets. – Cattle Market, School Lane, Thursday; Pannier Market, Town Centre, Saturday.

Population. – 2,860.

Post Office. – Fore Street.

The Torrington road from Bideford is one of the most beautiful in the district. It is sufficiently wide to permit parking to enjoy the glorious views over the curving river, where grey Tudor houses and manors are surrounded by gay gardens and backed by wooded cliffs. The low grey stone wall along the roadside is rich in ivy, harts' tongue ferns and shy wild strawberries, while on the landward side there are clear little springs tinkling down chines in woods of beech, oak and fir with a thick undergrowth of bracken and bramble.

Great Torrington, so called to distinguish it from Little and Black Torrington, is an old-fashioned municipal borough and market town, occupying the summit and slope of a high hill. It is of great antiquity and in the Domesday Survey is referred to as "Torritone". The mayoral records date from 1182.

The church was re-built in 1651 and the present tower at the west end added in 1830. It contains a peal of eight bell. Three thirteenth-century carvings are over the south-east window near the vestry. They are probably the oldest carvings on the building. In the south window of the vestry is some ancient glass.

In the centre of the Market Square is a prettily designed fountain. An interesting specimen of a double gabled building – rare in North Devon – is the *Black Horse Inn*, with a fine, studded door, and over the fireplace a plaster panel dated 1681. Another building of interest is Palmer House (1752) once occupied by Mary Palmer, who was often visited by her brother, Sir Joshua Reynolds. In the **Town Hall** are several interesting portraits, a fifteenth-century Town Seal and some fine Jacobean oak panelling. From the farther end of the Market one passes to the **Castle Hill**, which is also reached by way of South Street *(note the remains of an old cross)* and Castle Street. From the Hill there is a superb view of the surrounding country, the Torridge flowing peacefully at the foot of the hill, which was once crowned by a castle. Close to the flagstaff is a bowling green. A little to the south-east of the Castle Hill, at the edge of the escarpment above the river, is a curious **Obelisk** commemorating the battle of Waterloo.

The slopes above the Torridge, intersected with paths and dotted with seats, with extensive views of the surrounding country, are one of the attractions of Torrington, while on the other side of the town are extensive gorse-covered commons.

Between 2 and 3 miles eastward from Torrington is the beautiful park of **Stevenstone**, so long identified with the Rolle family.

Two miles west of Torrington is **Frithelstock** where the Priory and Church are well worth a visit. The priory ruins are remnants of a thirteenth-century Augustinian priory. Still almost intact is the lovely western gable end with three fine lancets. The church has some fine bench ends and an old chest once the property of John Gay of "Beggar's Opera" fame.

Holsworthy

From Torrington a good road runs south-west *via* Stibb Cross to the little town, very near the county boundary. From it are good views southward to the Dartmoor heights. Holsworthy is situated at the inland end of the old Bude canal and is a busy market town. It is most interesting on Wednesdays when booths for the sale of all kinds of wares occupy the market place. The cattle market is one of the largest in the south-west. The Early English church, SS Peter and Paul, was built in 1250 succeeding a Norman chapel of 1130. Additions were made in 1366. The tall pinnacled tower dates from about 1450.

BARNSTAPLE
Scale of 1/4 Mile
0
1/4
PILTON
DERBY
STICKLEPATH
Fort Hil
Little Herton
Herton
St. Mary the Virgin Ch.
To Lynton & Lynmouth
Pilton Ho.
A 39
NORTH RD.
HIGHER RALEIGH RD.
RALEIGH RD.
R. Yeo
PILTON LAWN
UNDER MINNOW R.
ABBEY R.
PRIORY CLO.
BULL HILL
THE ROCK
PILTON ST.
To Braunton & Ilfracombe
BRAUNTON RD.
A 361
FAIR VIEW
PILTON PARK
PILTON CAUSEWAY
ST. GEORGES RD.
RIDDELL AV.
GRANVILLE AV.
KINGSLEY AV.
CARLYLE AV.
YEO VALE
ST. MARYS RD.
LETHABY R.
BELMONT R.
DERBY R
School
ROLLE ST.
POTTINGTON RD.
MILL LANE
ROLLE QUAY
Sports Ground
NORTH WALK
C.P.
Civic Centre and Police HQ.
Municipal Offs.
Castle Mound
Cattle Mkt.
TULY
HIGH ST.
GREEN LANE
BOUTPORT ST.
JOY ST.
Market
BUTCHERS ROW
Guildhall
P.O.
HOLLAND ST.
CASTLE ST.
COMMERCIAL RD.
CROSS ST.
PATERNOSTER ROW
St. Peter's Ch.
Queens Hall
Ch.
Cinª
THE STRAND
RIVER TAW
CORONATION ST.
GEORGE ST.
K. EDWARD ST.
CHARLES ST.
H. MAUDLIN ST.
L. MAUDLIN S.
PRINCESS S.
VICARAGE ST.
VICARAGE LAWN
CORSER ST.
REFORM S.
Sch.
GAYDON S.
RICHMOND ST.
GROSVENOR
SUNFLOWER RD.
BICTON ST.
CHARLES DART CRE.
Ceme
BEAR STREET
ALEXANDRA RD.
Institutn
HILLS VIEW
To Simonsb
FORT ST.
FORT TER.
Schs.
Drill Hall
SOWDEN
QUEEN ST.
WELLS S.
SILVER S.
THE DIAMOND
CAR PARK
TRINITY ST.
SUMMERLAND ST.
CHURCH ST.
SALEM ST.
BARBICAN TER.
Athenæum
SQUARE
Clock Tower
LITCHDON ST.
OAKLEIGH RD.
ASHLEIGH RD.
ASHLEIGH CRES.
Sunny B
BARBICAN RD.
BARBICAN L
Raleigh Works
LONGBRIDGE
TERR.
CLIFTON TER.
STICKLEPATH
TAW VALE PARADE
Hosp.
Sch.
Gas Works
VICTORIA RD.
Coney
VICTORIA LAWN
Cut
To Bideford & Clovelly
STICKLEPATH HILL
B3232
War Memorial
ROCK PARK
Junction Sta. (Passenger)
Bandstand
NEWPORT RD.
John Gay Thea.
BROADFIELD RD.
GLOSTER RD.
PORTLAND ST.
CYPRUS TER.
Trafalgar Lawn
Tennis
Bowls & Putting
Swimming Pool
PARK LANE
To Taunton
Millenary Stone
Boating Lake
St. John's Ch.
SPRINGFLD. AV.
A 377
SOUTH PARK
SOUTH WALK
Sports Ground
Grammar Sch.
To Exeter
BISHOPS TAWTON

Barnstaple

Banks. – *Barclays, Lloyds, Midland, National Westminster, Devon and Exeter Savings.*

Bowls. – Public greens at Rock Park and Pottington. Barnstaple Bowling Club have green at Ashleigh Road.

Buses. – Buses start from the Strand. Services to Ilfracombe, Saunton and Croyde; Instow, Bideford and Westward Ho!; Swimbridge and South Molton; and many other places or connections thereto.

Cinemas. – *Classic*, Boutport Street; *Regal* Strand.

Concerts, Dancing, etc. – At Queens Hall, Boutport Street.

Distances. – Bideford, 9; Braunton, 5; Bude, 35; Croyde, 11; Exeter, 40; Ilfracombe, 12; London, 195; Lynmouth, 17; Mortehoe, 18; Swimbridge, 5; Torrington, 16.

Early Closing. – Wednesday.

Fair. – Annual Fair on Wednesday, Thursday and Friday preceding September 20.

Fishing. – In the estuary below the bridge. The Taw and Torridge are noted for salmon and trout. Both rivers under the jurisdiction of Devon River Authority. Local inquiries must be made for waters available.

Hotels. – *Royal and Fortescue, Imperial, Clarence, Wrey Arms, Bell, Queen's, Golden Anchor, Central, Waverley, Marshall, Lynwood,* and many guests houses.

Hunting. – Meets of the Devon and Somerset Staghounds, the Stevenstone Foxhounds and the Torrington Farmers Hounds are convenient from the town. There is also some otter-hunting.

Library. – Branch of county library at the Athenaeum, the Square.

Market Days. – Principal day is Friday, with half market-day on Tuesday. Pannier market (fruit, vegetables, cream, etc.), High Street; Modern cattle market, Castle Street.

Museums. – North Devon Athenaeum, The Square. Free. Also has good reference Library. St. Anne's Chapel Museum, off High Street, small charge.

Parking Places. – Queen Street; Pannier Market (except Fridays); North Walk; Derby; Congrams Road; The Square; Seven Brethren Bank.

Population. – 17,820.

Post Office. – General Post Office, Boutport Street.

Putting. – Putting and pitch and putt at Rock Park.

Swimming Baths. – Open air bath near south end of Rock Park.

Tennis. – Public courts in Rock Park. Barnstaple Tennis Club, Ashleigh Road, and Rock Park Tennis Club, Rock Park.

Prosperous market town and busy touring centre, Barnstaple is among the oldest boroughs in the British Isles. It is well situated on the north bank of the River Taw and has good road connections. For many years it has been a centre for those touring North and North-west Devon, but it has become increasingly popular as a place of residence and is gradually extending. There are numerous shops, both multiple stores and those of local origin; it is a thriving agricultural centre; and there are several important factories for cabinet making, lace-net manufacture, pottery (Barumware), milling and pre-cast concrete ware. There are the usual social activities and facilities for education and sport are excellent. The climate is good.

Those who approach the town by the 700-foot-long bridge which spans the Taw, get a pleasant first impression. The town proper lies alongside the river and the residential streets meander away from the industrial or business thoroughfares. To the right is the Taw valley, to the left the river widens out until at Instow 6 miles below, it joins the Torridge and, thus augmented, flows into the sea.

Barnstaple Bridge

The Long Bridge, so-called to distinguish it from the shorter Pilton Bridge over the Yeo, was built about 1350. It was widened in 1796, again in 1807 and in 1865, and was further improved in 1925. Its picturesque appearance has not been enhanced by a still further widening completed in 1964.

The Square. At the north end of the bridge is an open space called The Square, neatly laid out with lawns, flower beds and seats. In the middle is a fountain and the **Albert Memorial and Clock Tower.** To the left is the wide **Strand**, where the buses start, and Queen Anne's Walk.

Queen Anne's Walk. This colonnade derives its name from the statue of the queen placed over it in 1708, though it had previously been known as the Exchange or Merchant's Walk. The heraldic designs seen are the armorial bearings of contributors to its re-erection in 1713. Immediately beneath the statue of Queen Anne is a small "table" of stone standing on a small column. This is the "Tomb" or *Tome stone* which formerly stood on the quay and which was used by the merchants and Merchant Venturers when buying or selling. The act of placing the purchase money on the stone in the presence of witnesses was a part of the transaction, which thereby became binding on both parties. From the names of the mayor, ex-mayor, and alderman carved on the rim [John Delbridge(e), Richard Fer(r)is, and Nicholas Delbridg(e)] it is estimated that it dates from 1633, when it is supposed to have replaced an earlier stone. A similar custom obtained at Bristol where the Nayle, as it was called, gave rise to the expression "Paying on the Nail".

Opposite Queen Anne's Walk is Cross Street leading up to High Street. Continuing the line of the Strand, however, is Castle Street leading to the site, on the right, of the old **Castle**, of which interesting remains have been revealed. The original castle was founded in the eighth century and rebuilt in Norman times as a typical motte and bailey castle of the period. The motte, a great steep artificial mound, still exists, the bailey forms the adjacent public garden, and there are still traces of the great surrounding moats. On the top of the mound are parts of the 10-feet-thick walls of the keep.

Close by is Barnstaple's famous cattle market, now rebuilt, which on Friday mornings presents a spectacle of considerable interest.

At the end of the Strand is the modern **Civic Centre** housing offices of the Borough and Rural District Councils and the North Devon departments of the County Council. Adjoining are the new Police Station and Law Courts.

Immediately to the right of the Long Bridge is the **North Devon Athenaeum** (*open* 10–1, 2–6; *Saturdays* 10–1). The Athenaeum, endowed by the late W. F. Rock, a great benefactor of the town, has a large collection of local records, a geological museum, a considerable library and well-stocked reading room. On the ground floor is a branch of the County Library.

The Taw, Barnstaple

Adjoining the building is the **Taw Vale Parade**, a favourite promenade skirting the river as far as **Rock Park**, a pleasant open space and recreation ground. Just behind the park is a Sports Centre with swimming bath, tennis courts, bowling greens, putting and pitch and putt, and a model boating lake. Opposite the baths is the Millenary Stone, 930–1930, under which are buried examples of contemporary coins and copies of town records. From here the riverside promenade continues as far as the Sports Ground and the railway bridge over the Taw.

Running parallel with the Taw Vale Parade from the Square is **Litchdon Street** which leads past the Penrose Almshouses.

The **Penrose Almshouses** in Litchdon Street were erected in the seventeenth century and have been carefully preserved. Their most notable feature is a colonnade of granite pillars. There are twenty dwellings, each for two inmates, and with a small plot of ground attached. In one of the doors are bullet holes, a relic of the Civil Wars. There are other almshouses in Trinity Street, while in Church Lane are the Horwood Almshouses with a school attached – the Alice Horwood School which she "endowed for 20 poor children for ever, in 1659".

Also in Litchdon Street are the **Royal Barum Ware Potteries**, which are among the most cherished of Barnstaple's industrial possessions. The industry was established in the thirteenth century, when Cross Street was originally named Crock Street. The ware is now noteworthy for its artistic shapes and glazes. Examples may be seen at Messrs. Brannam's Pottery.

Meeting at the north-west corner of the Square are **Boutport Street** and **High Street**, the two busiest streets of the town. In the former, facing High Street, stood the Golden Lion Hotel, notable for its richly ornamented ceilings. The hotel has given place to the National Westminster Bank, but

St. Peter's, Barnstaple

its two famous ceilings remain, having been carefully preserved in their original positions during the erection of the bank. One is in the public part of the bank: the other is in the Manager's room, but it is willingly shown to visitors.

St. Peter's Church, a short distance up High Street, was built or re-built in 1318 and is the parish of the united benefice of St. Peter's with Holy Trinity. Curiosity is always aroused by its twisted steeple, much out of the perpendicular, a malformation caused by lightning in 1810. In 1910 this was strengthened, the lead sheets remade and replaced.

In the church are many interesting seventeenth-century monuments of Barnstaple worthies. There are some good stained-glass windows and the remains of a wall painting. A beautiful chasuble, used in the church in pre-Reformation days, was in 1910 restored to the church by the lady into whose possession it had passed. A "state seat" for the mayor stands in the church.

St. Anne's Chapel, in the churchyard, is used during the summer months for the exhibition of objects of local antiquarian interest. It is small in size, but of great historic interest, and the cause of much archaeological speculation. Some authorities believe it was the chapel of St. Sabinus, an early Irish missionary who came to preach Christianity and was wrecked at Woolacombe. The upper portion of the building is believed to date from 1456. The walls of the lower older part are pierced by slits, widely splayed within, and the crypt is a quaint structure. Previous to the Reformation it was used as a chantry of St. Anne, and after the Dissolution became by purchase the property of the Corporation, who for more than 300 years used a part of it as a Grammar School. Among the many distinguished men who were educated here were Bishop Jewell, John Gay, the poet, whose quaint writing chair is still preserved elsewhere, and John Doddridge, Solicitor-General to James I.

The Boys and Girls Grammar Schools are now in fine modern buildings south of Rock Park.

The **Pannier Market**, a few steps from the church, is on a Friday one of the sights of Barnstaple. It is a huge covered building occupying a space of about 45,000 square feet, connecting High Street with Boutport Street. Farmers' wives and daughters and a large number of cottagers bring in their produce, which is sold from low stalls at which the vendors sit. To the visitor, the scene is a remarkable one, and there is a pleasant sense of age-old tradition in spite of modern buildings, dress and speech, of the time when freemen of the town held rights to free stalls.

Adjoining is quaint **Butcher's Row**, where there are a number of butchers' shops, each with a uniform frontage, and "all in a row". Barnstaple is one of the few towns where the medieval practice still obtains, of placing shops of one kind together.

The **Guildhall**, at the High Street end of the Market, was erected in 1827. In the building there are portraits of townsmen painted in 1730 by Thos. Hudson and some modern additions and valuable civic plate and regalia. The latter are publicly displayed at the time of the annual Fair. Some of the pieces date from 1425. A punch-bowl or more correctly a monteith, with indentations at the rim so that glasses may be hung round, dates from 1745. Three silver-gilt goblets resembling church chalices are notable features of the collection. A treasure of comparatively recent acquisition is a Coronation Mayor's chain of beautiful design, with a community badge consisting of the borough arms and the three seals of the town, decorated with the Barnstaple ships of the Armada.

The Great Fair of Barnstaple has been called "The Saturnalia of North Devon". It is held on the Wednesday, Thursday and Friday preceding September 20 and is opened with civic ceremonial. The Mayor, aldermen and councillors assemble at the Guildhall, and, according to ancient custom, partake of spiced ale, toast, cheese and fairing – the latter being a special type of sweet prepared for the occasion. Then with a full-dress parade of the municipal officials, there is a procession to the High Cross, to the bottom of High Street and to the Strand, sites of the old west and south gates, where the Town Clerk formally proclaims the Fair open. It lasts three days – originally one for horned cattle, one for horses, and one for pleasure. The Fair has been shorn of many of its old-time characteristics, and the horse fair has died out, but the "pleasure fair" is as popular as ever, and attracts thousands of visitors to the town. While it lasts a large stuffed glove, signifying the Hand of Welcome, is displayed from a window in the Guildhall.

Pilton, on the northern side of the Yeo is within the borough. The Church is of great age and much interest, dedicated to St. Mary the Virgin. It originally formed part of a Priory which tradition says was founded by King Athelstan (925–40), whose figure and name were placed on the Prior's seal. (In the vestry there is an impression of the seal supposed to have been made in 1412–21.) The priory was dissolved in 1533, and with the exception of the church its buildings were destroyed or allowed to fall into decay.

Pilton Church

The present church was dedicated by the Bishop of Exeter in 1259. The tower was built (or re-built) in 1270. The upper part of it was pulled down during the Civil War, as recorded on a tablet in the south porch. It contains a very fine peal of eight bells. Six were placed there in 1712, the other two in 1853. They were tuned and rehung in 1970.

The church has been restored at various times, and in 1914 much was done to improve and beautify the chancel. A remarkable feature of the interior is that many of the columns and even the pulpit and screen are out of the perpendicular.

On the north side of the chancel is the memorial of Sir Robert Chichester (d. 1627) and his two wives, who, with their children, are represented upon it. There are other elaborate monuments, mostly with Latin inscriptions.

The Communion Table, dating from the reign of Queen Elizabeth, is of special interest through having sliding panels by which it could be lengthened, if a longer table than usual was necessary to accommodate the communicants who in the early days of the Reformed Church stood or sat round the table. The Communion rails have a book rest, an uncommon feature. The carved oak canopy and cover over the font are fine examples of fifteenth-century work, and the cover itself is considered by many the most beautiful in the West.

From the road the church is almost hidden by some **Almshouses** administered by trustees of the St. Margaret's Hospital Charity. St. Margaret's Leper hospital, connected with the Priory was situated lower down Pilton Street.

Excursions from Barnstaple

Good bus and coach services have greatly added to the advantages of Barnstaple as a centre. Ilfracombe, Combe Martin, Croyde and Saunton to the north of the estuary, and Bideford, Westward Ho! and Clovelly to the south-west, are but a few of the places which are linked with the town. There are, however, numerous delightful walks around and nearer to Barnstaple.

Tawstock is situated about 3 miles south of the town. It can be approached by **Seven Brethren Bank**, the bank on the west side of the river. Access is gained from the south side of the bridge. There is also a pleasant walk to the village by the road which from the bottom of Sticklepath Hill passes through **Lake**.

Those who arrive by road will come to a cottage at the head of an avenue, one of four cross-roads. The road opposite the avenue leads to the church. Rather more than half-way is a castellated gateway, dated 1574, the only remains of the former **Tawstock Court**, which was burnt down in 1787 and replaced by a handsome modern mansion.

The little **Church** of St. Peter is an ancient cruciform building in the Decorated and Perpendicular styles. It has a lofty embattled tower containing eight bells, and has also embattled aisles. The church contains two good screens and is famous for the costly sixteenth- and seventeenth-century altar tombs of the Bouchiers, Earls of Bath, of whom Tawstock Park was the seat from 1136 to 1654, when they were succeeded by the Wreys.

Bishops Tawton and Coddon Hill. Bishops Tawton is on the Exeter road, about 2½ miles from Barnstaple (bus service). The Parish Church (St. John the Baptist) in the centre of the village has some good stained-glass windows, two beautiful white marble tablets – the workmanship in the drapery of the figure is exquisite – and a tomb supposed to be that of Sir Lewis Pollard, a Justice of the Common Pleas in the fifteenth century. Immediately to the south of the church is a farmhouse with two small towers, the remains of one of the palaces of the Bishop of Exeter.

Coddon Hill (630 feet), the highest point in this district, is a furze-covered slope southward of the village. The view from the top well repays a climb. A broad path leads up the face of the hill from the roadway, at a point where the road forks, a short distance beyond the last houses in Bishops Tawton. The road skirting the hillside leads to Chittlehampton.

Chittlehampton

Chittlehampton lies 2½ miles eastward from Umberleigh, an uphill walk, and about the same distance from the Barnstaple–South Molton bus route, 8½ miles by road from Barnstaple through Bishops Tawton – a good road. The spacious square is believed to have been the "town place" of the original Saxon settlement of the neighbourhood. Of interest are the church and St. Teara's Well, at the eastern end of the village and traditional site of St. Hieritha's martyrdom.

The church is dedicated to St. Hieritha, over whose shrine it was erected, and has a notable tower. It is 114 feet high to the pinnacles, for the number of which both it and the church are remarkable – altogether between 80 and 90. Among the most interesting features of the light and spacious interior of the church are the wooden roofs of the Rolle and Giffard chapels (the transepts), the chancel roof, the mosaic reredos, the figure of St. Hieritha on north panel of pulpit, some good brasses to the Cobleigh family near the pulpit, the ancient font and carved capitals on the south side of the nave. A Giffard monument in the north transept is unique in commemorating five generations at once.

At **Winson**, half a mile south-east, and at **Eastacott**, a mile south-west, are to be seen ancient wayside crosses, the only examples of their kind in Devon.

Umberleigh and Atherington

Umberleigh is a pretty little village 8 miles south of Barnstaple on the main Exeter road. It is set amid lovely scenery, through which the Taw gushes with alternate courses of calm and weir water. A bridge, commanding a charming view of the river, connects the two parishes of Chittlehampton and Atherington. There is good fishing for salmon, sea-trout and trout, a three-mile stretch of the river being reserved to the *Rising Sun Inn*, a picturesque former coaching house.

The village of **Atherington** has a number of cottages in whitewashed stone and a great tree in the centre, together presenting an attractive appearance. The Church is mainly in the Perpendicular style and has a lofty and very richly carved oak screen, with rood loft, the only one in Devon. On most of the pew-ends in the nave are ancient carvings.

Swimbridge

Swimbridge is situated 5 miles south-east on the South Molton road. About 2 miles from Barnstaple the road makes a detour to the left at **Landkey**. Motorists should keep to the main road on the left above the village, but walkers may well use the right-hand one passing Landkey Church.

Swimbridge is an attractive village quite apart from its church, which is of extreme beauty and interest. Its peculiar name is said to be a corruption of Sawin of Birige, the name of a priest who founded a chapel here in the time of Edward the Confessor, and was its chaplain at the time of the Norman Conquest.

The tower of the church belongs to the Early Decorated period, and was probably erected about 1310. The short spire reaches to the height of 90 feet from the ground, and is of the "twisted" variety, like St. Peter's, Barnstaple, and St. Brannock's, Braunton.

The church contains one of the finest of Devonshire screens. This extends the whole width of the church, is of beautiful design and is especially noted for the amount of carving on the western side. It probably dates from about 1500. The roofs are exceptionally good. They are of cradle form, except that of the north transept, which is of a type unusual in North Devon.

The walk from Swimbridge to Bishops Tawton, 4 miles, is through pretty, narrow lanes, and is well worth the trouble of finding the right road, which starts at the back of the tannery.

Three miles beyond Swimbridge towards South Molton is the village of **Filleigh**, noted for the magnificent Castle Hill, the house now occupied by a member of the Fortescue family. It is set in a beautiful wooded park (not open). There are many memorials of the Fortescue family in the church.

A pleasant circular tour for motorists is Bishop's Tawton, Chapelton, Atherington, South Molton (with a detour to Chittlehampton) and back *via* Swimbridge.

Braunton

Braunton is on the old coast road, now a wide main road to Ilfracombe. At about 4½ miles from Barnstaple it cuts through **Wrafton.** The castle-like Heanton Court (now an hotel) figured prominently as "Narnton Court" in Blackmore's romance, The Maid of Sker. To the right is **Heanton Punch-**

ardon, where the postman-poet Capern lies buried. A feature of his tombstone is the inclusion of the bell he used to ring upon his rounds.

Braunton is a small but growing town which owes its origin to St. Brannock, who came from Wales on a preaching tour in the sixth century. The upper part, set back on the slopes of low hills, is a quaint little place with narrow streets and old inns and cottages, while the lower is modern and spreading rapidly along the main trunk road.

Braunton has the largest enclosed field in England – over 350 acres in extent – owned under the ancient system of strip tenure. Excellent views of it may be obtained from the Beacon and the top of East Hill. It is most impressive, surrounded as it is by hedge-bounded fields of the usual size.

Braunton Church is situated on the Ilfracombe road, about four minutes' walk from the cross-roads in the village near which the Barnstaple bus stops. It has been described as "the fayrest church in these parts of one span" and as "the strangest collection of odds and ends" but is of great beauty and interest.

The church is a large and ancient building with a tower surmounted by a spire and containing a clock and eight bells. The roof is fine and the old oak seats are unrivalled in the county. There is a palimpsest brass, and a chest on which are rudely delineated a man and woman in Portuguese costume of about 1500. Tradition claims this is an Armada chest washed up on Saunton Sands.

Much of the flat ground between Braunton and the sea is meadow and marshland. Some is used for camps, and during the war a large aerodrome was built here.

Near the sea, some 2 miles west of the town, is a large sandy tract, called **Braunton Burrows**, abounding with wild flowers and a wealth of rare sea and marsh birds. In 1964 it was declared a National Nature Reserve, and is one of the largest sand-dune systems in Great Britain. At the far southern end is a Trinity House light and a lighthouse.

Saunton Sands

Situation. – On the coast, about 3 miles west of Braunton, from which there is a good bus service.

Golf. – Saunton Golf Club, 18 holes.

Accommodation. – *Saunton Sands Hotel* (100 rooms); *Ashmead* (Boarding); *Knelle Lodge* (Private).

Saunton Sands, a popular summer resort, is an extension of Saunton (St. Anne's Town). A magnificent stretch of flat sands backed by sand-hills, in part towering to a considerable height, sets the scene for splendid surfing, swimming and beach games. On a portion of the sand-hills and adjoining land is the splendid 18-hole course of the Saunton Golf Club, attracting players from many parts and the venue of numerous championship events.

Off the main road at Saunton is the miniature St. Anne's Church, which in some measure replaces the old and vanished chapel of the same name once situated at the southern end of Braunton Burrows (see above).

It is a fine walk along the sands to the lighthouse and near-by beacon. In addition to the interest always attaching to a lighthouse, though this one is automatic and unmanned, there is the reward of a charming view.

Croyde

Beyond Saunton the road skirts the rocky coast at a considerable height above the sea and gives marvellous views across the bay to Clovelly and Hartland and eastward over Barnstaple. After rounding Saunton Down there comes a clear view of lovely Croyde Bay and then the road drops into **Croyde**, a charming and popular village at the northern end of the bay. Accommodation at farms and inns is booked up early in the year, as also are the various houses, bungalows and chalets that skirt the fine sandy bay. The situation of the village is delightful, up a sheltered combe with a stream running down one side of the road. In the bay, backed by marram-grassed sand dunes, can be enjoyed swimming and the exhilarating sport of surf-boarding, the breakers being ideal. At low tide bathers should take great care for the swirling tide causes many hidden pot-holes. The sands and the many pools amongst the rocks at each end of the bay provide a perfect playground.

Prominent **Baggy Point** (National Trust) separates Croyde Bay from the larger Morte Bay, consisting of **Putsborough Beach** and the vast Woolacombe sands (see p. 224). Putsborough may be reached either from Croyde or the quiet village of **Georgeham.** The latter is a bracing, secluded spot, 400 feet above sea-level and a little inland from Croyde. A bus service connects it with Ilfracombe, Barnstaple, Croyde and Saunton. The lofty fourteenth-century tower of the church stands up most impressively in the centre of the village. In 1876 the church underwent a drastic restoration. It contains much of interest. In the chancel is an unusually fine, though badly damaged, sculptured panel of the Crucifixion (*c.* 1300).

To Arlington Court ——

Situation. – 7 miles north-east of Barnstaple on the east side of A.39 (Barnstaple-Lynton Road).

Open. – April 1 or Easter Saturday to mid-October daily except Good Friday, 11–6. Last admissions 5.30. House and Carriage Exhibition close between 1 and 2 p.m. Charge. Restaurant.

The family of Chichester figures prominently in the history of Devon. Amyas Chichester in 1537 inherited Arlington through the Raleigh family. The house he refitted disappeared long ago. So did the late eighteenth-century house that succeeded it. The present Arlington Court was built, on a different site to those of its predecessors, in 1821. The architect was Thomas Lee, who also built the Wellington monument and several houses in the west country. Sir Bruce Chichester, the second and last baronet, who added about 1880 a long wing to the north of the house and made other alterations, was succeeded in 1881 by an only daughter, Rosalie Caroline Chichester.

Miss Chichester lived all her life at Arlington until 1949 when she left the whole estate of 3,471 acres, the house and its collections to the National Trust. During these long years Miss Chichester devoted her interests to the estate. In the park may still be seen a herd of her Shetland ponies and a flock of Spanish sheep. She cherished the heronry and made the estate into a bird sanctuary.

Porcelain, silver, snuff-boxes and bibelots of all sorts form part of the Chichester inheritance.

Miss Chichester's own collections, however, dominate the house. Model ships, sea-shells and pewter are the subjects most in evidence and the first two are among the largest and most complete private collections in England. Many of the ships, which number over 100, were made by French prisoners during the Napoleonic wars.

The stables house a large collection of horse-drawn vehicles. One of the carriages is used to give rides to visitors.

Arlington Court

Ilfracombe

Banks. – *Barclays, Lloyds, Midland, National Westminster*, all in High Street.

Bathing. – *Wildermouth Beach*, on immediate sea front; *Rapparee Cove* and *Larkstone Beach* at the base of Hillsborough; *The Tunnels*, opposite the foot of Northfield Road; *Broadstrand Beach* and *Blythe's Cove*, reached by paths down from Hillsborough; *Cheyne Beach*, between Capstone and Lantern Hill; *Hele Beach*, on far side of Hillsborough; *White Pebble Bay*, reached by steps from Torrs Walk.

Covered sea-water bath at West Promenade one of the largest covered salt-water baths in the West. Water is filtered and warmed. Galas and water-polo matches during season.

Boating. – Moorings available in harbour. Pleasure and fishing trips arranged by licenced boatmen.

Bowls. – The local club is in Highfield Road. Annual tournament in July.

Buses. – Regular services link Ilfracombe with Lynton on the east, and Woolacombe on the west, and throughout the year also provide communication with Barnstaple, Bideford, Braunton, Clovelly, Combe Martin, Lee Bay, Lynton, Saunton, South Molton, Woolacombe, Westward Ho! and all other places of interest in North-west Devon. Bus Station in Broad Street.

Coach Tours. – Excursions and services to all neighbouring places of interest. Towns farther afield such as Exeter, Bude, Plymouth, etc.

Early Closing Day. – Thursday.

Entertainments. – Summer shows at the Pavilion Theatre, Promenade, and at Alexandra Theatre, Market Street. Dances at Holiday Inn, and in several hotels. Clifton and Embassy Cinemas, in High Street.

Fishing. – For variety of fishing, North Devon is hardly excelled. Sea fishing for bass, pollack, rock whiting, grey mullet, cod, conger is popular. A good spot is just off shore from Hillsborough. Local boatmen usually supply bait and tackle. Another favourite place is Hele Bay, while the pier can offer good sport.

Trout fishing available in town reservoirs at Slade, subject to tickets obtainable at the Council Offices.

Golf. – *Ilfracombe Golf Club*, on cliffs beyond Hele Bay (bus service).

Hotels. – *Mount, Imperial, Dilkhusa Grand, Cliffe Hydro, Grosvenor, Candar, Collingwood, Runnacleave, Queens Court, Royal Britannia, Alexandra, Cavendish, Cecil, Clifton, Granville, Gilbert, Moonta, Wildersmouth, St. Helier* and many others.

Library. – Branch of County Library in Brookfield Place, off High Street.

Museum. – Near Council Offices. Charge.

Parking Places. – The Pier, West Promenade, Wilder Road, The Cove, Bicclescombe, Rapparee, Hillsborough, Hele, Oxford Grove. Some charges.

Population. – 9,350.

Post Office. – Chief Post Office in High Street. Several sub-offices.

Putting. – At Pavilion Pleasure Gardens (18 holes). There are miniature golf courses at Larkstone Sports Ground and at the Torrs. Pitch and putt at Rapparee.

Riding. – Several stables in the town.

Steamers. – Steamer services and excursions to Lynmouth, Clovelly, Minehead, Bristol, Cardiff, Barry and Swansea, etc., also channel cruises and trips to Lundy, Mumbles, Tenby, etc. Booking offices at Pier Road, and on sea front.

Tennis. – Numerous courts in the town, notably at Larkstone, The Torrs and Bicclescombe.

Theatres. – *Alexandra*, Market Street; *Pavilion*, Promenade – variety.

Zoo. – Comyn Hill, Worth Road.

Deep in the shelter of surrounding hills and facing the Bristol Channel, Ilfracombe has justifiable claim as the premier resort of North Devon. There are indeed few places to rival it in its variety of fine scenery, magnificent cliffs, grand sea views, attractive walks, sea trips and road excursions.

On first approach Ilfracombe presents a striking picture. Those who reach it by sea are at once interested in the boat-crowded harbour, and the long house-flanked quay which gives the place a quaintly Continental air.

Visitors arriving by road get their first views from higher ground.

To the west of Ilfracombe are the Torrs, a high switchback range whose green slopes this side give no idea of the grandeur on the other. To the east and topped by a flagstaff, is the Capstone, a huge rock 150 feet high, again with grassy slopes on the landward side. Stretching away north is the great sweep of the Bristol Channel, with a sight of the Welsh coast in the distance. Running back into the valley, or combe, away from the sea, is the residential part of Ilfracombe.

Holy Trinity Church, Ilfracombe's parish church is a venerable building presenting a variety of styles. The earliest known record of it is in connection with Bishop Stapledon's visit in 1321. Probably it then consisted of a plain Norman nave and chancel. The bishop ordered its enlargement by the extension of the nave and the construction of an aisle on either side. The octagonal pillars of the nave probably date from this time. In the following century the aisles are thought to have been extended to their present length by the construction of chantry chapels on each side of the chancel. At the same time the walls of the chancel would be pierced. Late in the same century, the fifteenth, the roofs of the aisles were raised to their present height and the windows received their Perpendicular tracery. This was removed from the east window in 1861, when a certain amount of restoration was undertaken.

The dormer windows, just west of the chancel, date from 1899. The oak panelling and decorative carving of the chancel roof were carried out in 1905.

The pulpit is Jacobean. It was restored in 1901 and of that date are the carved base, the stairs and the moulding around the top. The font is Norman, and is almost all that remains of the Norman church.

Adjoining the churchyard is a pleasant Garden of Remembrance which, with its granite column topped by a bronze Victory, represents Ilfracombe's War Memorial. It is a good spot at which to sit awhile on the seats provided.

From the parish church, **Church Road** winds round to **Wilder Road**, which leads to the **Capstone**; while to the right goes **Church Street**, the beginning of the main thoroughfare of the town. It soon merges into **High Street**, the site of many of the principal shops, the **Post Office**, and a few yards farther, the **Arcade**, from the end of which there is a glimpse of the Capstone and Wildersmouth Beach. At this point there goes to the right **Portland Street**, which soon gives place to **Hillsborough Road**. They are parts of the route to Barnstaple *via* Muddiford and Pilton.

From the Arcade, the line of High Street is continued by **Fore Street**, which slopes steeply down to –

The Pier and Harbour. The Pier and the outer and inner harbours are owned by the local authority. The strong concrete pier is busy with steamer traffic while the wide arm of the outer harbour makes a useful car park for this part of the town. The expansive inner harbour, often crammed with small craft, is lined on three sides with picturesque terraces of shops, cafés and restaurants and the houses of boatmen. On the fourth, the seaward side, is the old pier, protecting the inner harbour, and which was built, as an inscription tells, by the Wrey family when Lords of the Manor of Ilfracombe. The harbour even at low water is never lacking in interest and is an ever popular promenade.

The Harbour, Ilfracombe

Lantern Hill. To the west of the pier is the conical Lantern Hill which owes its name to the use made of the small building which crowns it. It is probably this, together with the quayside buildings, which helps to give Ilfracombe the quaint Continental appearance noticed when first seen from the east. Pride of "old" Ilfracombe, the structure dates back about seven hundred years. Originally a chapel dedicated to St. Nicholas, patron saint of sailors, it now serves as a lighthouse, showing a red light to point the harbour entrance. The summit of the hill is about a hundred feet above sea-level.

Opposite the pier is **Larkstone Beach** and a little farther east, the romantically named **Rapparee Cove** with popular bathing beach of rock-free sand. Both can be reached by a path round the harbour. Another approach is by Hillsborough Road and Quayfields.

Hillsborough Hill. Towering above Rapparee Cove is Hillsborough Hill, a noble headland. It rises almost perpendicularly from the sea but its other sides are gentle grass-covered slopes. A much-frequented pleasure ground of the town it is one of the few spots in England from which the sun can be seen to rise out of and set behind a sea horizon. As the hill is 447 feet high its summit commands a magnificent view of the town and surrounding countryside. The ascent is not difficult and signposts indicate the easiest route. The hill is reached by the path skirting the harbour and from Hillsborough Road. There are seats at frequent intervals and, useful on some occasions, storm shelters built into the rock.

For those who do not like hills, there is a pleasant walk round the base of Hillsborough. The path leads to the right or back of the hill and presently overlooks Hele. After passing **Blythe's Cove** a steep path descends to the beach opposite the pier. At low water here, several fine cavities in the rocks are uncovered, with chambers and halls worn by the waves.

The Capstone and Capstone Parade. North-westward of the harbour is the Capstone, a huge rock 156 feet high. Almost precipitous on the north, sea side, and dizzily sheer on the west, it has a steep grassy slope on the town side. On this side paths zig-zag to the top, from which again fine views are to be obtained.

Around the seaward side of the hill is a fine promenade, the **Capstone Parade**, from which, at intervals, steep steps lead on to the rocks below, with other steps cut here and there in the lower rocks themselves, a help when searching at low water for anemones and other sea treasures, of which many varieties are to be found. There are seats at all nooks and corners of the Parade, as well as along the paths which scale the Capstone. Comfortable shelters face the sea. Since one side or other of the hill will be protected on windy days, visitors can remain comfortably in the open air even on the roughest days. Indeed, watched either from the Capstone or the Parade, a rough sea at Ilfracombe is a magnificent sight.

Wilder Road, with its numerous attractive hotels, runs from the Parade parallel to and between the front and High Street. On the seaward side of the road are the attractive **Runnymede Gardens**. The large building between these and the Promenade is **Holiday Inn** (the one time Ilfracombe Hotel). There is regular dancing here, licensed bars and cafés. At the other end of the same building are the Municipal Offices and Information Bureau. Near by in a corner of the colourful **Southern Slope Gardens** is the **Museum** with collections illustrating the geology, flora and fauna of Devon. The Curator is always ready to help identify specimens. Beyond on the Promenade are the **Municipal Baths**, with a heated indoor sea water pool.

Beyond the Runnacleave in Wilder Road, where several roads converge, can be seen the entrance to the **Tunnels**, passages which pierce the cliff and provide easy access to a very popular bathing beach. By building up walls between rocks two pools have been made and there are changing boxes and spectators' seats. These pools provide excellent safe bathing.

Keeping to the left along Wilder Road the circuit of the main part of the town is completed at Church Street. Or Torrs Park Road on the right may be taken leading to Granville Road, again on the right, and the entrance to –

The Torrs Walks. This famous beauty spot at the western end of the town, since purchase by the local authority, is freely open to all. The distance from the entrance to the top is about one and a half miles, but there is a shorter route by which one may return if desired.

The hills rise abruptly one above another to a height of some 500 feet above the sea. Upon them is a succession of zig-zag paths. Ferns and all kinds of wild growth fringe the way, with occasional walls of bare solid rock, which often tower above the foliage. The paths slope gently enough for the walk not to be tiring. But in no case would one wish to hurry. The ever-changing views of the Channel, then glimpses of the Capstone, and the bathing beaches at the Tunnels below, compel countless pauses. In sheltered corners there are seats. From the summit there is an extensive view right over the town. Across in the direction of Bull Point Lighthouse stretch the Downs, through which the cliff path runs to Lee and Mortehoe.

Cairn Top is a 511-feet-high hill half mile back from the town off Cairn Road. Much of the ground is covered with Austrian and Scots pine. Walks bordered by rhododendron and laurel give access to the top and to numerous quiet nooks. Seats are placed at convenient open spots and viewpoints. The climb up is quite stiff, but there is good reward in the fine prospect opened up. At the summit is a pile of rocks giving the height its name.

Instead of returning by the outward route, the town may be regained by descending the western side of the hill to the hamlet of Slade, and thence either following the main road to the right or taking the footpath immediately opposite the point at which the main road is reached and leading through fields to the end of the Torrs Park Road.

Another alternative is to descend the eastern side of the hill to St. Brannock's Road and there turn to the left. The walk is about 3 miles.

Bicclescombe Park in the same direction is, however, reached from the foot of Station Road by following the lower road, St. Brannock's, which soon divides. The left-hand branch is Bicclescombe Park Road, which quickly leads to the ground from which it is named. The park has had much care and attention expended on it. Well laid out there are fine stretches of lawn and floral displays. The Wilder brook runs along the eastern side and opportunity has been taken to design ornamental gardens, waterfalls and lakes. There are tennis courts and facilities for various other sports, and a children's boating lake in the park.

Excursions from Ilfracombe

There are numerous trips to be had around Ilfracombe and each has its particular charm and variety. Typical high-banked Devon lanes, with here and there a glimpse of rich coloured earth between a wealth of ferns and foxgloves, alternate with open paths across wide moorland or slim cliff tracks with widespread views of sea and sky. It is useful to have a local time table in the pocket for there are several handy bus services to help one on one's way.

Most of the places described here can be reached by car, but access to and from can often be more enjoyable on foot for many of the beautiful byways or lanes are really unsuitable for motor traffic.

To Score Valley and Oakridge

These lie southward of Ilfracombe and at no great distance beyond Bicclescombe Park. Oakridge, the turning-point, being less than a mile farther along the lane which passes the old cemetery and crosses the East Wilder Brook. The second path on the right alongside Cleeve Wood divides and reaches the farm about half a mile from the brook. From the farm the path crosses a field and then follows the hedge of another field to the Barnstaple Old Road, which is struck about 1½ miles from the town to which there is a gradual descent.

On the return, after walking about a mile seaward along the Barnstaple Old Road, an alternative route along Worth Road can be taken to the right – by picturesque Comyn Hill House. In the garden here is an attractive **Zoo**.

From Comyn Hill the road descends to Highfield Road which, followed to the left, leads past the Bowling Green and St. Peter's Church to the junction of Church Street and High Street; or from the foot of Comyn Hill Road, Castle Hill leads to Portland Street and the centre of the town. The total length of this walk is about four miles.

To Lee

The road route is *via* Slade and Lincombe. There is a very steep descent into Lee. Those wishing to continue on to Mortehoe must first return up Lee Hill, turning to the right at Lincombe Cross, to join the Mortehoe road ¼ mile east of Mortehoe and Woolacombe Station.

Lee, one of the prettiest places near Ilfracombe, nestles westward of it in Borough Valley, often known as Fuchsia Valley, a deep combe where these charming bushes grow in profusion.

Walkers may approach it by the Coast Road across the Downs. By the Torrs Park Road or by proceeding over the Torrs Walks, the beginning of the Lee Downs is reached, from which there is a fine view of Bull Point Lighthouse and, in clear weather, Lundy, 20 miles away to the west.

At the Lee end of the Downs there is a gate opening into a lane which leads down to Lee Bay Hotel and the sea. Alternatively there is a public footpath to the left leading down across two fields to another lane which joins the main road by the Miramar Guest House, where refreshments may be obtained. By turning right and following the road the main part of Lee village is reached.

On the right is the little **Church of St. Matthew and St. Wardrede.** Although not old (1833–4), it contains some good carved furniture and panelling (sixteenth–seventeenth centuries) of which the pulpit and choir gallery are fine examples.

A little farther on is the thatched cottage of the **Old Maids of Lee.** This cottage is said to have been built in 1653. In the nineteenth century the Three Old Maids of Fred Weatherley's song are reputed to have occupied the cottage for a time.

A little way down, the road forks to the right and goes uphill for a short distance and then down to the sea. Alternatively, those walking can, instead of following the right fork, avoid traffic by forking left down a lane, passing some old cottages on the right and the Old Farm on the left. The *Old Farm Tea Garden* is popular and well known. From Old Farm a footpath leads down to the sea.

Lee Bay is pretty but small and cliffs tower on each side. Several old cottages front the bay including the Smugglers Cottage, parts of which are over 400 years old. The *Old Mill* dates from 1560. There is a pleasant beach at Sandy Cove about five minutes' walk from the front at low tide.

To Bull Point Lighthouse

Motorists go on the Braunton-Barnstaple road, turning to the right at Mullacott Cross a mile and a half beyond which bearing left and then taking right fork for Mortehoe.

Walkers: About 2 miles west of Lee. From Lee take the road to the beach and passing this go straight ahead to a field-gate in front on the right. From this cross the field to another gate at which the path goes to the right. At the next gate it goes to the left and at first runs close to the hedge. It leads to a plank bridge beyond which it winds up a low, steep hill. From the summit follow the road which will be

Old Cottage, Lee

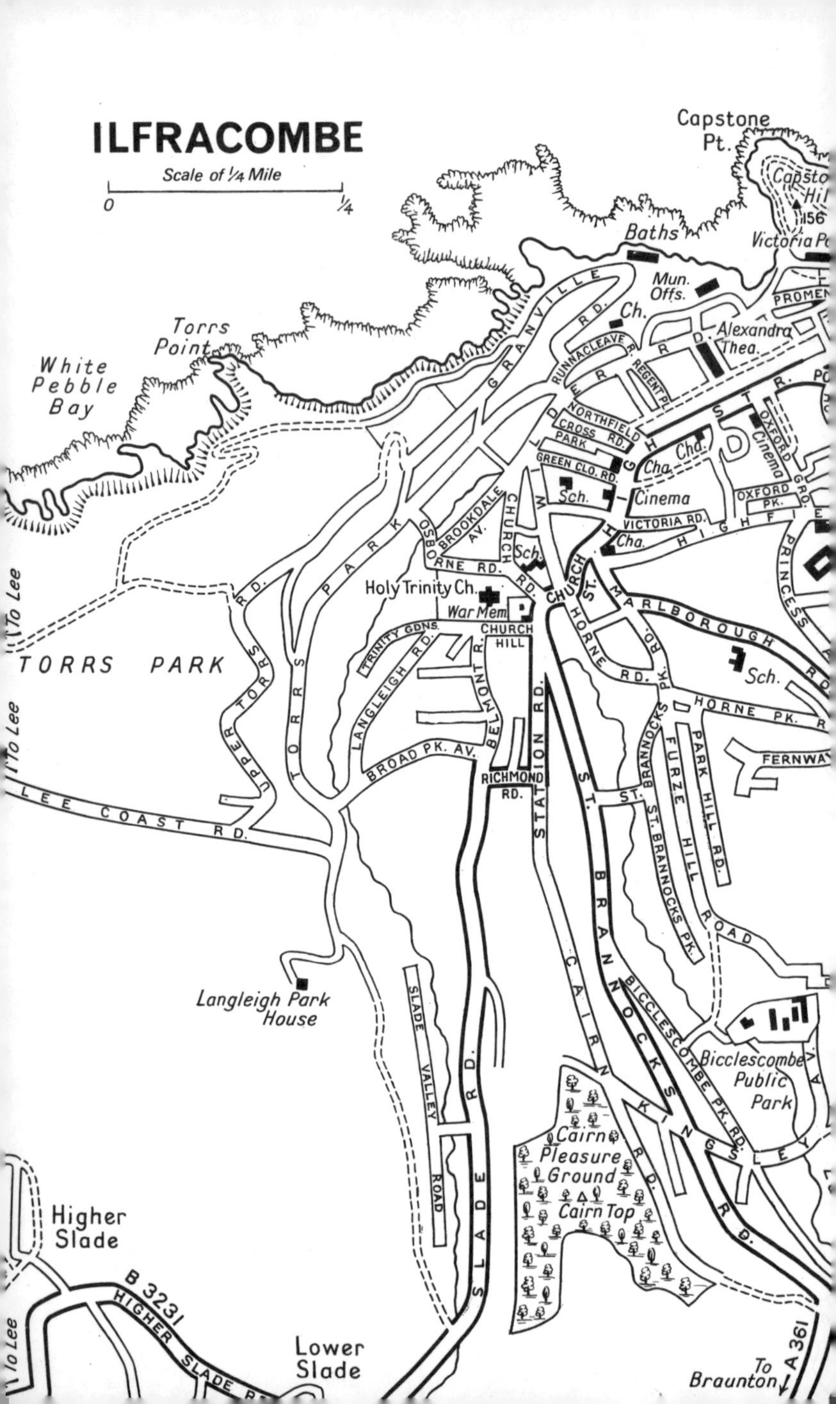

ILFRACOMBE
Scale of 1/4 Mile
0
1/4
Capstone Pt.
Capstone Hill
156
Victoria Pd
Baths
Mun. Offs.
Ch.
Promenade
Alexandra Thea.
Torrs Point
White Pebble Bay
Granville Rd.
Runnacleave Rd.
Regent Pl.
Northfield Rd.
Cross Rd.
Park
Green Clo. Rd.
Wilder Rd.
High St.
Oxford Gro.
Oxford Pk.
Cinema
Cha.
Sch.
Victoria Rd.
Highfield
Princess Av.
Brookdale Av.
Osborne Rd.
Church Rd.
Church St.
Holy Trinity Ch.
War Mem.
Church Hill
Marlborough Rd.
Horne Rd.
Horne Pk. Rd.
Fernway
Torrs Park
Park Rd.
Upper Torrs Rd.
Torrs Rd.
To Lee
Trinity Gdns.
Langleigh Rd.
Belmont Rd.
Broad Pk. Av.
Richmond Rd.
Station Rd.
St. Brannocks Rd.
St. Brannocks Pk.
St. Brannocks Pk. Rd.
Furze Hill Road
Park Hill Rd.
Lee Coast Rd.
Langleigh Park House
Slade Valley Road
Slade Rd.
Cairn Rd.
Kingsley Av.
Bicclescombe Pk. Rd.
Bicclescombe Public Park
Cairn Pleasure Ground
Cairn Top
Higher Slade
B 3231
Higher Slade Rd.
Lower Slade
To Braunton
A 361

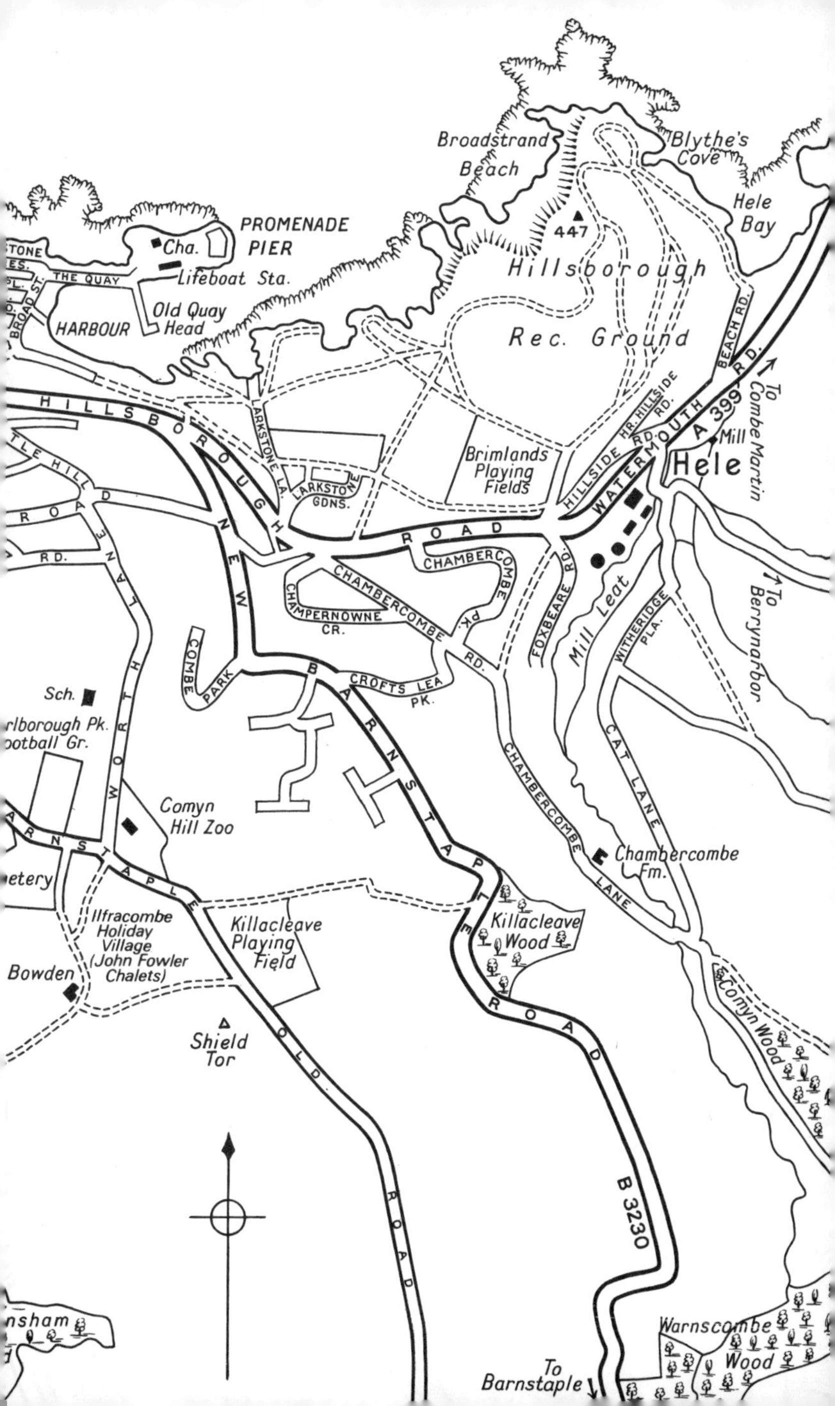

PROMENADE PIER
Cha.
Lifeboat Sta.
THE QUAY
BROAD ST.
HARBOUR
Old Quay Head
Broadstrand Beach
Blythe's Cove
Hele Bay
447
Hillsborough
Rec. Ground
BEACH RD.
HILLSBOROUGH
LARKSTONE LA.
LARKSTONE GDNS.
Brimlands Playing Fields
HR. HILLSIDE RD.
HILLSIDE RD.
WATERMOUTH RD.
A 399
To Combe Martin
Mill
Hele
ROAD
NEW
CHAMBERCOMBE PK.
CHAMBERCOMBE RD.
CHAMPERNOWNE CR.
FOXBEARE RD.
Mill Leat
WITHERIDGE PLA.
To Berrynarbor
COMBE PARK
CROFTS LEA PK.
BARNSTAPLE ROAD
Sch.
Football Gr.
WORTH LANE
Comyn Hill Zoo
CHAMBERCOMBE LANE
CAT LANE
Chambercombe Fm.
Killacleave Playing Field
Killacleave Wood
Ilfracombe Holiday Village (John Fowler Chalets)
Bowden
Comyn Wood
Shield Tor
OLD ROAD
B 3230
Warnscombe Wood
To Barnstaple

seen running through open country and leading to the lighthouse, about a mile distant. Admission is generally obtainable in the afternoon.

From the lighthouse there is a gated road, with a public right of way for walkers only, to Mortehoe, a distance of 1½ miles. About half-a-mile to the west of this road is **Morte Point**, now National Trust property, with extensive picturesque walks. Immediately below the ridge on the north side about 200 yards west of the auxiliary coastguard station is an ancient British cromlech. The upper stone, weighing some 2 tons, has collapsed due to weathering of the supporting stones. Access to Morte Point is ¼ mile along a narrow road immediately to the north of Mortehoe Church and through memorial gates commemorating the gift of the Point to the Trust by the late Miss Chichester.

The return to Ilfracombe may be made by bus from Mortehoe.

To Mortehoe

By coast 5 miles *via* Lee (p. 214): by road 6 miles. There is a bus service. From the old station the road to the left goes to Woolacombe, 2 miles; that to the right goes to the main road which, followed to the left, leads to the vicinity of Mortehoe Church, over two miles distant. At first there is a short easy rise and then the way is all downhill.

Various legends connect Mortehoe with the scene of the supposed perpetual doom of the family of Tracy, Norman lords of the barony of Barnstaple, on account of the participation of Sir William de Tracy in the murder of Thomas à Becket.

The **Church** contains the tomb of "Sir William Tracy", but it has been conclusively shown that this "Sir" William was a priest of the church, not a knight militant. He was, in fact, rector of Mortehoe from 1257 to 1322, and died 146 years later than Becket's assassin. It was an old-world custom to bestow the title of Sir on clergy in priests' orders who were not university graduates.

From the vicinity of the church there is a steep descent to the coast, where is the newer part of Mortehoe. A short distance down the hill is the Methodist Church. At the foot of the hill is the **Combesgate** portion of this extensive parish. Here is a public path to a safe and pleasant bathing beach of sand, enclosed by rocks which, farther southward, adjoin the quaint and narrow little rocky cove of **Barricane**, in Woolacombe. It is noted for its beach of shells.

Very soon the rocks suddenly end and are succeeded by the magnificent sandy beach of Woolacombe.

To Chambercombe Valley

This is a delightful walk within easy distance of the town and presenting charming and varied scenery. The way is by Portland Street to Hillsborough Road, east of the town. Pass the Larkstone Gardens on the left and the thatched Cottage Inn on the right and follow Chambercombe Road to the old manor-house and Comyn Farm, little more than a mile from the centre of Ilfracombe.

The historic old manor-house at **Chambercombe** (*teas*) was formerly the manor-house of Ilfracombe. The date of the earliest record of it is 1162 though Domesday Book contains a reference to a Chambercombe Manor probably acquired by the Champernoune family soon after the Norman Conquest. *House and gardens open* *to visitors*. Lady Jane Grey is said to have slept in the room above the hall when on a visit to the Champernounes. This room is notable for the wagon-top ceiling, the Tudor Rose in the carved scroll work and the carved coat of arms over the fireplace. There is a collection of Tudor and Jacobean furniture including two fine oak chairs, a twelfth-century *Peters Pence Box*, and a 400-year-old cider press. There is also a Benz motor car of 1889. A secret chamber, a furnished bedroom, discovered in 1865, contained the skeleton of a woman. Her ghost is said to haunt the old manor. Legend ascribes her as being Kate Oatway, daughter of a wrecker of Chambercombe.

At **Comyn Farm**, near by, is the entrance to the Valley and Woods, which are private property, but open to visitors.

As there is no outlet through the woods, return again to Comyn Farm and take a path to the left leading over fields to the Barnstaple Road, by which the return may be made to Ilfracombe, or the walk extended to the **Sterridge Valley**.

To Berrynarbor

This walk of 3 miles is *via* Hele village. Berrynarbor takes its name from Berry de Nerbert, the former family name of the lord of the manor here. One of the principal members of this family is commemorated by a memorial in the church, in which are also memorials to other Berrys. The Church, dedicated to St. Peter, is of Norman origin, has a fine tower, 89 feet high, and an interesting interior.

A link with ancient days is an old farmhouse known as **Bowden**, and notable as the birthplace in 1522 of Bishop Jewell, whose *Apologia Ecclesiæ Anglicanæ* so pleased Queen Elizabeth that it was ordered to be chained in the parish churches.

The return to Ilfracombe can be made by either of the following routes.

(*a*) *Via* Goosewell, a cluster of cottages reached by leaving Berrynarbor from the opposite end to that at which it was entered. The road passes to the left of the church in a north-westerly direction. After descending the hill and crossing the stream, take the first turning to the left, then immediately to the right and uphill to Goosewell. In a mile and a half it joins the Hillsborough Road, and rather more than 3 miles from Berrynarbor Church the High Street of Ilfracombe is reached.

(*b*) *Via* Watermouth, a rather longer route, but buses run over the greater part of it. Berrynarbor is left as above, but after crossing the stream continue along the road for approximately half a mile to Saw Mills, where the Ilfracombe–Combe Martin road is reached.

To Woolacombe

Access. – By bus from Woolacombe and Mortehoe, 2 miles. Bus services from Ilfracombe. Coach services.

Banks. – *Lloyds* (Mon., Tues., Thurs., Fri., 10–1); *Barclays* (Mon., Tues., Thurs., Fri., 10–1); *National Westminster* (Tues. and Fri. 10–12.30).

Bathing. – Generally safe, but dangerous at low tide. Surfing is popular and boards may be hired. Beach huts let by the week, etc. Swimming pool at Woolacombe Bay Hotel open to public.

Car Parking. – Near Esplanade and at Challacombe Hill Road.

Hotels. – *Woolacombe Bay, Narracott Grand, Combe's, Rathleigh, Atlantic, Beach, Headlands, Pandora, Sands, Little Beach, Hartland* and others.

Occupying the greater part of Morte Bay, between Baggy Point and Morte Point, is the two-mile golden stretch of **Woolacombe Sands**, one of the finest beaches in the West Country. Croyde and Saunton, farther south, are the only other places on the North Devon coast where such sands are found. At the northern part of the bay, backed by Mortehoe, olive-tinted, white-fringed rocks pointing finger like to sea are separated by lovely sandy coves. The sands make a magnificent playground and bathing and surfing under normal conditions are perfectly safe. Attention must, however, be paid to warnings not to bathe at low tide.

In Woolacombe itself there are some first-rate hotels and boarding houses, holiday flats, some attractive property, banks and shops. Nearby are extensive caravan sites. Dances and film shows are held in the Village Hall.

Woolacombe has grown up at the end of the usual Devon combe, which, however, in this instance is much more open and less wooded than some, giving a consequent impression of freedom. Here and there are gleaming white quartz veins in the grey cliffs, gloriously crowned with grass and yellow sea flowers.

It is claimed that Woolacombe, being sheltered from the north, east, and south-east, facing due west, and overlooking the open Atlantic, has a far more bracing air than any place on the south coast open only to the south.

The church, consecrated in 1912, is dedicated to St. Sabinus, a missionary from Ireland who was wrecked at Woolacombe.

At the northern end of the sands is **Barricane** or **Shell Beach**. Above it is the Esplanade from which there is an expansive view. Running parallel with the sands is the Marine Drive. The road climbing Challacombe Hill leads over Pickwell Down to the village of Georgeham.

To Watermouth

Distance from Ilfracombe. – 3 miles (on Combe Martin bus route).

About half-way between Ilfracombe and Combe Martin is the pretty castellated **Watermouth Castle**, formerly the home of the Bassets, an old Devonshire family whose estate covered several square miles and included the village of Berrynarbor. Part is now in use as a holiday bungalow centre. On the opposite side of the road is a gate leading to the **Watermouth Caves**. A boatman is usually waiting to take visitors on a little tour of inspection. This is perhaps the best way of seeing the caves, although they can easily be reached on foot at low tide. The formation of the rocks here, especially at **Briery Cave**, is most peculiar. Caravan centre at Watermouth Caves.

Combe Martin

Combe Martin

Banks. – *Lloyds, Midland, National Westminster.*
Bathing. – Safe beaches. All bathing is free. Shingle gives way to sand at low tide.
Boating. – Rowing-boats for hire. Trips by launch.
Bowls. – Green in King Street.
Buses. – Services to Lynton, Ilfracombe, Barnstaple, etc. numerous coach trips.
Early Closing Day. – Wednesday.
Fishing. – Good sea fishing. Fly fishing at Hunter's Inn.
Hotels. – *Channel Vista, Lion, Delve's, Sea View, Pack of Cards, Kingston House, London Inn, George* and others.
Police. – High Street.
Population. – 2,207.
Post Office. – High Street. Sub-office at Seaside.
Putting. – At "Brooklands".
Tennis. – Hard courts.

Combe Martin, a popular holiday centre, is situated amid some delightful scenery. The view from the hill on the Ilfracombe side particularly is charming. Green fields, tidy market gardens, quaint cottages and pleasant houses make a comforting picture contrasting well with the wild scenery of the coast.

The little bay, tucked away among the cliffs, is picturesque. A stream trickles across the sands, seaward, at low tide. Overlooking the bay on the west side and part shaded by trees, is the **Parade**. It is a good place from which to watch the wonderful sea and sky effects, especially beautiful towards evening when the setting sun deepens the colour contrasts of the land.

The village consists principally of a single long street, a little over a mile and a half long, narrow and nearly all on an incline. For those wanting a quiet place, this is an ideal choice, while it is also a good centre for motoring, cycling and walking. There are a good number of shops, houses which are let furnished during summer months, and numerous houses offering accommodation and board.

Market gardening and fruit growing are important local industries, while a ready market for produce is found at Ilfracombe, Lynton and Barnstaple. Strawberries, for which the district is famous, are dispatched in quantity to London, South Wales and other large centres in early summer. In spring the fields of daffodils are like sheets of fairy gold.

The western end of Combe Martin, that part at which one first arrives from Ilfracombe, is known as *Seaside*. Once but a few fishermen's cottages, there are now more modern houses at which there is good accommodation for visitors. Close at hand are Newberry Beach, the Parade with car park, seats and shelters, and Combe Martin Beach, a large stretch of level sand outside a long ridge of stones known as the Breakwater. The sea here for some distance out is free of currents and the beach popular for bathing. There is also good bathing at the foot of Hangman Hill. **Sandy Bay**, to the left of Newberry Beach and reached by Sandy Bay Lane, off the Ilfracombe–Combe Martin road, belies its name, for there is no sand, but the spot is favourite for a picnic. Steps lead down to the beach.

Although most of the buildings in the long street are unremarkable, one immediately arrests attention on account of its unusual shape. This is *The Pack of Cards*, said to have been built in the eighteenth century from winnings at card-playing. It has four floors; on each are thirteen doors, and originally there were fifty-two windows, one for each card. The old table on the ground floor is said to have been used in the days of the press gangs. Three men can hide in the space below the false top. Those who have read Marie Corelli's *The Mighty Atom* may remember that it contains a reference to this building.

Farther along the street is **High Cross**, a busy road junction where the market, now discontinued, was held in olden times. The *War Memorial*, a grey granite cross, occupies a well-tended site at the end of Church Street. Behind it –

The Parish **Church**, dedicated to St. Peter ad Vincula, consists of nave and chancel, north and south transepts, a north aisle extending into a chancel aisle or chapel, and at the west end a fine tower, 99 feet high to its battlements. The oldest parts are the chancel, nave and south transept. The tower was probably begun in the reign of Henry II (1154–89). The interior of the church has some highly interesting features, the most striking perhaps being the beautiful carved screen.

In the window nearest the screen on the south side of the chancel is a bit of old glass representing the Seraphim of *Isaiah vi* 2. and the wheels of *Ezekiel i.* 15–20. The modern window on the south side, donated in 1949, portrays the three Bishops connected with Combe Martin and neighbourhood – Bishop Martin of Tours,

Great and Little Hangman

Bishop Jewell born at Berrynarbor, and Bishop Hannington of Trentishoe. In the Lady chapel are curious old benches of oak or Spanish chestnut carved at the ends and surmounted by mutilated carved figures. Here also may be noticed a brass of 1587 to William Hancock and the elaborately sculptured monument to Judith Hancock (1637), the lace on her dress being particularly noteworthy. An old door, its age somewhat doubtfully given as 800 years, leads into the vestry. The lofty tower arch is Early English, but the capitals of its pillars are Norman or Transitional. The bells were recast in 1827 and again in 1922, when the number was increased to eight.

The High Street leads into Castle Street where are the remains of an ancient manor hall of the early twelfth century, often referred to as the Tithe Barn, though its early history is obscure. The fine Norman arch still stands.

The distant high ground eastward of the church comprises the Hangman Hills, Great and Little. The building on the ridge was connected with the mines of silver and lead, which were worked here at least as far back as the reign of Edward I, when 337 workmen were brought from the Peak of Derbyshire.

Camden states that Combe Martin silver helped to pay the cost of the French wars in the reigns of Edward III and Henry V. From that period to the reign of Elizabeth the mines appear to have been neglected; but then Adrian Gilbert discovered a new lode, which was subsequently worked by Sir Beavis Bulmer, Kt., with such skill that the mines again yielded a considerable revenue. At the Mansion House in London there are three tankards made from silver mined here at that time. After Bulmer's time the mines fell into disuse. Since 1648 repeated attempts have been made to work them, but without permanent success. Combe Martin, however, is still regarded by many eminent geologists as a highly valuable, though neglected, mineral district.

Walks from Combe Martin

Combe Martin abounds in delightful walks. The favourite is to the **Great Hangman Hill** which starts at the junction of Borough Road and Cross Street. A notice board indicates the lane to the *Hangman Walk*. After passing the school, bear left to Lester Point, the cliff above Wild Pear Beach. The coast route continues to the top of Little Hangman Hill (716 feet), then on to Great Hangman (1,044 feet). An alternative route is *via* Shute Lane nearly opposite *The Pack of Cards* leading to Rocky Lane, of which the line is continued from Netherton Cross by Knapp Down Lane. Beyond the track to Girt (great) Farm the ascent is less steep; and soon there is seen on the left a wide field-path leading to Sherracombe Waterfall and the Great Hangman.

A circular tour can be made by going *via* the field path and returning by the coast route. The top of Great Hangman (1,044 feet) is marked by a rough cairn. The total distance is about 5½ miles, and there are seats and shelters on the way up.

On the way to Great Hangman a path is passed which leads down the face of the cliff to **Wild Pear** or **Hangman Beach**, a delightful spot for picnics, with varying sand or pebble shore for bathing. The tide comes right up to the rocks. Steps have been cut in the cliff down to the beach, but the descent and climb back is quite arduous. On the north side of the beach is a stream of drinking water.

Hunter's Inn (*see* p. 225), about 6 miles of heavy going eastward, can be reached by going up Shute Lane, turning right and continuing on to Stony Corner, from which are the lovely views of the harbour and the Combe Martin valley, and taking the Trentishoe road, which follows the slight dip between Holdstone and Trentishoe Downs, passing a little below Trentishoe Barrows and through the village of **Trentishoe**. Shute Lane, the old coaching way, is now fit for cars. Alternatively, Trentishoe village can be avoided by keeping to the right at the fork beyond the Barrows, and walkers may be recommended to go one way and return by the other, which will afford dissimilar views. Stony Corner can also be reached through Buzzacot Lane, near the top of the village. There is a good bus service between Combe Martin and Hunter's Inn, during the summer, by way of Buzzacot Road, Stony Corner, Holdstone Down. A bus may also be taken to Parracombe Hill, walking the rest of the way to Hunter's Inn by Killington and Kittitoe.

Another delightful walk is to **Berry Down** by way of the Barnstaple road, and back to Combe Martin through the pretty Sterridge Valley and Berrynarbor village.

Watermouth Caves are about 2¼ miles along the road to Ilfracombe. This walk will be enhanced by taking the diversion along the Old Road beyond Sandy Cove.

The top of **Clorridge Hill** (481 feet) is reached by passing through a wicket gate on the right-hand side of the Barnstaple road, about ¼ mile beyond the church. A path leads through a disused quarry to the top of the hill, where are seats from which glorious views of the church, village, sea and country may be obtained.

Hunter's Inn, Heddon's Mouth and Woody Bay

The scenery in this district is generally considered the most romantic in Devon; it is impossible to speak in too glowing terms of its beauty.
Hunter's Inn is an idyllic spot in the combe which runs down to **Heddon's Mouth.**

The **Inn** is a picturesque building, and a good centre for fishing and sketching. Fishing tickets for the **Heddon** are obtainable at the hotel.

There is a marked contrast between the wooded loveliness of the valley near the Inn and the bare rocks where the combe opens to the sea at Heddon's Mouth. Seawards the hills close in, making it a narrow glen, varying in aspect with the seasons, softer in summer, when the greens hide much of the rock, than in winter, when the growth dies down and the rusty reds and browns with a full stream foaming over the boulders give it an air of wild grandeur. The valley can be followed on either side of the stream, that on the left or west bank (approached by keeping to the road on the left of the Inn and taking a gate beyond a subsidiary stream) being more level than that on the right or east (the path starts close to the back of the Inn). Farther on this path forks, one climbing the hillside and forming the cliff path to Woody Bay, which should only be traversed by those with good heads for heights, the other keeping more or less beside the stream until the shore is reached. Care must be taken in clambering up the steep hillside, as falls of cliff sometimes occur.

The Martinhoe Cliff Drive which starts to the right of Hunter's Inn, and is the wider of the two roads there seen, affords a fine view of the Heddon's Mouth gorge. It is a rough road which quickly peters out to a mere bridle path or footpath. It gradually ascends, winding round subsidiary combes and then, turning **High-veer Point**, comes out on the open coast, with sheer drops to the sea in places. It is some distance from the Point before this path comes out on to the tarmac road between **Martinhoe Common** and Woody Bay. From the road, which continues to Lynton, another goes down to Martinhoe Manor and Woody Bay, while to the right a rough, narrow throughfare, for those on foot only, mounts steeply to Martinhoe church and thence to Hunter's Inn.

Woody Bay

a charming glen, has, like every true Devonshire combe, a rushing torrent. The cliffs, covered with foliage to the water's edge, fall steeply to the sea,

Heddon's Mouth

and perhaps more enjoyment can be obtained by looking at the scene from the paths which encircle it high on the down than by exploring the various descending zigzags through the trees, although occasional charming glimpses may be obtained here and there.

Round the west side of the bay the downs soar some hundreds of feet, and are dotted with attractive houses. Below, near the strand, is *Martinhoe Manor*. The precipitous western horn of the inlet, wooded from the base to summit, is **Wringapeak**.

The beach may be reached by turning to the left at the top of the zigzag at the crossways.

Lower down from the road, a turn to the right leads to the stream, which is crossed by *Inkerman Bridge*. Thence the road goes on to join the drive through the grounds of Lee Abbey, 2 miles from Woody Bay Hotel. In a hollow a quarter-mile short of it are pleasant tea gardens.

To Lynton and Lynmouth

From Combe Martin there is a stiff climb almost to the summit of **Kentisbury Down** (1,105 feet). At the cross-roads by *Blackmore Gate* turn left. A mile on, the old road descends to the pretty village of **Parracombe** (*Fox and Goose Inn*), and then rises again, but the new road, part of the magnificent Lynton–Barnstaple highway, by missing the village, avoids the hill, though it passes close to the ancient church of St. Petrock, dating from the tenth century. A stop should be made to examine its very interesting interior. There are old oak benches and high pews, a three-decker pulpit and minstrels' gallery, with a piece of wood cut out for the bow arm of the double bass player. Close by are two old cottages where ale used to be brewed for thirsty worshippers. Beyond Parracombe the road passes Martinhoe Cross and thence continues over Caffins Heanton Down to **Lynton**, on high ground, and **Lynmouth** at the outlet of the West Lyn torrent.

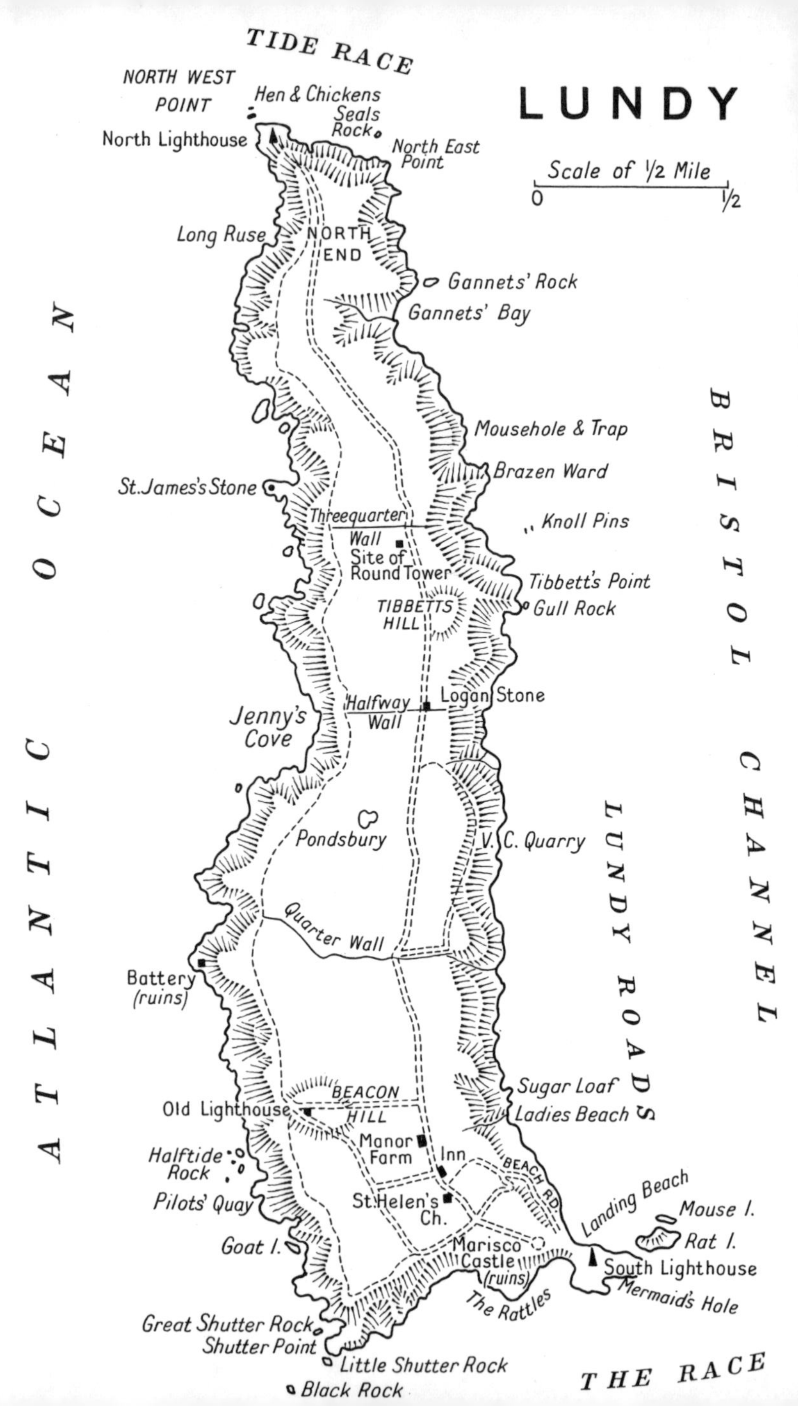
LUNDY
Scale of ½ Mile
0
½
TIDE RACE
NORTH WEST POINT
Hen & Chickens
Seals Rock
North Lighthouse
North East Point
Long Ruse
NORTH END
Gannets' Rock
Gannets' Bay
ATLANTIC OCEAN
BRISTOL CHANNEL
Mousehole & Trap
Brazen Ward
St. James's Stone
Threequarter Wall
Knoll Pins
Site of Round Tower
Tibbett's Point
Gull Rock
TIBBETTS HILL
Halfway Wall
Logan Stone
Jenny's Cove
Pondsbury
V. C. Quarry
LUNDY ROADS
Quarter Wall
Battery (ruins)
Sugar Loaf
Ladies Beach
BEACON HILL
Old Lighthouse
Manor Farm
Halftide Rock
Inn
BEACH RD
Pilots' Quay
St. Helen's Ch.
Landing Beach
Mouse I.
Rat I.
Goat I.
Marisco Castle (ruins)
South Lighthouse
Mermaid's Hole
The Rattles
Great Shutter Rock
Shutter Point
Little Shutter Rock
Black Rock
THE RACE

Lundy

Access By Sea. – A motor vessel leaves twice a week from Ilfracombe from April to September inclusive. For the remainder of the year sailings every seven to ten days. Steamers and other boats make trips from Cardiff, Swansea and other Bristol Channel ports during summer months, all calling at Ilfracombe. Landing from steamers is accomplished by motor-boats. When an easterly wind is blowing a landing is impossible. Fares include landing fee.

Accommodation. – The Hotel and some furnished cottages. Enquiries to The Agent, Lundy, Bristol Channel, *via* Ilfracombe.

Landing Fee. – The island is private property and a landing fee is payable.

Refreshments. – At the Marisco Tavern. A tea garden is open on steamer calling days.

A Quick Tour

The time allowed on a day trip is not usually sufficient for leisured exploration of the island or to reach the extreme north where the rarer birds nest. The quarter, half and threequarter walls built by convict labour under Benson are useful indications of the distance if the time has to be watched for the return. A short tour could start with the steep climb from the landing beach to the Marisco Castle ruins. From here the westward path leads past the granite formation known as Benjamin's chair and bears right to Beacon Hill and the old lighthouse. Northward, the footpath along the cliff top gives wonderful views of the west coast. To return, cross to the east coast path and walk south past the quarries and the quarterwall cottages. Two fields ahead is the Manor Farm, the Hotel and the Marisco Tavern (light refreshments and drinks, no licensing hours) and the general stores where postcards, stamps, etc., may be bought. To the west is the Church and to the east, Millcombe House annexe to the Hotel, from which a good road leads to the landing beach.

Lundy Island lies in the Bristol Channel 11¾ miles north-west of Hartland Point and 23 miles due west of Ilfracombe. It is a huge rock, volcanic in origin, three miles long and averaging half a mile in width. A sloping tableland of just over a thousand acres its cliff sides rise to a height of from 300 to 400 feet. The eastern side is clad with heathery combes, grassland, trees and flowering shrubs, and is intersected with sparkling springs and rivulets. Westward the scenery is rugged with sheer precipices, pinnacled cliffs, rocky coves and a magnificent coastline.

Lundy was long owned by the Harman family but in 1969 was gifted by purchase to The National Trust and leased to the Landmurk Trust.

The soil is light, and only a small part of the island is under cultivation, but about a quarter of the area is permanent pasture, sheep, cattle and ponies being reared, while the rest is moorland. Lobsters are caught in large quantities. Fresh water is supplied in abundance by the springs. Snow and ice are rare.

On Lundy

Botanically Lundy is of great interest, wild flowers growing in great number and variety. *Brassicella Wrightii*, named after its discoverer, Dr. Elliston Wright of Braunton, is a plant found nowhere else in the world, and it is supposed to be the ancestor of all the *brassicella* (cabbage) on the mainland. The fauna, too, is remarkable. Rat Island, an island of about an acre situated off the south-east point, is one of the few remaining strongholds of the black rat, which is also fairly numerous in the main part of the Island, and is also the home of trap-door spiders, found nowhere else in or around the British Isles. Rabbits are said to have been introduced to England from Lundy, the first documentary reference dating from about the year 1200. Ponies of an excellent type are numerous and there are some Japanese Sika deer, wild goats and Soay sheep. Seals breed on and are frequently seen in great numbers near Lundy, and one large cave is known as the Seal's Hole. The birds, past and present, are intensely interesting. Strict measures exist to preserve the many rare birds which nest in the island at the present time, the peregrine falcon, cormorant, puffin and oyster-catcher, regarded as rarities in other parts of the British Isles, being common on Lundy. One theory is held that the name *Lundy* is derived from the Scandinavian: *lunde*-puffin; *ey*-island. There are no snakes, frogs or toads on the island, tradition crediting St. Patrick with having stayed there *en route* for Ireland.

In a cliff at the south-west corner there is a curious funnel-shaped cavity, about 370 feet deep, called the **Devil's Lime Kiln**, at the bottom of which are two small passages leading to the sea. Close at hand is a huge conical-shaped rock called **Shutter Rock**, near which the battleship *Montagu*, practically a new vessel, was wrecked in 1906, a loss to the country of a very costly ship. The rock is referred to in *Westward Ho!* as that upon which the Spanish galleon struck when pursued by Amyas Leigh. Lying off the north end of Lundy is a cluster of rocks called the **Hen and Chickens**. Vessels give these a wide berth. In the same neighbourhood, but on the island, is the **Constable Rock**. On the east side is the **Templar Rock**, which bears a marvellous resemblance to the human face.

The **Church**, erected in 1897 and dedicated to St. Helena, is of grey stone and has a clock in its square tower. There is a finely carved alto-relievo reredos.

Close to the church are the principal buildings on the island, the Manor House combining a comfortable hotel, and the Marisco Tavern and stores.

There are three **Lighthouses**, but that on the highest point of the island has no longer a lantern. The light was hidden when mist capped the top of the island, as frequently happens. It is now used as a bird observatory and can be rented by organized parties. Visitors who ascend the tower will be well rewarded by a view of the whole of Lundy.

High above the landing beach stand the remains of the keep of the Castle of the Mariscos, its lords in the twelfth century. Close by is **Benson's Cave**, used as a storehouse by the former owner of that name (of whom more below), but probably made by the Mariscos. A granite quarry, opened in 1864, has yielded stone for many important buildings in London and elsewhere. The quarry has since been named "V.C. Quarry" in memory of J. P. Harman, who was posthumously awarded the Victoria Cross for gallantry in Burma in 1944. A fine memorial stone was unveiled in 1949.

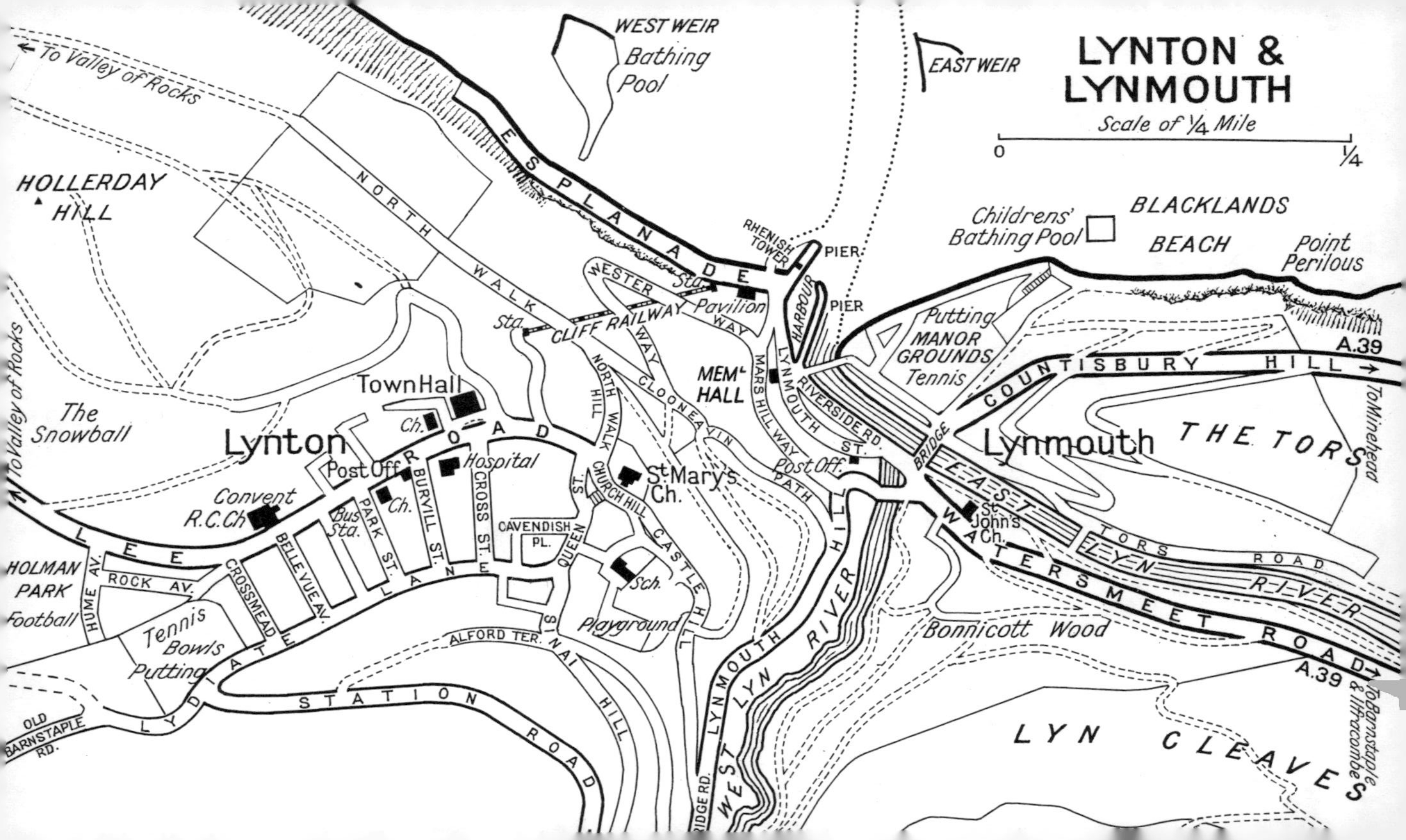

LYNTON & LYNMOUTH
Scale of 1/4 Mile
0
1/4
WEST WEIR
Bathing Pool
EAST WEIR
Childrens' Bathing Pool
BLACKLANDS
BEACH
Point Perilous
To Valley of Rocks
HOLLERDAY HILL
The Snowball
Lynton
Lynmouth
THE TORS
ESPLANADE
NORTH WALK
RHENISH TOWER
PIER
HARBOUR
Sta.
CLIFF RAILWAY
WESTER WAY
Pavilion
MEM'L HALL
Town Hall
Ch.
ROAD
Post Off.
Hospital
Convent R.C.Ch
Bus Sta.
PARK ST.
BURVILL ST.
CROSS ST.
CAVENDISH PL.
QUEEN ST.
NORTH WALK HILL
CHURCH HILL
St. Mary's Ch.
CLOONEAVIN
MARS HILL WAY
LYNMOUTH ST.
RIVERSIDE RD.
PATH
HILL
CASTLE HILL
Sch.
Playground
SINAI HILL
ALFORD TER.
LEE
LANE
HOLMAN PARK
Football
HUME AV.
ROCK AV.
CROSSMEAD
BELLE VUE AV.
Tennis
Bowls
Putting
LYDIATE
STATION ROAD
OLD BARNSTAPLE RD.
BRIDGE RD.
WEST LYN RIVER
LYNMOUTH
Putting
MANOR GROUNDS
Tennis
COUNTISBURY HILL
A.39
To Minehead
BRIDGE
EAST LYN RIVER
TORS ROAD
St. John's Ch.
WATERSMEET ROAD
Bonnicott Wood
To Barnstaple & Ilfracombe
LYN CLEAVES

Lynton and Lynmouth

Bank. – *Lloyds,* Lee Road, Lynton, and branch office at Lynmouth.

Bathing. – The sea at Lynmouth is beautifully clear and, having a uniform temperature, is rarely really cold even in winter.

Sillery Sands, a good stretch of beach about a mile east of Lynmouth, is a favourite place for bathing. It is approached by way of a path zigzagging down the hillside from about half-way up Countisbury Hill, or by boats which run daily in summer. Bathing may be enjoyed at Wringcliffe (about 1½ miles), under the Castle Rock: and there is good bathing at Lee Bay (2 miles).

Boating. – Motor-, sailing- or rowing-boats may be hired.

Cricket. – *Lynton Cricket Club* ground in the Valley of Rocks. Visitors are invited to play.

Entertainments. – In the season dances, cinema and theatrical performances are given in the Town Hall, Lynton. There are Amusement Centres in the Pavilion, Lynmouth and at Lee Road, Lynton.

Early Closing Day. – Thursday.

Fishing. – Both sea and river fishing are extremely good, forming indeed one of the chief attractions of the district.

Hotels. – Lynton: *Royal Castle, Valley of Rocks, Seaward, Queens, Woodlands, Imperial, Fairholm, Olde Cottage Inn, Channel View, Crown,* etc.

Lynmouth: *Tors, River Lyn View, Bath, Rising Sun, Oakleigh, Tregonwell.*

Library. – Lending library at the Town Hall.

Park and Pleasure Grounds. – **Lynmouth Park**, on the slope of the hill at the foot of the Cliff Railway, and the **Manor Grounds** on the sea-front, command fine views of the East Lyn Valley, the Foreland, and the sea.

At the entrance to the Valley of Rocks is the **Holman Park** and the Lynton tennis courts and putting green.

Some of the finest views around Lynton are to be gained from Southcleave, or **South-cliff**. The site is the hill on the left (south) of and overlooking the Valley of Rocks.

The grounds of **Hollerday House** were presented to Lynton by the late J. W. Holman.

Population. – 1,770.

Post Offices. – Lee Road, Lynton and Lynmouth Street, Lynmouth.

Putting. – At Lee Road and in Manor Grounds.

Steamer Trips. – In summer there are steamer trips from Lynmouth to Minehead, Weston, Ilfracombe and Clovelly; sometimes also to Lundy, the South Wales coast and distant Newquay.

There is no landing-stage at Lynmouth. Motor-boats put off and take passengers to and from the steamers.

Tennis. – At Lee Road, Lynton and at Manor Grounds, Lynmouth.

It has been said that Lynton and Lynmouth constitute an epitome of the scenery of Devon. Perhaps more songs of praise have been sung of these twin villages than of any other English holiday resort, but, owing their charm partly to their picturesque site and natural beauty of surroundings and partly to the almost dramatic contrast between modern Lynton above, and ancient Lynmouth tucked away at the water's edge, they fully justify all that has been said of them.

Lynton crowns a steep and lofty hill, about 600 feet high, and seems to mount guard over her smaller sister Lynmouth nestling in the valleys and woods beneath. The name is believed to be derived from the Celtic *lyn* or *line*, "a pool", and those Exmoor rivers, the East and West Lyn, which unite in Lynmouth itself, are essentially streams of pools and rocks.

Southey passed through Lynmouth on his way to Ilfracombe, and his graphic description of the meeting of the two rivers, the contrast between the bare stones of one combe and the rich woods of the other, the magnifi-

Lynton

cent view from Summerhouse Hill between, is as true now as when he wrote it. Gainsborough, too, spoke of the district as the landscape artist's ideal.

The Ideal Holiday Resort

For many years Lynton-Lynmouth was content to be a showplace, the bourne of excursions from Ilfracombe, Minehead and other resorts. A show-place it still is, but its charm cannot be fully absorbed in a day and it now attracts large numbers of visitors who stay. For its size it has more and better hotels than any other place in Devon; there are numerous boarding houses and holiday flats, and every hamlet and farmhouse in the neighbourhood offers additional accommodation in the season. For walkers it would be hard to beat as headquarters; motorists might find better centres, but nowhere will they find greater use for the car, which easily surmounts hills which seventy years ago defined almost any loaded vehicle and so kept much of the neighbouring scenery a closed book. The bus and coach services are admirable. Delightful expeditions can be made by them entirely, or partly on foot and partly by bus. Those who have no cars or prefer not to use them need not therefore miss any of the beauty spots. The drivers are generally most helpful in giving information and pointing out places of interest. Cyclists must be careful of the steep hills. Anglers and sportsmen of all kinds will find Lynton and Lynmouth good headquarters, while tennis, boating and bathing are among other recreations.

Lynton

In Lynton is the **Parish Church** (St. Mary's), standing amid the hotels and business houses. It has been so many times altered, enlarged and repaired that scarcely anything remains of the original structure except part of the tower; this is mainly thirteenth century. The nave was re-built in 1741, and the church has been enlarged since; a beautiful side chapel having been added for weekday celebrations and services. Two interesting monuments at the west end record the death of Hugh Wichehalse, of Ley, in 1653, and Thomas Grose, nearly a century later. The wording on both is curious. There are other monuments and tablets to the Browning, Knight, Vellacott, Kekewich and Herries families. The font is of Caen stone. A battle flag of the Indian Mutiny period hangs on the west wall. The registers date from 1569. In a glass case is the Bishops' Bible issued by Anglican bishops in the sixteenth century. The tower contains a beautiful peal of six bells, two of which are medieval.

In the south porch are the old **Village Stocks,** in a fair state of preservation, and a well-preserved stoup, found at Furzehill, an old Exmoor farmhouse, where stood an ancient chapel of St. John the Baptist. A reproduction of the stocks stands in the south-west corner of the Churchyard.

From the Church, Lee Road leads to the **Town Hall**, a Tudoresque building set well back from the roadway. It was given by the late Sir George Newnes, Bart., to celebrate the coming of age of his son, the late Sir Frank Newnes. In front stands a memorial to Lynton and Lynmouth men who fell in the two world wars. The Hall contains the Council Chamber and offices of the Urban District Council. It also houses a Branch County Library. Upstairs is the Assembly Hall, with a good dance floor, and where film and theatrical performances are given in the season.

Behind the Town Hall rises **Hollerday Hill** (variously spelt Haliday and Holiday), on the slopes of which stood the ruins of Hollerday House (destroyed by fire in 1913), for many years the North Devon residence of Sir G. Newnes. The late J. W. Holman generously gave the grounds to Lynton, and the Council are very wisely keeping them in their original state – delightful, shady, pine-scented walks leading gently up to the open heath country, with springy turf, foxgloves and pennywort on the banks. From the top of this crowning beauty, glorious views are obtained of the rugged coastline, and inland to the wilds of Exmoor.

Farther along Lee Road are the **Methodist Church**; the **Lynton District Hospital**; the **Post Office**; the **Convent of St. Clare**; the **Roman Catholic Church**, and the **United Reformed Church**, the gift of Sir George Newnes. A short distance farther, in the lych-gate porch of the Churchyard extension, stands a *Shrine* to the memory of Lynton's war dead. The **Lee Road Recreation Club** has a billiard-room available to visitors for a small charge.

From the centre of Lynton, near the Church and the Town Hall, there is a choice of several ways down to Lynmouth, namely the steep Lynmouth main road, the devious elbow way over the Cliff Railway bridges, and the Clooneavin path.

Each of the zigzag paths is beautiful, but many visitors prefer to use –

The Cliff Railway

Services. – Cars run at intervals of a few minutes from 8 a.m. to 8 p.m. in June, 8 a.m. to 9 p.m. in July, August and September, and to 7 p.m. in winter. It is closed for part of the winter, usually January and February.

Sunday service (July to September only): 10 a.m. to 8 p.m.

The line comprises a double set of rails running sheer down the side of the cliff from the level of the Town Hall at Lynton, close to which is the lift head, to the Esplanade at Lynmouth, a distance of 901 feet, the gradient being 1 in 1¾.

The two cars by which the ascent and descent are made are fixed, equidistant, on an endless wire cable. To set the cars in motion a triangular-shaped tank beneath the top car is charged with water (of which there is a natural and plentiful supply) and the tank of the bottom car is simultaneously emptied. When the brakes are released one car runs down by the force of gravitation while the other is dragged up. Danger is reduced to a minimum by automatic brakes and an emergency brake. Should the wire rope snap, which is highly improbable, the brakes would automatically grip the rails and bring the cars to a standstill.

Lynmouth

From the west or from one of the cliff-paths a sight of great beauty is presented. The mouth of the united rivers forms a small tidal harbour, sheltered by stone jetties. On the western jetty is the modern replica of the Rhenish tower, originally built a hundred years ago. It was destroyed in the disastrous flood of 1952 but has been rebuilt. It is, in fact, an actual imitation of a tower on the Rhine. Originally intended as a beacon light for local mariners and fishermen, it still fulfils the duty, but instead of the tar-barrel flare of old, the iron cradle at the top contains a powerful electric lamp showing a white light visible for ten miles. There is no lifeboat now at Lynmouth, as it is quicker to launch a motor lifeboat from Ilfracombe or Minehead.

Overlooking the harbour is the Memorial Hall, erected in 1958 in memory of the 1952 flood. There are reading and rest rooms.

Westward from the tower the Esplanade runs along the foot of the cliff, with a public **Car Park** at the western end, and the **Old Bathing Pool** which refills at each high tide. But the eye involuntarily turns towards the lovely glen down which the rivers rattle. High on either hand rise steep and closely wooded hillsides, and among the trees are charmingly situated houses and hotels. Lynton seems to peer over the edge of the hill on the right, and the narrow strip of relatively level ground between the foot of the cliff and the river is closely filled with hotels, garages, restaurants and shops which do an enormous trade in postcards and souvenirs. The tide-fed **New Bathing Pool** stands on the Eastern Beach facing the Manor Grounds. The **Manor House**, used as a school during the Second World War, now serves as a Holiday Fellowship centre during the summer months. **Mars Hill** is the most picturesque of the steep little streets of Lynmouth, a glorious medley of colour-washed cottages, fuchsias and roses.

Lynmouth

Three bridges cross the stream; the more important being just above the point where the West Lyn comes in: this is the bridge by which all road traffic crosses; it is one of the busiest corners in Lynmouth, where the greatest care is necessary.

There are not many villages in England where the seaside shops and garages can be seen on one side of the main street and on the other a brawling salmon and trout stream with all the fascination that running water always exerts.

St. John's, nearby, is a well-built modern structure of squared stone – a little over a hundred years old. There is a fine stone grained roof over the chancel and a beautifully carved altar given by a mother in memory of her young daughter.

Opposite the Church is what is known as *Shelley's Cottage* (now a hotel and café). The poet is believed to have stayed here in 1812 while writing many poems and pamphlets. Some of the latter were of a seditious character – one was a "Declaration of Rights" – and it was his custom to place them in bottles and throw them into the sea – a curious form of "propaganda". The authorities ordered his arrest, but, being warned, he bribed a local boatman to pull him across to Wales and escaped.

The ravine down which the *West Lyn* roars in a succession of falls before joining its sister river and the open sea is known as **Glen Lyn**. It is extremely beautiful and may be visited on payment of a small charge.

Excursions from Lynton and Lynmouth

For the better enjoyment of the many delightful short excursions in the immediate vicinity it is necessary to walk, although, apart from the coach tours, there are many convenient bus services. It is useful to carry a bus time-table. The following list of distances from Lynmouth will be helpful in calculating probable time occupied, but it should be remembered that the hills are very steep and progress is necessarily much slower than in flatter country.

Distances from Lynmouth

	Miles
Barbrook	1½
Brendon, *via* Countisbury	3½
Brendon Church, *via* Watersmeet	3
Combe Park Gate	2½
Countisbury Church	1½
Countisbury Lighthouse	2¼
County Gate, *via* Countisbury	5
Glenthorne: Entrance Gate on main road	4
Hunter's Inn, Heddon's Mouth, *via* Slattenslade	5¾
Hunter's Inn, *via* Woody Bay	6¼
Lee Abbey	2¼
Lee Bay (bathing)	2¼
Lyn Bridge (Mill)	¾
Lynton Church	½
Malmsmead (for Badgworthy)	7¼
Martinhoe Church, *via* Slattenslade	4¼
Parracombe	5¼
Oare Church	8¾
Rockford, *via* Watersmeet	3½
Sillery Sands (bathing)	1
Valley of Rocks	1
Watersmeet	2¾
Woody Bay	3¼

Hollerday Hill (800 ft.) is so nearly a part of Lynton that directions are hardly required. Walk up Lee Road, Lynton, and just before reaching the Town Hall turn to the right up the hill. The one-time ruins of Hollerday House occupy a commanding site a little below the summit, nearly 800 feet above the sea, but are hidden by tall firs. The well-made road winds through deep cuttings and pleasant shrubberies to the top. The view is magnificent. The sterile Valley of Rocks, the jagged cliffs, Ragged Jack, Castle Rock, Duty Point with its tower, the beautiful sweep of Woody Bay, and Wringapeak and Highveer Point, stretching far out and away to the west, are well seen. On the east, beyond the East Lyn Valley and Tors Hill, is the long point of the Foreland, beyond which wide stretches of Exmoor are revealed. Far below is the broad Channel, rimmed by the faint white line of the South Wales coast. If the path is followed from the summit it turns to the right and leads back by a different route to Lynton, the whole hill being thus encompassed.

Summerhouse Hill (850 ft.) rising between the East and West Lyn rivers, also affords good views. It is approached by the zigzag path from Lynbridge or from the East Lyn Valley. From the latter the path starts opposite Lynmouth Church and winds up the hill through lovely **Glen Lyn Wood**. Half-way up, the woods cease, and the path is broad and safe to the topmost crag, from which is obtained an uninterrupted view of sea, mountain, valley, wood and moorland.

From the top of the hill a well-defined path (to the right approaching from Lynmouth) leads to Lynton *via* **Lynbridge**. Another equally well-defined path to the left leads to a lane running down to the Lyn Down road, and West Lyn Farm.

The Valley of Rocks

From Lynton take the North Walk downhill turning by the west gate of the Churchyard, and in about 100 yards bear to the left over the bridge crossing the Cliff Railway. The **North Walk** is a mile-long terrace–cut midway down the face of the cliff. The path is about five feet wide and commands along its entire length uninterrupted views of the Channel and the Welsh coast. Four hundred feet below is the sea, a glorious sight with gulls wheeling over the water. The sheer face of the cliff affords scanty foothold for the goats which browse on the tufts of grass peeping out amid the stones. Just over the jagged peaks on the left is the Valley of Rocks. The path here forks and by bearing right **Castle Rock** is sighted, with Duty Point in the distance. Between Castle Rock and **Ragged Jack** the path dips a little, to enter–

The Valley of Rocks. Southey described this vast amphitheatre admirably:

"Imagine a narrow vale between two ridges of hills, somewhat steep; the southern hill turfed; the vale, which runs from east to west, covered with huge stones and fragments of stone among the fern that fills it; the northern ridge completely bare, excoriated of all turf and all soil, the very bones and skeletons of the earth; rock reeling upon rock, stone piled upon stone, a huge terrific mass. I ascended, with some toil, the highest point; two large stones inclining on each other formed a rude portal on the summit".

The Castle Rock. The ascent is easier now than in Southey's day, for at the topmost heights has been made a rough stone stairway just wide enough to scramble up. The rock is nearly 800 feet high, and the seaward view is magnificent. On scaling the last fifty feet the peculiar formation of the rock is revealed, for the summit is composed of stupendous masses of stone piled one above the other, the strata running in all directions. Southey's "rude portal"–an enormous rock resting on another, standing endways–provides shelter beneath for a score of persons.

Looking along the valley The **Devil's Cheesewring** (otherwise Cheesering and Cheesepress) is seen almost opposite. From this elevation it looks quite diminutive, but when the level of the valley is regained, the fantastic pile of rocks assumes greater magnitude.

Some antiquaries think it probable, from the way the rocks are placed, that the site was occupied by an ancient temple. A circle of rocks can be distinctly traced and at one time there were several such circles here. The valley here has a notable echo.

In the Castle Rock is a peculiar formation, which when viewed from the Lee Abbey road about thirty yards from the lodge gate gives the appearance of a **White Lady**. The figure is formed by the sky beyond a hollow in the rocks.

On the western side of Castle Rock a hollow, or goyal, running down to Wringcliff Bay gives a grand view of the true dimensions of the "Castle", and of the vast wooded and rocky sweep of Duty Point. The Point is private property, so the road must be rejoined here. There is a toll for cars on the Lee Abbey road.

Passing through the gateway, by which stands a pretty lodge, the public road enters the demesne of picturesque **Lee Abbey**, a Church of England holiday and conference centre. Visitors are permitted but permission must be requested at the front door.

The "Abbey" previously had no ecclesiastical associations, having been built as a private residence in 1850, but romance attaches to the place, for it was erected on the site of an ancient gabled farmhouse which was the home of the Wichehalses – a name familiar in the pages of *Lorna Doone*. They were an old Devonshire family who, leaving Barnstaple in fear of the Plague, in 1628, came to live at Lee; and reigned as squires of Lynton for over a century. Another version of their removal to Lee is related below, in connection with Duty Point.

The magnificent views from the lofty conical height of **Duty Point** which the road skirts, can only be enjoyed by those fortunate enough to obtain permission; but the picture from the road in front of the Abbey is very delightful and impressive. On the right the land slopes down for 200 feet to **Lee Bay**; on the left it rises hundreds of feet. In front towers the round wooded knoll called **Bonhill Top**; beyond is **Crock Point**, forming the eastern side of Woody Bay; and, approaching the romantic little bay, the west side of Duty Point towers high on the right, a vast wall of wood, capped by a picturesque tower. It is said that the point derives its name from the fact that it was once one of the principal points of duty for coast-guards watching for smugglers.

At Lee Abbey, the branch drive on the left leads to *Sixacre Farm,* through beautiful woodland scenery down which falls a tiny murmuring rivulet. This bridle path takes the first turning to the left and zigzags up through the woods to a gate. It is worth following both for its own sake and for the fine views of Duty Point which it gives. The road leads through a gate to a lane by which the return to Lynton may be made. Follow the lane, turn left at the cross-roads and left again at the fork a little farther on. The road is joined by another track bearing to the right downhill, which leads direct to Lynton; the complete tour is about six miles. To extend the walk to Caffin's Heanton Down, bear right instead of left, at the cross-roads after passing *Sixacre Farm*. From the zigzag path through the Lee Abbey woods a public footpath branches off and climbs over the hills to Lynton. This path is steep but well marked and gives magnificent panoramic views of the coastline.

On the way back from Lee by the main road the **Cricket Ground** will be observed, 300 yards up and right in the cup of the valley. The return is made through the valley road to Lynton.

Lynbridge and Barbrook

This is a pleasant walk by way of the Barnstaple road. From Lynton descend Castle Hill; from Lynmouth ascend Lynmouth Hill. Thence the route lies through the beautiful gorge of the *West Lyn*, which is more open than that of the East Lyn and presents a different type of scenery. At **Lynbridge** (¾-mile) a path to the left of the road leads up to **Summerhouse Hill**.

Continuing along the main road for another mile, the pretty, soft scenery around **Barbrook** is reached. Here is the intake for the Lynton and Lynmouth water supply. The bed of the stream is 600 feet above sea-level. Barbrook Bridge leads to a much-used road which winds up and round by Lyn Down and descends to Hillsford Bridge and the East Lyn Valley at Watersmeet. On the right a short distance from Barbrook Bridge is the prodigious **Beggar's Roost Hill**, steep and rough.

By crossing **Cherrybridge**, on western side of petrol station, the left bank of the West Lyn can be followed southward for miles to its source by a lofty road, 1,200 feet high in places, passing East Ilkerton, Thornworthy and Shallowford (to the east of which, on **Ilkerton Ridge,** there are two tumuli and some hut circles), with bare, breezy commons and ridges all around.

Or the stream can be followed from Barbrook, by the road above the opposite bank, passing the old entrenchment called **Stock Castle**, and thence over Stock Common and Furzehill Common, where, striking to the left by several hut circles, the *Hoar Oak* branch of the Combe Park stream will be met beneath Cheriton Ridge; then, following this stream down, beneath **Roborough Castle** (another old entrenchment) on the left, and by Combe Park, the road to the left at Hillsford Bridge can be taken for Lynbridge. Or the Combe Park stream can be followed down to Watersmeet, and the East Lyn thence to Lynmouth.

Taking the right-hand (westward) road at Barbrook, by the side of the tributary stream, for about three-quarters of a mile, ascend the hill and, where the river turns south, turn to right through Dean hamlet. Turn left at the cross-roads and then right down Sixacre Lane past **Sixacre Farm** through woods by a zigzag path to Lee Abbey. **Caffin's Heanton Farm** is away to the left.

From the cross-roads, the road known as **Lydiate Lane** now leads for a mile and a half northwards over bare downs, the higher slopes of **Mount Sinai** (1,000 feet high), descending to Lynton between Southcliff on the left and Station Cleaves on the right, at the back of Rock Lodge.

To Watersmeet

Road Route.–The Watersmeet Road (A39) follows the south bank of the East Lyn from the bottom of Lynmouth Hill. To vary the return to Lynmouth or Lynton, follow the road upstream from Watersmeet to Hillsford Bridge, about $\frac{3}{4}$ mile farther, turn up sharply to right and follow the road crossing Lyn Down and descending to the West Lyn Valley at Barbrook Bridge. This route passes close to Beggar's Roost Hill.

Car Park above Watersmeet.

Over the years the National Trust have acquired much of the land of the East Lyn river, including Watersmeet and Barton Woods. On the south of the river from Lynmouth to Rockford, Summerhouse Hill (now known as "The Cleaves") and the Combe Park Estate are controlled by the Trust. Various paths have been cut, notably one leading to Countisbury Hill and affording beautiful views over the valley.

WATERSMEET

So great is the just fame of Watersmeet, where the tumbling waters of the *East Lyn* are joined by the *Combe Park Water*, amid sylvan scenery of extraordinary beauty, that no one, whatever else is omitted, will miss the excursion. With the aid of a car it is possible to see Watersmeet in an hour or less, but the delightful walk (about 1½ miles) by the banks of the East Lyn is infinitely to be preferred, the scenery all the way being of a most romantic character.

The wooded gorge of the East Lyn, lying between the Tors Hill and Summerhouse Hill, can be entered in two ways. Proceed up Lynmouth's main street, cross the bridge on left, then turn right up Tors Road, then riverside path to Watersmeet. At the fork, keep right, and crossing the bridge at Black Pool, Watersmeet is reached.

The stream is here broad and shallow, and for a short distance is lined by cottages, along Tors Road. Since the 1952 flood the National Trust have cut a path through the wood and across Myrtleberry Combe, and which rejoins the river at Chiselcombe Bridge.

The **Tors** rise sheer on the left to a height of 735 feet, and in common with the hills about are covered with gorse and heather to their very summits. **Myrtleberry Cleave**, on the opposite bank, is of equal height. Among the recesses of its rocks the badger is still to be found. Occasionally the water runs quietly in deep pools in which salmon and trout are plentiful, but in a few yards giant boulders are again encountered, forming numerous cascades up which salmon may often be seen leaping on their way from the sea to their spawning beds. The river is, in fact, a succession of falls, waterslides, rapids, and deep, quiet pools, each variety being found every successive hundred yards. The Lynrock spring may be seen gushing out at a point halfway to Watersmeet.

Countisbury may be reached by going up the little green valley which joins that of the *East Lynn* at Myrtleberry. The path begins on the right bank downstream from the new Chiselcombe Bridge, and winds up the valley to the Countisbury road, joining it near the Farm. This makes an excellent return route, the walk down the steep Countisbury Hill affording magnificent views of Lynmouth and its harbour nestling below Lynton and Hollerday Hill.

Continuing up the East Lyn Valley, the path runs through a pleasant meadow, where the goyal (an Exmoor term meaning a narrow valley) is wider and more open, and the river is spanned by the stone bridge. A short distance farther, over a narrow rocky pathway–

Watersmeet

comes into view, a miracle of varied beauty. To the right, facing upstream, the rushing *Combe Park (or Hoarock) Water* plunges down a succession of falls, between two high woods, to meet the *East Lyn*, flowing in more peacefully on the left. The smaller stream is the more impatient. A mass of foam and spume, it comes leaping ledge to ledge from a point 50 feet above, to lose itself in the larger stream which steals gently round the bend from the left. The sharp peak of the central wooded hill divides the two channels and the other lofty timbered hills enclose the scene in sweeping curves.

Watersmeet

If time allows, the walk should be continued from Watersmeet either (*a*) to Rockford and Millslade, or (*b*) to Hillsford Bridge, as follows.

(*a*) **Watersmeet to Rockford and Millslade.** The Lyn is followed by taking the path on the *right* bank of the river. A short distance upstream disused limekilns on the bank are relics of the time when farmers used more lime on their soil than is now the case. At a point where the narrow track threads the steep bank, the stream falls over a narrow ledge ten feet high, and splits on the edge of a great boulder into two white torrents. Uniting, these plunge convulsively over ragged rocks penned in between natural walls only a few feet apart, and then stretch out in a long, silent, black line to the outlet below, out of sight. This is the **Long Pool**. "Shut in by abrupt cliffs" says Ward, "draped and festooned with fern and hanging creepers, dark and sunless almost always, for a length of a hundred yards and more the river creeps along, exhausted seemingly by the turmoil of its previous course".

Pools and falls without number occur for another half-mile, and then a thinning of the trees on the left hand, and a green belt between the stream and the fir plantations above on the right, mark the approach to the quiet little hamlet of **Rockford** *(Rockford Inn)*.

The footbridge here leads to the main road. For Brendon Church (*see* (3) below), cross the bridge and turn to the right on reaching the main road; for Millslade turn to the left, but it is preferable to keep to the riverside path on the opposite bank of the East Lyn, crossing the river by a footbridge at Countisbury Mill, nearly opposite the *Staghunter's Inn*. The fishing here is good.

The return to Lynmouth can be made by:

(1) Retracing the riverside path.
(2) Crossing the East Lyn a hundred yards from the *Staghunter's Inn*, turning to the left, ascending Combe Girt, across Countisbury Common and down Countisbury Hill. This is the nearest route and there is the possibility of a seat on a Lynmouth-bound bus.
(3) Returning to Rockford by road, ascending the hill leading to Brendon Church, and thence down Barton Hill to Hillsford Bridge, from which a direct road leads to Lynmouth.

(*b*) **Watersmeet to Hillsford Bridge.** Hillsford Bridge is about a mile south of Watersmeet.

The higher path on the right at Watersmeet follows the Combe Park Water to Hillsford Bridge, at the junction of the *Hoar Oak* and *Farley Waters*. These, together, make the *Combe Park Water*.

Here are busy cross-roads. That to the right runs to the north of Combe Park, dividing in about a mile and a half, the right-hand branch going to Lynbridge by way of West Lyn hamlet, the left-hand or Exmoor branch running southward over Lyn Down and Stock Common, and the one straight ahead going to Barbrook by way of Beggar's Roost Hill. This is part of the motor road, but turning to the right it avoids the dangerous Beggar's Roost Hill and descends to Barbrook by an easier gradient.

The left turning crosses the new motor road bridge to join the Simonsbath (right)–Brendon Valley (left) road; the latter fork brings one past Brendon Church and down the steep Church Hill to Rockford. The road straight across passes Combe Park and beyond a small bridge, leads up the beautifully wooded valley of *Farley Water* for about a mile to the pretty hamlet of **Bridge Ball**. Here the road again divides, one branch turning to the right, up Cheriton Hill, through **Cheriton** hamlet and across Cheriton Bridge down to the *Hoar Oak* stream. Crossing this, the road runs up and across *Stock Common* and on to the *West Lyn* stream, just two miles above Barbrook.

The branch to the left at Bridge Ball crosses the Farley stream and one of its tributaries and climbs **Scob Hill**, reaching the Simonsbath road at the top.

Turning left and passing Brendon Barton, this road joins that from Barton Hill.

At Brendon Barton a path to the right leads across Tippacott Ridge down to Malmsmead.

To Countisbury Foreland

Road Route. – Except as a means of getting easily up and down the long and steep Countisbury Hill, which starts from Lyndale Bridge, Lynmouth (*see* plan), a car is of little use on this excursion as the Foreland is about a mile from the road and must be explored on foot. The Minehead–Lynmouth buses pass along this way.

The distance from Lynmouth is 2½ miles – a magnificent walk, though as the road rises over 800 feet in little more than a mile many visitors prefer to drive up and reserve their energies for an exploration of the Foreland. Those who walk should either take the main road or follow for the greater part of the way the old **Pack-horse Path**. In the earlier years of the last century this was the only route between Lynmouth beach and Porlock, and up it toiled pack-horses and mules loaded with lime, fish and merchandise, much of the last-named being smuggled

Countisbury Hill

through Lynmouth Bay. Take the wide grassy path on the right up the slope, starting from the entrance to Beacon Guest House. Following this the earthwork, an ancient camp 900 feet above sea-level, which crowns Countisbury Hill, is passed. North, south and west the ground slopes precipitously to sea and river, while the east, where the approach is level, is defended by an enormous earthen rampart 40 feet in height. Soon afterwards the main road is reached. *The cliff path above Sillery Sands is unsafe.*

The highlands of the Foreland are covered with gorse and heather, but the lower slopes of the eastern side are cultivated, particularly **Caddow Combe**, down which falls the pretty little *Caddow* stream. A **Lighthouse**, 50 feet high, stands on the Foreland, at a height of 220 feet above the sea. The light has an intensity equal to 190,000 candles, and is visible 21 miles in clear weather. Four flashes are given in quick succession every fifteen seconds. In foggy weather a 36-unit fog-signal sounds three 2-second blasts every 30 seconds. The Lighthouse, which is well worth a visit (1 p.m. to an hour before sunset, weekdays only), is easily accessible by a private road (available for pedestrians) which leaves the main Countisbury–Porlock road on the left about half-a-mile from Countisbury, or by a footpath from the *Blue Ball Inn* (signposted). Cars may be left at the free car parks at the inn or at the commencement of the approach road to the lighthouse. (Distance to lighthouse is about one and a half miles.)

It cannot be too strongly stressed that it is dangerous to approach too closely the cliff edge hereabouts.

A beautiful return route from the Foreland – made increasingly beautiful by its contrast with the open country – is along the narrow, sylvan valley of the East Lyn. From Countisbury Church take the road through Countisbury village and leave it 150 yards down on the left. This path leads southward to Myrtleberry, whence the route is unmistakable, along the right bank of the river.

If desired the return may be made by bus from the *Blue Ball Inn*, a sixteenth-century building formerly used as a coaching inn. Or those who are reluctant to leave the breezy, heather-clad cliffs may work eastward towards Glenthorne, possibly picking up a bus on the return journey.

In the nave of little **Countisbury Church** is a tablet to John Fry, dated 1762, suggestive of *Lorna Doone*. Parts of the church date back to the thirteenth century and noteworthy features are the altar rails, pre-Reformation panel, and a fifteenth-century font.

Below the west side of the Foreland, and reached by boat or by a hazardous clamber along the coast over large rocks from Lynmouth, are the **Sillery Sands**, a favourite spot for picnics and bathing. *(Visitors should watch, however, that they are not cut off by the swiftness of the tide at this point.)* A stream of pure water tumbles down the cliffs, and there is plenty of driftwood with which to boil the kettle. Prawns abound in the rocky pools beyond the sands. Motor-boats ply to and from Lynmouth and offer a further variation of the return journey.

To Glenthorne and Yenworthy

Road Route. – The walk described below may be begun at Countisbury Church and ended at various points on the main road. As in the foregoing excursion, a car is useful for negotiating Countisbury Hill; but otherwise it is apt to prove superfluous.

Buses and coaches are available.

Good walkers can visit Glenthorne in conjunction with Countisbury (*see* above) or with the Doone Country (see p. 248), but everyone should endeavour to do the fine coast walk described below.

The main Porlock road is followed up Tors Hill to **Countisbury**, where, by the little church, the way strikes across the Foreland.

The path bears away to the right, but if it is desired to go down to the shore of **Countisbury Cove** on its east side (care is required), and the track is missed, it does not matter, for the path can be seen winding along the face of the cliffs high overhead, and can be regained by a scramble up and across the field slopes and over the stone fences.

For several miles this glorious **Coast Path** to **Glenthorne** is cut in the hillsides at a general height of about 300 feet, with great slopes stretching five, six, and seven hundred feet higher. As point after point is rounded, beautiful and majestic views of wooded combes, steep, bare cliffs, and gaunt hillsides stretch before one, while across the Channel rises the dim white coast of South Wales. It is difficult to conceive a more splendid walk than the springy turf path over these gigantic escarpments, with their abrupt transitions from rugged sterility to a wealth of foliage.

Just before reaching a bare point thickly strewn with rocky débris, **Desolation Point**, another path goes off to the right higher up the hill. This will lead to the upper gate in the glen we are approaching.

The lower path presently bends back westward a few yards and then descends again to the right, with a seat in the angle. A small gate here gives access to the fair domain of–

Glenthorne. The grounds are private property. Visitors desirous of passing through them should previously write to A. J. B. Halliday, "Glenthorne", Lynton, N. Devon requesting permission. Glenthorne ("The Valley of Thorns") is a beautiful hollow or scoop in a lofty hill facing the Channel, clothed for hundreds of feet with firs. The path leads across the side facing east, through trees, flowering shrubs, brambles, ferns and heather, with great boulders and jagged rocks breaking through here and there, the strata being sometimes almost perpendicular. A picturesque arched gateway leads to the grounds surrounding the residence, described in Page's *Exmoor* as "a pretty Tudoresque mansion pitched upon a tiny plateau, the only level spot for miles. On every side dark woods climb the giant hills, watered occasionally by diminutive streams, which tumble down to the beach over mossy rocks half concealed by fern brakes". The house was actually built in 1830 and is hardly Tudor, however. A charming stream, with a path by its side, runs to the sea east of the house. The road passes this stream and continues up to the stables, but the former cliff-path beyond is now impracticable.

From the stables the road winds back to the west, and then for three miles zigzags up through the beautiful glen to the Lynton and Porlock high-road, 1,000 feet above. But the walker may save half the distance by taking, about a quarter of a mile above the lodge, a broad, grassy path on the left. Some distance up, on the right-hand side, is the gate of the higher path before mentioned, and above this is the lodge.

Just before reaching the high-road, where the car may be rejoined, **Oldburrow**, a circular entrenchment, is passed on the right. Excavations have shown it to have been a Roman military outpost built A.D. 48–54.

The main road is rejoined about half a mile west of **County Gate**, 6 miles from Lynmouth. Only the name perpetuates the gateway which originally marked the boundary between Wessex and Devonia and which until a few years ago reminded travellers that here Devon joins Somerset. The return to Lynton can be made either by the higher cliff-path, by the main road, or *via* Oare and the Brendon Valley. A Nature Trail has been marked out starting from County Gate, descending to Glenthorne beach and returning by another route. The route extends for about 3 miles and includes the Pinetum and other interesting features on the estate.

About ¾ mile north-east of County Gate, between the road and the sea is Yenworthy Farm, with intimate associations with the Doones.

From Yenworthy, Oare Church can be reached fairly easily by a short route. Ascend to the main road, and take the path by *Clannors* leading southward across the common to Oare (*see* below). The views of Exmoor from this route are magnificent.

Or from Yenworthy a beautiful walk leads eastward by Broomstreet and Silcombe to **Culbone Church**. The bus time-table should be consulted for a lift on the return journey along the main road.

To Oare and the Doone Valley

Road Route. – There is no road up the Doone Valley, but cars can be left at Malmsmead. The lane down to Oare leaves the main Lynmouth-Porlock road ¼ mile east of County Gate (as described below), and a narrow but charming road follows the East Lyn valley from Oare to Brendon and Hillsford Bridge, whence the way back to Lynmouth is by Watersmeet or up to the left and over Lyn Down.

Motor-coaches run from Lynton and Lynmouth, Minehead and other centres to the Doone Valley, Oare, and other places described in this excursion.

As a preliminary to this excursion one should re-read *Lorna Doone*, as a knowledge of the doings of the "girt Jan Ridd" adds considerably to the enjoyment of a ramble through the neighbourhood so picturesquely described by Blackmore. Many admirers of *Lorna* are unaware that the novelist followed up his greater work by a stóry *Slain by the Doones*, in his *Tales from the Telling House*.

This forms a very fine circular trip of about 15 miles. One half of the route is by the main road to County Gate, the other is along the lovely Brendon Valley to Hillsford Bridge and Watersmeet. Some prefer to start with County Gate; others prefer to walk out *via* Watersmeet and pick up a homeward-bound bus at County Gate in the evening. The walk is good enough (traffic notwithstanding) to be taken both ways; but good walkers should devote at least a day to the Doone Valley, returning over Brendon Common.

The road from County Gate runs southward down the long slope to the valley of the East Lyn, now become the *Oare Water*. With glimpses of the beautiful gorge winding away to Watersmeet on the right, of the long break in the moors which marks the channel of the *Badgworthy Water* southward, and of other combes at right angles to this, **Oare** parish is entered. There are few houses here, and the original of Plover Barrows Farm cannot be found, for if it ever did exist, and there is doubt, it is non-existent now; though some point to the farm at Oareford (*see* p. 250). Near the church is Oare Manor, long the residence of the late Nicholas Snow, whose family held property in the parish for 1,000 years.

Oare Church is a small plain stone building, with a low square tower at the west end and filled with Georgian high pews. It is entered by the north porch, facing the Malmsmead road. The ceiling is rounded and plastered. The church contains a very old piscina of quaint design, a Norman font-bowl and an Elizabethan chalice.

The Doone Valley

At Malmsmead, a mile west of Oare, the Lyn is joined by the **Badgworthy Water**, which, as John Ridd told us, "brings a good stream down, as full of fish as of pebbles". On the same excellent authority "the Badgworthy Water ran out of the Doone Valley a mile or so from the mouth of it"; and not the least interesting feature of the excursion up the Badgworthy Valley today is the endeavour to "place" the valley of the Doones. The route lies through Badgworthy Wood to Lankcombe near the famous Waterslide. Continuing up the valley for another 50 yards, the remains of a hunting gate is reached, referred to as "The Doone Gate". The generally accepted "Doone Valley" lies about 500 yards beyond this and can be recognized by the few traces of ruins.

Let it be said at once that the maps which mark a "Doone Valley" running from the west into the main Badgworthy Valley some two miles south of Malmsmead merely perpetuate the error of an early surveyor. Not only does this valley differ more markedly than any other in the neighbourhood from Blackmore's description, both in general ruggedness and in other particulars, but there is not the slightest ground for linking the overgrown walls near its mouth with the Doone dwellings.

On the other hand, the *Lank Combe*, half a mile nearer Malmsmead, does boast a veritable waterslide, down which the water pours impressively after heavy rain, and those who penetrate upstream will find that the valley beyond the slide answers far more nearly to Blackmore's valley. The waterslide, however, is the most interesting link between the scenery and the story.

John, it will be remembered, had been poaching up the Badgworthy stream when he discovered the Doone Valley. His story runs:

> "I stood at the foot of a long pale slide of water, coming smooth by to me without any break or hindrance, for a hundred yards or more, and fenced on either side with cliff, sheer and straight and shining. The water neither ran nor fell, nor leaped with any spouting, but made one even slope of it, as if it had been combed or planed, and looking like a plank of deal laid down a deep black staircase. However, there was no side-rail nor any place to walk upon, only the channel a fathom wide, and the perpendicular walls of crag shutting out the evening."

But we look in vain for Lorna's Bower, though there are half a dozen possible sites for the Doone Gate. There is a strong local tendency to regard the Doone Valley as situated in the main Badgworthy Valley – indeed, the interest of the search is so high that one concludes with some reluctance that Blackmore's Doone Valley was a composite picture into which were woven various features and in which some details were enormously magnified, others almost obliterated.

From the head of the Lank Combe or the so-called Doone Valley farther south the return may be made *via* Millslade in the Brendon Valley, but it is advisable to make inquiries there for exact directions, as the paths across the moors are confusing and in places boggy and the way might be easily lost if mist or darkness descends.

By following Badgworthy Water to the junction with the next stream, crossing to the left-hand side beyond the junction, shortly climbing the hill (keeping the tributary stream below on the left), then bearing slightly half-left from some perpendicular stones which form a mysterious kind of avenue, crossing a bare down, and, when over a local fence, bearing to the half-right, the valley of the *Chalk Water* will be reached. This Ward calls "the finest little bit on Exmoor", and Page "a fine specimen of the border combes of Exmoor". Following the stream down for about a mile and a half, the *Weir Water* (as the higher part of the East Lyn is called) is reached at **Oareford**. Here the streams form almost a right-angle, containing two or three cottages, and a farm supposed by some to be the original Plover Barrows – a little community amid the most charming surroundings.

The road from Malmsmead to Lynmouth passes through the straggling but pretty village of **Brendon** and then **Rockford**. The inns, farmhouses and cottages in this delightful valley are favourite holiday quarters for walkers and anglers. Cross the footbridge at Rockford and follow the right bank of the stream to Watersmeet and Lynmouth by the path described on p. 243. Or from Rockford climb the long, steep Church Hill, crowned by Brendon Church with its interesting porch sundial dated 1707. The left-hand branch at the fork just beyond is the Exmoor Road, leading to Simonsbath and Dulverton. This should be remembered for use in future rambles over the moor. Walkers take the right-hand branch, which soon makes a steep and winding descent to Hillsford, but cars take the newer road of easier gradient which leaves the Simonsbath and Dulverton road on the right just before Scob Hill is reached. The two routes rejoin at **Hillsford Bridge** (*see* p. 244) and cross *Farley Water* by the new stone bridge and *Combe Park Water* by the stone-built single arch.

In a few yards the road down the Combe Park Water to Lynmouth strikes off to the right. That which climbs the hill to the left comes to Barbrook, passing the path to East Lyn Farm and Summerhouse Hill.

To South Molton

Follow the A39 past Parracombe to the Blackmore Gate cross-roads (*see* p. 227). Turn left along the B3226 which leads through Brayford to **South Molton**. This ancient market town has many attractive buildings. The church, approached through beautiful avenues, is Perpendicular in style and the dominating feature is the great fifteenth-century tower. The interior is notable for the intricate stone carving on the font, the pulpit and the capitals in the chancel.

The return journey may be made through **North Molton**, where the church contains the elaborate alabaster Bampfylde monument to the knight, his wife and a great number of children, and **Simonsbath**, in Somerset.

Index

Abbotsham Cliffs, 190
Abbotskerswell, 120
Aish, 129
A la Ronde, 40
Aller, 121
Alma Bridge, 50
Anchor Stone, 145
Anstey's Cove, 113
Appledore, 187
Arlington Court, 207
Ashburton, 153
Ashcombe, 76
Ash Hole, 134
Atherington, 205
Aveton Gifford, 166
Axminster, 63
Babbacombe, 117, 114
Badgworthy Water, 248
Baggy Point, 207
Bampton, 68
Bantham, 167
Barbrook, 240
Barnell, Branscombe, 53
Barnstaple, 197
Barricane Beach, 218, 220
Barton, 121
Batson, 161
Bayard's Cove, 141
Beacon Quay, 107
Bearscove Castle, 141
Beer, 54
Beer Head, 53
Beesands, 159
Beggar's Roost Hill, 241
Benson's Cave, 231
Bere Ferrers, 171
Berry Castle, 129
Berry Down, 224
Berry Head, 53, 134
Berrynarbor, 219
Berry Pomeroy Castle, 127, 151
Bicclescombe Parl, 213
Bickleigh, 66
Bicton, 46
Bideford, 183
Bigbury, 167, 166
Bishop Blackall School, 32
Bishops Court, 61
Bishops Tawton, 203
Bishopsteignton, 85
Bishops Walk, 113, 114
Bitton Park, 81
Black Hill, 41, 47
Blackpool, 143, 159
Blackpool Mill, 179
Blagdon, 129
Blundell's School, 67
Blythe's Cove, 212
Boat Cove, 74
Bolt Head, 165
Bolt Tail, 165
Bone Hill, Northam, 187
Bonhill Top, 240
Bovey House, 55
Bovey Tracey, 93
Bow Bridge, 178
Bow Creek, 145
Bowden, 219
Bradley Manor, 90
Bradninch, 66
Branscombe, 52
Braunton, 205, 206
Brenden, 250
Bridge Ball, 244
Bridgetown, 148, 151
Briery Cove, 219
Britannia Royal Naval
College 141, 145
Brixham, 131
Broad Clyst, 66

Broadsands, 127
Brookhill, 138
Brunel Manor, 118
Brutus Stone, 147
Buckfast Abbey, 151
Buckfastleigh, 151
Buckland, 167
Buckland Abbey, 171
Buckland Brewer, 192
Buckland-in-the-Moor, 153
Buck Mills, 174
Budleigh Salterton, 43
Bull Point, 215
Burgh Island, 167
Burton Art Gallery, 184
Bury Camp, 53
Butterwalk, Dartmouth, 139
Butterwalk, Totnes, 150
Cadbury Castle, 65
Caddow Combe, 245
Cadhay, 61
Caffin's Heanton Farm, 241
Cairn Top, 213
Castle Cove, 143
Castle Dyke, 76
Castle Rock, 239
Chagford, 93
Chambercombe, 218
Chapel Hill, 110
Chapman Rocks, 177
Charleton, 161
Cheriton, 244
Cherrybridge, 241
Chit Rocks, 59
Chittlehampton, 204
Chivelstone, 161
Chudleigh, 85
Chudleigh Fort, 186
Chudleigh Rocks, 85
Chulmleigh, 69
Church Living, Branscombe, 52
Churchstow, 168
Churscombe, 113
Churstow Quay Cove, 133
Citadel, Plymouth, 169
Clennon Hill, 127
Cliff Field, Sidmouth, 50
Cliff House, 164
Clorridge Hill, 225
Clovelly, 173
Clovelly Dykes, 174
Coburg Field, 51
Cockington, 112
Coddon Hill, 203
Coffinswell, 121
Cofton, 76
Colaton Raleigh, 47
Colcombe Farm, 62
Colyford, 62
Colyton, 62
Combe Martin, 221
Combesgate, 218
Compass Cove, 143
Compton, 119, 127
Comyn Farm, 219
Constable Rock, 231
Cookworthy Museum, 157
Coombe Cellars, 84
Corbyn Head, 102
Coryton Cove, 74
Countess Weir, 32
Countisbury Foreland, 242, 244
County Gate, 247
Courtenay Walk, 165
Cow and Calf Rocks, 180
Crediton, 69
Crockern Tor, 97
Crock Point, 240
Croyde, 207
Culbone, 247
Cullompton, 66
Daccombe, 121
Daddy Hole Plain, 115
Damehole Point, 180
Dart, The, 145
Dartington Hall, 151
Dartmeet, 153
Dartmouth, 137
Dawlish, 73
Dawlish Warren, 75
Dean Court, 153
Dean Prior, 153
Denbury, 90
Desolation Point, 246
Devil's Cheesewring, 239
Devil's Lime Kiln, 230

Devil's Point, 113
Dittisham, 143
Dodbrooke, 157
Doddiscombsleigh, 96
Doone Valley, 248
Dousland, 98
Downes, 69
Dowrich, 69
Duncannon, 145
Dyer's Wood, 91
Eastacott, 204
East Budleigh, 45
East Ogwell, 90
East Portlemouth, 158
East Prawle, 158
East-the-Water, 186
Edge Barton, 53
Egge, 53
Elberry Cove, 127
Eldern Point, 177
Elephant Rock, 75
Ermington, 170
Exeter, 15
Exmansworthy, 177
Exminster, 70
Exmouth, 35
Fernworthy, 94
Filleigh, 205
Fishcombe Beach, 133
Forde House, 88
Frithelstock, 195
Frogmore, 161
Furzeham, 133
Gallantry Bower, 176
Galmpton, 166
Galmpton Bay, 145
Georgeham, 207
Giant Rock, 118
Gidleigh, 93, 95
Glen Lyn, 237
Glenthorne, 246
Golden Chair, 85
Gommerock, 138
Goodrington, 126
Great Haldon, 76
Great Hangman, 224
Great Hill, 121
Great Torrington, 194
Greenway House, 145
Grimspound, 96
Haccombe, 91, 84
Haldon, 77, 85
Hameldown Tor, 153
Ham Stone, 165
Hangman Beach, 223
Harberton, 153
Harbourne, 145
Harpford, 47, 170
Harpford Wood, 47, 59
Hartland, 178, 177
Hatherleigh, 172
Hayes Barton, 45
Heaton Punchardon, 205
Heddon's Mouth, 225
Hele's School, 32
Hembury Castle, 153
Higher Ashton, 96
Higher Dittisham, 145, 143
Highweek Church, 89
High Willhays, 172
Hillsborough Hill, 211
Hillsford Bridge, 244, 250
Hobby Drive, 174
Holcombe Down, 77
Hole Head, 81
Hollerday Hill, 238, 235
Holsworthy, 195
Honiton, 63
Hope, 166
Hope's Nose, 115, 116
Hunter's Inn, 225, 224
Ideford, 86
Ilbertstow Point, 161
Ilkerton Ridge, 241
Ilfracombe, 209
Ilsham Grange, 117
Instow, 190
Ipplepen, 91
Ivybridge, 170
Jacob's Ladder Beach, Sidmouth, 50
Kenn, 71
Kentisbury, 227
Kenton, 71
Kent's Cavern, 110
Kes Tor, 95

Kingsbridge, 156
King's Gardens, Torquay, 102
Kingskerswell, 120, 121
Kingsteignton, 85
Kingswear, 137
Kipling Tors, 189
Kirkham House, 126
Knightstone Farm, 61
Labrador, 83
Ladies Mile, 75
Ladram Bay, 46, 59
Lake, 203
Landcross, 194
Landkey, 205
Land's End, Torbay, 115
Landslip, 64
Langstone Cliffs, 74
Lannacombe, 158
Lantern Hill, 211
Lapford, 69
Leadstone, 115
Lea Mount, 74
Lee, 214
Lee Abbey, 240
Lee Bay, 215, 240
Lidwell, 77
Lincombe Drive, 117
Lindridge, 86
Little Haldon, 76, 86
Littleham, Bideford, 192
Littleham, Exmouth, 39, 41, 44
Littlehempston, 151
Livermead Sands, 102
Livery Dole, 31
London Bridge, Torbay, 115
Long Park, 51
Long Pool, 243
Lower Dittisham, 145, 143
Lundy, 229
Luscombe Park, 76
Lydford, 171
Lydiate Lane, 241
Lympstone, 40
Lynbridge, 238, 240
Lynmouth, 233
Lynton, 233
Maer, Exmouth, 36
Magdalen Almshouses, 31
Maidencombe, 118
Malborough, 166
Mamhead House, 76
Mamhead Point, 76
Mansands, 135
Manstone, 51
Marldon, 119
Mars Hill, 236
Marsland Mouth, 181
Mary Tavy, 171
Mattiscombe, 158
Mayflower Stone, 169
Maynard's School, 32
Meadfoot, 116, 115
Metherall, 93
Milber Down, 92
Mill Bay Cove, 135
Millslade, 244
Modbury, 166
Monkleigh, 193
Moretonhampstead, 93, 96
Mortehoe, 218
Morte Point, 218
Mount Pleasant, Clovelly, 174
Mount Pleasant, Dawlish, 75
Mount Ridley, 137
Mount Sinai, 241
Mouth Mill, 177
Myrtleberry Cleave, 242
Ness Point, 83
Nether Exe, 65
Newton Abbot, 87
Newton Bushel, 88
Newton Poppleford, 59
Norman Lockyer Observatory, 51
Northam, 187
North Bovey, 96
North Molton, 250
Notre Dame Convent, 81
Nutwell Court, 40
Oakridge, 214
Oare, 248
Oareford, 250
Oarstone, 115
Oddicombe Beach, 117
Ogwell, 90
Oldbarrow, 247
Old Mill Creek, 143, 145

Oldway, 126
Otterton, 46
Ottery St. Mary, 59, 60
Overbecks, 165
Paignton, 123
Parkham, 193
Parliament House, 128
Parracombe, 227
Parson and Clerk Rock, 75
Peak Hill, 50
Peartree Point, 158
Pebble Ridge, 189
Peter Tavy, 171
Pettitor Cliffs, 117
Phear Park, 37
Pilton, 201
Pixie's Cave, 85
Plymouth, 168
Plympton, 171
Point-in-View, 40
Porch House, Sidford, 61
Portlemouth, 163
Postbridge, 97
Poultry Walk, Totnes, 150
Powderham, 70
Prawle Point, 158
Preston, 126
Princetown, 97
Puritan's Pit, 90
Putsborough, 207
Queen Anne's Walk, 198
Ragged Jack, 239
Rapparee Cove, 211
Rattery, 151
Redgate Beach, 113
Rickham, 158
Ringmore, 83
Roborough Castle, 241
Rockford, 243, 250
Rock Park, Barnstaple, 199
Rock Walk, Torquay, 106
Rougemont Castle, 29
St. Anne's Almshouses, 31
St. Clement's, Dartmouth, 140
St. Edmund-on-the-Bridge, 31
St. John in the Wilderness, 39
St. Leonard's Tower, 88
St. Margaret's Hospital, 64
St. Marychurch, 118
St. Mary's Bay, 135
St. Mary Steps, 30
St. Nectan's, Hartland, 179
St. Petrox, Dartmouth, 140
St. Saviour's, Dartmouth, 140
Salcombe, 163
Salcombe Hill, Sidmouth, 51
Saltram House, 170
Saltstone, 161
Sandridge House, 145
Saunton, 206
Scabbacombe Sands, 135
Scob Hill, 244
Score Valley, 214
Scorhill Circle, 95
Seahill, Seaton, 57
Seale-Hayne College, 89
Seaton, 57
Seven Brethren Bank, 203
Shag Rock, 115
Shaldon, 82
Shambles, Kingsbridge, 156
Sharpham, 145
Sharpitor, 165
Shell Beach, Woolacombe, 220
Shell Cove, 74
Sherbrooke Chine, 44
Shipload Bay, 177
Shoalstone Beach, 133
Shorton, 127
Shorten Valley, 113
Shutter Rock, 230
Sidbury, 61
Sidbury Castle, 61
Sidford, 61
Sidmouth, 49
Sillery Sands, 246
Sixacre Farm, 240
Slapton, 143, 159
Slapton Ley, 158
Slapton Sands, 159
Smeaton's Lighthouse, 169
Smuggler's Lane, 77
South Brent, 170
South Down, 53
South Hams, 155
South Milton, 166

South Molton, 250
South Pool, 161
Spanish Barn, 103
Speke's Mouth, 181
Starcross, 71
Start Point, 158
Stepcote Hill, 31
Sterridge Valley, 219
Stevenstone, 195
Stock Castle, 241
Stoke Fleming, 143, 159
Stoke Gabriel, 145
Stoke-in-Teignhead, 84
Stokemouth, 145
Stokenham, 143
Stonycombe, 120
Straight Point, 36, 41
Strete, 143, 159
Sugary Cove, 143
Summerhouse Hill, 238, 240
Sutton Pool, 169
Swimbridge, 205
Tacket Wood, 161
Tame, 81
Tapeley Park, 192
Tavistock, 171
Tawstock, 203
Taw Vale, 199
Teign, 82
Teignmouth, 79
Teign Valley, 85
Templar Rock, 231
Thatcher Pines, 114
Thorn, 93
Thorverton, 65
Three Boys, 94
Thurlestone, 167, 166
Ticket Wood, 161
Titchberry Farm, 177
Tiverton, 67
Topsham, 33
Torbay, 102
Torbryan, 91
Torcross, 143, 158
Torquay, 99
Torre Abbey, 103
Torridge, 186
Torrs Walk, Ilfracombe, 212
Torwood Gardens, 117
Totnes, 147
Trentishoe, 224
Tuckenhay, 145
Two Bridges, 97
Ugbrooke Park, 86
Umberleigh, 204
Valley of Rocks, Lynton, 239
Valley of Rocks, Torquay, 118
Waldon Hill, 103
Walla Brook, 95
Walls Hill, 113
Warberry Hill, 113
Warfleet Creek, 141
Washbrook Mill, 157
Watcombe, 118
Waterhead, 161
Watermouth, 220
Watersmeet, 241
Weare Giffard, 193
Welcombe, 181
West Dart, 97
Westdown Beacon, 39, 44
West Ogwell, 90
Westward Ho!, 189
White Cliff, 57
Widecombe-in-the-Moor, 153
Widecombe Ley, 158
Wide Gates, 161
Wilderness, 176
Wild Pear Beach, 224
Willoughby Field, 50
Windbury Head, 177
Winson, 204
Wistman's Wood, 97
Withycombe, 39
Withycombe Raleigh, 39
Wolborough Church, 88
Woodbury, 40
Woodbury Castle, 41
Woody Bay, 225
Woolacombe, 219
Woolfardisworthy West, 176
Wringapeak, 227
Wynard's Hospital, 31
Yelverton, 98, 171
Yenworthy, 246
Yes Tor, 172